The returning sunwalkers crowd onto the loading platform as the city nears it.

Some have been out for weeks, or even the months it would take to make a full circumambulation. When the city slides by, its locked doors will open and they will step right in.

That is soon to occur, and Swan should be there too. Yet still she stands on her promontory. More than once she has required retinal repair, and often she has been forced to run like a rabbit or die. Now it will have to happen again. She is directly south of the city, and fully lit by horizontal rays, like a silver flaw in one's vision. One can't help shouting at such rashness, useless though it is. Swan, you fool! Alex is dead—nothing to be done about it! Run for your life!

And then she does. Life over death—the urge to live—she turns and flies. Mercury's gravity, almost exactly the same as Mars's, is often called the perfect g for speed, because people who are used to it can careen across the land in giant leaps, flailing their arms for balance as they bound along. In just that way Swan leaps and flails—once catches a boot and falls flat on her face—jumps up and leaps forward again. She needs to get to the platform while the city is still next to it; the next platform is ten kilometers farther west.

She reaches the platform stairs, grabs the rail and vaults up, leaps from the far edge of the platform, forward into the lock as it is halfway closed.

BY KIM STANLEY ROBINSON

The Memory of Whiteness

Icehenge

Three Californias
The Wild Shore
The Gold Coast
Pacific Edge

The Planet on the Table

Remaking History

Escape from Kathmandu

A Short Sharp Shock

Mars Trilogy
Red Mars
Green Mars
Blue Mars

The Martians

Antarctica

The Years of Rice and Salt

Science in the Capital
Forty Signs of Rain
Fifty Degrees Below
Sixty Days and Counting

Galileo's Dream

2312

Shaman

2312

KIM STANLEY ROBINSON

www.orbitbooks.net

Orbit
Hachette Book Group
1290 Avenue of the Americas
New York, NY 10104
www.orbitbooks.net

Orbit is an imprint of Hachette Book Group. The Orbit name and logo are trademarks of Little, Brown Book Group Limited.

The Hachette Speakers Bureau provides a wide range of authors for speaking events. To find out more, go to www.hachettespeakersbureau.com or call (866) 376-6591.

The publisher is not responsible for websites (or their content) that are not owned by the publisher.

Printed in the United States of America

First oversize mass market edition: May 2013
10 9

OPM

CONTENTS

CONTENTS

2312

Prologue

The sun is always just about to rise. Mercury rotates so slowly that you can walk fast enough over its rocky surface to stay ahead of the dawn; and so many people do. Many have made this a way of life. They walk roughly westward, staying always ahead of the stupendous day. Some of them hurry from location to location, pausing to look in cracks they earlier inoculated with bioleaching metallophytes, quickly scraping free any accumulated residues of gold or tungsten or uranium. But most of them are out there to catch glimpses of the sun.

Mercury's ancient face is so battered and irregular that the planet's terminator, the zone of the breaking dawn, is a broad chiaroscuro of black and white—charcoal hollows pricked here and there by brilliant white high points, which grow and grow until all the land is as bright as molten glass, and the long day begun. This mixed zone of sun and shadow is often as much as thirty kilometers wide, even though on a level plain the horizon is only a few kilometers off. But so little of Mercury is level. All the old bangs are still there, and some long cliffs from when the planet first cooled and shrank. In a landscape so rumpled the light can suddenly jump the eastern horizon and leap west to strike some distant prominence. Everyone walking the land has to attend to this possibility, know when and where the longest sunreaches occur—and where they can run for shade if they happen to be caught out.

Or if they stay on purpose. Because many of them pause in their walkabouts on certain cliffs and crater rims, at places marked by stupas, cairns, petroglyphs, inuksuit, mirrors, walls, goldsworthies. The sunwalkers stand by these, facing east, waiting.

The horizon they watch is black space over black rock. The superthin neon-argon atmosphere, created by sunlight smashing rock, holds only the faintest pre-dawn glow. But the sunwalkers know the time, so they wait and watch—until—

a flick of orange fire dolphins over the horizon

and their blood leaps inside them. More brief banners follow, flicking up, arcing in loops, breaking off and floating free in the sky. Star oh star, about to break on them! Already their faceplates have darkened and polarized to protect their eyes.

The orange banners diverge left and right from the point of first appearance, as if a fire set just over the horizon is spreading north and south. Then a paring of the photosphere, the actual surface of the sun, blinks and stays, spills slowly to the sides. Depending on the filters deployed in one's faceplate, the star's actual surface can appear as anything from a blue maelstrom to an orange pulsing mass to a simple white circle. The spill to left and right keeps spreading, farther than seems possible, until it is very obvious one stands on a pebble next to a star.

Time to turn and run! But by the time some of the sunwalkers manage to jerk themselves free, they are stunned—trip and fall—get up and dash west, in a panic like no other.

Before that—one last look at sunrise on Mercury. In the ultraviolet it's a perpetual blue snarl of hot and hotter. With the disk of the photosphere blacked out, the fantastic dance of the corona becomes clearer, all the magnetized arcs and short circuits, the masses of burning hydrogen pitched out at the night. Alternatively you can block the corona, and look only at the sun's photosphere, and even magnify your view of it, until the burning tops of the convection cells are revealed in their squiggling thousands, each a thunderhead of fire burning furiously, all together torching five million tons of hydrogen a second—at which rate the star will burn another four billion years. All these long spicules of flame dance in circular patterns around the little black circles that are the sunspots—shifting whirlpools in the storms of burning. Masses of spicules flow together like kelp beds threshed by a tide. There are nonbiological explanations for all this convoluted motion—different gases moving at different speeds, magnetic fields fluxing constantly, shaping the endless whirlpools of fire—all mere physics, nothing more— but in fact it looks *alive*, more alive than many a living thing. Looking at it in the apocalypse of the Mercurial dawn, it's impossible to believe it's *not* alive. It roars in your ears, it *speaks* to you.

Most of the sunwalkers over time try all the various viewing filters, and then make choices to suit themselves. Particular filters or sequences of filters become forms of worship, rituals either personal or shared. It's very easy to get lost in these rituals; as the sunwalkers stand on their points and watch, it's not uncommon for devotees to become entranced by something in the sight, some pattern never seen before, something in the pulse and flow that snags the mind; suddenly the sizzle of the fiery cilia becomes audible, a turbulent roaring—that's your own blood, rushing through your ears, but in those moments it sounds just like the sun burning. And so people stay too long. Some have their retinas burned; some are blinded; others are killed outright, betrayed by an overwhelmed spacesuit. Some are cooked in groups of a dozen or more.

Do you imagine they must have been fools? Do you think you would never make such a mistake? Don't you be so sure. Really you have no idea. It's like nothing you've ever seen. You may think you are inured, that nothing outside the mind can really interest you anymore, as sophisticated and knowledgeable as you are. But you would be wrong. You are a creature of the sun. The beauty and terror of it seen from so close can empty any mind, thrust anyone into a trance. It's like seeing the face of God, some people say, and it is true that the sun powers all living creatures in the solar system, and in that sense *is* our god. The sight of it can strike thought clean out of your head. People seek it out precisely for that.

So there is reason to worry about Swan Er Hong, a person more inclined than most to try things just to see. She often goes sunwalking, and when she does she skirts the edge of safety, and sometimes stays too long in the light. The immense Jacob's ladders, the granulated pulsing, the spicules flowing . . . she has fallen in love with the sun. She worships it; she keeps a shrine to Sol Invictus in her room, performs the *pratahsamdhya* ceremony, the salute to the sun, every morning when she wakes in town. Much of her landscape and performance art is devoted to it, and these days she spends most of her time making goldsworthies and abramovics on the land and her body. So the sun is part of her art.

Now it is her solace too, for she is out there grieving. Now, if one were standing on the promenade topping the city Terminator's great Dawn Wall, one would spot her there to the south, out near the horizon. She needs to hurry. The city is gliding on its tracks across the bottom of a giant dimple between Hesiod and Kurasawa, and a flood of sunlight will soon pour far to the west. Swan needs to get into town before that happens, yet she still stands there. From the top of the Dawn Wall she looks like a silver toy. Her spacesuit has a big round clear helmet. Her boots look big, and are black with dust. A little booted silver ant, standing there grieving when she should be hustling back to the boarding platform west of town. The other sunwalkers out there are already hustling back to town. Some pull little carts or wheeled travois, hauling their supplies or even their sleeping companions. They've timed their returns closely, as the city is very predictable. It cannot deviate from its schedule; the heat of coming day expands the tracks, and the city's undercarriage is tightly sleeved over them; so sunlight drives the city west.

The returning sunwalkers crowd onto the loading platform as the city nears it. Some have been out for weeks, or even the months it would take to make a full circumambulation. When the city slides by, its lock doors will open and they will step right in.

That is soon to occur, and Swan should be there too. Yet still she stands on her promontory. More than once she has required retinal repair, and often she has been forced to run like a rabbit or die. Now it will have to happen again. She is directly south of the city, and fully lit by horizontal rays, like a silver flaw in one's vision. One can't help shouting at such rashness, useless though it is. Swan, you fool! Alex is dead—nothing to be done about it! Run for your life!

And then she does. Life over death—the urge to live—she turns and flies. Mercury's gravity, almost exactly the same as Mars's, is often called the perfect g for speed, because people who are used to it can career across the land in giant leaps, flailing their arms for balance as they bound along. In just that way Swan leaps and flails—once catches a boot and falls flat on her face—jumps up and leaps forward again. She needs to get to the platform while the city is still next to it; the next platform is ten kilometers farther west.

She reaches the platform stairs, grabs the rail and vaults up, leaps from the far edge of the platform, forward into the lock as it is halfway closed.

SWAN AND ALEX

Alex's memorial ceremony began as Swan was straggling up Terminator's great central staircase. The city's population had come out into the boulevards and plazas and were standing in silence. There were a lot of visitors in town as well; a conference had been about to begin, one that had been convened by Alex. She had welcomed them on Friday; now on the following Friday they were holding her funeral. A sudden collapse, and they hadn't been able to revive her. And so now the townspeople, the diplomat visitors: all Alex's people, all grieving.

Swan stopped halfway up the Dawn Wall, unable to go on. Below her rooftops, terrace patios, balconies. Lemon trees in giant ceramic pots. A curved slope like a little Marseilles, with white four-story apartment blocks, black iron-railed balconies, broad boulevards and narrow alleys, dropping to a promenade overlooking the park. All crowded with humanity, speciating right before her eyes, each face intensely itself while also a type—Olmec spheroid, hatchet, shovel. On a railing stood three smalls, each about a meter tall, all dressed in black. Down at the foot of the stairs clustered the sunwalkers who had just arrived, looking burnt and dusty. The sight of them pierced Swan—even the sunwalkers had come in for this.

She turned on the stairs and descended, wandered by herself. The moment she had heard the news, she had dashed out of the city onto the land, driven by a need to be alone. Now she couldn't bear to be seen when Alex's ashes were scattered, and she didn't want to see Mqaret, Alex's partner, at that moment. Out into the park, therefore, to wander in the crowd. All of them standing still, looking up, looking distraught. Holding each other up. There were so many people who had relied on Alex. The Lion of Mercury, the heart of the city. The soul of the system. The one who helped and protected you.

Some people recognized Swan, but they left her alone; this was more moving to her than condolences would have been, and her face was wet with tears, she wiped her face with her fingers repeatedly. Then someone stopped her: "You are Swan Er Hong? Alex was your grandmother?"

"She was my everything." Swan turned and walked off. She thought the farm might be emptier, so she left the park and drifted through the trees forward. The city speakers were playing a funeral march. Under a bush a deer nuzzled fallen leaves.

She was not quite to the farm when the Great Gates of the Dawn Wall opened, and sunlight cut through the air under the dome, creating the usual horizontal pair of yellow translucent bars. She focused on the swirls within the bars, the talcum they tossed up there when they opened the gates, colored fines floating on updrafts and dispersing. Then a balloon rose from the high terraces under the wall, drifting west, the little basket swaying under it: Alex; how could it be. A surge of defiance in the music rumbled up out of the basses. When the balloon entered one of the yellow bars of light, the basket blew apart in a poof, and Alex's ashes floated down and out of the light, into the air of the city, growing invisible as they descended, like a shower of virga in the desert. There was a roar from the park, the sound of applause. Briefly some young men somewhere chanted, "A-lex! A-lex! A-lex!" The applause lasted for a couple of minutes, and arranged itself as a rhythmic beat that went on for a long time. People didn't want to give it up; somehow that would be the end, they would at that very moment lose her. Eventually they did give it up, and lived on into the post-Alex phase of their lives.

She needed to go up and join the rest of Alex's family. She groaned at the thought, wandered the farm. Finally she walked up the Great Staircase, stiffly, blindly, pausing once to say, "No, no, no," for a time. But that was pointless. Suddenly she saw: anything she did now would be pointless. She wondered how long that would last—seemed like it could be forever, and she felt a bolt of fear. What would change to change it?

Eventually she pulled herself together and made her way up to the private memorial on the Dawn Wall. She had to greet all those who had been closest to Alex, and give Mqaret a brief rough hug, and withstand the look on his face. But she could see he was not home. This was not like him, but she could fully understand why he might depart. Indeed it was a relief to see it. When she considered how bad she felt, and then how much closer Mqaret had been to Alex than she had been, how much more of his time he spent with her—how long they had been partners—she couldn't imagine what it would feel like. Or maybe she could. So now Mqaret stared at some other reality, from some other reality—as if extending a courtesy to her. So she could hug him, and promise to visit him later, and then go mingle with the others on the highest terrace of the Dawn Wall, and later make her way to a railing and look down at the city, and out its clear bubble to the black landscape outside it. They were rolling through the Kuiper quadrant, and she saw to the right Hiroshige Crater. Once long before, she had taken Alex out there to the apron of Hiroshige to help with one of her goldsworthies, a stone wave that referenced one of the Japanese artist's most famous images. Balancing the rock that would be the crest of the breaking wave had taken them a great number of unsuccessful efforts, and as so often with Alex, Swan had ended up laughing so hard her stomach hurt. Now she spotted the rock wave, still out there—it was just visible from the city. The rocks that had formed the crest of the wave were gone, however—knocked down by the vibration of the passing city, perhaps, or simply by the impact of sunlight. Or fallen at the news.

A few days later she visited Mqaret in his lab. He was one of the leading synthetic biologists in the system, and the lab was filled with machines, tanks, flasks, screens bursting with gnarled colorful diagrams—life in all its sprawling complexity, constructed base pair by base pair. In here they had started life from scratch; they had built many of the bacteria now transforming Venus, Titan, Triton—everywhere.

Now none of that mattered. Mqaret was in his office, sitting in his chair, staring through the wall at nothing.

He roused himself and looked up at her "Oh, Swan—good to see you. Thanks for coming by."

"That's all right. How are you doing?"

"Not so well. How about you?"

"Terrible," Swan confessed, feeling guilty; the last thing she wanted was to add to Mqaret's load somehow. But there was no point in lying at a time like this. And he merely nodded anyway, distracted by his own thoughts. He was just barely there, she saw. The cubes on his desk contained representations of proteins, the bright false colors tangled beyond all hope of untangling. He had been trying to work.

"It must be hard to work," she said.

"Yes, well."

After a blank silence, she said, "Do you know what happened to her?"

He shook his head quickly, as if this was an irrelevance. "She was a hundred and ninety-one."

"I know, but still . . ."

"Still what? We break, Swan. Sooner or later, at some point we break."

"I just wondered why."

"No. There is no why."

"Or how, then . . ."

He shook his head again. "It can be anything. In this case, an aneurysm in a crucial part of the brain. But there are so many ways. The amazing thing is that we stay alive in the first place."

Swan sat on the edge of the desk. "I know. But, so . . . what will you do now?"

"Work."

"But you just said . . ."

He glanced at her from out of his cave. "I didn't say it wasn't any use. That wouldn't be right. First of all,

Alex and I had seventy years together. And we met when I was a hundred and thirty. So there's that. And then also, the work is interesting to me, just as a puzzle. It's a very big puzzle. Too big, in fact." And then he stopped and couldn't go on for a while. Swan put a hand to his shoulder. He put his face in his hands. Swan sat there beside him and kept her mouth shut. He rubbed his eyes hard, held her hand.

"There'll be no conquering death," he said at last. "It's too big. Too much the natural course of things. The second law of thermodynamics, basically. We can only hope to forestall it. Push it back. That should be enough. I don't know why it isn't."

"Because it only makes it worse!" Swan complained. "The longer you live, the worse it gets!"

He shook his head, wiped his eyes again. "I don't think that's right." He blew out a long breath. "It's always bad. It's the people still alive who feel it, though, and so . . ." He shrugged. "I think what you're saying is that now it seems like some kind of mistake. Someone dies, we say why. Shouldn't there have been a way to stop it. And sometimes there is. But . . ."

"It *is* some kind of mistake!" Swan declared. "Reality made a mistake, and now you're fixing it!" She gestured at the screens and cubes. "Right?"

He laughed and cried at the same time. "Right!" he said, sniffing and wiping his face. "It's stupid. What hubris. I mean, fixing reality."

"But it's good," Swan said. "You know it is. It got you seventy years with Alex. And it passes the time."

"It's true." He heaved a big sigh, looked up at her. "But—things won't be the same without her."

Swan felt the desolation of this truth wash through her. Alex had been her friend, protector, teacher, step-grandmother, surrogate mother, all that—but also, a way to laugh. A source of joy. Now her absence created a cold feeling, a killer of emotions, leaving only the blankness that was desolation. Sheer dumb sentience. Here I am. This is reality. No one escapes it. Can't go on, must go on; they never got past that moment.

So on they went.

There was a knock at the lab's outer door. "Come in," Mqaret called a little sharply.

The door opened, and in the entry stood a small— very attractive in the way smalls often were—aged, slender, with a neat blond ponytail and a casual blue jacket—about waist high to Swan or Mqaret, and looking up at them like a langur or marmoset.

"Hello, Jean," Mqaret said. "Swan, this is Jean Genette, from the asteroids, who was here as part of the conference. Jean was a close friend of Alex's, and is an investigator for the league out there, and as such has some questions for us. I said you might be dropping by."

The small nodded to Swan, hand on heart. "My most sincere condolences on your loss. I've come not only to say that, but to tell you that quite a few of us are worried, because Alex was central to some of our most important projects, and her death was so unexpected. We want to make sure these projects go forward, and to be frank, some of us are anxious to be sure that her death was a matter of natural causes."

"I assured Jean that it was," Mqaret told Swan, seeing the look on her face.

Genette did not look completely convinced by this reassurance. "Did Alex ever mention anything to you concerning enemies, threats—danger of any kind?" the small asked Swan.

"No," Swan said, trying to remember. "She wasn't that kind of person. I mean, she was always very positive. Confident that things were going to work out."

"I know. It's so true. But that's why you might remember if she had ever said anything out of keeping with her usual optimism."

"No. I can't remember anything like that."

"Did she leave you any kind of will or trust? Or a message? Something to be opened in the event of her death?"

"No."

"We did have a trust," Mqaret said, shaking his head. "It doesn't have anything unusual in it."

"Would you mind if I had a look around her study?"

Alex had kept her study in a room at the far end of Mqaret's lab, and now Mqaret nodded and led the little inspector down the hall to it. Swan trailed behind them, surprised that Genette had known of Alex's study, surprised Mqaret would be so quick to show it, surprised and upset by this notion of enemies, of "natural causes" and its implied opposite. Alex's death, investigated by some kind of police person? She couldn't grasp it.

While she sat in the doorway trying to figure out what it could mean, trying to come to grips with it, Genette made a thorough search of Alex's office, opening drawers, downloading files, sweeping a fat wand over every surface and object. Mqaret watched it all impassively.

Finally the little inspector was done, and stood before Swan regarding her with a curious look. As Swan was sitting on the floor, they were about eye level. The inspector appeared on the verge of another question, but in the end did not say it. Finally: "If you recall anything you think might help me, I would appreciate you telling me."

"Of course," Swan said uneasily.

The inspector then thanked them and left.

What was that about?" Swan asked Mqaret.

"I don't know," Mqaret said. He too was upset, Swan saw. "I know that Alex had a hand in a lot of things. She's been one of the leaders in the Mondragon Accord from the beginning, and they have a lot of enemies out there. I know she's been worried about some system problems, but she didn't give me any details." He gestured at the lab. "She knew I wouldn't be that interested." A hard grimace. "That I had my own problems. We didn't talk about our work all that much."

"But—" Swan started, and didn't know how to go on. "I mean—enemies? Alex?"

Mqaret sighed. "I don't know. The stakes could be considered high, in some of these matters. There are forces opposed to the Mondragon, you know that."

"But still."

"I know." After a pause: "*Did* she leave you anything?"

"No! Why should she? I mean, she wasn't expecting to die."

"Few people are. But if she had concerns about secrecy, or the safety of certain information, I can see how she might think you would be a kind of refuge."

"What do you mean?"

"Well, couldn't she have put something into your qube without telling you?"

"No. Pauline is a closed system." Swan tapped behind her right ear. "I mostly keep her turned off these days. And Alex wouldn't do that anyway. She wouldn't talk to Pauline without asking me first, I'm sure of it."

Mqaret heaved another sigh. "Well, I don't know. She didn't leave me anything either, as far as I know.

I mean, it would be like Alex to tuck something away without telling us. But nothing has popped up. So I just don't know."

Swan said, "So there wasn't anything unusual in the autopsy?"

"No!" Mqaret said, but he was thinking it over. "A cerebral aneurysm, probably congenital, burst and caused an intraparenchymal hemorrhage. It happens."

Swan said, "If someone had done something to—to cause a hemorrhage . . . would you necessarily be able to tell?"

Mqaret stared at her, frowning.

Then they heard another tap at the lab's outer door. They looked at each other, sharing a little frisson. Mqaret shrugged; he had not been expecting anyone.

"Come in!" he called again.

The door opened to reveal something like the opposite of Inspector Genette: a very big man. Prognathous, callipygous, steatopygous, exophthalmos—toad, newt, frog—even the very words were ugly. Briefly it occurred to Swan that onomatopoeia might be more common than people recognized, their languages echoing the world like birdsong. Swan had a bit of lark in her brain. *Toad.* Once she had seen a toad in an amazonia, sitting at the edge of a pond, its warty wet skin all bronze and gold. She had liked the look of it.

"Ah," Mqaret said. "Wahram. Welcome to our lab. Swan, this is Fitz Wahram, from Titan. He was one of Alex's closest associates, and really one of her favorite people."

Swan, somewhat surprised that Alex could have such a person in her life without Swan ever hearing of it, frowned at the man.

Wahram dipped his head in a kind of autistic bow. He put his hand over his heart. "I am so sorry," he said. A froggy croak. "Alex meant a great deal to me, and to a lot of us. I loved her, and in our work together she was the crucial figure, the leader. I don't know how we will get along without her. When I think of how I feel, I can scarcely grasp how you must feel."

"Thank you," Mqaret said. So strange the words people said at these moments. Swan could not speak any of them.

A person Alex had liked. Swan tapped the skin behind her right ear, activating her qube, which she had turned off as a punishment. Now Pauline would fill her in on things, all by way of a quiet voice in Swan's right ear. Swan was very irritated with Pauline these days, but suddenly she wanted information.

Mqaret said, "So what will happen to the conference?"

"There is complete agreement to postpone it and reschedule. No one has the heart for it now. We will disperse and reconvene later, probably on Vesta."

Ah yes: without Alex, Mercury would no longer be a meeting place. Mqaret nodded at this, unsurprised. "So you will return to Saturn."

"Yes. But before I go, I am curious to know whether Alex left anything for me. Any information or data, in any form."

Mqaret and Swan shared a look. "No," they both said at once. Mqaret gestured. "We were just asked that by Inspector Genette."

"Ah." The toad person regarded them with a pop-eyed stare. Then one of Mqaret's assistants came into the room and asked for his help. Mqaret excused himself, and then Swan was alone with their visitor and his questions.

Very big, this toad person: big shoulders, big chest, big belly. Short legs. People were strange. Now he shook his head and said in a deep gravelly voice—a beautiful voice, she had to admit—froggy, yes, but relaxed, deep, thick with timbre, something like a bassoon or a bass saxophone—"So sorry to bother you at a time like this. I wish we could have met under different circumstances. I am an admirer of your landscape installations. When I heard that you were related to Alex, I asked her if it might be possible to meet you. I wanted to say how much I like your piece at Rilke Crater. It's really very beautiful."

Swan was taken aback by this. At Rilke she had erected a circle of Göbekli T-stones, which looked very contemporary even though they were based on something over ten thousand years old. "Thank you," she said. A cultured toad, it seemed. "Tell me, why did you think Alex might have left a message for you?"

"We were working together on a couple of things," he said evasively, his fixed gaze shifting away. He didn't want to discuss it, she saw. And yet he had come to ask about it. "And, well, she always spoke so highly of you. It was clear you two were close. So . . . she didn't like to put things in the cloud or in any digital form—really, to keep records of our activities in any media at all. She preferred word of mouth."

"I know," Swan said, feeling a stab. She could hear Alex say it: We have to talk! It's a face world! With her intense blue eyes, her laugh. All gone.

The big man saw the change in her and extended a hand. "I'm so sorry," he said again.

"I know," Swan said. Then: "Thank you."

She sat down in one of Mqaret's chairs and tried to think about something else.

After a while the big man said in a gentle rumble, "What will you do now?"

Swan shrugged. "I don't know. I suppose I'll go out on the surface again. That's my place to ... to pull myself together."

"Will you show it to me?"

"What?" Swan said.

"I would be very grateful if you were to take me out there. Maybe show me one of your installations. Or, if you don't mind—I noticed that the city is approaching Tintoretto Crater. My shuttle doesn't leave for a few days, and I would love to see the museum there. I have some questions that can't be resolved on Earth."

"Questions about Tintoretto?"

"Yes."

"Well ..." Swan hesitated, unsure what to say.

"It would be a way to pass the time," the man suggested.

"Yes." This was presumptuous enough to irritate her, but on the other hand, she had in fact been searching for something to distract her, something to do in the aftermath, and no _____ come to her. "Well, I suppose."

"Thank you very _____

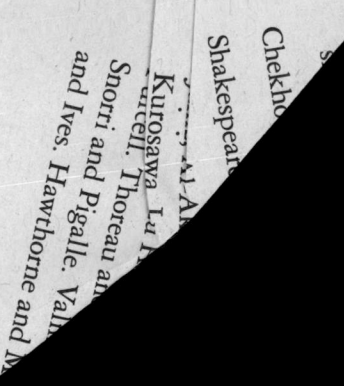

Lists (1)

Ibsen and Imhotep; Mahler, Matisse; Murasaki, Milton, Mark Twain;

Homer and Holbein, touching rims;

Ovid starring the rim of the much larger Pushkin;

Goya overlapping Sophocles.

Van Gogh touching Cervantes, next to Dickens. Stravinsky and Vyasa. Lysippus. Equiano, a West African slave writer, not located near the equator.

Chopin and Wagner right next to each other, equal size.

v and Michelangelo both double craters.

e and Beethoven, giant basins.

khṭal. Aristoxenus, Ashvaghosha.
lsün, Ma Chih-yüan. Proust and
d Li Po, Rūmī and Shelley,
niki, Whitman. Brueghel
elville.

It's said the naming committee of the International Astronomical Union got hilariously drunk one night at their annual meeting, took out a mosaic of the first photos of Mercury, recently received, and used it as a dartboard, calling out to each other the names of famous painters, sculptors, composers, writers—naming the darts, then throwing them at the map.

There is an escarpment named Pourquoi Pas.

SWAN AND WAHRAM

It was not difficult to spot the Titan, standing there by the city's south lock door at the appointed hour. He was in form spherical, or perhaps cubical. As tall as Swan, and Swan was pretty tall. Black hair in tight curls like sheep's wool, cut close to his round head.

Swan approached him. "Off we go," she said gracelessly.

"Thank you again for this."

Terminator began to glide past the platform that held the Tintoretto tram station. They walked through the lock directly into a waiting tram, along with about a dozen other people.

The tram, when it departed, moved much faster than Terminator did, zipping off west on ordinary tram tracks and soon reaching a couple hundred kilometers an hour.

Swan identified a long low hill on the horizon as the outer wall of Hesiod Crater. Wahram consulted his wristpad: "We slide between Hesiod and Sibelius," he announced with a little smile. His pop eyes had brown irises, flecked with radial streaks of black and pumpkin. His wristpad meant he probably did not have a qube stuck in his head, and if he did, it would not be a bitch trying to ruin his day. Pauline was murmuring stuff in her ear, and when Wahram got up to look out the other side of the tram, Swan muttered, "Don't bother me, Pauline. Don't interrupt me, don't distract me."

"Exergasia is one of the weakest of the rhetorical devices," Pauline opined.

"Be quiet!"

After another hour they had a good lead on Terminator, and the tram glided up to the outer wall of Tintoretto Crater, where the tracks led into a tunnel in the rugged wall of old ejecta. As they exited the tram, it announced they had two hours before it would return to the city. Through the vestibule of the museum, then to a long arcing gallery. The inner curve of the chamber was a single recessed window wall, giving them an excellent view of the crater's interior. It was a small but steep-walled crater, a handsome circular space under the stars.

But her Saturnian did not appear to be interested in Mercury. He walked facing the outer wall of the gallery, moving slowly from painting to painting. He planted himself in front of them each in turn, stood staring impassively.

The canvases ranged in size from miniatures to gigantic wall-fillers. The palette of Renaissance Italy fleshed out crowded scenes from the Bible: the Last Supper, the Crucifixion, Paradise, and so on. Mixed in was a bit of classical mythology—including a portrait of Mercury himself, with stylish gold shoes covering his feet, the shoes sporting slots through which Mercury's wings emerged. There were also many portraits of individual sixteenth-century Venetians, vivid to the point of breaking into speech. Most of the paintings were the originals, moved here for safekeeping; the rest were copies so perfect that it would take a chemical analysis to tell them from the originals. As with many of Mercury's single-artist museums, the hope was to gather all the original paintings here and locate only copies on Earth, to take on the intense assault of that most volatile environment—oxidation, corrosion, rust, fire, theft, vandalism, smog, acid, daylight. . . . Here, in contrast, everything was controlled, benign—safer. Or so it was said by Mercurial curators. The Terrans were not always so sure.

Toad Man was very slow on his feet. He stood right next to the paintings, for a long time, sometimes with his nose only a centimeter from the paint. Tintoretto's *Paradise* was twenty meters wide and ten tall—the notes said it was the largest painting ever painted on canvas— and very crowded with figures. Wahram moved all the way back to the clear inner wall to look at this one for a while, then took his more usual position nuzzling it. "Interesting how he has angels' wings as being black," he murmured, breaking his silence at last. "It looks good. And look here, see how the white lines in this one angel's black wings actually form letters. *C H E R*, see? Then the rest of the word is hidden in a fold. That's what I wanted to check. I wonder what that was about."

"Some kind of code?"

He didn't reply. Swan wondered if this was his usual response to art. He ambled on to the next painting. Possibly he was humming to himself. He was not interested in her response to these paintings, even though he knew she was an artist. She wandered on her own, looking at the portraits. The big crowd scenes were too much for her, like epic movies all jammed into a single frame. The subjects of the portraits, on the other hand, looked at her with expressions she recognized immediately. "I am always me, I am always new, I am always me"—for eight centuries they had been saying it. Nothing but women and men. One woman had her left nipple exposed, just under the curve of a necklace; in most periods that would have been transgressive, she seemed to recall. Almost all the women were very small-breasted and big-waisted. Well-fed, under-exercised; didn't nurse their own babies; not working people. The bodies of nobles. Beginning of speciation. Tintoretto's *Leda* looked quite fond of the swan ravishing her, in fact was protecting the swan from an intruder. Swan had once or twice been swan to a Leda, not violently of course—at least not physical violence—and she recalled some of the Ledas had liked it. Others not.

She returned to Wahram, who was again inspecting *Paradise*, this time from as far away as he could get, thus at a slant. To Swan it still seemed a mess. "It's very crowded," she said. "The figures are in too symmetrical a pattern, and God and Christ look like doges. Indeed the whole thing looks like a Venetian senate meeting. Maybe that was Tintoretto's idea of paradise."

"Hmm," he said.

"You don't agree. You like it."

"I'm not sure," he said, and walked a few meters away from her.

He didn't want to talk about it. Swan went off to look at more Venetians. For her art was something to make, first and foremost, and after that something to talk about. Ineffable aesthetic responses, *communing* with a work—these struck her as too precious. One of the portraits glowered, another tried to suppress a little ironic smile; they agreed with her. She was out here with a stick of a toad. Mqaret had said Alex revered this man, but now she doubted it could be true. Who was he? What was he?

A low recorded announcement informed them it was time for the tram to take them back to Terminator, which would soon be catching up to their longitude— as would the sun. "Oh no!" Wahram exclaimed faintly as he heard the announcement. "We've only just started!"

"There are over three hundred paintings here," Swan pointed out. "One visit will never do. You'll have to come back."

"I hope," he said. "These are really magnificent. I can see why they called him Il Furioso. He must have worked every day."

"I think that's right. He had a place in Venice that he rarely left. A closed shop. His assistants were mostly his children." Swan had just read this on one of the notes.

"Interesting." He sighed and followed her to the tram.

On the ride back to the city, they passed a group of sunwalkers, and Swan pointed them out. Her guest roused himself from his reverie and looked.

"So they have to keep moving," he said. "How do they rest, eat, sleep?"

"We eat on our feet, and sleep in carts pulled by companions," Swan said. "We take turns at that, and on it goes."

He gave her a look. "So you have an inexorable spur to action. I can see the appeal."

She almost laughed. "Do you need such a spur?"

"I think everyone does. Don't you?"

"No. Not at all."

"But you join these ferals," he said.

"That's just to do it. To see the land and the sun. I check out things I made, or do a little crack mining. I don't need to find reasons to stay busy."

This was exactly backward, she realized, and shut her mouth.

"You're lucky," he said. "Most people do."

"Do you think?"

"Yes." He gestured at the sunwalkers, whom they were rapidly leaving behind. "What happens if you run into an obstruction that keeps you from continuing westward?"

"You have to avoid those. In some places they've built little ramps that go up cliffs, or trail systems that get through chaotic terrain quickly. There are routes established. Some people stick to certain routes, some do them all. Others like to try new terrain. It's pretty common to do a complete circumnavigation."

"Have you done that?"

"Yes, but it's too long for me. I usually go out for a week or two."

"I see."

It was pretty clear he didn't.

"We were made to do this, you know," she said suddenly. "Our bodies are nomads. Humans and hyenas are the two predators that chase their prey down by wearing it out."

"I like walking," he allowed.

"So what about you? What do you do to occupy your time?"

"I think," he said promptly.

"And that's enough for you?"

He glanced at her. "There's a lot to think about."

"But what do you *do*?"

"I suppose I read. Travel. Listen to music. Look at the visual arts." He thought some more. "I work on the Titan project, that's very interesting, I find."

"And the Saturnian league, more generally, Mqaret tells me. System diplomacy."

"Yes, well, my name came up in the lottery and I had to do my time, but it's almost over now, and then I plan to return to Titan and get back to my waldo."

"So . . . what were you and Alex working on?"

His pop eyes took on a look of alarm. "Well, some of it she wouldn't want me to talk about. But she spoke of you often, and now that she's gone, I just wondered if she might have left you a message. Or even arranged things such that you might be able to step in a bit in her absence."

"What do you mean?"

"Well, you designed many of the terraria out there, and now they form the bulk of the Mondragon Accord. They would listen to you, perhaps, knowing you were one of Alex's closest confidantes. So . . . possibly you could go out with me and meet some people."

"What, to Saturn?"

"To Jupiter, actually."

"I don't want to do that. My life is here, my work. I traveled the system enough when I was young."

He nodded unhappily. "And . . . you are quite certain Alex didn't leave anything for you? Something to give to me, in case something happened to her?"

"Yes, I'm sure! There's nothing! She didn't do things like that."

He shook his head. They sat in silence as the tram slid over the dark face of Mercury. To the north some hilltops were just sparking white with the rising sunlight. Then the top of Terminator's dome appeared over the horizon, like the shell of a transparent egg. As it cleared the horizon, the city looked like a snow globe, or a ship in a bottle—an ocean liner on a black sea, caught in a bubble of green light. "Tintoretto would have liked your city," Wahram said. "It looks like a kind of Venice."

"No it doesn't," Swan said crossly, thinking hard.

.

TERMINATOR

Terminator rolls around Mercury just like its sun-walkers, moving at the speed of the planet's rotation, gliding over twenty gigantic elevated tracks, which together hold aloft and push west a town quite a bit bigger than Venice. The twenty tracks run around Mercury like a narrow wedding band, keeping near the forty-fifth latitude south, but with wide detours to south and north to avoid the worst of the planet's long escarpments. The city moves at an average of five kilometers an hour. The sleeves on the underside of the city are fitted over the track at a tolerance so fine that the thermal expansion of the tracks' austenite stainless steel is always pushing the city west, onto the narrower tracks still in the shade. A little bit of resistance to this movement creates a great deal of the city's electricity.

From the top of the Dawn Wall, which is a silvery cliff forming the eastern edge of the city, one can see the whole town stretching out to the west, green under its clear dome. The city illuminates the dark landscape around it like a passing lamp; the illumination is very noticeable except at those times when high cliffs west of the city reflect horizontal sunlight into town. Even these mere pinpricks of the dawn more than equal the artificial lights inside the dome. During these cliff-blinks nothing has a shadow; space turns strange. Then the mirrors are passed; that light fades. These shifts in illumination are a significant part of the sensation of movement one has in Terminator, for the glide over the tracks is very smooth. Changes in light, slight tilts in pitch, these make it seem as if the town were a ship, sailing over a black ocean with waves so large that when in their troughs, the ship drops into the night, then on high points crests back into day.

The city sliding at its stately pace completes a revolution every 177 days. Round after round, nothing changing but the land itself; and the land only changes because the sunwalkers include landscape artists, who are out there polishing mirror cliffs, carving petroglyphs, erecting cairns and dolmens and inuksuit, and arranging blocks and lines of metal to expose to the melt of day. Thus Terminator's citizens continuously glide and walk over their world, remaking it day by day into something more expressive of their thoughts. All cities, and all their citizens, move in just such a way.

SWAN AND ALEX

The next day Swan returned to Mqaret's lab. Again he was in his office staring at nothing. Suddenly Swan realized it was a relief to have something to be angry at.

Mqaret roused himself. "How was your trip out with Wahram?"

"He's slow, he's rude, he's autistic. He's boring."

Mqaret smiled a little. "Actually it sounds like you found him interesting."

"Please."

"Well, I can assure you Alex found him interesting. She spoke of him pretty often. A few times she made it clear they were involved in things she thought were very important."

This gave Swan pause, as it was meant to. "Gran, can I have another look around her study?"

"Of course."

Swan went down the hall to Alex's room at the end, entered, and closed the door. She went to the one window and looked out at the city, all roof tiles and greenery from this vantage point.

She wandered around the study, looking at things. Mqaret had not yet changed anything. She wondered if he would, and if so, when. All Alex's things, scattered as always. Her absence was a kind of presence, and again grief stabbed through Swan's middle and she had to sit down.

After a while she stood and began a more methodical examination. If Alex had left something for her, where would she have put it? Swan could not guess. Alex had wanted always to keep her business offline, out of the cloud, unrecorded, live only, in real time only. But if she had done anything like this, she would have to have figured out some kind of method. Knowing her, it might be a purloined-letter type of thing: a paper note, for instance, right there on her desktop.

So Swan hunted through small stacks of paper on her desk, still thinking it over. If she had had information she wanted Swan to pass along, without Swan necessarily knowing what it was... if there were a lot of data... possibly it would be more than a paper note. And possibly she would want only Swan to find it.

She began to wander the room, talking to herself, and looking closely at things. The room's control AI would know the room was occupied by only a single person and, with voice and retina, could certainly be set to identify the person.

There was a little toilet room attached to the study, with a sink and mirror, so now she went into it. "I'm here, Alex," Swan said sadly. "I'm here if you want me."

She looked into the wall mirror, then into a little oval mirror on a stand next to the sink. Sad Swan's bloodshot eyes.

A jewelry box next to the oval mirror fell open; Swan jumped back into the wall, then collected herself.

She looked in the box. Jewelry tray; take it out; and under it were three small white paper envelopes. All had written on one side *In Case of My Death*; on the other sides they were marked *For Mqaret*, *For Swan*, and *For Wang on Io*.

Hands trembling, Swan took the one marked for her and tore it open. Two little data tabs fell out. One of them was murmuring, "Swan, Swan, Swan." Swan put it to her ear, her teeth clenched, tears starting to her eyes.

"My dear Swan, I am sorry you are hearing this," Alex's voice said. It was just like hearing a ghost, and Swan clutched her hands over her chest.

The little voice went on: "Very sorry, in fact, because if you're hearing this, it means I'm gone. My room AI has heard about my death, and it knows to open this box if you come in here alone. It's the best plan I could think of. Sorry to intrude on you like this, but it's important. This is kind of an insurance policy, because I've got some things going on that need to continue even if I die, and I don't want to tell anyone else here about them. And really at our age you can go any time, so I'm setting this up. If you're hearing this, I need your help. Please take the envelope for Wang out to Io and give it to him in person. Wang and I and a few others are working on a couple of very important projects together, and we've been trying to keep completely offline with them, which is very difficult to do when we live so far apart. You can help me hugely by taking him his envelope. But please keep the matter entirely to yourself. Also, if you would let your Pauline read the other chip in your envelope and then destroy the chip, that would serve as a secure backup. They both are one-reads. I hate to do even this much. But I know you don't usually link Pauline to other qubes, and if you would keep it that way, it would be better for our plan. Wang will explain more to you, as will Wahram from Titan. Good-bye, my Swan. I love you."

That was it. Swan tried to listen to it again, but it was inert.

She put the other tab up to Pauline's membrane, in the skin at the base of her neck. When Pauline said "Done" she put the inert tabs and the two remaining envelopes into her pocket and went to find Mqaret.

He was in his office, poking around in a 3-D image of what looked like a protein. "Look what I found," Swan said. She explained what had happened.

"That box was locked," Mqaret said. "I knew it was her jewelry, and I figured I would run into the key some time or other."

He stared blankly at his envelope, seeming in no hurry to open it; possibly even a little afraid of it. Swan let him be, went out of the room. "Pauline," she said after she left, "you got the contents of that tab?"

"Yes."

"What was on it?"

"I am instructed to convey the information to Wang's qube, on Io."

"But tell me just generally what's on it."

Pauline did not reply, and after a while Swan cursed her and turned her off.

Both tabs were now inert; Alex's ghost had departed. Swan was not entirely sorry. The shock of hearing Alex's voice speaking to her was still causing her to tremble.

She went back into Mqaret's office. He was white-faced, his mouth a little knot. He looked up at her.

"She gave you something to take to Io?"

"Yes. Do you know what it's about?"

"No. But I do know Alex had an inner group of especially close associates. Wahram was one of them, and Wang too."

"And what were they up to?"

Mqaret shrugged. "She spared me that kind of thing. But I could see she thought it was important. Something about Earth, I think."

Swan thought it over. "If it was important, and she was keeping things off the record, she would have known her death might cause problems. So she left us these little recordings."

"It was like her ghost," Mqaret said shakily. "She spoke to me."

"Yes," Swan said, unable to say more. "Well...I guess I'm going to take the third envelope she left to Io, like she told me to."

"Good," Mqaret said.

"Wahram already asked me to go out there, now that I think of it. And he kept asking if she left us anything for him."

Mqaret nodded. "He was part of it."

"Yes. And that inspector too. So I guess I'll go. But I don't think I want to tell him about these messages. Alex didn't say anything about that."

"He may guess, just by the fact you're going."

"Let him guess."

Now Mqaret regarded her with a sympathetic squint. "You're going to have to figure things out as best you can. You may even have to step in and do some of the things Alex would have done."

"How can I do that? No one can do that."

"You don't know. Pauline will help you, and maybe this Titan of yours also. And if you have to act in Alex's place—she would have liked that."

"Maybe." Swan was not so sure.

"Alex will have had a plan. She always did."

Swan sighed, lanced again by the thought of Alex's absence. These ghostly messages were not even close to an adequate replacement for her. "All right, then. I'll go out to see this Wang."

"Good. And be ready to act."

Swan found out where the offworld diplomats still in town were staying, went to the terrace where the Saturnian delegation had been housed. When she entered the courtyard of the place, she immediately came on Wahram, head down as he conferred with the little police inspector, Jean Genette. The sight of the two of them together gave her a shock, and something in their body language said they were well acquainted. Co-conspirators, by the look of them.

Cheeks burning, Swan approached them. "What's this?" she demanded. "I didn't know you two knew each other."

Neither of them at first replied.

Finally the small waved a hand. "Fitz Wahram and I often work together on various system issues. We were just now deciding to visit a mutual acquaintance."

"Wang?" Swan said. "Wang of Io?"

"Why . . . yes," the inspector said, looking up at her curiously. "Wang is an associate of ours, as he was of Alex. We were working together."

"As I mentioned to you," Wahram said in his low croak. "When we were coming back from Tintoretto."

"Yes, yes," Swan said sharply. "You asked me to join you on that trip, without really explaining why."

"Well . . ." The toad man's broad face was looking a little discomfited. "It's true, but you see, there are reasons to be discreet...." He looked down at Genette as if hoping for help.

"I'm going," Swan said, interrupting their glance. "I want to go."

"Ah," Wahram said with another quick glance at Genette. "Good."

Extracts (1)

Take an asteroid at least thirty kilometers on its long axis. Any type will do—solid rock, rock and ice, metallic, even ice balls, although each presents different problems.

Attach a self-replicating excavator assembly to one end of the asteroid, and with it, hollow out your asteroid along its long axis. Leave the wall at least two kilometers thick at all points except for your entry hole. Assure the interior integrity of the wall by coating it with a dura of suitable strength.

As your assembly hollows the interior, be aware that ejection of the excavated material (best aimed toward a Lagrange salvage point, to collect the salvage fee) will represent your best chance to reposition your terrarium, if you want it in a different orbit. Store excess ejecta on the surface for later use.

When the interior is hollowed out, leaving an empty cylinder at least five kilometers in diameter and ten kilometers long (but bigger is better!), your excavator assembly will return to the access hole and there reconfigure itself into your terrarium's propulsion unit.

Depending on the mass of your new world, you may want to install a mass driver, an antimatter "lightning push" engine, or an Orion pusher plate.

Beyond the forward end of the cylinder, on the bow of your new terrarium, attach a forward unit at the point of the long axis. Eventually your terrarium will be spinning at a rotational rate calculated to create the effect of gravity on the inner surface of the interior cylinder so that when you are inside, you will be pulled to the floor as if in a gravity field. This is the g equivalent, or gequivalent. The forward unit will then be connected to the bow of the terrarium by a geared axle, to allow the forward unit not to spin but instead to stay fixed. It will be nearly weightless in this bowsprit chamber, but many functions of the terrarium will go better without the spinning, including docking, viewing, navigating, etc.

It is possible to build an interior cylinder that spins freely inside an asteroid that does not spin—the so-called prayer wheel configuration—and this does give you both an interior with g effect and a non-spinning exterior, but it is expensive and finicky. Not recommended, though we have seen some good ones.

When stern and bow are properly installed and configured, and the asteroid is set spinning, the interior is ready to be terraformed.

Begin with a light dusting of heavy metals and rare earths, as specified for the biome you are trying to create. Be aware that no Terran biome ever began with the simple ingredients you will be starting with on an asteroid. Biospheres need their vitamins right from the start, so be sure to arrange for the importation of the mix you want, usually including molybdenum, selenium, and phosphorus. These are often applied in "puff bombs" set off along the axis of the cylindrical space. Don't poison yourself when you do this!

After that, string the axis of the cylinder with your terrarium's sunline. This is a lighting element, on which the lit portion moves at whatever speed you choose. The lit portion of the sunline usually starts the day in the stern of the cylinder, after a suitable period of darkness (during which any streetlights overhead will serve as stars). The lit portion of the line, appropriately bright, then traverses the sunline from stern to bow (or east to west, as some describe it), taking usually the same time as a Terran day, as measured by the latitude of your biome on Earth. Seasons inside your terrarium will be rendered accordingly.

Now you can aerate the interior to the gas mix and pressure you desire, typically somewhere between 500 and 1100 millibars of pressure, in something like the Terran mix of gases, with perhaps a dash more oxygen, though the fire risk quickly rises there.

After that, you need biomass. Naturally you will have in your spice rack the complete genetic codes of all the creatures you intend to introduce into your biome. Generally you will be either recreating some Terran biome, or else mixing up something new, hybrid biomes most people call Ascensions, after Ascension Island on Earth, the site of the first such hybrid (started inadvertently by Darwin himself!) All the genomes for all the species of your particular biome will be available for print on demand, except for the bacteria involved, which are simply too numerous and too genetically labile to categorize. For them you will have to apply the appropriate inoculant, usually a muck or goo made of a few tons of the bacterial suite that you want.

Luckily bacteria grow very fast in an empty ecological niche, which is what you now have. To make it even more welcoming, scrape the interior wall of your cylinder, then crumble the rock of the scrapings finely, to a consistency ranging from large gravel to sand. Mixed with an edible aerogel, this then becomes the matrix for your soil. Put all the ice gathered in your scraping aside, except for enough when melted to make your crumbled rock matrix moist. Then add your bacterial inoculant and turn up the heat to around three hundred K. The matrix will rise like yeasted dough as it becomes that most delicious and rare substance, soil. (Those wanting a fuller explanation of how to make soil are referred to my bestselling *All About Dirt*.)

With a soil base cooked up, your biome is well on its way. Succession regimens at this point will vary, depending on what you are looking for at climax. But it's true to say that a lot of terraria designers start out with a marsh of some kind, because it's the fastest way to bulk up your soil and your overall biomass. So if you are in a hurry to occupy, this is often a good way to start.

When you've got a warm marsh going, either freshwater or salt, you are already cooking good. Smells will rise in your cylinder, also hydrological problems. Fish, amphibian, animal, and bird populations can be introduced at this point, and should be if you want maximum biomass growth. But here you have to watch out for a potential danger: once you get your marsh going, you may fall in love with it. Fine for you, but it happens a bit too often. We have too many estuarine biomes now, and not enough of the other biomes we are hoping to cook out here.

So try to keep your distance at this point; keep a depopulate marsh, or stay away from it during this part of the process. Or join a trading scheme in which you trade asteroids when they are at the marsh point, so that you come into a new one wanting to change things, unattached to what's already there.

With the hefty biomass created by a marsh, you can then build up land using some of your excavated materials, saved on the surface of the asteroid for this moment. Hills and mountains look great and add texture, so be bold! This process will redirect your water into new hydrologies, and this is the best time to introduce new species, also to export species you no longer want, giving them to newer terraria that might need them.

Thus over time you can transform the interior of your terrarium to any of the 832 identified Terran biomes, or design an Ascension of your own making. (Be warned that many Ascensions fall as flat as bad soufflés. The keys to a successful Ascension are so many that I have had to pen another volume, *How to Mix and Match Biomes!*, now available.)

Ultimately you will need to make many temperature, landscape, and species adjustments, to get to the kind of stable climax community you want. Any possible landscape is achievable; sometimes the results are simply stunning. Always the entire landscape will be curving up around you, rising on both sides and meeting overhead, so that the look of the land will envelop you like a work of art—a goldsworthy inscribed on the inside of a rock, like a geode or a Fabergé egg.

Obviously it is also possible to make interiors that are all liquid. Some of these aquaria or oceanaria include archipelagoes; others are entirely water, even their walls, which are sometimes refrozen transparently so that in the end when you approach them, they look like diamonds or water droplets floating in space. Some aquaria have no air space in their middles.

As for aviaries, every terrarium and most aquaria are also aviaries, stuffed with birds to their maximum carrying capacity. There are fifty billion birds on Earth, twenty billion on Mars; we in the terraria could outmatch them both combined.

Each terrarium functions as an island park for the animals inside it. Ascensions cause hybridization and ultimately new species. The more traditional biomes conserve species that on Earth are radically endangered or extinct in the wild. Some terraria even look like zoos; more are purely wilderness refugia; and most mix parkland and human spaces in patterned habitat corridors that maximize the life of the biome as a whole. As such, these spaces are already crucial to humanity and the Earth. And there are also the heavily agricultural terraria, farmworlds devoted to producing what has become a very large percentage of the food feeding the people of Earth.

These facts are worth noting and enjoying. We cook up our little bubble worlds for our own pleasure, the way you would cook a meal, or build something, or grow a garden—but it's also a new thing in history, and the heart of the Accelerando. I can't recommend it too highly! The initial investment is nontrivial, but there are still many unclaimed asteroids out there.

WAHRAM AND SWAN

Although no doubt they were simply the result of an engineering response to an engineering problem, regarded as an aesthetic matter the Mercurial launching gyres were interesting. A maglev tube twisted in a cone set on its point, increasing in size as it rose. The tip of the cone was secured to a platform that moved in a circle, about the size of the widest part of the cone. The movement of the platform exaggerated very effectively the force of acceleration on the ferries as they were being magnetically thrown up the tube. Thus the ferry they were in had them seated sideways to the ground, but as it careened around and up, their floor became most definitely down, and then with dizzying speed they were launched into space, going so fast that if there had been an atmosphere they would have burned to a crisp the moment they left the tube. The effect as seen from the spaceport resembled some kind of antique carnival ride. From inside the ferry it proved to be a quite serious acceleration, very near the maximum allowed in commercial travel, which was 3.5 g.

Swan Er Hong had strapped herself into the seat

beside Wahram just before takeoff, grimacing apologetically at the cliché of her lateness. Now she leaned toward him to look out the little window at the rapidly receding craterscape of her home world. Quickly the land changed from a plane to a ball, a thin crescent of it bathed in sunlight, the gibbous nightside black. Mercury was an interesting place, but Wahram was not unhappy to leave; despite the locals' best efforts to spruce it up with art, the landscape was a cindery clinker. And the truth was that when he was inside its marvelous gliding city, the sudden blink of illumination on high points to the west always reminded him of the sun, following them relentlessly, always about to burst over the horizon and torch everything.

Their ferry was going to catch the terrarium *Alfred Wegener*, which was moving so fast that the ferry would have to make another long three-g burn to catch up. During this time, Wahram shifted his seat into bed mode and endured like everyone else. Across the room Swan groaned and curled around herself on her bed. Wahram forbade himself to think about the studies that had been made on the effect of g-forces on the human brain, delicate goo that it was, trapped without much padding inside its hard prison walls. Then the *Wegener* caught them and reeled them in with a final little squish of g, as if to emphasize the problem.

After that Wahram and the other passengers had to adjust to the sudden weightlessness, and pull themselves from the ferry into the terrarium's dock, then through the neck and down broad padded stairs to the cylinder floor.

The interior space in the *Wegener* was pretty substantial, about twenty kilometers long and five across, spun to a one-g equivalent. The great majority of the interior space was park, with a few small towns scattered mostly fore and aft. The mix of savanna and pampas was very attractive, Wahram thought as he walked toward the first village, looking up at the land overhead. Grass prairie and patches of forest arched like a giant Sistine Chapel overhead, a Sistine on which Michelangelo had painted a version of Eden—a savanna, the first human landscape, appealing to something very deep in the mind. Although terrarium topology always made Wahram feel as if he were inside a map that had been rolled into a tube. As one looked along the longitude line one occupied, the land always appeared as a long U-valley, with nearby trees topped by higher, more distant trees, tilting toward the valley bottom in a curve of ever-steepening parkland, up to vertical side walls, as in certain great glacial U-valleys—but then the walls continued up and folded over, breaking past verticality in a manner very distinct to the eye. Above that line the landscape was simply overhead, and quite undeniably upside down. As now, for instance, when beyond a cloud he saw the tops of a sheet of flocking birds, flying over the surface of a lake hanging directly over his head.

Wahram went to a little Saturn House in the first town, called Plum Lake, and checked in. They kept a restaurant in the ground floor, so he signed up for kitchen duties (he liked all the simplest chores), and after showering he took a walk around the town. It was a handsome place, with a lakefront and a hill, and a tram station at its eastern end. Trams ran through parkland to the other towns. The central plaza was full of Venusians, presumably on their way home: tall broad-shouldered young Chinese, for the most part, with intent eyes and big smiles. They were working on Venus hip deep in dry ice, doing dangerous things. Wahram engaged in similar work when he was home on Titan, but Titan had only .14 g, and this had often saved him from little accidents; Venus, at .9 g, impressed him as dangerous.

At the edge of town he came to a line of trees and a fence. He signed in at a little kiosk and read on a plaque that his new acquaintance Swan Er Hong had designed the biome here some seventy years before. This was a surprise; he had heard she had once been a designer, but she had shown no interest in the *Wegener* when they arrived.

Wahram took a little stun gun out of a box of them, put it in the pocket of his coat, and let himself through the gate into the park. He walked at an angle up the curve of the land. The soil was a thick black loam, with a mixed Tanzanian and Argentinian provenance, he had read at the kiosk. A stand of broad-topped acacia trees showed signs of elephant damage on their trunks. Treetops directly overhead looked like round bumps of lichen. Tall clumps of grass obscured the view beyond his immediate locality; one could see more up where the park curved over the nearby treetops. Up to his left, over the trees, a little knoll of rocks looked like a good lookout; although of course that might have occurred to a puma or a hyena, so he was careful as he approached. Most animals were wary of humans, but he didn't want to surprise anybody. You don't need danger to get your thrills, his mother used to tell him. That would be decadent, and I don't like decadence! The rest of his parents had not been so judgmental, perhaps considering that as they were all living around Saturn, their take on danger might be skewed. But his mother had made her point, and Wahram was not decadent; he was continually shocked by the new; and now his heart was pounding a little.

The knoll was empty, however. The rocks were spotted with actual lichen, as if sprayed with a surfacing of semiprecious stones, yellow and red and pale green. He crouched in a crack and had a look around.

There were a mother cheetah and two cubs, below him in clumps of bunchgrass. The mother's attention was focused on some pampas deer grazing in the mid-distance. Wahram wondered what pampas deer made of cheetahs—whether there had been any predator that fast in South America. It seemed unlikely.

He felt lucky to see cheetahs on their feet, as it seemed they were usually asleep. It looked like this mother was trying to teach her cubs how to hunt; she squashed one down with a forepaw to get it to flatten. The chiral wind was rushing down from the left, so he was crosswind to the cats; they would not smell him. Or so it seemed, although in fact many animals' senses were so sharp as to make humans seem deaf and dumb.

He settled down to watch. The cubs, still brindled, were looking confused, as if they didn't even comprehend the concept of a lesson. They batted each other still, as if wanting to play. The peak point of brain growth was also the peak point of playfulness.

They were downwind of the deer, who looked unruffled and were coming their way. The mama cheetah crouched in the grass, and now her cubs were doing likewise, their tails twitching uncontrollably.

Then the mama was off in a burst of grass blades, and the cubs bounded after. The deer dashed away in great pronging leaps, leaving the cheetahs in the dust; but then the deer had to diverge around some trees, and the mother cheetah intercepted the last deer in one group and knocked it over in a tangle of fur that ended with her on top, teeth sunk in the spine at the deer's neck, holding on. The deer heaved up a little and then was still. The sight of blood was its usual red shock. The cubs arrived late, and Wahram wondered if their lesson had taught them anything but the need to grow up, the need to run fast.

He found he was standing. And now, looking left at some motion, he saw another person: Swan. Surprised, he waved to her, and she lifted her chin as she continued to watch the cheetah kill. The mother was now teaching the kittens how to eat a deer, not that they needed much instruction there. Wahram surveyed the scene. The lit part of the sunline was now far toward the fore end of the terrarium, its light slanting back with a sunset tint. Masses of grass clumps waved in the wind. It felt like an ancient moment.

Swan walked over to him and ascended the knoll. It was going to be a little embarrassing to be found out here alone, which in some parks was not legal, and in general was not considered prudent. Then again, here she was too.

He nodded his greeting, formal but not unfriendly. "Unusual luck to see such a thing," he remarked as she approached.

"Yes," she said. "Are you out here alone?"

"I am. And you?"

"Alone, yes." She was looking at him curiously. "I'm surprised to find you out here, I must confess. I didn't know you liked this kind of thing."

"Mercury isn't really where you would find out."

She gestured at the cats. "You aren't worried?"

"They're scared of people, I find."

"Well, but if they're hungry..."

"But they never are, that's the thing. There's so much easy prey."

"That's true. But if they have never run into people before, they'll just think of you as a kind of chimp. Very tasty, no doubt. A delicacy. You hear of it happening. They have no experience of being hunted."

"I'm aware we could be prey," Wahram said. "I carry a little stunner just in case. Don't you?"

"I don't," she admitted after a pause. "I mean, sometimes I do, but mostly to avoid spending a night in jail."

"Indeed."

She tilted her head, as if listening to a voice in her ear. She had had her qube implanted, Alex had told him, back when the idea was fashionable. "Speaking of eating," she said, "shall we get something?"

"My pleasure."

They returned to the perimeter fence. When they reached it, they found a little group at the kiosk; these people saw Swan and crowded around her, greeted her cheerfully. "What do you think?" they asked her. "How do you like it now that it's all grown up?"

"It's looking good," she told them in a reassuring tone. "We saw a cheetah take down a pampas deer. I thought maybe there were too many deer, actually, what's that about?"

One of the group said deer were high because cats were still low, and Swan asked some questions about that. Wahram gathered that predator-prey populations went up and down in sine wave patterns tied together, and predators moved up or down a quarter of a cycle behind prey; there were further complications that Wahram couldn't follow from what they were saying.

When Swan was done with her conversation, she led him along the street back to the town.

"So they knew you designed this terrarium," Wah ram said as they walked.

"Yes, I'm surprised anyone remembers. I hardly do myself."

"So you were an ecologist?"

"A designer. It was a long time ago. I don't like a lot of what I did, to tell the truth. These Ascensions are too much. We need all the terraria to be conserving species gone on Earth. I don't know what I was thinking. But I wouldn't say that to the people who live here. They're into this, it's their place."

They hiked up the curve of the cylinder several degrees. A cloud they had seen overhead at sunset, hugging the land above like an orange shawl, had come round the cylinder and now immersed them in a diffuse fog. Things lost their shadows in the misty twilight, and the land above went invisible, the few lights on the other side like blurred stars. It seemed a different world now, an outie rather than an innie.

Wahram explained that he had signed up to run dishwashers in the Saturnian restaurant, so they made their way back to the Saturn House in Plum Lake and ate there. Swan hadn't signed up for any work; she seldom did, she said. As they sat there she grew quiet and distracted, looked out the window, then around the room, always moving just a little, tapping a foot, rubbing fingertips together. They ate and she went completely silent. No doubt she was still grieving for Alex. Wahram, often pierced by the thought of the loss himself, could only wordlessly sympathize; but then she tilted her head to the side and said, "Quit talking to me, I don't want to hear you."

"What's that?" Wahram said.

"I'm sorry," she said. "I'm talking to my qube."

"Can you make it so that it speaks aloud?"

"Of course," Swan said. "Pauline, you can speak up."

A voice coming from the right side of Swan's head said, "I am Pauline, Swan's faithful quantum computer." It sounded like Swan's voice, except, as it was projected from speaker buds in her skin, a little muffled.

Swan made a face and began to spoon soup into her mouth. Nonplussed, Wahram focused on eating. Then Swan snapped, "Well then you talk to him!"

The voice from the side of her head said, "I understand you are traveling to the Jupiter system."

"Yes," Wahram said warily. If Swan had just assigned her qube to do her talking for her, that did not seem like a good thing. But he wasn't sure that was what was happening.

"What kind of artificial intelligence are you?" he asked.

"I am a quantum computer, model Ceres 2196a."

"I see."

"She is one of the first and weakest of the qubes," Swan said. "A feeb."

Wahram pondered this. Asking How smart are you? was probably never a polite thing. Besides, no one was ever very good at making such an assessment. "What do you like to think about?" he asked instead.

Pauline said, "I am designed for informative conversation, but I cannot usually pass a Turing test. Would you like to play chess?"

He laughed. "No."

Swan was looking out the window. Wahram considered her, went back to focusing on his meal. It took a lot of rice to dilute the fiery chilies in the dish.

Swan muttered bitterly to herself, "You insist on

interfering, you insist on talking, you insist on pretending that everything is normal."

The qube voice said, "Anaphora is one of the weakest rhetorical devices, really nothing more than redundancy."

"*You* complain to *me* about redundancy? How many times did you parse that sentence, ten trillion?"

"It did not take that many times."

Silence. Both of them appeared to be done with speech.

"Do you study rhetoric?" Wahram asked.

The qube voice said, "Yes, it is a useful analytic tool."

"Give me an example, please."

"When you say exergasia, synathroesmus, and incrementum together in a list, it seems to me that you have thereby given an example of all three devices in that same phrase."

Swan snorted at this. "How so, Socrates?"

" 'Exergasia' means 'use of different phrases to express the same idea,' 'synathroesmus' means 'accumulation by enumeration,' and 'incrementum' means 'piling up points to make an argument.' So listing them does all three, yes?"

"And what argument would you be piling up points in?" Swan asked.

"That I was giving you too much credit in thinking you were using many different devices, when really you only have the one method, because these are distinctions without a difference."

"Ha-ha," Swan said sarcastically.

But Wahram had only just kept himself from laughing.

The qube went on: "One could also argue that the classical system of rhetoric is a false taxonomy, a kind of fetishism—"

"Enough!"

The silence stretched on.

"I'm going to help in the kitchen," Wahram said, and got up.

After a while she followed him in and emptied dishwashers next to the window, looking out at the fog. There was a bottle of wine and she poured a glass. The wet clank of kitchen work always struck him as a kind of music.

"Say something!" she commanded at one point.

"I'm thinking about those cheetahs," he said, startled, hoping she was speaking to him, even though there was no one else in the room. "Have you seen very much of them?"

No answer. They went out and washed down the tables, which took a while. Swan muttered; it sounded like she was arguing with her qube again. Once she bumped into Wahram and said, "Come on, move it! Why are you so slow?"

"Why are you so fast?"

Of course this kind of nervous rapidity was a notorious characteristic of qubeheads; but one couldn't say that, and besides, she seemed worse than most. And possibly she was still distracted by grief and deserved a break. She did not answer him now but merely chucked away her apron and walked out into the fog. He went to the door to look after her; she veered suddenly toward a bonfire in the center of the square, around which people were dancing. When she was no more than a silhouette against the firelight, he saw her skip into the dance.

Habits begin to form at the very first repetition. After that there is a tropism toward repetition, for the patterns involved are defenses, bulwarks against time and despair.

Wahram was very aware of this, having lived the process many times; so he paid attention to what he did when he traveled, on the lookout for those first repetitions that would create the pattern of that particular moment in his life. So often the first time one did things they were contingent, accidental, and not necessarily good things on which to base a set of habits. There was some searching to be done, in other words, some testing of different possibilities. That was the interregnum, in fact, the naked moment before the next exfoliation of habits, the time when one wandered doing things randomly. The time without skin, the raw data, the being-in-the-world.

They came a bit too often for his taste. Most of the terraria offering passenger transport around the solar system were extremely fast, but even so, trips often took weeks. This was simply too much time to be banging around aimlessly; doing that one could easily slide into a funk or some other kind of mental hibernation. In the settlements around Saturn this sort of thing had sometimes been developed into entire sciences and art forms. But any such hebephrenia was dangerous for Wahram, as he had found out long before by painful experience. Too often in his past, meaninglessness had gnawed at the edges of things. He needed order, and a project; he needed habits. In the nakedness of the moments of exfoliation, the intensity of experience had in it a touch of terror—terror that no new meaning would blossom to replace the old ones now lost.

Of course there was no such thing as a true repetition of anything; ever since the pre-Socratics that had been clear, Heraclitus and his un-twice-steppable river and so on. So habits were not truly iterative, but pseudoiterative. The pattern of the day might be the same, in other words, but the individual events fulfilling the pattern were always a little bit different. Thus there was both pattern and surprise, and this was Wahram's desired state: to live in a pseudoiterative. But then also to live in a *good* pseudoiterative, an interesting one, the pattern constructed as a little work of art. No matter the brevity of a trip, the dullness of the terrarium or the people in it, it was important to invent a pattern and a project and pursue it with all his will and imagination. It came to this: shipboard life was still life. All days had to be seized.

So the next morning he left the Saturn House after breakfast and walked back to the park, and at the kiosk joined a group going out to track a little elephant herd. After a while Swan too joined them, coming from farther in the park and looking a little flushed, as if she had been running. Their group had with them a device that shifted the elephants' subsonic vocalizations up to human hearing levels, and Swan now frowned as she listened to them talking, or singing, as if she understood their language. When the elephants went silent, she asked the zoologist leading their group to explain why the sunline's twilight had gone on so long the previous evening. Quickly Wahram gathered that this biome, being equatorial, should have had a very short twilight, as on Earth the equatorial sun dropped almost perpendicularly to the horizon, no matter the season. The zoologist, surprised that Swan had noticed, explained rather defensively that they were running an experiment that placed their terrarium at a twenty-three-degree latitude equivalent, because there were great swaths of Earth's northern hemisphere along that latitude that were now as hot as the equator had been before Earth's warming. Forests were turning into grassland, there was widespread desertification, so the assisted migration movement was investigating the possibility of relocating tropical semiarid populations like this one up to those latitudes. In the hope of giving them some preliminary data, the sunline regime in *Wegener* had been adjusted accordingly.

Swan did not look too satisfied with this explanation, and soon afterward she took off again on her own, ignoring the disappointment of the zoologist and the disapproval of some of the other guests. Wahram saw her later that evening at his restaurant; probably she too practiced some form of the pseudoiterative, as she too traveled a lot; and it was a natural human impulse. Wahram ate at the table next to hers and then went to wash dishes, and though he nodded politely to her, she did not speak. When he was done in the kitchen and went back out for a drink, she had gone. Down the street the bonfire was again burning, the dancers dancing.

So that second day had some elements of new habit; but the next afternoon the *Wegener* was making a close passby of Venus, using it as a gravity handle to help sling it faster out to Jupiter. Wahram took a tram forward to the bulkhead, then with the help of handholds pulled through the nearly weightless passageway to the observation room that bubbled out from the forward end of the asteroid. This chamber had a steady view of the hemisphere of stars arched over them—and there, swelling visibly ahead of them, was Venus. Wahram, who at home spent a fair bit of time in micro g like this, balanced happily with one hand holding a strap, eager to watch the second planet pass under them. Swan came in just as they made their final closing, hurrying as usual to avoid being late.

Venus's atmosphere was now so reduced in density from its native state that it was transparent, and even though the whole planet was in the shadow of its sun-shield and therefore in perpetual night, one could make out the dim white dry ice seas, and the black rock of the two continents partially blown and scraped free. Cloud patterns familiar from Earth and Mars swirled over snowy plains and the dry ice oceans, making a salt-and-pepper effect that could not be comprehended even with the most intense effort. The observation chamber rang with the sounds of excited and puzzled viewers. Black as high and white as low didn't work very well for the human eye, and it was not that simple anyway. Even at their closest approach it was still a mess of stippling. They angled in at it and then *Wegener* shot by just above the atmosphere, maximizing the gravity sling. Below passed a cluster of lights that someone said was Port Elizabeth. Nearby there was a town called Billie Holliday, where Wahram had once worked in a giant waldo, covering the dry ice in the lowlands with foamed rock. Now they were doing similar things on Titan. Venus and Titan were really the best remaining candidates to join Mars as fully terraformed worlds—shirtsleeve worlds, as some called them, with free atmospheres humans could breathe. The example of Mars showed what could happen: an independent new world, free from all the troubles of the old one.

Swan was dancing by herself. "I want to go back," she was chanting to no one in particular, or perhaps to her qube. "I want to feel the poison wind slap the poison sea."

The Venusians had debarked before the swingby, so now *Wegener* was not as humanly interesting. No bonfires, no all-night dances. Wahram spent most of his days in the park; it became the heart of this particular pseudoiterative. They were trying to do a census of its birds and mammals. Often they spotted Swan out there, running by herself. She definitely slept out there, and one night in the kitchen remarked that she never slept indoors if she could avoid it, although of course the entire terrarium was indoors in a certain sense. Out in the park he saw signs that she was also trying to catch some of her food. They once found a rabbit caught in a little snare set by the creek side that spiraled through the park. This kind of thing was illegal, and, more importantly, not done. A few times they also saw the ashes of little fires, with little bones in them not fully burned. Rabbit or fawn, cooked over a little fire. One would have to keep an eye out for hyenas if one did that. Surely the excellent south Indian food in his restaurant was preferable.

Then one morning they came on Swan still crouched by her little fire, her face greasy and streaks of blood still on her hands, with a small mass of fur there between her feet. She looked up at them with a feral glare, very like the look one would have gotten from a hyena caught in the same moment, and for a long time no one knew quite what to say. Poaching was no more popular with the authorities than it had ever been, Wahram saw with a quick glance at the zoologist, although Swan would not get hung for it; and indeed, because of her founder status here, the locals, all half her age at most, were shuffling around, trying to find a way out of the situation.

"I guess this is what they meant by the phrase getting caught red-handed," Wahram said in his most jovial voice. "But please, I want to see those elephants while I can, and they are moving away from us. I'm sure the situation here will soon revert to normal." And he walked off in a way that shepherded his guides with him.

Better to explore the park in the other direction. Or he could track the little cheetah family. Once he saw Swan doing that too, but did not approach her. It was clear by now that she felt like being alone. In the town, if she came by his restaurant, she ate by herself. Wahram found that a little disappointing.

In the pseudoiterative, one performs the ritual of the day attentive to both the joy of the familiar and the shiver of the accidental. To be out at dawn was important. The sunny point in the sunline cast shadows up the cylinder, and overhead flocks of birds flew from one lake to another. The migratory birds pretended to migrate, he was told; they took off at dawn and flew around for most of the day, then came back to where they had begun. Perhaps all his movement was a similar thing.

He went forward to the observation bubble when *Wegener* passed the famous asteroid *Programming Error*. Here one of the excavators had missed one of its commands—the AI error perhaps caused by the unlucky hit of a cosmic ray, some postulated—so that after coring its large iron-nickel asteroid and leaving the interior space floored by steel, the machinery had looped back on itself and begun to eat the remaining rock of the asteroid across the tube of the first cavity; then every time it broke through to the surface of the asteroid, it turned and dived back in, building and leaving behind more tubing as it went. After a few years it had become clear that this process was never going to stop on its own, as the entire asteroid, considerably reduced, had ended up looking like braided steel rope tied in a knot. Some advocated letting the process go on to see what would happen, but there must have been someone who hadn't agreed with this, because an explosion with an intense electromagnetic pulse had shattered the AI and frozen the thing in the middle of a turn, leaving the excavator snout sticking out of the side like the head of a snake. Indeed at that point the asteroid was a kind of Medusa's head, a pretzel sculpture that some considered beautiful and others horrifying, the very image of AI foolishness, or the futility of human effort.

Now *Wegener* flashed by it so fast that the people in the observation bubble could not blink without missing it; it grew from a dot to a basketball to a dot in the course of a single indrawn breath. There were gasps, then cheers. It was in fact a very striking accidental artwork, Wahram judged, so bulging with curves that it seemed to be still squiggling, as if the head of Ouroboros were chasing a reluctant tail, or, as it occurred to him when describing it back in the kitchen, like a tangle of Klein bottles.

The next day they flashed by another famous error, and more went forward to see this one than had seen *Programming Error*, which Wahram found depressing. This terrarium, *Yggdrasil*, had suffered a catastrophic break; an unnoticed ice-filled crack had blown open, in more of an explosion than a leak. Only a few of the inhabitants had survived, something like fifty out of three thousand. It could happen to anyone who did not live on Earth or Mars. Wahram did not care to look.

Lists (2)

Lying naked on a block of ice under a heat lamp

Spending five hours in a spacesuit with only four hours of air

Running around Mercury on the equator

Cutting a solar system diagram into the skin of her chest with a laser knife

Falling slowly (all day) down the Great Staircase, naked, as in Duchamp

Flying in a popper up from the terminator into the light of a coronal flare, ejecting, and crash-landing on spacesuit jets only

Sitting in a chair and staring into the eyes of people who sit down across from her, for a year

Dancing on fire in a flame-resistant clear bodysuit

Rolling bowling balls down the Great Staircase from the top of the Dawn Wall, for an entire day (Pachinko Day)

Spending a week in a worm box

Hanging in an upside-down crucified position in the light of the sun when the gates of the Dawn Wall are opened

Sitting for a week in a pile of onions, peeling one after the next

Leaving shelter in a spacesuit with air but no heat, to see how long she could stay out (fourteen minutes)

Leaving shelter in a spacesuit with air but no heat, to see how long she could stay out while walking in partial sunlight and its radiative heating (sixty-one minutes)

Leaving shelter in a spacesuit with heat but only a helmet full of air, to see how long she could stay out (eight minutes)

SWAN AND A CAT

Swan got off the *Wegener* feeling embarrassed and depressed by the horrid ideas of her youth, in this case the savanna-pampas Ascension—not to mention her own poaching in same, caught red-handed indeed, the smart-ass. But then it got even worse when their taxi unloaded them into a terrarium headed Jupiterward, and it turned out to be the *Pleistocene*, another of her youthful indiscretions, an ice age north with any number of spavined megafauna resurrected and clomping around in pathetic mutant versions of themselves. Giant short-faced bears, looking around in openmouthed confusion—also dire wolves, saber-toothed tigers, American cheetahs, mastodons, and woolly mammoths, most of them only semi-genuine revivals from ancient DNA, really synthetics, birthed from elephants or lions or Kodiak bears, and thus uneducated in the ways of their kind. It was sad. Swan cursed herself and went feral to get through the remaining week to Jupiter, and almost paid for it with her life; for one thing, it was painfully cold, and then one morning she woke up in a stupidly uncomfortable perch in a tree to find it shaking under the weight of a cat climbing it, a big cat, a who-knew-what—possibly just a mountain lion, maybe a snow leopard, it had such long fur—intent to get to her, and as it was no heavier than she was, it seemed like it could climb the tree high enough to make it happen. Maybe twelve meters to the ground, terrarium spinning at one g—for a second she cursed the long-ago shift away from Martian g in terraria, which at first had been the norm—then fear drove all thought from her head. Get out of the nest. Get higher than a cat your own weight can get: obviously a problem. She pulled herself up onto the branch over her, which pronged up much more vertically than her sleeping branch. The cat eyed her calmly, not moving yet. Topaz eyes in brindled long white fur; upper lip drawn back, teeth white and hungry. No malice in it. Up the vertical branch, feet deep in forks, painful twists to free herself, up and up. Swaying now in the canopy, all the branches around her equally thin and flexible. Some kind of oak. If she kicked it on the snout when it attacked, possibly it would miss and fall. Foreclaws would latch on to her; her kick would have to twist away—maybe up. She tried to get higher, couldn't.

She was on the *Pleistocene*. She carried a stun gun.

But she had left it in the nest. "Shit."

The cat began to shift onto Swan's branch. Quite a weight to sway it that much.

"Pauline, any suggestions here?"

"Scare it," Pauline said. "Adrenalate fully, then do something bizarre."

Swan twisted and let go, fell feetfirst into the face of the cat, screaming as loud as she could. When her feet hit something else, she clasped branches to her and felt something smash into her ribs. Air knocked out of her, no more scream. She scrabbled with her feet for some purchase, found none, looked down. The cat was on the ground, looking up at her. Swan screamed again, felt the stab of a cracked rib. She changed to a raging shout, cursing the cat foully. Kill it like Archilochus. Grating, painful snarl of a voice, bitter shrieking that hurt her throat and screeched unbearably in her own ears, the sound making her aware she had lost it. The cat heaved a heavy sigh and padded away.

She climbed back to her nest and retrieved the stun gun. Getting down out of the tree hurt like hell.

She avoided Wahram completely after that, and by the time they were dropped off on Callisto, she had become a little fond of that stab in her side. It made her feel better; it was an expression of her grief, her anger. The moment of dread involved was not forgotten, but digested into something else, some kind of triumph. She had almost been eaten for breakfast! She had been a fool and survived yet again—how often it had happened. Surely it was a fate. Surely it would keep on happening.

"This is the most basic of false syllogisms," Pauline assured her when she spoke the thoughts aloud.

The Jovian moons were huge, with Jupiter itself a gargantuan oil painting of overelaborate genius, viscous blobs swirling around from one gorgeous paisley orangerie to the next; every border between the bands was a fantasia beyond compare. Swan loved the sight of it, and the city from which she viewed it wasn't bad either: the Fourth Ring of Valhalla, built on the eponymous rim of the great multi-ringed crater. Valhalla had six rings, splashed into the side of Callisto like concentric waves on a pond after a rock is thrown in. The city was located on the top of the fourth ring, extending all the way around; now cities were beginning on the tops of the third and fifth rings as well. It was said that they would eventually tent the entirety of Valhalla and, after that, maybe all the rest of Callisto; and it was a big world. There were even those arguing it could be properly terraformed, despite the lack of a starter atmosphere.

It was one big world of four, in fact, because all the Galilean moons were gigantic. But there was some kind of a curse on them, it seemed to Swan; one of them was almost useless, another contested. Io orbited so far within Jupiter's ferocious radiation belts that it was never going to be occupied at all except by a few small hardened scientific stations. Europa, a big beautiful ice moon, had a great depth of ice for people to delve into to escape the Jovian radiation, strong even there: wondrous ice palaces, with giant Jupiter always gnarling overhead—or everyone had thought at first. But it hadn't happened, because there had proved to be aliens living in the ocean below, a complete ecology of algae, chemotrophs, lithotrophs, methanogens, scrapers, suckers, fans, scavengers, and detrivores, all swimming or crawling or holding on or burrowing in; and they created a problem. Some thought they had already contaminated this ocean by their exploratory intrusion into it, because examining it with a drill had been the Lake Vostok problem writ large. But they had done their best to sterilize the probes, and then, having discovered and sampled the full ecology, they had sealed off the hole, and now sat on the surface in scientific stations, culturing and studying their sample populations and pondering whether they should stay or go, and if they stayed, what kind of presence they should have. Possibly the proposed ice palaces would be perfectly fine, with the life below completely sequestered by the ten kilometers of glaciosphere that lay between the moon's surface and its ocean. On the other hand, life being life, spermatozoically wriggling into every place it could reach, contamination might almost certainly be assumed to follow any occupation of the moon. And yet, given that these creatures appeared to be cousins of theirs anyway, long separated by meteor voyage—and now already recontaminated by a visit—would living above them and continuing to be a minor contaminant clearly be such a bad thing? When there were already people out there swallowing the alien microscopic life, and shooting it into their veins? And when life had been bouncing around the solar system and interacting with its cousins all along? These were open questions, interesting and vivid to the Europans and the other Jovians, less so to the rest of the system. Swan remained somewhat interested from her design days, and she approved their recent decision to go ahead and settle Europa, only perching unobtrusively on top of the internal indigenous aquaria.

Now she spent her time walking the High Road that ran all the way round the Fourth Circle of Valhalla, waiting for their flight to Io. She was still avoiding Wahram, who watched her these days with a look of alarmed concern that she could not stand. Jupiter overhead was its usual lurid magnificence. Possibly the Jovians were right to be so self-absorbed; they had a whole little solar system here, full of different things. Between the rings of the crater, the surface of Callisto was a vast knobbly white plain, and Jupiter and the three other moons were up there performing their dance. It was a gorgeous space.

But they were here to see Wang, so soon she grew impatient for the Io shuttle, and tired of the view overhead. Jove squiggling its buffooneries over and over— it was not art but chemistry, mere fractal repetition. The saving grace was that they had recently lit great gas lamps in the upper Jovian atmosphere, to better illuminate the towns located on the Galileans' Jovian sides. One could see how these painfully brilliant diamond points were distorting Jupiter's cloud tops, adding new swirls and eddies; that made it art, the whole thing a kind of mad goldsworthy.

Finally the time came for the shuttle to Io.

Swan said, "Pauline, are you going to be all right down there?"

"I will be if you are. You definitely need to stay inside the Faraday cage there to stay safe. The Jovians will no doubt tell you that."

And during the trip they did, at great length. In a box inside a box, like Russian dolls: they were so proud. Down then to Io, shedding a furious aurora behind their spacecraft, a blaze of transparent blue and green electric banners and flares arcing away as they flew.

10

Io, the innermost moon of Jupiter, as big as Luna. The yellow slag world, awesome upchucking of a moon's guts, regurgitation over and over until everything more volatile than sulfur has long since burned off. Sulfur, sulfur everywhere, and nary a place to stand. Four hundred live volcanoes bursting through the slag like angry boils, geysering sulfur dioxide hundreds of kilometers into the air. A moon with an interior hotter than Earth's—and try putting your hand in front of the steam coming out of the volcanic vent on Néa Kaméni, in the caldera of Santorini, to feel just how hot Earth is; it looks like the steam on your stove top, but you will quickly find it is three times hotter. Even though you snatch your hand away instantly, your skin will blister. And Io's interior is thirty times hotter than that.

It looks it. A hellworld, flexed hugely in the immense tidal pull between Jupiter and Europa, almost torn apart. That's gravity at work. Then also Jupiter's radiation field is so vast and so strong that Io sizzles inside it; even *Deinococcus radiodurans* perishes in it. Nothing lives on Io.

Except humans, and the little suite of biota they carry

everywhere they go. For it is possible to find islands of hard rock in the highlands of the enormous volcanoes, and bore into that rock, and hide a little station. A cube to hold Wang's qube. Everything there must be triply protected, first by physical walls, then by a magnetic field strong enough to counteract Jupiter's radiation; but this field itself would be enough to kill, so inside that field a Faraday cage is necessary, to protect you from your protection.

Descend in a blue magnetic aurora, a fire of electrons. Below, the moon spreads from a ball to a plain to a tumultuous mountainscape of overlapping volcanoes, the bulky cones hard to spot in all the overlapping swaths of yellow on tan on white on black on brick on bronze, swaths of every burnt color, but most of all, yellow. Here and there scattered rings of black or red or white reveal active vents, pouring out the guts of the interior in irregular circles around the vents; but most of the patches are much less regular, and taken altogether, the surface is a jumble that cannot be resolved by the eye into a topography. It is what it looks like, a molten world, a world on fire. The names humans have applied are redundant. Fire gods, thunder gods, lightning and volcano gods, every combustible deity, from Agni the Hindu god of fire to Volund the German blacksmith of the gods: all these names attempt to humanize the moon, but fail. Io is not a human place. The hard crust on its surface, cooled only by contact with the chill vacuum of space, is so thin that in many places it would not support a standing person. Some early explorers found this out the hard way: walking too far away from their lander, they plunged through the sulfurous ground into red-hot lava and disappeared.

We think that because we live on cooler planets and moons, we live on safer ground than that. But it is not so.

SWAN AND WANG

The station on Io holding Wang's qube and its support team was located high on the flank of Ra Patera, one of the biggest mountains in the solar system. As the ferry descended, the tilt of Ra's broad apron came to seem barely off the horizontal. The ferry dropped into a gap in a concrete pad, and a roof then closed over them; from then on they were mostly underground. Everything they could see of the moon on the station's various viewscreens, and through the little windows in the station's little conning tower, was part of the apron of Ra.

There were several people in the station's bridge, up in the conning tower. None of them looked up at Swan and Wahram, nor at Wang when he came in.

Wang Wei turned out to be a round person with an innocuous manner. A real principal investigator, as Mqaret would have said: one of the system's foremost experts on qubes. Sometimes such individuals were sovereign to quite remarkable little Ruritanias. Swan wondered if Alex had been right in her notion that the solar system's balkanization was a deliberate but unconscious human reaction to qubes, some kind of resistance to their incipient power.

Wang greeted Swan and Wahram, and with a quick "Ah, thank you," took the envelope from Alex that Swan offered to him. It appeared he had already known about it. He read the letter in it, then plugged the tab that fell from it into the nearest desk. He stared at the desk console for a long time, reading carefully, using a forefinger to keep his place.

"So sorry to lose Alex," he said to Swan finally. "Condolences from the heart. She was the hub of our little wheel, and now we spin off like broken spokes."

Surprised at this, Swan said, "She told me in her note to me that I should come to you. The messages were left for me in her study. A kind of contingency plan, I guess. And part of it was this envelope for you."

"Yes. She told me she might do this. And you also loaded a tab into your internal qube, Alex suggests in her note here."

"That's right. But my qube won't tell me about it."

"That was no doubt Alex's instruction. The data are specialized. What you have is a kind of backup," Wang explained apologetically.

Swan glared at Wang, and then Wahram, and saw that they were in cahoots, like Wahram and Genette back on Mercury. "Tell me what's going on," she demanded. "You two were working with Alex on something."

The two of them hesitated, and then Wang said, "Yes. For many years. Alex was the hub, as I said. We were working with her."

"But she didn't like being in the cloud," Swan said, gesturing around her at the station. "She kept things in her head, right? But you work with qubes, isn't that right? Wang's qube, Wang's algorithm?"

"Yes," Wang said.

Wahram said, "To stay off the record, Alex had to stay clear of qubes. And for that she needed a qube's help. That's just the way it is now, and she knew that."

Wang nodded. "So she chose me. I can't say why. Possibly she thought I have more contact than I really do with what she used to call the league of unaffiliated worlds. I do have a network of contacts like that, but it's not comprehensive. No one has an accurate description of the system as it exists now."

"Is that what Alex wanted?" Swan asked.

Wahram shook his head. "She knew the system as well as anyone could. Wang knows the unaffiliateds, but more importantly, to my mind, his qube is sequestered here. Its contact with the rest of the system is controlled by Wang. Alex liked that, because she was trying to shift all her dealings over to direct human communication."

"But she left these messages," Swan said. "For if she couldn't talk. So she wanted *us* to talk. For you two to talk to me."

"Evidently."

"So tell me what you're up to!"

The two men glanced at each other. For a long time they stared at the floor.

Then Wang looked her in the eye, which caught Swan by surprise. His gaze was intense. "No one knows exactly how to deal with this situation, because it has to do with qubes, and you have a qube embedded in you. So Alex would not tell you about this part of things, and I don't want to either. Now that Alex's list of contacts is safely here, we who were working with her can try to proceed with her plans."

Swan said, "So you have information from Alex, and

my qube has information from Alex, but I can't have any information from Alex."

Wang looked at Wahram. Wahram's broad face looked as if pins were being stuck into him somewhere. His pop-eyed stare, Wang's basilisk intensity: they stood there looking at her. They didn't know what to say to her. They weren't going to tell her anything.

With a sudden snort Swan waved them away and left the room.

There wasn't anywhere to go in this little station to get away, something that occurred to Swan only after she had made her exit. She badly needed to run off her anger in some hills, and here she was trapped in a qube cube, a box of rooms, only a few of which even had windows. Claustrophobia lay always just under her surface, and now, with her anger at the two men and her grief for Alex (and anger at Alex for keeping things from her just because of Pauline), the trapped feeling jumped her and she banged around cursing until she went up in the conning tower to a small room with a view window and was able to slam the door and pound her fists on a table for a while. Her rib hurt quite a bit as she did so, but that was just part of the mix now, the stab of all these other feelings combined. She hurt!

Then a movement outside caught her eye. She interrupted her fit and went to the window to look: through her tears she saw the blurry blinking image of a human figure, out on the yellow slag, walking toward the station. It moved oddly, wavering, staggering, blinking from one position to another.

"Pauline, can someone walk on the surface here? Outside the station?"

"Their suit would have to be as protective as the station

is," Pauline said. "Please—inform station security of your sighting immediately."

"Surely they'll have seen it?"

"That suit out there may be shielded in many ways. Your visual sighting may be the only indication they have. Please hurry. Arguing with me now is untimely."

Swan growled and left the room. After some hurrying around, getting lost, she came to the room Wahram and she had entered first.

"There's someone approaching your station on foot," she said to the startled people inside. A few of them began scanning screens very closely. Swan couldn't tell them which direction her window had been facing, and had to take them back to it (just barely recalling the way) to show them. By that time nothing was visible on the slaggy landscape extending downhill from the station. Apparently the people back in the control room weren't seeing anything either.

"Pauline, tell them," Swan said.

Pauline said, "There was something about three hundred meters downslope. Footprints should still be visible. The figure was moving irregularly—"

Wang hurried into the room, summoned, no doubt. "Lock it down," he said curtly to his people: Ringing alarms went off in every room, painfully high and loud. Quickly the halls filled with people. Swan and Wahram were hustled along a hallway to the lockdown shelter. By the time they got there it was already crowded, and after they pushed their way in, the door was closed; apparently everyone was accounted for. Now they were inside the smallest Russian doll of all.

There were screens on one wall, and Pauline helped the station AI direct the station's surveillance cameras. Soon enough one screen zoomed in on a view downslope: there, far down the rumpled and tilted plain of slag, a tiny figure was hopping downhill.

"Not a good idea," Wang said. "The crust thins down there."

And then the distant figure sank into a brief flare and disappeared.

"Keep looking around the station," Wang said after a shocked silence. "See if there is anyone else out there. And put up a drone to have a look around for a hopper."

The people in the room watched the screens in a grave silence. If the Faraday cage were to lose power, they would be cooked very quickly, every cell in them burst by Jupiter's radiation.

But nothing seemed to have happened. The station's power seemed secure, and there was no one else to be seen in the surrounding area.

Then there was a stir across the room. "Call from a ship requesting to land!" someone said.

"Who are they?"

"It's an Interplan ship, *Swift Justice*."

"Make sure it's really them."

The image of an incoming ship was shifted to a larger screen, and everyone watched as a small spaceship flared down into the hole in the station's landing pad. Shortly thereafter a helmeted face appeared right in front of a surveillance camera lens in the landing bay, filling the screen to provide a retinal scan, then waving and giving them a brief thumbs-up. Friends, apparently.

They were let in, and there in the doorway stood three people, helmets off, one of them a small. Swan was startled to recognize the inspector who had visited them at Mqaret's laboratory: Jean Genette.

"You're late," Wang said.

"Sorry," Genette replied. "We were detained. Tell me what happened."

Wang made his account brief, ending, "It appears to have been a single intruder. It approached and then went downslope and fell through the crust. We haven't found any hoppers yet."

Genette's head was tilted to the side. "It just ran downslope to its death?"

"Apparently so."

The inspector looked up at the others. "We need to pull whatever remains of it out of the lava." Then, to Wang and the others: "Back shortly. Maybe you should stay in lockdown a little longer."

And the three of them disappeared back toward the station lock.

All right," Swan said heavily, staring hard at Wahram in particular. "Tell me what's going on."

"I'm not sure," Wahram said.

"We were just attacked!"

"I guess so."

"You guess so?"

Wang spoke while still reading their screens. "A very ineffective attack, I must say."

"So who would want to attack you?" Swan asked. "And how did this Inspector Genette get here so fast? And does this have anything to do with what you were doing with Alex?"

Wahram said, "It's hard to tell at this point," and Swan interrupted by punching him in the arm.

"*Quit it*," she said viciously. "Tell me what's going on!"

She looked around the packed room: twelve or fifteen people all crowded in there, but now ostentatiously focused on their own affairs, leaving Wang and his visitors alone at a small table in a corner. "Tell me or I'll start screaming." She let out a little shriek to show them what could happen, and people all over the room jumped and looked their way, or tried not to.

Wahram glanced at Wang. "Let me try," he said.

"All yours," Wang said.

Wahram tapped on the table screen and called up a schematic of the solar system, a three-dimensional image that seemed to float inside the table. Spheres of bright holographic colors made something like the familiar solar system orrery, though this one had many more colored spheres in it, Swan saw, and a great number of colored lines connecting these spheres. Also, the spheres were not sized in proportion to the real sizes of the planets and moons.

"This image was generated from Alex's analysis," Wahram told Swan. "It's an attempt to show power, and the potential for power. A kind of Menard graphic. The size of the spheres is determined by a compound function of the factors Alex considered important."

Swan spotted Mercury, down by the sun, small and red. The Mondragon members were all red, making a constellation of red dots scattered through the system—all small, but there were a lot of them. Earth was huge and multicolored, a bundling of spheres, like a bunch of helium balloons tugging at a fist. Mars was a single green sphere, almost as big as Earth. Colored lines connecting spheres made webs that were dense through the system out to Saturn, sparser beyond that.

"What factors?" Swan asked, trying to calm herself. She was still rattled, more by the appearance of Genette than by the attack.

Wahram said, "Accumulated capital, population,

bioinfrastructure health, terraforming status and stability, mineral and volatile resources, treaty relations, military equipment. We can give you the details of the heuristic later. What you can see immediately is that Mars, and Earth, considered as a collective, are tremendously larger than any other powers at this point. And China, the big pink ball, is a very big fraction of Earth's power. Venus, meanwhile, has such great potential that it's hard to represent, because at present it has nothing like the power it's going to have. Venus and China are colored pink because they both have good relations with the Mondragon. You can see that there is potential in the China-Venus-Mondragon nexus for the largest power of all. Alex often said that Chinese dominance is the default norm throughout history, except for the brief period of subjugation to Europe. That may be putting it too strongly, but the image speaks for itself concerning the current situation.

"Also, notice the smallness of almost all the other space settlements. Even taken together, they are still small. However, if you amp up their terraforming potential in the calculation, as I will do now—then look: Venus, Luna, the Jovian Galileans not counting Io, Titan, and Triton get much bigger. They represent the largest opportunities for more power in space. The asteroids are for the most part filled. So in near-term potential, Venus and the big moons are the new powers. And Venus will soon be fully habitable and experiencing a growth spurt, so things are already getting strange there and destabilizing things on Earth."

"So what was Alex's concern?" Swan asked. "And what was she proposing to do about it?"

Wahram took a deep breath, let it out. "She saw an unstable system, headed for a crash unless some corrections were made. She wanted to stabilize things. And she thought the fundamental source of trouble was Earth."

He stared at the image for a while, which made the point very effectively; there, in the middle of all the clear primary colors, the party balloon jumble that represented Earth was so garish it almost vibrated.

"So she wanted to do what?" Swan asked, feeling a stab of worry. "Are you saying she wanted to change things on Earth?"

"Yes," Wahram said firmly. "She did. She knew, of course, that this desire is a famous mistake for spacers to make. An impossible project, sure to go wrong. But she thought we might have enough leverage by now to make a difference. She had a plan. A lot of us felt like it was a bit of the tail wagging the dog, you know. But Alex was persuasive that we would never be safe until Earth was in better shape. So we were going along with her."

"What does that mean?"

"We've been stockpiling food and animals in the terraria, and setting up Terran offices in friendly countries there. There were agreements. But now that's been complicated by Alex's death, because she did so much of it in person. They were verbal agreements."

"She didn't trust qubes, I know that."

"Right."

"Why not?"

"Well, I . . . Perhaps I shouldn't really say now."

After an uncomfortable pause, Swan said, "Tell me." When he raised his eyes and met her gaze, she gave him the look Alex would have given him—she could feel it coursing through her. Alex had been able to make people talk with a look.

But it was Wang who answered her. "It has to do with some funny stories about qubes," he said carefully. "On Venus and in the asteroid belt. Those incidents are being looked into by Inspector Genette and his team. So"—he gestured at the doorway—"this may be another part of that. So until they learn more, let us leave that matter alone for now. Also . . . assuming your internal qube is recording all this? If you could get it to keep the recording locked, that would be best."

Wahram said to Wang, "Show Swan the image of the system with qube power included."

Wang nodded and tapped at the table's image. "This one tries to include both qubes and classical AIs. It hopes to give an image of how much of our civilization is run by artificial intelligence."

"Qubes don't run anything," Swan objected. "They don't make any decisions."

Wang frowned. "Some things they do decide, actually. When to launch a ferry, for instance, or how to allot the goods and services in the Mondragon—things like that. Most of the work of the system's infrastructure, as it turns out."

"But they don't *decide* to run it," Swan said.

"I know what you mean, but look at the image."

In this version, he explained, red designated human power, blue the power of computers, with light blue marking classical computers, and dark blue quantum computers. A big dark blue ball appeared near Jupiter, and there were other blue dots scattered everywhere, most netted in a single web. Humans appeared as clumps of red, fewer and smaller than the blue dots, with far fewer red lines between them.

"What's the blue ball around Jupiter?" Swan asked. "Is that you?"

"Yes," Wang said.

"And so now someone has attacked this rather immense blue ball."

"Yes." Wang was frowning heavily as he stared into the table. "But we don't know who, or why."

After a silence, Wahram said, "Images like this one were part of what concerned Alex. She initiated some efforts to come to grips with the situation. Let's leave it at that for now, please. I hope you understand."

His froggy eyes popped more than ever with the force of his entreaty. He was sweating.

Swan glared at him for a while, then shrugged. She wanted to argue and realized again that it felt good to find something besides Alex's death to be angry at. Pretty much anything would do. But in the end it wouldn't help.

Wahram tried to return the subject to Earth: "Alex said we should think of Earth as our sun. We all revolve around it, and it exerts a huge drag on us. And because of the individual need spacers have for their sabbaticals, we can't just ignore it."

"For any number of reasons we can't do that," Wang pointed out.

"True," Wahram said. "So. We are determined to keep her projects going. You can help with that. Your qube now has her contact list. It'll take a big effort to keep that whole group on board. We could use your help."

Swan, unsatisfied with this kind of generality, inspected the new image again. Finally she said, "Who did she work with most on Earth?"

Wahram shrugged. "Many people. But her main contact there was Zasha."

"Really?" Swan said, startled. "My Zasha?"

"Yours in what sense?"

"Well, we were partners once."

"I didn't know that. Well, Alex certainly relied on Zasha for a sense of the situation on Earth."

Swan had been vaguely aware that Zasha did things with the Mercury House in Manhattan, but she had never heard Alex or Zasha speak of each other. It was another new thing to learn about Alex, and it suddenly occurred to Swan that this was the way it would happen from now on; she would not learn things from Alex, but about her. That was the way Alex would live on, and small though it was, it was better than nothing. Better than the void. And if Zasha had been working with her—

"All right," Swan said. "When your inspector lets us out of here, I'm going to Earth."

Wahram nodded uncertainly.

Swan said, "What will you do?"

He shrugged. "I have to go to Saturn and report."

"Will I see you again?"

"Yes, thank you." Although he looked a little alarmed at the idea. "I'll soon be returning to Terminator. The Saturn League council has been contacted by the Vulcanoids, who it turns out also had some verbal agreements with Alex. There are Vulcanoid light transfers out to Saturn in the works, and I am currently the league's inner planet ambassador. So I'll see you when you return to Mercury."

Extracts (2)

to simplify history would be to distort reality. By the early twenty-fourth century there was too much going on to be either seen or understood. Assiduous attempts by contemporary historians to achieve an agreed-upon paradigm foundered, and we are no different now, looking back at them. It's hard even to assemble enough data to make a guess. There were thousands of city-states out there pinballing around, each with its presence in the data cloud or absence from same, and all of them adding up to—what? To the same mish-mash history has been all along, but now elaborated, mathematicized, effloresced—in the word of the time, *balkanized*. No description can be

instability nodes, when many pressured stresses rupture at once—in this case the withdrawal of Mars from the Mondragon, its counterimperial campaign on Earth, and the return of the Jovian moons to the larger interplanetary scene. As the first settlements beyond Mars, the Jovians were hampered by path dependency on earlier, less powerful settlement technology, also the discovery of life inside Ganymede and Europa, as well as Jupiter's intense radiation. Later more powerful settlement strategies, and terraforming efforts on Venus and Titan, caused the Jovians to reevaluate their stations, domes, and tented Luxembourgs as inadequate. Even with Io permanently off-limits, the three other Galilean moons constituted together an enormous potential surface area, and it was the resolution of their inner conflicts and their common commitment to full terraformation that threw the volatiles markets into disarray and triggered the nonlinear breaks of the following two decades

they were now their own unavoidable experiment, and were making themselves into many things they had never been before: augmented, multi-sexed, and most importantly, very long-lived, the oldest at that point being around two hundred years old. But not one whit wiser, or even more intelligent. Sad but true: individual intelligence probably peaked in the Upper Paleolithic, and we have been self-domesticated creatures ever since, dogs when we had been wolves. But also, despite that individual diminution, finding ways to accumulate knowledge and power, compiling records, also techniques, practices, sciences

possibly smarter therefore as a species than as individuals, but prone to insanity either way, and in any case stuck in the moment—a moment now lost to us—when people lived in the almost-forgotten technology and culture of the Balkanization, the years just before 2312—

except wait: that is yet to tell

Lists (3)

alcohol, fasting, thirsting, sweat lodges,
   self-mutilation,
sleep deprivation, dance, bleeding, mushrooms,
   immersion in ice water,
kava, flagellation with thorns or animal teeth, cactus
   flesh, tobacco,

exposure to the elements, long-distance running,
   hypnosis,
meditation, rhythmic drumming and chanting,
   jimsonweed, nightshade,
Salvia divinorum, pungent or aromatic scents, toad sweat,
   tantric sex,

spinning in circles, amphetamines, sedatives, opioids,
   hallucinogens,
nitrous oxide, oxytocin, holding one's breath,
   jumping off cliffs,
nitrites, kratom, coca leaves, cocoa, caffeine, entheogens—

ethylene, an entheogenic gas, escapes from the ground
   under Delphi

SWAN IN THE DARK

When they were free to leave Io Station, Swan headed to Earth.

It turned out that the first transport heading down-system was a blackliner. Feeling the blackness of Alex's absence inside her, Swan decided to take it. Wahram saw her off with his now characteristic expression of alarm.

Inside the blackliner, darkness reigned. It was as black as could be, the black one would find inside a cave deep inside the earth. The terrarium was just barely rotating, so there was very low g throughout. People therefore floated in the dark, naked or dressed in clothes or spacesuits. Around buildings and float-ing pods a blind society bounced carefully, living in a world of sound. Bat people. Sometimes there were interactions, conversations, embraces; sometimes one heard cries for help, and there were sheriffs on patrol to provide aid, using infrared goggles to see what was going on. But for most passengers the point was to be blind for a while. It could be a penance, it could be a bit of mental voyaging; it could be a new kind of sex. Swan didn't know what she wanted out of it. It had sounded right for the way she felt.

Now she floated in pure and complete blackness. Her eyes were open and yet she didn't see a thing: not her hand before her face, not a glint of light anywhere. The space she was in seemed as infinite as the cosmos itself, or else just a bag around her head. There were voices here and there, coming from various distances. They all sounded hushed, as if in the dark people naturally whispered—although forward along the centerline, it seemed by the faint pull of the g, there was some kind of game or sport being played, with whistles and beeps and shouts of laughter. From another direction came the sounds of guitar and oboe, playing a baroque duet. She jetted toward it cautiously, hoping to hear it better. Halve the distance, double the sound. On the way she passed the paired breath of a couple having sex, or so it seemed. This was a noise that could draw a crowd as much as music or sport. There had been assaults in blackliners; people had done unspeakable things, or so one heard. In fact it was hard to believe anyone would care enough to impinge so drastically on anyone else. Why care that much? What would it do?

The continuous pure dark soon began to be marked in her vision by blotches of color, then by memories of sights that seemed to be there in her eye. She closed her eyes, and colored bars redoubled. Color everywhere; it reminded her of that time years before when she had ingested the Enceladan suite of aliens, a crazy act which she usually managed not to remember. The votaries sitting around lit candles; Pauline, newly inside her, warning her not to do it; the little chalice full of *Enceladusea irwinii* and other Enceladan microscopic lifeforms; the votary giving it to her and saying, "Do you understand?" and Swan replying that she did, the biggest lie of her life; the taste of the infusion, like blood; the heave in her stomach; the way after a moment of blackout the candlelight returned and grew too bright to look at; the waves-on-the-beach roar all through her, everything becoming brilliantly stuffed with color, Saturn looking like a confection of mint and cantaloupe. Yes, a period of synesthesia, with all her senses on fire; and at one point she had had the sudden realization that she would never be the same. Infecting herself with an alien, was it wise? No, it was not! Crying out then as if poisoned, trapped in a kaleidoscope, a roaring in her ears, exclaiming over and over, *But I was—I was Swan—I was—I was Swan—*

Now she did her best to throw the vivid memory into darkness away from her. She spun weightlessly with the effort, which had caused her to wrench her body into a knot. As she spun, it began to seem that the guitar and oboe she heard were actually at quite a distance from each other. Was it really a duet at all? How would that work if the two of them were half a kilometer apart? There would be a distinct time lag, each for the other. She tried to focus on them, hear if they were in concert or not. In the pure black she would never know.

Miserably she realized that this was going to go on for as long as she was in here. No face to cling to with one's gaze, nothing at all to see—her memory and imagination would run riot, her starved senses left to spin hungrily, making things up—nothing but her unhappiness for company. Pure being, unadulterated thought, revealing what the phenomenal world could hide but not change: the blank at the heart of things.

Her stomach grumbled and she ate part of her belt. She relieved herself in a bag inside her suit and cast the

sealed bag toward the ground, janitorbots would sniff
it out and take it away. She kept seeing images of Alex's
face, and she clung to them as precious memories she
would need to hold to forever, but they made her groan
too. She mewed like a hurt beast, she couldn't help it.

"You are perhaps experiencing an episode of hypotyp-
posis," Pauline said aloud. "The visionary imagination
of things not present before the eyes."

"Shut up, Pauline." Then, after a while, she said,
"No, I'm sorry. Go on, please."

"An aporia in some rhetorics is a pretended dubitation before coming back to the attack, as in Gilbert on
Joyce. But Aristotle has it as an insoluble problem in an
inquiry, arising from equally plausible but inconsistent
premises. He writes that Socrates liked to reduce people
to aporia to show them they didn't really know what
they thought they knew. The plural that Aristotle uses
in his book on metaphysics is 'aporiai.' 'We should first
review the things about which we need from the out-
set to be puzzled,' he writes. The word *aporia* was later
adapted by Derrida to mean something like the blank
spots in our understanding that we don't even know are
there, with the idea we should try to see these. It is not
quite the same idea, but joins a constellation of mean-
ings for the word. The *Oxford English Dictionary* refer-
ences a quote from J. Smith's *Mystical Rhetoric* of 1657,
which says *aporia* refers to the problem of 'what to do or
say in some strange or ambiguous thing.'"

"Like now."

"Yes. Listen further. The Greek comes from *a*, 'not,'
and *poros*, 'passage.' But in the Platonic myth, Penia,
the child of poverty, chooses to become impregnated by
Poros, the personification of plenty. Their child is Eros,
who combines the attributes of its parents. Pointed out

as strange here is the vision of Penia as resourceful, and prosperity as drunk and passive—"

"That's not strange."

"So that although Penia is not Poros, she is also not a-poria. She has been called neither masculine nor feminine, rich or poor, resourceful or without resources. And so *aporia* becomes even more an untranslatable term."

"I am an aporia. And I am in an aporia. This blackliner."

"Yes."

All very well, to talk and think—"Thank you, Pauline"—but at the end of it, there was still a week more to live through, and Alex's death never gone away. She was floating in the bardo, trying to think like someone unborn would think. Full of dubitation, child of a poverty. Would be reborn some other Swan.

But then later—it seemed much later, there in the suspended space of no-time, banging around in her thoughts as they looped over and over—later she came to understand that when the chime in her suit rang and signaled that this trip was over, they would decant the same Swan that went in. There was no escape.

"Pauline—tell me more. Talk to me. Please talk to me."

Pauline said, "Max Brod once had a very interesting conversation with Franz Kafka, which he later recounted to Walter Benjamin...."

Extracts (3)

Homo sapiens evolved in Terran gravity and it is still an open question what effects time spent in less than one g will have on the individual

decrease in bone strength from 0.5 percent to 5 percent per month in 0–.1 g

repeated exposure to gravity incidents greater than 3 g has been shown to create micro-strokes and raise the incidence of major strokes

the biomedical research community has changed its mind about these questions more than once through the years

aerobic and resistance exercise partially compensates for physiological effects of long-term residence in moderate low g (defined as between Luna's .17 g and Mars's .38 g) but there are problems left unaddressed

maintaining a vigorous physical life substantially mitigates

below Luna g, physical etiolation occurs in some organs and tissues no matter how much exercise

statistically very significant results in actuarial tables suggest longevity beyond historical norms is impossible without frequent return not just to a one-g environment, but to Earth itself. Why this should be so is a matter of dispute, but the fact itself is very clear in the data. We propose to show

one year in every six spent on Earth, with no time away longer than ten years, greatly increases longevity. Neglect of this practice leads to a high risk of dying many decades before

oversterile environments cannot

the famous or notorious sabbatical has been proposed as an example of hormesis or Mithridatism, in which brief exposure to toxins strengthens the organism against greater

Earth's continuing clutch on space-dwelling humans is physiological and will not go away unless it is fully characterized and all components of it effectively ameliorated

inoculations of helminths (ringworm), bacteria, viruses, etc., impossible to catalog and yet

possible psychological effects also, which means extreme difficulty in defining causation or treatment

not dissimilar to other five-hundred-year projects in intrinsic difficulty

effects are cumulative and lead to dysfunction

increase in longevity is a statistical fact but no guaran-
tee for any particular individual. Life choices shift the
probabilities of

regenerative therapies continue to improve

the biggest jump in the longevity graphs came at the
start of the Accelerando, and many feel this was not
a coincidence. There is a surge of energy that comes
when you realize you may live much longer than you
had thought possible. Problems that later complicate
the picture don't become evident until

the statistics are suggestive but the causes are not yet

life is a complex

STD, sudden traumatic death, insoluble

people should minimize their time in the lowest and
highest gs if they want to maximize their chance at
newly normative extended lifetimes, which keep getting longer

no real sense of what might be possible if improvements continue

could we live for thousands of

people compromise, they cut corners. They want
to do things, they indulge their desires, their love of
adventure

to have to return to Earth, so dirty and old, so oppressive, such a failure. So much the sad planet

they swore they would live by accident, but they were young at the time

most older spacers go home to Earth as advised, one year every seven, because these are the ones living the longest and the effect is self-reinforcing

the hunt continues for a fuller explanation

SWAN AND ZASHA

Earth's thirty-seven space elevators all had their cars full all the time, both up and down. There were still many spacecraft landings and ascents, of course, and landings of gliders that then reascended on the elevators; but all in all, the elevators handled by far the bulk of the Earth-space traffic. Going down in the cars were food (a crucial percentage of the total needed), metals, manufactured goods, gases, and people. Going up were people, manufactured goods, the substances common on Earth but rare in space—these were many, including things animal, vegetable, and mineral, but chiefly (by bulk) rare earths, wood, oil, and soil. The totals came to quite a flow of physical mass up and down, all powered by the counterbalanced forces of gravity and the rotation of the Earth, with a bit of solar power to make up the difference.

The anchor rocks at the upper ends of the elevator cables were like giant spaceliners, as very little of their original asteroidal surfaces were left visible; their exteriors were covered with buildings, power units, elevator loading zones and the like. They were in effect giant harbors and hotels and, as such, extremely busy places. Swan passed through the one called Bolivar and settled into one of the hotel cars without even noticing it; to her it had just been a complicated set of doors and locks and corridors, getting her into yet another set of rooms. She was resigned to the long ride down to Quito. It was an irony of their time that the trip down the elevator cable was going to take longer than many interplanetary voyages, but that's the way it was. Five days stuck in a hotel. She spent the days attending performances of Glass's *Satyagraha* and *Akhnaten*, also dancing hard in a grueling class designed to get people toughened up for one g, which sometimes hit her pretty hard. Looking down through the clear floor, she got familiar again with the great bulge of South America, gaining definition below them: blue oceans to each side; the Andes like a brown spine; the little brown cones of the big volcanoes, bereft of all their snow.

It was almost an ice-free planet now, with only Antarctica and Greenland holding on to much, and Greenland going fast. Sea level was therefore eleven meters higher than it had been before the changes. This inundation of the coastline was one of the main drivers of the human disaster on Earth. They had immensely powerful terraforming techniques off-planet, but here they usually couldn't be applied. No slamming comets into it, for instance. So they bubbled their ship wakes with surfactants to create a higher albedo, and had tried various levels of sulfur dioxide injected into the stratosphere, imitating volcanoes; but that had once led to disaster, and now they couldn't agree on how much sunlight to block. Much that people advocated, and many of the smaller projects that were in action already, cut against other proposed or ongoing projects. And there were still powerful nation-states that were also corporate conglomerates, the two overlapping in Keynesian disarray, with the residual but powerful capitalist system ruling much of the planet and containing within it its own residual feudalism, there to fight forever against the serfs, meaning also against the horizontalized economy emerging within the Mondragon. No, Earth was a mess, a sad place. And yet still the center of the story. It had to be dealt with, as Alex had always said, or nothing done in space was real.

In Quito Swan took the train to the airport and got on an airplane flight to New York. The Caribbean's cobalt and turquoise and jade were brilliantly vivid; even the brown underwater outline of drowned Florida had a jasper sheen. The stunning gloss of Earth itself.

A much steelier ocean crashed whitely into Long Island as they descended over it, bumping and slipping in the air. Then they were landing on a runway somewhere on the mainland north of Manhattan, and at last she was out of the various travel containers, the rooms and vehicles and corridors and hallways, and under the open sky.

Simply to be outdoors in the open air, under the sky, in the wind—this was what she loved most about Earth. Today puffy clouds were massed overhead at about the thousand-foot level. Looked like a marine layer rolling in. She ran out into some kind of paved lot filled with trucks and buses and trolley cars, and jumped around screaming at the sky, then kneeled and kissed the ground, made wolf howls, and, after she had hyperventilated a bit, lay on her back on the pavement. No handstands—she had learned long before that handstands on Earth were really hard. And her rib still hurt.

Through gaps in the cloud layer she could see the light-but-dark blue of the Terran sky, subtle and full. It looked like a blue dome flattened at the center, perhaps a few kilometers above the clouds—she reached up for it—although knowing too that it was just a kind of rainbow made it glorious. A rainbow that was blue everywhere and covered everything. The blue itself was complex, narrow in range but infinite within that range. It was an intoxicating sight, and you could breathe it—one was always breathing it, you had to. The wind shoved it into you! Breathe and get drunk, oh my, to be free of all restraint, minimally clothed, lying on the bare surface of a planet, sucking in its atmosphere as if it were an aqua vitae, feeling in your chest how it kept you alive! No Terran she had ever met properly appreciated their air, or saw their sky for what it was. In fact they very seldom looked at it.

She collected herself and walked over to the dock. A big grumbling water ferry took on her and many others, and after negotiating a crowded canal, they were out in the Hudson River and going down to Manhattan. The ferry moved into a dock on Washington Heights, but Swan stayed on it as it plied its way down the Hudson side to midtown. A few parts of Manhattan's ground still stood above the water, but most of it was drowned, the old streets now canals, the city an elongated Venice, a skyscraper Venice, a super Venice—which was a very beautiful thing to be. Indeed it was an oft-expressed cliché that the city had been improved by the flood. The long stretch of skyscrapers looked like the spine of a dragon. The foreshortening effect as they got closer made the buildings look shorter than they really were, but their verticality was unmistakable and striking A forest of dolmens!

Swan got off the ferry at the Thirtieth Street Pier and walked on the broad catwalk between buildings to the High Line extension, where people filled the long plazas stretching north and south. Manhattan on foot: workers pushing narrow handcarts on crowded skyways, connecting island neighborhoods suspended between skyscrapers at differing heights. The rooftops were garnished with greenery, but the city was mostly a thing of steel and concrete and glass—and water. Boats burbled about on the water below the catwalks, in the streets that were now crowded canals. All the aerial plazas and catwalks were jammed with people. As crowded as ever, people said. Swan dodged between the bodies of the crowd, working the border between the two directions of traffic, glorying in all the faces. They were just as heterogeneous as any spacer crowd, but the people were very much closer to an average size—rather short at that—with many fewer smalls and talls. Asian faces, African, European—everyone but Native Americans, as she always thought in Manhattan. Talk about invasive biology!

A building she passed had pumped out its old floor and now operated down there in a kind of big bathtub of air. She had heard that submarine and intertidal real estate was booming. Some spoke of pumping out the subway system, which still worked wherever it had run aboveground. Below her the slop of water threw up a big ambient sound. Human voices, and water splashing, and the cries of gulls back on the docks, and the rush of wind through the canyons of buildings; these were the sounds of the city. The water below was completely chopped up with intersecting wakes. Behind her, down the avenue to the west, mirrorflakes of broken sunlight bounced on the big river. This was the thing she loved—she was outdoors, truly in the open. Standing on the side of a planet. In the greatest city of all.

She hopped down some stairs and got on a vaparetto going down Eighth Avenue. The ferry was a long low-slung thing, with seats for about fifty people and room for another hundred to stand. It stopped every few blocks. She hung over the rail and gazed up and down the canal: a river canyon, with buildings for canyon walls. Very Futurismo in appearance. She got off at Twenty-Sixth Street where it was bridged by a long esplanade, extending east all the way to the East River. Lots of the east-west streets had overhead platforms like this, and the crowded canals under them were shaded almost all day long. When the sunlight slanted through slots, it laid a bronze glaze on things, and the blue water turned pewter. The New Yorkers did not seem to notice this effect, but on the other hand, there were twenty million people living here despite the flood, and Swan thought that beauty was not completely irrelevant to the phenomenon, even if people chose to keep mum about it. Tough guys, it made her laugh. Swan was not a tough guy, and not a New Yorker, and this place was astonishing and she knew the locals knew it. Talk about landscape art! "'The geography of the world is unified only by human logic and optics,'" she chanted, "'by the light and color of artifice, by decorative arrangement, by ideas of the good, the true, and the beautiful!'" You could sing Lowenthal's entire oratorio on the catwalks of Manhattan, and no one would care.

She moved into the sun whenever she could. That was the direct radiation of Sol, slamming into her naked skin. It was amazing to stand in the light of the sun without dying of it. This was the only place in the solar system where that could happen; the bioshell surrounding a star was as thin as a soap bubble. Thickening the life bubble—maybe that was the human project. That they had pulled the bubble out around Mars was a remarkable thing. If they pulled it inward to Venus, even more so. This, however, would always be the sweet spot. No wonder the mystics of this old world, stunned by all life's changes. Metamorphosis suited Earth, and never stopped. The great flood had become a fortunate fall, had brought on an exfoliation into a higher state. The world had been watered. Flowers popping out of the leafy branch. She was back

The Mercury House was down by the Museum of Modern Art. Many of the museum's paintings were now on Mercury, only copies left behind, and in an unusual gesture, a room here was devoted to Mercurial art. The Group of Nine was prominently displayed, of course. It was a little too much sun and rock for Swan. And she always found it odd to see canvas used as the medium, a bit like looking at scrimshaw or other antique exotica. When you had the world and your body as canvases, why deal in squares of wallpaper? It was peculiar, but as a result perhaps interesting as well. Alex and Mqaret had held a reception for the Nine once, and Swan had met many of them and enjoyed talking to them.

Up on the roof patio of the Mercury House building, maybe thirty stories above the water, she found a number of Mercurials gathered at the bar. Most of them wore exoskeletons or body bras, which, whether hidden by clothing or not, were evident to Swan by the way the people wearing them stood, resting comfortably slightly off true, as if in water. The ones without were more or less heroically erect, holding off the weight of the Earth with a strained look. Swan felt a little that way herself. No matter what you did, one g imposed itself on your attention for a while.

Their New York office was headed by an ancient Terran named Milan, who had a sweet smile for everyone. "Swan, darling, so good of you to come."

"Oh my pleasure, I *love* New York."

"Well, bless your ignorance, child. I'm glad you like it. And I'm glad you're here. Come meet some of my new people."

So Swan met some of the local team and endured their condolences about Alex, and gave them a brief inaccurate account of her trip to Jupiter. They had ideas about the Mondragon above and beyonds that they shared with her.

When they were done, Swan said to Milan, "Is Zasha still around?"

"Zasha will never leave this town," Milan said. "You must know that. Haven't you been to Z's latest scheme? It's on one of the Hudson piers."

So Swan took the ferry back up Eighth Avenue, got off, and climbed stairs until she reached a catwalk she could take west.

With all the old piers eleven meters underwater, a new set had had to be built. Some were old ones salvaged and stilted; others had been built anew, sometimes using the drowned ones as foundations. Smaller floating docks filled gaps and were attached to piers or nearby buildings at what used to be their fourth floors.

Some of these docks were mobile and became like barges as they moved around. It was a tricky shoreline.

Some of the submerged docks now held aquaculture pens, and Swan's old partner Zasha apparently now ran a pharm on one of these piers, growing various piscean drugs and bioceramics while also doing things for the Mercury House—and for Alex.

Swan had called ahead, and Zasha appeared at the fence that cut a floating dock off from the big plaza complex west of Gansevoort Street, at the south end of the High Line. After a brief hug, Z led her to the end of the dock and then out on the Hudson River in a boat, a smooth little hummer that soon had them midriver.

Everything on the water moved at a watery pace, including the water itself. The Hudson River here was wide; the entire city of Terminator would have fit in New York Harbor. Bridges were visible all over the place, including one on the distant southern horizon. There was so much water Swan could hardly believe it; even the open sea did not seem to have so much; and yet it was not even a very big river, compared to the really big ones. Earth!

Zasha was observing the scene with a contented expression. Banks of windows at the tops of the highest skyscrapers blazed with reflected sunlight, and all the buildings glowed. Skyscraper island: it was the classic Manhattan look, unlikely and superb.

"How are things with you?" Swan asked.

"I like this river," Zasha said, as if it were a reply. "I motor up to the top of the island, or even to the Palisades, and then just float on down. Throw a line over. Hook the most amazing stuff sometimes."

"And at Mercury House?"

Zasha frowned. "Spacers are getting blamed for a

lot these days. The people down here are resentful. The more we help, the more resentful they get. However, their capital funds keep on investing in us."

"As always," Swan said.

"Yes, well, perpetual growth. But nothing lasts forever. The solar system is just as finite as Earth."

"Do you think it's filling up? Hitting carrying capacity?"

"More like investment return peak. But people may be feeling pinched by it. Anyway, they're acting like they're pinched."

Zasha's boat drifted in the ebb tide until it passed the Battery, and the view to the Brooklyn shore opened up. The skyscrapers at the foot of Manhattan looked like a cluster of giant swimmers, gathered knee-deep to charge into cold water. Between buildings the water sheeted like glass, and the canals were filled with little boats; the harbor bay too, although not as densely. At any given moment hundreds of watercraft were visible. They could see up both rivers, the Hudson and the East, and between those ran the smaller, straighter rivers of the streets, all under a cloudy sky. A Canaletto vision. Cloud reflections whitened the bay's watery sheen. It was so beautiful that Swan felt like she had been cast into a dream, and she reeled a little with the boat's rocking.

"Feeling the g?" Zasha asked.

"I am kind of."

"Want to spend the night at my place? I'm getting kind of hungry."

"Sure. Thanks."

Zasha piloted the boat west across the river to a channel on the Jersey side that led west. It was hard to tell if it was a canal or a creek. Inland the waterway opened up to the north, and Zasha turned up that way and docked at a wooden pier sticking into what looked like a shallow lake. Whole neighborhoods sloped right down into water. The east side of North America had always been a drowned coastline, but now more than ever.

A walk up a rise under a violent sunset sky, which was tastelessly mashing orange and pink together. At times like these it was the eastern sky that really put on a show, subtler but more glorious. But no one looked that way.

Zasha's place was a tiny squat next to a line of trees, as handmade and run-down as any favela or shantytown Swan had ever seen.

"What is this place?"

"Part of the Meadowlands."

"And you're free to make your own home here?"

"As if! Actually my rent is stupendous, but Mercury House gives me a little supplement to keep me out here away from them."

"Hard to believe."

"Anyway, it's fine. I like my commute."

Swan sat gratefully in a beat-up armchair and watched her old partner putter about in the gloom. It had been a long time since they had banged around the solar system, building terraria and raising Zephyr; it had even been a long time since Zephyr had died. And they had never gotten along very well, separating soon after Zephyr went off. Still, Swan recognized the way Zasha hovered over the stove, waiting for the teapot to boil, harboring a secretive knowing look she also recognized.

She said, "So did you work with Alex?"

"Well, sure," Zasha replied, glancing at her briefly. "She was my boss. So you know how that goes."

"What do you mean?"

"I mean she loved you and took care of you, and you did exactly what she wanted you to."

Swan had to laugh. "Well, yes." She thought it over, ignoring the pain. "Somehow she conformed herself to what you needed. Helped you to get what you needed."

"Uh-huh. I know what you mean."

"But listen—now she's gone, and she left me a message. Basically she used me as a courier to Wang, on Io, and also dumped something into Pauline. It was all in case something happened to her, she said."

"What do you mean?"

Swan described the visitation from Alex's ghost—the envelopes—her trip out to Jupiter, and the interloper on Io.

Zasha said, "I heard about that. I didn't know you were there," frowning at the teapot, face blue in the stove top glow.

"What were you and Alex working on?" Swan asked. "And why didn't she tell me about it in this message she left? She—it's like I was just a courier for her, and Pauline some kind of safe-deposit box."

Zasha didn't reply.

"Come on, tell me," Swan said. "You can tell me. I can take it from you. I'm used to you telling me how bad I am."

Zasha expelled a breath, poured two cups of tea. Steam in gloom, catching light from somewhere. Z handed her one, then sat down on a kitchen chair across from her. Swan warmed her hands on her cup.

"There's stuff I can't talk about—"

"Oh come on!"

"—and stuff I can. She got me involved in a group that is hunting down some odd qubes. That's been interesting. But it was something she wanted kept confidential, along with some other things she had going. So, maybe she thought that you aren't very good at keeping things confidential."

"Why would she think *that*?"

But even Zasha knew of three or four examples of Swan's being indiscreet, and Swan herself knew of several more.

"Those were accidents," Swan finally added. "And not very big accidents either."

Zasha sipped the tea cautiously. "Well, but maybe they seemed to be becoming more frequent. You are not the same person you used to be, you have to admit. You've stuffed your brain with augmentations—"

"I have not!"

"Well, four or five. I didn't like it right from the beginning. When you grow the religious part of the temporal lobe, you can turn into a very different person, not to mention risking epilepsy. And that was only the start. Now you've got the animal stuff in there, you've got Pauline in there, recording everything you see—it is not insignificant. It can do damage. You end up being some kind of post-human thing. Or at least a different person."

"Oh come on, Z. I'm the same as I always was. And everything you do can damage you! You can't let that stop you. Every thing I've done to myself I consider part of being a human being. I mean, who wouldn't do it if they could? I would be ashamed not to! It isn't being *post* human, it's being *fully* human. It would be stupid not to do the good things when you can, it would be *anti*human."

"Well," Zasha said, "you did those things and you immediately stopped designing terraria."

"I was done! We were past the design phase anyway; they were just going to build more of the same. And a lot of what we did was stupid anyway. We shouldn't have been making Ascensions at that point, we needed to get the traditional biomes past the extinction. We still need that! I don't know what we were thinking, frankly."

Zasha was surprised at this. "I like the Ascensions. They help genetic dispersion."

"Too much so. Anyway that's not the point. The point is I wanted to try different things, and I did."

"You became an artist."

"I was always an artist. I just changed media. And hardly even that. Just a focusing in. It was what I wanted. Come on, Zasha. I'm just living a human life. You refuse these opportunities, that doesn't make you more human, it just makes you regressive. I don't go anywhere near as far as some people. I don't have a third eye and I don't break my ribs when I have an orgasm. I just . . ."

"Just what?"

"I don't know. Try things that sound good."

"And have they all worked out for you?"

Swan sat there in the gloom, somewhere in New Jersey. Outside was the open air of Earth. "No." Long pause. "In fact I've done worse things than what you know about, if you want to know the truth."

Zasha stared at her. "I'm not sure I do."

"Ha-ha. And Alex knew about it too, now that I think of it, because I told Mqaret about it."

"He wouldn't automatically tell her."

"I didn't ask him not to."

"Well," Zasha said. "So maybe she knew. Something worse than animal brains? Something worse than a qube in your skull? Never mind, I *don't* want to know. But maybe Alex did, and maybe she had stuff that she..."

"That she didn't trust me with."

"That she needed to keep to herself. And here you are, kind of a mess."

"I am not a mess!" Though her rib did hurt, squeezed by her indignation. And she was full of grief for Alex—and now a little angry at her too.

"Seems like you're saying you are messed up," Z observed. "You've had five or six or seven brain tweaks over the years, a qube in your head—in fact, whatever was fashionable at the time."

"Yeah yeah."

"Well think about it!"

Swan put her teacup on the table. "I think I'll go out for a walk."

"Good. Don't get lost. I'll cook up something while you're out, say about forty-five minutes."

Swan left the hut.

Outside the door she took her slippers off and stuffed them into her pocket, dug her toes into the dirt and wriggled them around. Leaned over from the waist like a dancer and dug her fingers in, put hands to face and breathed. Dirt, the ultimate ambrosia. Tasted like muddy mushrooms.

It was after sunset. There was an asphalt road running next to a marsh, green and yellow, the wind bouncing the reeds out there. She walked on the dirt by the side of the road and looked at the marsh and the sky. On the other side of the road some old buildings were nestled under a stand of trees. Rows of old apartment blocks beyond. Croak of frog. She sat on the edge of the marsh and saw the black dots half in and half out of the water under her. A chorus of frogs, croaking. She listened for a while, watching the marsh in the wind, and heard suddenly that they were performing a call-and-response. If one frog said "ribbit," then all the others would repeat it for a while, up and down the road for as far as she could hear, until in a momentary pause one croaked "robot," and they would all repeat that for a while. Then it changed to "limit," and off the others went, as if speaking to her like some Greek chorus, transmogrified to frogs. So many limits! So many robots. The lump nearest her contributed only once in a while, puffing under his chin briefly, then croaking. Otherwise it was perfectly still, except for a little shift of the eyeballs she could see in the dusk, a liquid blink, always alert. "Romper!" it croaked in a pause, and Swan exclaimed, "Good for you!" and said it with them for a while.

October on the northern hemisphere of Earth, so glossy and full. All her body-planet interfaces humming. Suddenly life in space seemed a stark nightmare, an exile to the vacuum, everyone locked in sensory-deprivation tanks, separate, virtual, augmented. Here the real was real.

"Robber!"

"Robber robber robber robber . . ."

The moment itself, robbed from them as it happened. Here she was, passing through a space. Flit of the now. Dusk in a marsh in a transient universe, so strange, so mysterious. Why should anything be like this? The wind was cool, the clouds had a little twilight left in them. Looked like rain. The leaves of the thorny vine on the ground were as red as maple leaves. The marsh was like a person out there breathing. Crows flew over cawing, headed into the town and its heat islands. Swan knew a little of the crow language; they would say to each other, "Caw, caw, caw," as now, just chatting, and then one would shout a word out so clearly that it had become an English word—"Hawk!"—and they would scatter. Of course the word *crow* also came from their language. In Sanskrit they had it as *kaaga*. Imported words from another language.

There were some people, standing by the buildings next to the trees. They were small somehow. Weighted down. Could this be so close to the great city? Was it indeed part of the city, part of what made it work, not just the wetlands but the legions of poor marginal people, living in the half-drowned ruins? The weight of the planet began to drag her down. Those people over there were like figures out of Brueghel, people from the sixteenth century, bowed down with time. Maybe these were the people living a real life, and what she did in space nothing more than the dilettantism of a gaga aristo. Maybe what she really needed to do was to live here and build things, maybe houses, little but functional, a different kind of goldsworthy. Under the sky, in the full light of the sun—the utter luxury of the real. The only real world. Earth, heaven and hell both—natural heaven, human hell. How could they have done such a thing, how could they have not tried harder?

Maybe they had. Maybe the trying included the flight to space, as some kind of desperate hope. Cast from Earth as if in a seed pod, out to where one was sure to freeze and rot and turn back into soil. This dirt by the side of the road. She lay on it, avoiding the thorny vine; squirmed around as if to burrow into it. A spacer fucking the dirt—they must see that all the time, not be impressed anymore. Those poor lost people, they must think. Because there was nothing like this in space, not really—not the wind and the big sky over her, almost night now, with moisture that was not yet cloud—Oh how could they have left! Space was a vacuum, a nothingness. They had inhabited it only by deploying little rooms, little bubbles; the city and the stars, sure, but it wasn't enough! There needed to be a world in between! This was what city people forgot. And indeed off in space they had better forget, or they would go mad. Here one could remember and yet not go mad—not exactly.

But how sad it was. Grubby, tawdry, beaten down. Pitiful. Sad to distraction, to a stabbing despair. That they had let it come to this. That she had done what she had done to herself. Even Zasha thought she had gone too far, and Z was a very tolerant person. Would have stayed with her, maybe, if she hadn't gone off. And now she was no longer the person Zasha had parented a child with, she could feel that, even though she didn't know exactly what had changed. Unless it was the Enceladan bugs in her . . . In any case a strange person. A person for whom the only place that made her truly happy also made her deeply sad. How was she to reconcile this, what did it mean?

She sat up. Sat there on the dirt, feeling it lumpy under her.

She saw a motion from the corner of her eye and tried to leap to her feet, misjudged the g and crashed back down. She peered into the gloom:

A face. Two faces: mother and daughter. Here it was such a clear thing; it looked like parthenogenesis. Moonlight just now breaking over the skyglow of the city.

The younger stepped toward Swan. Said something in a language Swan didn't recognize.

"What is it?" Swan said. "Don't you speak English?"

The woman shook her head, said something more. She looked around her, called quietly behind her.

Two more figures appeared next to her, taller than her and broader. Two young men. They leaned over and muttered to the daughter.

"You have antibiotics?" one of them said. "My coz is sick."

"No," Swan said, "I don't carry those on me." Although possibly her belt had something, she wasn't even sure.

They took a step closer. "Who are you?" one said. "What are you?"

"I'm visiting friends," Swan said. "I can call them."

The young men approached her, shaking their heads. "You're a spacer," the first speaker said, and the other added, "What you doing here?"

"I have to go," Swan said, and started for the road— but the two of them grabbed her by the arms. Their grips were so strong that she didn't even try to jerk free. "Hey!" she said sharply.

The first speaker called out toward the dark behind the two women: "Kiran! Kiran!"

Soon another figure appeared out of the dark— another young man, the tallest yet, but willowy. The two holding Swan had grips that felt to her like something they had done before.

The new young man was startled at the sight of Swan and said something sharp to the two holding her, in a language she didn't recognize. A quick urgent conversation passed between them; this Kiran was not pleased.

Finally he looked at Swan. "They want to keep you for money. Give me a second here."

More urgent talk in their tongue. Kiran appeared to be making them nervous or defensive; then he approached and took Swan by the upper arm, squeezing once as if to send a message, and gestured the others away with a flick of his head. He was telling them what to do. The other two finally nodded, and the one who had spoken first said to her, "Back soon." Then the first two slipped away into the night.

Swan looked Kiran in the eye, and he grimaced and let go of her arm. "Those are my cousins," he said. "They had a bad idea."

"A stupid idea," Swan said. "They could have just asked me for help. So what did you tell them?"

"That I would keep you here while they got their mother's car. So now I think you should get out of here."

"Come walk me back," Swan said. "I want you along, in case they come back."

His eyebrows shot up his forehead, and he regarded her closely. After a while he said, "All right."

They walked quickly on the road. "Will you get in trouble for this?" Swan asked at one point.

"Yes," he said gloomily.

"What will they do?"

"They'll try to beat on me. And tell the old guys."

Her arms were still burning where they had been gripped, and her cheeks were hot. She regarded the gloomy youth walking next to her. He looked good. And he had without a moment's hesitation removed her from a bad situation. She recalled how sharp his voice had been when he'd spoken to his cousins. "Do you want to leave?"

"What do you mean?"

"Do you want to go into space?"

After a pause he said, "Can you do that?"

"Yes," she said.

They stopped outside Zasha's, and Swan looked him over. She liked the look of him. He looked at her with an expression curious, wondering—eager. She felt a shiver run down her.

"My friend who lives here is a diplomat for Mercury. So...come in if you want. We can get you up there if you want," she said, looking skyward briefly.

He hesitated. "You won't...get me in trouble?"

"I *will* get you in trouble. Trouble in space."

She started toward Zasha's, and after a moment, he followed her. She opened the door. "Zasha?" she said.

"Just a sec," Zasha called out of the kitchen.

The boy was staring at her, clearly wondering if she was on the level.

Swan said, "They called you Kiran?"

"Yes, Kiran."

"What language were you speaking?"

"Telugu. South India."

"What are you doing here?"

"We live here now."

So he was already an exile. And there were all kinds of immigrant residency requirements on Earth; possibly he was not in compliance.

Zasha appeared in the doorway to the kitchen, washcloth in hand. "Uh-oh. Who's this?"

"This is Kiran. His friends were kidnapping me, and he helped me to escape. In return I told him I would get him off Earth."

"But no!"

"But yes. So...here we are. And I need to keep my word."

Zasha looked at Swan skeptically. "What is this, Stockholm syndrome already?" Z glanced at the youth, whose gaze was fixed on Swan. "Or Lima syndrome?"

"What are those?" Kiran said without shifting his gaze.

Zasha made a little grimace. "Stockholm syndrome is where hostages become sympathetic to their captors and advocate for them. Lima syndrome is where the kidnappers become fond of their victims and let them go."

"Isn't there a Ransom of Red Chief syndrome?" Swan said sharply. "Come on, Z. I told you, he rescued me. What syndrome is that? I want to repay a favor, and I need your help. Quit trying to take over the situation like you always do."

Zasha turned away with an annoyed look; thought it over; shrugged. "We can get him off if you really want it. I'll have to do it through a friend who helps me with this kind of thing. He's at the Trinidad-Tobago elevator, it's a hawala. We have a kind of pass-through agreement, although after this I'll owe him. Meaning you'll owe me."

"I always owe you. How will we get to Trinidad?"

"Diplomatic pouch."

"What?"

"Private jet. We'll have to get a worm box too."

"A what?"

"We have a system. It's always supposed to be a box of soil or worms, and there's an understanding that it doesn't get inspected."

"Worms?" Kiran said.

"That's right," Zasha told him with a grim little smile. "I'm going to get you off-planet, because of Ms. Stockholm here, but given the circumstances, we have to do it off the record. That takes using the systems we have. So you might have to go up in a big box of worms, all right? Are you going to be okay with that?"

"No problem," said Kiran.

Extracts (4)

At the end of the period of planetary accretion, about 4.5 billion years ago, there were more planets than there are now, all slung around by close calls and orbital resonances and pulled together by gravity, so that they sometimes collided. They had been doing it for a billion years to get to this point, and this was the last stage of that process of accretion. During this period every one of the inner planets took at least one very big hit.

A planet called Theia grew at Earth's L5 point until it was about the size of Mars, then drifted into a collision with Earth. It hit at a forty-five-degree angle, at something less than four kilometers per second—not fast in astronomical terms. Theia's iron core plunged in and merged with Earth's core, and Theia's mantle and some of Earth's mantle were thrown into orbit. The angular momentum imparted by the hit spun Earth to a five-hour day. Two moons accreted from the ejected material rather quickly; estimates range from a month to a century. Eventually the smaller moon splatted onto the larger one, leaving behind the jagged mountains on the anti-terran side of the resulting moon, Luna.

Around the same time, a small planet about three thousand kilometers in diameter struck Mars and created the Borealis Basin, which is basically Mars's northern hemisphere, still six kilometers lower than the southern hemisphere.

Venus was struck by a Mars-sized planet, creating a moon like Earth's, called Neith; ten million years later, another impactor gave Venus its slow retrograde motion. This change in rotation slowed Neith and caused it to plunge back into Venus and merge with it.

Mercury was struck by a protoplanet half its size, at such a speed and angle that Mercury's mantle was stripped off and cast throughout Mercury's orbit. Ordinarily Mercury would have swept these pieces back up, but in the four million years this process would have taken, most of the material was pushed outward by solar radiation and thus never made it back to Mercury. About sixteen quadrillion tons of Mercury's crust eventually ended up on Earth, and more on Venus. In the end only the heaviest 70 percent of Mercury remained, essentially the planet's core. Thus the Mars g for a diameter smaller than Titan's.

Somewhat later, the young Jupiter and Saturn fell into a one-to-two orbital resonance, with Jupiter spinning through two of its years for every one of Saturn's. This created a very powerful combined gravity wave, swinging around the solar system at varying strength, depending on where the two giants were in relation to each other. This new wave at its strongest caught Neptune, which had grown just outside Saturn, and threw it away from the sun! Neptune flew out past Uranus, pulling Uranus outward too, also onto its side. Only at that point did the two smaller gas giants end up in the orbits they now occupy.

Inside Jupiter's orbit, meanwhile, that same Jupiter-Saturn resonance wave caught asteroids and threw them like pinballs all over the system, in the period called the Late Heavy Bombardment, 3.9 billion years ago. All the inner planets and moons were pummeled with impacts, to the point where the surfaces of these planets often were seas of molten rock.

The Era of Big Hits! The Late Heavy Bombardment! Never let it be said that the great merry-go-round is entirely fixed and regular in its motion—that it doesn't sometimes resemble more a swirl of bumper cars. Gravity, mysterious gravity, immutably following its own laws, interacts with matter, and somehow the result is complex motion. Invisible waves slinging rocks this way and that.

What if human history has such invisible waves? Because ultimately the same forces apply. What big hits made us what we are? Will some new resonance create a wave and throw us in a new direction? Are we entering our own Late Heavy Bombardment?

KIRAN AND SWAN

From the moment Kiran saw the woman his cousins had grabbed, everything changed. She was old, tall, good-looking. She moved as if she were swimming. He knew immediately that she was a spacer, and that kidnapping her was a terrible idea. After that everything went a bit too fast for him actually to be deciding what to do. This is what happened to him when he was in a pinch: he watched himself do what he did from just behind and to one side. People said he was cool, but really he was slow. And yet good things still seemed to happen.

Her hair was black; she looked Chinese or Mongol. Her eyes were brown, with a little blue patch at the bottom of one eye; and really it was her eyes that captured him. Some kind of coincidence—the girls back home had those same dark eyes with luminous whites, in a dark face—it was very compelling to him. She had looked to him the moment he had taken her arm, to show how much she wanted to be free—a very passionate look, as if she knew what being held captive was like, and was afraid. It shocked him how expressive her face was, how firmly she grabbed his attention. Her friend Zasha had called it Lima syndrome—maybe so. Maybe now he was an incompetent Peruvian.

But he was going to space. That meant leaving—but he could send money back to his relatives. They were tired of putting him up anyway. He could go and see what he had always dreamed of seeing—which was really just anywhere, but space in particular, ever since he was a small boy. Mars, the asteroids—anywhere out there. Everyone heard stories.

The woman drove them out to Newark. Jammed in the little seat behind them, he began to realize it was really happening—something, anyway. His idiot cousins were not going to be able to find him and beat him. A new life: he began to quiver slightly, as if *he* were the hostage who had been kidnapped. In a way it was almost true. Captured by a look, stuffed into the backseat of a car.

They came to an airport that did not look like Newark. They drove out to a hangar and were escorted up a stand of stairs into a small jet. He had never been in anything like it, and was impressed by its speed as they took off. They gave him a window seat and he watched Manhattan below, like a great ship of light. Off they went into the night.

Eventually he leaned his head on the window and fell asleep. Later he woke with a stiff neck, watched the ocean get closer. The jet landed on a green island with reddish soil.

Out into a pungent evening, humid air like mid-August in Jersey, almost like his childhood home in Hyderabad. Rice fields. Childhood memories sparked out of what he saw and smelled, and again he walked as if a little beside himself. He was very distracted as they entered a building. Mercury House, a sign said.

Inside, they took him to a big room, where immense white plastic tubs like those used in industrial kitchens were being sealed and loaded onto a pallet. "All right, young man," said Swan's friend Zasha, clearly still a little disgusted to have to be doing this for Swan. "In you go. Put on this spacesuit first, then the helmet. After that we're going to cover you in dirt and worms, and up you go." To Swan: "My friend won't inspect the boxes that have my sign on them. He's got the next shift."

"Why the worms?"

"It's a way to show I'm not using it casually. I only send up a couple people a year like this. And naturally he gets favors back from me."

"What about the AI inspections?"

"What about them? We do a lot of stuff outside that system." Zasha grinned fiercely at her. "This is a hawala elevator, the whole thing is set up to skip certain scans."

Then Kiran was in a crinkly one-piece and had a helmet on and was breathing cool coppery air. They helped him in and laid him out in the tub as if in his coffin, and a wriggling mass of worms and black dirt was dumped over his body and face. He was going to leave Earth buried in worms. "Thank you!" he called out to the woman and her friend.

It was a long trip. Kiran lay there thinking. He could feel the worms writhing all over him. When he freaked out and hyperventilated, the helmet and suit seemed to be able to take it. Eventually he always had to calm back down. There were water and food tubes that would come out of the neck of the suit to where he could suck on them, and though the food was a paste, it was very sustaining. He was not too cold or too hot. The sensation of movement over him was disconcerting, sometimes horrible. This must be what it was like to be dead and buried. The worms would eat you. Or it was like the purification rites in certain festivals—in the Durga-puja, for instance, in which you were steeped in ash or manure until it was time for the cleansing. He liked that holiday. So here he was. As he had to eat and drink, then shit and pee, all in this suit, he was for the moment pretty much like the worms. We are poor forked worms on this Earth, his grandfather used to say. Birds pick us off.

As time passed he went entirely weightless. He had heard it took five days to ascend. It seemed longer. He began to get bored. When he felt a jolt upward, and then light flooded the dirt and the lid disappeared, he struggled up as carefully as he could, thinking the worms in the box were fellow travelers who deserved no harm. "Careful!" he commanded the people helping him out of the box, and Swan laughed at him.

She led him to a little bathroom. Once out of his suit, he showered. In the hot water he thought, Ah yes, this is the cleansing. Next came the purification; what would it be? Was this woman who had seized him a manifestation of Durga, mother of Ganesh—also sometimes manifested as Kali?

"You look good," Swan said when he emerged from the bathroom. "Not too traumatic?"

Kiran shook his head. "Time to think. Where to next?"

Again she laughed. "This ship is going to Venus," she told him. "I'm on my way to Mercury, so I'll drop you off."

Kiran said, "Isn't Venus a Chinese place?"

"Yes and no," Swan said.

Kiran persisted: "So I become Chinese?"

"No. There are all kinds of people there. My friends will give you an ID. After that, anything can happen. But Venus is a good place for you to start."

They were traveling in a terrarium called the *Delta of Venus*, an ag asteroid dedicated to growing food for Earth—mostly enhanced rices but also other crops that liked it warm and wet. The internal gravity felt like Earth; Kiran couldn't detect the famous Coriolis push to the side.

They spent their days out in the upcurving fields, working alongside water buffalo, tractors, canal boats, and many other workers, most of them passengers. After an hour the work became hard on the back, and as the passengers—some of them only a little taller than the rice sprouts, while others were taller than giants, which was at first startling to see—sloshed up and down the rows, they talked to pass the time. Complaint and desire to be elsewhere were natural themes. "I'm festivalled out." "I've tried them all." "The only place terraforming matters is on Earth, and they're terrible at it." "It's all turning out to be face business." "We could have taken the *Grindewald* and gone mountain climbing. The Mönch, the Eiger, the Jungfrau, they've reproduced every damn crack." "I'd rather go in an aquarium and swim around. Live with a mermaid for a week."

Beachworlds were wonderful, all agreed. With Earth's beaches gone, the ones inside aquaria were much beloved.

Others advocated cloud forest worlds; these were visits to arboreal heaven and an earlier stage of primate life. "Such bliss to be a monkey!"

Someone said, "Or a bonobo. I wish *I* had gone on a sexliner."

This broke a little dam of reticence and brought the talk immediately around to sex on those sexliners, which were often designed to look like Caribbean resorts. Dionysian dances, perpetual tantric orgies, Kundalini panmixia, everyone had a story. One of them said mournfully, "I could have spent the whole trip in a touchy-feely box, and here I am wielding a hand hoe."

"Touchy-feely box?" Kiran couldn't help asking.

"You get in a box that has holes cut in it about as big around as your hand, and then people reach in the holes and do what they want."

"I'm surprised people would do that."

"Lines always seem pretty long, for both inside and outside."

"I should have thought of the worms that way," Kiran said to Swan. "Could have been happy all the way up that elevator."

"I'd rather be in here than in one of those," someone else called. "Farms are sexy! All this fertilizer!"

Many groaned at this. It was not a joke that resonated.

Someone else said, "Last time I was on a sexliner, this group of bisexuals ran out to the pool, about twenty of them, all with the biggest tits and cocks you ever saw, and all of them with erections, and they got in a circle one behind the next and plunged into the one in front of them and away they went. It was like when you see insects clumping together on a summer day, keep fucking till they fall to the ground."

This brought on quite a silence until someone said heavily, "Wish I had seen that," which got the others laughing, or loudly protesting that any such image had ever been put in their heads. "I'm just saying," the witness insisted. "These things happen. It's a regular sport."

And it seemed to Kiran that after the talk about sexliners the rice planting hurt less. And when these people were done for the day and back at the dorm, it seemed like the farm might turn into a sexy place after all. There was a look in people's eyes Kiran thought he recognized.

Extracts (5)

Take raw Venus. CO_2 atmosphere of ninety-five bar, temperature at surface would melt lead, hotter even than Mercury's brightside. A hellish place. On the other hand, .9 g, and just a tad smaller than Earth. Two continental rises on the surface, Ishtar and Aphrodite. Earth's sister planet. There's real potential here for a great new creation.

Take one Saturnian ice moon—Dione will do fine. Dismantle with Von Neumann self-replicating excavators, cutting it into chunks about ten kilometers on a side. Attach mass drivers to the chunks and send them down to Venus.

While doing this, build a round sunshield of lunatic aluminum, very thin material, only 50 grams per square meter and yet still totaling 3×10^{13} kilograms, the largest thing ever built by humans. Concentric strips give the sunshield flexibility and allow it to tack up into the solar wind to hold its position at the L1 point, where it will shadow Venus entirely. Deprived of insolation, the planet will cool at a rate of five K a year.

After 140 years, the CO_2 atmosphere will have

rained and snowed to the surface and frozen as a layer of dry ice. Scrape all the dry ice that landed on Ishtar and Aphrodite down to the lowlands, being careful to keep a smooth surface. While clearing off the continents, release another suite of Von Neumann self-replicating chemical factories designed to break oxygen out of the frozen CO_2; these will create 150 millibars of oxygen for the atmosphere, in about the same time it takes for all the CO_2 atmosphere to freeze. A purely oxygen atmosphere would be too flammable, so add a buffer gas, preferably nitrogen, to make a more stable mix. Titan may be oversubscribed for its excess nitrogen, so be prepared to seek substitutions. Argon mined on Luna would also serve in a pinch.

When you have the oxygen you want, and the dry ice all flat on the lowlands, cover the dry ice with foamed rock, so that the CO_2 is a completely sequestered feature of the lithosphere.

Now take the chunks of Dione you have been saving and crack them against each other in the oxygen-and-buffer atmosphere at the correct height to create steam and rain. This will add back to the planet some heat, which at this point has been taken below the human-friendly range. Possibly some light can be let through the sunshield if needed to help heating. It will only take two years for the greater part of the impact water to rain and snow onto the surface, so be ready to work fast.

The water on the surface after this Dione infusion will be equal to about 10 percent of Earth's water. It will be freshwater; salt to taste. The water will cover 80 percent of Venus, which is much flatter than Earth, to an average depth of 120 meters. If deeper seas are preferred, but also a maximum amount of land, consider digging an oceanic trench with some of the Dione impactors. Remember this will complicate the CO_2 sequestration if you choose to do it, so make adjustments accordingly. If it is done carefully, however, Venus could ultimately end up with about twice the land surface that Earth has.

At this point (140 years freezing and preparation, 50 years scraping and poaching, so be patient!) you might think that the planet is ready for biological occupation. But remember, combining the Venusian year of 224 days with its daily rotation period of 243 days, you get a screwball curve (retrograde motion, sun rising in the west) in which the solar day for any particular point on the planet is 116.75 days. Tests have long since determined that that's too long for most Terran life-forms to survive, tweaked or not. So at this point, two main options have been identified. First is to program the sunshield so that it lets through sunlight to the surface and then blocks it off again, flexing like a circular venetian blind to make a more Terran rhythm of night and day. This would make it easy on the new biosphere, but would require that the sunshield work without fail.

The second option would call for another round of impactor bombardments, this time striking the surface of the planet such that their angular momentum spins the planet up to something like a fifty-hour day, which is considered within the tolerance limit for most Terran life-forms. The problem with this option is the way it would delay occupation of the planet's surface, by its release of a considerable amount of the sequestered dry ice under the foamed rock layer. Biosphere establishment would have to be put off for another two hundred years, effectively doubling the time of terraformation. But there would be no further reliance on a sunshield. And a properly constituted and maintained Venusian atmosphere could handle full sunlight without green-housing or other spoilage.

Which option you choose is your preference. Think about what you want in the end, or, if you don't believe in endings, which process you prefer.

KIRAN AND SHUKRA

A few days later they were approaching Venus. Kiran was pleased to see Swan joining him on the ferry ride down. She wanted to talk to a friend; she would introduce Kiran to him, then be on her way.

There were no space elevators on Venus, because the planet rotated too slowly for such a system to work. So their ferry sprouted wings, and as they tore down through the atmosphere the windows torched yellow-white. They landed on a huge runway next to a domed city, then got into a subway car, and came up from that short ride into the city. There they found what seemed like the entire population in the streets. Kiran followed Swan through the crowds, and in a side street they went up some stairs into a little Mercury House, set over a fish shop. They dropped off their bags, then went back out to join the crowd.

The faces of the city were mostly Asian. People shouted, and in the din no one could hear well, so they shouted even louder. Swan looked at Kiran and grinned at his expression. "It isn't always like this!" she shouted.

"Too bad!" Kiran shouted back.

Two big ice asteroids were apparently headed for a collision at the upper edge of the new Venusian atmosphere, roughly above the equator. This city, Colette, was three hundred kilometers north of the collision, and would therefore be quickly enveloped in a downpour. The rain would not stop for a couple of years, Swan said, after which they would let a little light through their sunscreen and have more ordinary weather.

But first the big rain. Crowds stood around them waiting for it, singing and cheering and shouting. And right at midnight the southern sky lit up white, then incandescent yellow, then all the reds ever seen. The inside of the city looked briefly like they were seeing it in the infrared. The noise of the cheering was stupendous. Somewhere a brass band was playing—Kiran spotted the musicians, on risers across the square— several hundred trumpets, French horns, baritones, trombones, tubas, all the euphoniums, everything from miniature cornets to alphorns, playing immense dissonant chords that blatted in the air and shifted ceaselessly toward harmonies that never came. Kiran didn't know whether to call it music; it sounded like they played without a plan. The effect was to make people shout and howl, leap and dance. They were making their sky.

Within the hour a wild rain had erased the stars and was drumming onto the dome as if trying to wash it away. They might as well have been at the bottom of a waterfall. The city's lights bounced off the dome glass and came back somehow liquefied, so that shadows ran over people's faces.

At some point Swan squeezed Kiran's upper arm in a manner very like the way he had hers the night they had met. He felt the pressure, he knew what she meant; his blood burned up and down from the spot she held. "All right already!" he shouted to her. "Thank you!"

With a little smile she let him go. They stood in the streaming light, the dome a dim milky white over them. The roar of voices was like waves breaking on a beach of cobbles. "You'll be all right?" she said.

"I'll be fine!"

"So now you owe me."

"Yes. But I don't know what I can give you in return."

"I'll think of something," she said. "For now, I'll introduce you to Shukra. I worked for him a long time ago, and now he's moved into some very high circles here. So if you work for him and do your best, and he likes you, then you'll have your chance. I'll give you a translator to help you."

Back in Colette's Mercury House they ate breakfast, then Swan took Kiran across town to meet her friend Shukra. He proved to be a middle-aged man with a round cheerful face under a shock of white hair.

"Sorry about Alex," he said to Swan. "I enjoyed working with her."

"Yes," Swan said. "Seems like everyone did."

She introduced Kiran: "I met this young man when I went out to Jersey, and he got me out of a mess. He wanted a job, and I thought he might be someone you could use."

Shukra heard this impassively, but Kiran could see from the bunching of his eyebrows that he was interested. "What can you do?" he said to Kiran.

"Construction, retail, janitorial, bookkeeping," Kiran said. "And I can learn fast."

"You'll need to," Shukra said. "I've got jobs that need doing, so we'll get you into something."

"Oh," Swan said, "and he needs papers."

"Ah," Shukra said. Swan met his gaze without flinching. Now she was going to owe him, Kiran saw. "If you say so," he said at last. "You are my black swan. I'll see what I can do."

"Thanks," Swan said.

After that she needed to get out to the spaceport to catch her flight. She took Kiran aside and briefly hugged him. "I'll see you again."

"I hope so!" Kiran said.

"It will happen. I get around." She smiled briefly. "Anyway, we'll always have New Jersey."

"Lima," he said. "We'll always have Lima."

She laughed. "I thought it was Stockholm." And gave him a kiss on the cheek and was gone.

Extracts (6)

The economic model of the space settlements developed in part from their origins as scientific stations. In this early model, life in space was not a market economy; once you were in space, your housing and food were provided in an allotment system, as in Antarctic scientific stations. What markets existed tended to be private unregulated individual enterprises in nonessential goods. Capitalism was in effect relegated to the margin, and the necessities of life were a shared commons

exchange between Earth and individual space colonies was on a national or treaty-association basis, thus a kind of colonial model, with the colonies producing metals and volatiles, knowledge useful for Earth management, and later on, food

once the space elevators were in place (first at Quito, 2076) traffic between Earth and space increased by a factor of a hundred million. At that point the solar system became accessible. It was too big to inhabit rapidly, but the increasing speed of space travel meant that over the course of the twenty-second century the entire solar system came within easy reach. It is not a coincidence that the second half of this century saw the beginning of the Accelerando

the space diaspora occurred as late capitalism writhed in its internal decision concerning whether to destroy Earth's biosphere or change its rules. Many argued for the destruction of the biosphere, as being the lesser of two evils

one of the most influential forms of economic change had ancient origins in Mondragon, Euskadi, a small Basque town that ran an economic system of nested co-ops organized for mutual support. A growing network of space settlements used Mondragon as a model for adapting beyond their scientific station origins to a larger economic system. Cooperating as if in a diffuse Mondragon, the individual space settlements, widely scattered, associated for mutual support and

supercomputers and artificial intelligence made it possible to fully coordinate a non-market economy, in effect mathematicizing the Mondragon. Needs were determined year to year in precise demographic detail, and production then directed to fill the predicted needs. All economic transactions—from energy creation and extraction of raw materials, through manufacturing and distribution, to consumption and waste recycling—were accounted for in a single computer program. Once policy questions were answered—meaning desires articulated in a sharply contested political struggle—the total annual economy of the solar system could be called out on a quantum computer in less than a second. The resulting qube-programmed Mondragon, sometimes called the Albert-Hahnel model, or the Spuffordized Soviet cybernetic model, could be

if everyone had been working in a programmed Mondragon, all would have been well; but it was only one of several competing economies on Earth, all decisively under the thumb of late capitalism, still in control of more than half of Earth's capital and production, and with its every transaction tenaciously reaffirming ownership and capital accumulation. This concentration of power had not gone away but only liquefied for a while and then jelled elsewhere, much of it on Mars, as Gini figures for the era clearly reveal

in residual-emergent models, any given economic system or historical moment is an unstable mix of past and future systems. Capitalism therefore was the combination or battleground of its residual element, feudalism, and its emergent element—what?

with the success of the Martian revolution and the emergence of its single planetwide social-democratic system, the gates were opened for the rest of the solar system to follow. Many space settlements remained colonies of Terran nations and combines, however, so the ultimate result was a patchwork of systems somewhat resembling anarchy. Much of the space economy came to be dominated by a league of settlements called the Mondragon Accord. The Accord was renewed at a conference every five years, and annually the Accord's AIs called out its economy, thereafter correcting it frequently (several times a second)

the longer the Mondragon Accord went on, the more robust it got. Confident in the Accord's support of the necessities, individual settlements' enterprise markets made more and more side deals, the so-called above and beyonds, all working on the margin. If not for Mars and its

as feudalism is the residual on Earth, capitalism is the residual on Mars

the margin itself grows with prosperity, resulting in increasing sophistication and culture

the existence of the marginal economy, semiautonomous, semi-unregulated, resembling anarchy, filled with fraud, double-dealing, and crime, delighted all free marketeers, libertarians, anarchists, and many others, some enjoying the bonobo barter and others the machismo of a wild west and wealth beyond need

marginal capitalism is a tough-guy sport like rugby or tackle football, suitable mostly for people slightly overdosed on testosterone. On the other hand, with some rule and attitude changes, it has proven it can be an interesting game, even beautiful, like baseball or volleyball. It is a valid project at the margin, a form of self-actualization, not to be applied to the necessities, but on the margin a nice hobby, even perhaps an art form

confining capitalism to the margin was the great Martian achievement, like defeating the mob or any other protection racket

WAHRAM AND SWAN

Wahram was back in Terminator before Swan returned from Earth. At that point the city was sliding over the immense plain of Beethoven Crater, and Wahram screwed his courage to the sticking point and when she got into town, asked Swan if she wanted to go out with him to a facility in the west wall of Beethoven, to hear a concert and catch up on things. As he made the call, he was, he had to admit, nervous. Her quicksilver manner left him uncertain what to expect; he could not even predict whether he would be going out to Beethoven with her or with Pauline. On the other hand, he liked Pauline; so hopefully it would be all right either way. And with luck Swan would no longer be so intent to learn all there was to know about Alex's plans concerning the qubes. That, Inspector Genette had made very clear, they had to keep from her.

In any case, the chance to hear some Beethoven was enough to spur him on. He made the call; and Swan agreed to go.

After that Wahram looked up the program for the performance they were to attend, and was excited to see it was a triple bill of rarely played transcriptions: first a wind ensemble playing a transcription of the *Appassionata* piano sonata; then Beethoven's opus 134, which was his own transcription for two pianos of his *Grosse Fugue* for string quartet, opus 133. Lastly a string quartet was to play a transcription of their own for the *Hammerklavier* sonata.

Brilliant programming, Wahram felt, and he joined Swan at the south lock of Terminator with an anticipation so strong that it overwhelmed the uneasiness he felt both about her and about being outside Terminator, on the surface of Mercury. Necessary movement westward—well, this was always true in some sense, he told himself, and focused his thoughts on the concert. Maybe there was no real reason for concern. It was interesting to think that he might be irrationally afraid of the sun.

At the little museum in the west wall of Beethoven, he was astonished to see that they were almost the only people in the audience, aside from the musicians not playing, who sat in the front rows to listen. The facility had an empty main room that would have held a few thousand people, but happily this concert was in a side hall with just a couple hundred seats, arced around a small stage in Greek theater style. Acoustics were excellent.

The wind ensemble, slightly outnumbering its audience, rollicked its way through the finale of the *Appassionata* in a way that made it one of the greatest wind pieces Wahram had ever heard, fast to the point of effervescence. The transcription to winds made it a new thing in the same way that Ravel had made Mussorgsky's *Pictures at an Exhibition* a new thing.

When they were done, two pianists got up, and

sitting at grand pianos snuggled into each other like two sleeping cats, they played Beethoven's own opus 134, his transcription of his *Grosse Fugue*. They had to pound away like percussionists, simply hammering the keys. More clearly than ever Wahram heard the intricate weave of the big fugue, also the crazy energy of the thing, the maniacal vision of a crushing clockwork. The sharp attack of struck piano keys gave the piece a clarity and violence that strings with the best will and technique in the world could not achieve. Wonderful.

Then some other transcriber had gone in the opposition direction, arranging the *Hammerklavier* sonata for string quartet. Here, even though four instruments were now playing a piece written for one, it was still a challenge to convey the *Hammerklavier*'s intensity. Broken out among two violins, viola, and cello, it all unpacked beautifully: the magnificent anger of the first movement; the aching beauty of the slow movement, one of Beethoven's finest; and then the finale, another big fugue. It all sounded very like the late quartets to Wahram's ear—thus a new late quartet, by God! It was tremendous to hear. Wahram glanced around at the audience and saw the wind players and the pianists were standing on their feet behind the chairs, bouncing, swaying in place, faces uplifted and eyes closed, as if in prayer; hands sometimes spastically waving before them, as if conducting or dancing. Swan too was back there dancing, looking transported. Wahram was very pleased to see that; he was out there himself in the space of Beethoven, a very great space indeed. It would have been shocking to see someone immune to it; it would have put her outside his zone of sympathy or comprehension.

Afterward, as an encore, the musicians announced they

wanted to try an experiment. They separated the two pianos, and the string quartet then sat between them, in a circle facing inward; then they reprised the two big fugues, all playing at the same time. The two pieces overlapped with the wrong instruments applied to each, increasing the cognitive confusion; and the quiet parts in each came at the same time, in an urgent eye of the storm, revealing the structural similarity of the two monsters. When both returned to their main fugues, the six instruments sawed or pounded away in their own worlds, lashing out six different tunes in a crisscross fury, with Messiaenic crashes. They ended together somehow. Wahram wasn't certain which of them had been extended or curtailed to make that happen, but in any case they finished together with a big crash, and everyone there, already on their feet, could only clap and cheer and whistle.

"Wonderful," Wahram said afterward. "Truly."

Swan shook her head. "Too crazy at the end, but I liked it."

They stayed around to join the congratulations and the discussion among the musicians, who were as interested as could be in what it had sounded like from the outside; more than one said they had been able to focus only on their own parts. Someone played back a recording made of it, and they listened along with the rest, until the musicians began to pause the recording and discuss details.

"Time to get back to Terminator," Swan said.

"All right. Thanks ever so much for this, it was very fine."

"My pleasure. Listen, do you want to walk back over to the city tracks? It's nice after a wild concert like this one. They've got suits here we can use. It gives you a chance to walk it out a little."

"But—do we have time?"

"Oh yes. We'll get to the platform well ahead of the city. I've done this before."

She must not have noticed his discomfort at being out on the surface of Mercury. Well, so he had to agree. Even though every other member of the audience, and the musicians too, took the tram back. On which they were almost certainly continuing the interesting discussion of the concert, of transpositions in Beethoven, and so on.

But no. A walk on a burned world. When their borrowed spacesuits had confirmed integrity, they exited the hall's air lock and headed back north toward Terminator's tracks.

Beethoven Crater had as smooth a surface as he had seen on Mercury. Little Bello was under the horizon to the east. Wahram walked along nervously. Their headlamps illuminated long ellipses of black desert. Fines lofted from the fronts of their boots and drifted back to the baked ground behind them. Their boot prints would last for a billion years, but they were on a track of prints, and the damage to the surface had long since been done. Flanking the dusty trail, the knobby granulated rock caught their headlamps' beams and reflected them in little diamond pricks of light that looked like frost, though they must have been minute crystal surfaces. They passed a rock with a Kokopelli painted on it; the figure appeared to be holding a telescope rather than a flute and was pointing the glass to the east. For a while Wahram whistled the theme of the *Grosse Fugue*, half speed, under his breath.

"Do you whistle?" Swan asked, sounding surprised.

"I suppose I do."

"So do I!"

Wahram, who did not think of himself as someone who whistled for others, did not continue.

They topped a small rise, and before them lay Terminator's tracks. No city in sight yet; one had to assume it was still over the horizon to the east. The nearest track blocked the view of most of those paralleling it on its other side. It was made of a particular kind of tempered steel, he had heard, and gleamed a dull silver in the starlight. Its underside stood a few meters above the ground, and the thick pylons supporting it were set every fifty meters or so. A loading platform abutted the outer track to the northwest of them, he was happy to see. The tram from the concert was already there.

Sunlight pricked a high point on the west wall of Beethoven. Everything in the landscape was lit by that burnished cliff edge. Dawn was on its way, slow but sure. When it came over the eastern horizon Terminator would make a grand sight. Possibly that was the dome of the globe, already visible as a curved glint.

A stupendous flash of light blazed up from the tracks where the loading platform had been. A bloodred afterimage split his vision in two halves; as it was pulsing back to a less vivid vertical blob, rocks began crashing down around them, kicking up puffs of dust that moved like splashed water. They both cried out, although Wahram had no idea what either said; then Swan was crying, "Get down, guard your head!" and tugging at his arm. Wahram kneeled next to her and put an arm around her shoulders; she seemed to be trying to put her arms over his helmet while ducking hers against his chest. Looking over her, he saw that the tracks where the platform had been had disappeared in a big ball of dust, and the very top of the dust cloud was now high enough to be up in the sunlight. The brilliant yellow of the sunlit part of the cloud illuminated the land around it like a beacon of fire. The land at the foot of the cloud was glowing with a light of its own; it appeared to be a pool of smoking lava.

"A meteor," he said stupidly.

Swan was talking on the common band. A few more rocks fell on the land around them, invisible until announced by an explosion of dust. It looked like the land was exploding, as if mines were going off. Occasionally a falling rock was hot and looked like a shooting star. Some ember blinks were still up there flying among the stars. They would get hit or they wouldn't: an awful feeling. Guarding their helmets did not seem like it was going to do much good.

Dust flew up over them, fell back to land in lazy sheets and veils. Gray topped by yellow; but when the top of the dust cloud fell back below the horizontal beams of approaching sunlight, they were plunged into the darkness of Mercurial night, with only the distant lit crater wall to illuminate them with its reflection. Red bars still pulsed vertically in the middle of Wahram's sight. It seemed much dimmer than it had before.

"There's a group of sunwalkers just south of here, up under the crater wall," Swan said grimly. She asked a question on the common band. "One of them's been hit, and they need help. Come on."

He followed her away from the tracks, feeling blind and confused. "Was it a meteor strike?"

"Looks like it. Although the tracks have a detect-and-deflect system, so I don't know what happened. Come on, we've got to hurry! I want to get back to the city. It's . . . ohhh. . . ." She groaned as the realization appeared to strike her that the city was doomed. "No!" she cried as she dragged him southward. "No, no, no, no, no, no, no." Over and over as they stumbled along. Then: "How could it *be*."

He couldn't tell if it was a rhetorical question. "Don't know," he said. She tugged at him and he kept his eyes on the ground to keep from kicking a rock and falling. Rocks littered the land. He tried to remember what he had seen; had it been a flash? From above? Hadn't it risen? No—a downward motion. He closed his eyes, but the red bar and light red clouds still bounced around on the black backdrop of the insides of his eyelids. He opened his eyes, glanced at Swan. Later perhaps they could review her qube's visual record, assuming it kept one. She was muttering now in the irritated tone of voice she seemed to use only when addressing it.

She led him around a hillock, and when they had cleared it, they spotted a group of three people in spacesuits, all three walking, which was good to see, but with one holding one arm with the other hand, and walking awkwardly as a result. The other two flanked this one, helping or trying to.

"Hey!" Swan said on the common band, and they looked up and saw them approaching. One waved. Swan and Wahram joined them a few minutes later.

"How are you?" Swan said.

"Happy to be alive," said the one holding an arm. "I got hit on the arm!"

"I can see. Let's get back to the city."

"What happened?"

"A meteor hit the tracks, it looked like."

"How could that be?"

"I don't know. Come on!"

Without further discussion the five of them began walking at speed toward the tracks, striding along in a Martian lope that made the best of the local g. Wahram was all right at it because of his time on Titan, which was about half as heavy as this, but similar enough. Together they bounded down the mild slope, angling eastward to intercept the city as soon as possible. There was a strange keening in Wahram's ear, an animal moan of distress; at first he thought it was the hurt sunwalker, but then realized it was Swan. Of course it was her city, her home.

They came over a rise that gave them a view of the top half of the city's dome, bulging over the horizon like the blue bubble of a pocket universe. The city appeared to be moving still. "The tracks ahead of it are damaged," he said.

"Yes, of *course*!"

"Is there a way for it to get past a section of broken track?"

"No! How would that work?"

"I don't know, I'm just . . . wondering. It seems like most support systems try to avoid criticalities."

"Of *course*. But the tracks are protected, there's an anti-meteor system!"

"It must not have worked?"

"Apparently not!" Again she cried out, a piercing sound in his ear even when damped by his suit's intercom.

The sunwalkers were chattering among themselves, sounding worried.

"What will we do when we get to it?" Wahram asked on the common band.

Swan stopped groaning and said, "What do you mean?"

"Are there lifeboats? You know—rovers to drive to the nearest spaceport?"

"Yes, of course."

"Enough for everyone?"

"Yes!"

"And are there spaceships enough at the nearest spaceport? Enough for the whole population of Terminator?"

"There's shelter in all the spaceports, enough to hold a lot of people. And vehicles to go west to the next ones. And some hoppers can handle being on the brightside."

As they hurried across the black rubbly plain, Terminator slowly hove up over the horizon. The upper half of the interior of the Dawn Wall was now visible, looking much steeper than it really was, all whitewashed walls and trees. A thick bar of green marked the treetops of the park. Extending forward from the trees were the crops of the farm. A snow globe on silver tracks, headed to its doom. They could see no people in the city, even though it was now looming above them. Certainly no one was on the terraces of the Dawn Wall anymore. It looked abandoned.

And there was no way to get up into it. The platform had been in the impact zone. Everyone who had been at the concert must have been killed. Inside the city they could see a trio of deer: buck, doe, fawn. Swan's cries pitched up an octave. "*No. No!*"

It was strange to be standing there, looking up at the empty city's Mediterranean calm.

Swan ran under the tracks to the north side of the city, and the rest of them followed. From that side they could see a little convoy of ground vehicles far to the north and west, rolling away from them through the break in Beethoven's northwest wall. The cars were fast, and soon over the horizon.

"They've left," Wahram observed.

"Yes yes. Pauline?"

"I suppose we could walk to the spaceport?" Wah ram said, worried.

Swan was talking to her internal qube, however, and Wahram couldn't follow the gist of the exchange. Her tone of voice was utterly caustic.

She broke off that argument and said to him, "The cars aren't coming back. The city will stop automatically when it hits the break in the tracks. We have to leave. Every tenth platform has elevators that go down to shelters under the tracks, so we have to get to one of those."

"How near is the closest one to the west?"

"About ninety kilometers. The town just passed one back to the east."

"Ninety kilometers!"

"Yes. We'll need to go east. It's only nine kilometers. Our suits will handle the sunlight for the time it will take us."

Wahram said, "Maybe we could walk the ninety."

"No we couldn't, what do you mean?"

"I think we could. People have done it."

"Athletes who have trained for it have done it. I do enough walking to know, and maybe I could do it, but you couldn't. You can't do it by willpower alone. And this sunwalker is hurt. No, listen, we'll be all right going into the sunlight. It's just the corona we'll be exposed to, and no more than an hour or a little more. I've done it often."

"I'd rather not."

"You have no choice! Come on, the longer we dither, the longer we'll be exposed!"

That was true.

"All right, then," he said, and felt his heart pound inside him.

She turned around, held out her arms up to the city, groaned like an animal. "Oh, my town, my town, *ohhhh* . . . We'll come back! We'll rebuild! *Ohhhhh* . . ."

Behind the glassy face mask her face was wet with tears. She noticed him watching her and swung a hand back as if to strike at him. "Come on, we have to go!" She gestured to the three sunwalkers. "Come on!"

As they started running east, Swan howled over the common band, a sound like an alarm siren that had done its duty but continued on in the emptiness after a disaster. The figure running before him did not seem capable of generating such a terrible sound, which stuck him like pins in the ears. A lot of animals had no doubt been left behind inside—the whole little terrarium, a community of plants and animals. And she designed such things. And this one was her home. Suddenly her howl made it clear to him that saving the humans of the place was not really enough. So much got left behind. A whole world. If a world dies, its people don't matter anymore—so the howl seemed to say.

Dawn kept coming, as always.

Now this was an interesting matter: could he modulate his fear, rein it in and use it to impel him at the optimum pace for the quickest arrival at the platform out there to the east, in the raw light of daybreak? And did that pace match the pace that was going to be set for him by the person he was following? For Swan was moaning still, crying and cursing, keening in a rhythm that was keyed to her running; she bounced forward on the impact of her strides, perhaps helpless to go slower; and yet she was moving faster than he could match. He had to give ground and keep to his own pace, and hope that he would at least be able to keep the distance close enough that he wouldn't lose her over the horizon. Although of course the tracks would lead him right to the platform, so even if she disappeared over the horizon, that should not matter. And yet he did not want to lose sight of her. The three sunwalkers were already a considerable distance ahead of her, even the one with the hurt arm. So maybe the unhappy noise she was making was in fact slowing her down.

The land dipped and rose here in such a way that he could see many kilometers to the north, and the highlands in that direction were now all ablaze with sunlight. That lit part of the landscape threw light over the shadowed terrain they ran in, and Wahram saw the rumples in the land, and the rubble on it, better than he had ever seen anything before, not just on Mercury but anywhere. Everything looked coated by a layer of friable powder, no doubt the result of the daily bake and freeze.

The light from the north grew so bright he had to look away to preserve his vision for the dark places underfoot and before him. Ahead the moaning silhouette bounded against the stars. He forced his breath into a rhythm with his feet, watched the ground he was running on, focused on a rapid efficient gait. One-third g could be deceptive, being neither light nor heavy. It had the potential for speedy running, but a fall was not a trivial thing, especially in this situation. Swan was on home ground and did not appear to be thinking of him at all.

He ran on. Normally the distance involved would be for him a matter of about forty-five minutes of running, he reckoned, depending on terrain. That was long enough to call for restraint from full speed, even for runners. Was she going out too fast? He saw no signs of deceleration.

On the other hand, she was not getting farther ahead. And he was now in a pace he thought he could sustain. It was neither fast nor slow. He huffed and puffed, watched the ground carefully. Quick glances showed Swan always well short of the horizon. It was all going to work out—then he stumbled and had to catch himself up by way of some desperate windmilling of the arms, after which he kept his head down and focused on the ground more than ever.

It was one of those moments when the shock of the unexpected throws one into a different space. He could see Swan's boot prints superimposed on the palimpsest of earlier prints. Her stride was shorter than his. He flew over her steps, even though he was losing ground on her. The sunwalkers were halfway over the horizon. Swan's moaning still filled his ears, but he refused to let himself turn down the volume or turn it off.

Then the sun blinked over the horizon, and again he felt his heart pounding. At first, licks of orange fire popped over the horizon and disappeared. The corona was hotter than the actual surface of the sun by a great deal, as he recalled. Magnetic surges, bowing up in characteristic loops of fire, rising majestically over the horizon and hanging there before blasting off to one side or the other. The sun's flames, in effect, flying up in stupendous explosions guided by the magnetic fields that roiled in the burn. He ran on looking down at the ground, but the next time he glanced up most of the horizon ahead of him was orange—the sun itself, its orangeness stuffed and writhing with bubbles and banners of yellow. To stop it down to something his eyes could handle, his faceplate had to render the rest of the cosmos black. The horizon was the only thing that could be clearly picked out, a line out there not very high, not smooth, various hills and dips that bounced and blurred. Swan stood out blackly, a runner imago, her silhouette thinned by white light pouring around her. The ground underfoot was now a salt-and-pepper pattern impossible to read, aching white and deep black all jumbled together so that the white parts pulsed and shimmered in his vision. He had to trust it was flat enough to run, because it didn't look like it. And then after another while it became a black-chipped white that looked flat as a sheet. They were out in full day.

He began to sweat. Probably this was just fear, and the sudden helpless acceleration in his pace. His suit began to hum audibly in its effort to cool him, a slight but terrible sound. His sweat would slide down his flanks and legs and collect at a seal above the boots. He didn't think enough could collect to drown him, but he wasn't sure. The black flicker of Swan in the sun had become a sort of spectre of the Brocken, exploding in and out of existence in vibrant pulses. He thought he saw her look over her shoulder at him, but he did not dare wave to her lest he lose his balance and fall. She seemed short, and suddenly he saw she was visible now only from the knees up. The horizon was about as far away as it would be on Titan. That meant he was probably only five or ten minutes behind her.

Then the platform top appeared over the horizon just to her left, next to the southernmost track, and he quickened his pace yet again. In any physical endeavor a little kick at the end could usually be found.

This time, however, it seemed he was truly stretched to his maximum. Indeed it very quickly turned into something more like a desperate attempt to hold what speed he had. He was gasping, and had to force himself to a breath pattern in a rhythm coordinated with his pounding heavy legs, one gasp for two strikes. It was very frightening to look up and see almost the whole visible stretch of the eastern horizon topped by the corona; the slight curve of it seemed to suggest it would eventually fill most of the sky, as if what was rising before them was some kind of universal sun. Mercury looked like a bowling ball rolling into that light.

His sweat now filled his suit to his thighs, and he wondered again if he could drown in it. But then again, he could drink it and save himself. Happily his air supply was still cool in his face.

His faceplate polarization shifted, and the texture of the sun through the black glass of his faceplate articulated into thousands of tongues of flame. Big fields of tendrils moved in concert, whole regions swirling like cats' paws on water. It looked like a living being, a creature made of fire.

The platform was a block of black in the black, Swan a black movement beside it. He reached her, stopped, gasped for a while with his hands on his knees, his back to the sun. Her keening had stopped, although from time to time she still moaned. The sunwalkers apparently had already taken the elevator down; she was waiting for it to come back up.

"I'm sorry," he said when he could speak. "Sorry I'm late."

She was looking at the sun, now four fingers high over the jagged black horizon. "Oh my God, look at it," she said. "Just look at it."

Wahram tried, but it was too bright, too big.

Then a loop of the corona flew hugely higher than any they had yet seen, as if the sun were trying to reach out and burn them with a touch. "Oh no!" Swan cried out, and pulled Wahram over to her and against the door, moving to his sun side and pulling him down to shield him with herself, punching elevator buttons over his shoulder and cursing.

"Come on hurry!" she yelled. "Oh that's a big flare, that's *bad*. By the time you see one of those it's already zapped you."

Finally the elevator doors slid open and the two of them rushed in. The doors closed. They felt the elevator car drop.

When Wahram's faceplate and eyes had adjusted to the ordinary light, he saw that Swan's face under her faceplate was wet with tears and snot.

She sniffed hard. "Damn that was a big flare," she said, wiping her face. When the elevator stopped and they got out, she said to the sunwalkers, "Any of you have a dosimeter on you?"

One of them replied as if quoting: "If you want to know, you don't want to know."

She looked at Wahram, her expression grim in a way he had never seen. "Pauline?" she said. "Find the dosimeter in this suit." She listened for a while, then clutched her chest, staggered down to one knee. "Oh shit," she said faintly. "I'm killed."

"How much did you get?" Wahram exclaimed, alarmed. He checked his wristpad; it showed a radiation spike of 3.762 sieverts, and he hissed. They would be needing a lot of DNA repair the next time they got their treatments—if they could make it. He repeated his question: "How much did you get?"

She stood up and would not look at him. "I don't want to talk about it."

"That was quite a slice of the sun," he said.

"It's not that," she said. "It was that flare. Bad luck."

The sunwalkers nodded at this, and Wahram felt a little queasy jolt slither down his spine.

They were in a lock. The elevator doors closed behind them, the door on the other side of the lock slid open, followed by a little whoosh of air. They went into a low room of some considerable size, with several doors and passageways leading out of it.

"Is this a refuge?" Wahram asked. "Do we have to stay here through the brightside crossing? Can we?"

"This is part of a whole system," Swan explained. "It was built to help with the construction of the tracks. Every tenth platform has a unit like this under it, and there's a utilidor that connects them all. A work tunnel." The sunwalkers were already checking some of the cabinet doors on one wall.

"So we could hurry underground in this tunnel and catch up to the nightside? Get to help?"

"Yes. But I wonder if the part under the meteor strike is still passable. I guess we can go see."

"It's all heated and aerated?"

"Yes. After some people died when they came down to take shelter, the stations have been made minimally survivable. Actually, I think you have to re-aerate the utilidor section by section as you go along. It's like turning on the lights."

One of the sunwalkers gave a thumbs-up, and Swan took off her helmet and Wahram did too.

"Do either of you have radio comms?" one of them asked. "Ours aren't working, and we're thinking maybe the sun fried them. And the phone here isn't working. We won't be able to tell people we're down here."

"Pauline, are you all right?" Swan said aloud, and fell silent.

"How is your qube?" Wahram asked after a while.

"She's all right," Swan said dismissively. "She says my head served as good insulation for her."

"Oh dear."

They followed the sunwalkers down the hall, took stairs down to a set of large rooms below.

The biggest room down there contained a scattering of couches and low tables, and the long bar of a communal kitchen. Swan introduced herself and Wahram to the three sunwalkers, who were people of indeterminate age and gender. They nodded politely at Swan's introduction, but did not identify themselves. "How is your arm?" Swan asked the hurt one.

"It's broken," the person said simply, and held it out a little. "Clean hit, but the rock was small and just falling, I guess. Tossed up in the big hit."

Now it seemed to Wahram that this one at least was young.

"We'll wrap it," one of the others said, also young "We can try to straighten it, and then wrap it with a support, no matter how straight it is."

"Did any of you see the meteor strike?" Swan asked.

They all three shook their heads. All young, Wahram thought. These were the kinds of people who walked around Mercury right before sunrise, torching themselves with solar visions. Although apparently Swan was also one of them. The young in spirit, then.

"What are we going to do?" he asked.

"We can take the utilidor west till we get to the next spaceport on the nightside," one of them said.

"Do you think the utilidor is still passable under the hit?" Swan asked.

"Oh," the one said. "I didn't think of that."

"It might be," said the one with the broken forearm. The third one was looking in cabinets against the wall. "You never know."

"I doubt it," Swan said. "But I guess we can go look. It's only about fifteen klicks away."

Only fifteen! Wahram didn't say. They stood there looking at each other.

"Well, shit," Swan said. "Let's go take a look. I don't want to just sit here."

Wahram suppressed a sigh. It was not as if they had a great number of choices. And if they could get through to the west, and hurried, they could catch up to the night, and hopefully the spaceport where the people from Terminator had gone.

So they went to a door at the west end of the room and went through it into a passageway, lit dimly by a string of overhead lights that were part of the ceiling. The walls of the tunnel were raw faces of rock, in some places cracked, in others bare walls with drill bit marks angling upward on their left and downward on their right. They hiked west at a good clip. The one with the broken arm seemed to be the fastest of them all, although one of the other sunwalkers stuck close by the hurt one. No one spoke. An hour passed; then, after a short rest sitting on some cubical blocks of rock in the tunnel, another hour. "Did your Pauline get an image of the strike?" Wahram asked Swan when they were walking again. The utilidor was wide enough for three or four people to walk abreast, as the sunwalkers were proving ahead of them.

"I've looked, but it's just a flash to one side. Only a few milliseconds of light before the explosion upward and out, coming down fast and hot. But why hot? There's no atmosphere to heat it, so that doesn't make sense. It kind of looks like it came from, I don't know, somewhere else. From some other universe."

"Seems like some other explanation will be forthcoming," Wahram could not help saying.

"Well, you explain it," she said sharply, as if speaking to her qube.

"I can't," Wahram said calmly.

They walked on in silence. Presumably at some point they were walking underneath the city. Above them, Terminator would be burning up in the day's rain of light.

Then the tunnel ahead of them appeared to end. They had all put their helmets back on, as it was the easiest way to carry them, and now they shone their helmets' headlamps into the darkness before them. A mass of rock rubble filled the tunnel, floor to roof. It was cold here, and suddenly Swan said, "We'd better seal our helmets," and her faceplate slid down. Wahram did the same.

They stood there looking at the blockage.

"All right," Swan said grimly. "Can't go west. We'll have to go east, I guess."

"But how long will *that* take?" Wahram said.

She shrugged. "If we sit here, it will be eighty-eight days till sunset. If we walk, it will be less."

"Walk around half of Mercury?"

"Less than half, because we will be walking and the planet will be rolling. That's the point. I mean, what else are we going to do? I'm not going to sit here for three months!" She was almost in tears, he saw.

"How far is it again?" he asked, thinking *half of Titan* as he said it. His stomach contracted within him.

"About two thousand kilometers. But if we walk east at, say, thirty kilometers a day, we shorten the wait time to something more like forty days. So we can cut it in half. That seems worth it to me. And it doesn't have to be continuous walking. I mean, it's not like the sunwalkers. We walk a day's worth, eat, sleep a night, then walk again. Set a daily schedule. If we hiked for twelve hours out of every twenty-four, that would be a lot, but it would save even more days. What, Pauline?"

"Can you turn up Pauline's voice again?" Wahram requested.

"I don't want to now. She says twelve-hour days of walking would shorten our time down here by around forty-five days. That's enough for me."

"Well," Wahram said. "That's a lot of walking."

"I know, but what are you going to do? Sit here for over twice as long?"

"No," he said slowly. "I guess not."

Although really it would not be so very long. A rereading of Proust and O'Brian, a few times through the Ring cycle; his little wristpad was very well stocked. But the way she stood there looking at him, these were not thoughts he felt comfortable expressing.

"I'll turn up Pauline," she said, as if giving him something in exchange for his agreement.

"*Solvitur ambulando*," Pauline said. "Latin for 'It is solved by walking.' Diogenes of Sinope."

"Thus you prove motion is real," Wahram supposed.

"Yes."

Wahram sighed. "I was already convinced."

Back at the first underground station they took stock. The three sunwalkers were perfectly happy to walk for six or seven weeks; it was very like their usual mode of existence. Their names were Tron, Tor, and Nar. They were gender nondescripts as far as Wahram was concerned, and seemed to him very young and simple. They lived only to hike around Mercury; they seemed to know nothing more than that, or perhaps they didn't speak much to strangers. But what they did say seemed childlike to him, or provincial in the extreme. There were whole terraria filled with such folk, of course, but he had gotten used to thinking of the Mercurials as highly sophisticated, steeped in history and art and culture. Now he was learning that it was not universally true. He realized he had thought sun worshippers would be followers of the various early solar religions of ancient Egypt, Persia, the Inca—but no. They just liked the sun.

It looked like they were going to have to spend a couple of nights sleeping on the floor of the unimproved tunnel in between each way station. "Every third day," Swan said, "we can resupply. It sets a good goal."

"We might even be able to go farther," Tron said shyly.

Tron was the one with the broken arm, so Wahram refrained from mentioning that for him personally, thirty-three kilometers a day might prove enough, or too much. That he might be the drag on this group was discouraging. In any case Swan was overseeing the filling of backpacks she had found in the emergency supply cabinets: their spacesuit helmets, some emergency air, water bottles, food, air mattresses, a little pot and stove. A roll of aerogel blankets, not very warm-looking, but the utilidor would stay at this temperature, Swan said; and it was pretty warm.

So: tunnel walk. Possibly similar to spelunking expeditions of long duration. Little headlamps were included in the packs too, although for now they were not necessary, as the ceiling held a warm square of yellow-white light every twenty meters or so, illuminating the rough rock of the utilidor very well. They were about fifteen meters underground, Swan said. The tunnel had been drilled through bedrock or regolith, with a heat finish that had imparted frequent swirls and dashes of mineral color, reminiscent of the cut surfaces of certain meteorites. In some stretches silver curves lay over pewter, then jet black. The floor had been chipped to a texture that made for a good grip underfoot. The tight curve of Mercury meant that the most distant overhead lights merged into a single bar of light. It was as if they could see the arc of the planet, which Wahram found vaguely encouraging. He was finding the idea of thirty-three kilometers a day, for more than forty days in a row, daunting. Must recall they were down around the forty-fifth latitude south here, so the distance was not as far as it would have been if they were on the equator. Sometimes Terminator's tracks went even farther south, as he recalled. Things could be worse.

So. Walk for an hour, in a tunnel that changed very little, and only in iterative ways. Stop, sit on the ground, rest for a while; then walk an hour more. At the end of three hours, stop and eat. Already that interval felt very long, something like a week or more in ordinary human time, in the time of thinking. But they did that three times before stopping to eat a larger meal, then slept for eight or nine hours.

Hour, hour, hour; hour, hour, hour; hour, hour, hour.

The sensation of lengthening time grew very strong in Wahram. Why it should feel so long was hard to tell; the repetition of the elements of the day he would have thought might streamline and thus speed the hours; but no. Instead it was protraction, a very pronounced feeling of protraction. At the end of each day, as he settled down, footsore and exhausted, to sleep, he could stretch out on his air mattress and say, "One down, thirty-seven to go," or even "thirty-three to go," and feel a little stab of despair. Every hour felt like a week! Could they endure it?

The sunwalkers usually hiked a bit ahead, and by the time Wahram and Swan joined them at a stop, they were always prepping tea. Then, well before Wahram was ready to get up and go again, the young ferals were off, almost apologetically, with a nod and a wave. His days, therefore, were spent mostly with Swan.

She was clearly not happy at the prospect of this hike, even though it was her idea. She was doing it only because the alternative was worse, in her estimation. It was something to be endured, in misery mute or voluble. Some days she went ahead, some days fell behind. "I'm going to get sick at some point," she said once. It became clear to Wahram that she liked the situation even less than he did—far less than he did, as she told him herself. She hated it, she said; suffered from claustrophobia; could not stand to be indoors; needed copious daily sunlight; needed lots of variety in her daily routines and in her sensory stimuli. These were *necessities*, she told Wahram, and in no uncertain terms. "This is so horrible," she exclaimed often, making the word an emphatic three syllables with fore and aft stresses. "Horrible, horrible, horrible. I won't be able to make it."

"Let's talk about something else," Wahram would suggest.

"How can I? It's horrrr-i-bull."

Endless repetition of these points would still occupy only the first hour of their twelve-hour day of walking and rests. After such a first hour, Wahram would usually decide it was appropriate to point out that they would need to talk about something else if they were to avoid undue repetition stress on both their parts.

"Tired of me already?" Swan concluded from these observations.

"Not at all. Vastly entertained. Even interested. But this motif, of the unhappy voyage of necessity, it's limited. It's played out. I want a different story."

"That's lucky for you, because I was going to change the subject."

"Lucky for me indeed."

She trudged on ahead of him. There was no reason to hurry to say the next thing; they had all day. Wahram watched her walk ahead of him: her stride was graceful and long, she was in her home g and sinuous, efficient. Very quickly she could get well ahead of him. She did not seem ill yet. From behind he sometimes heard her having conversations with her qube. For whatever reason, she had shifted Pauline's voice to exterior audibility; maybe she was keeping that little promise to him. The conversations between the two almost always sounded like arguments; Swan's voice was clearer and more hectoring, but Pauline's alto, slightly muffled by Swan's own skin, was somehow mulishly contentious as well. Depending on how one programmed them, qubes could be real fiends for argument, quibblers to the highest degree. Once Wahram caught up enough to be able to eavesdrop on them, and came in on something that had been going on for a while; Swan was saying, "Poor Pauline, if I were you I would be so sad! I feel so sorry for you! It must feel terrible to be nothing but a packet of algorithms!"

Pauline said, "This is the rhetorical device called anacoenosis, in which one pretends to put oneself in the place of one's opponent."

"No, not at all," Swan assured her. "I really am sympathetic. To be so few qubits, to be just algorithms grinding it out. I mean considering that, you do very well."

Pauline said, "This is the rhetorical device called synchoresis, in which one makes a concession before renewing the assault."

"Maybe you're right. I don't really know why I thought you were stupid, given the huge power of these arguments of yours. And yet—"

"This is both sarcasm and aporia in the bad sense I mentioned before, of a momentary expression of doubt, often faked, before renewing the attack."

"And *this* is the defense called casuistry, where when you've got *nothing* you retreat into a cloud of verbiage. Maybe you're *right*, maybe it's just smart consciousness and stupid consciousness. That would explain a lot."

Pauline did not seem to be deterred. "Happy to submit our speech acts to a double-blind study to see if any distinctions at all can be made between yours and mine."

"Really?" Swan said. "Are you saying you can pass a Turing test?"

"It depends who's asking the questions."

Swan laughed scornfully, but she really was amused, Wahram could hear it. So at least the qube was good for that.

The two of them swapped the lead every half hour, just to mark time and change the view, such as it was. They did not always talk; it would have been impossible, he thought. In any case they hiked in silence for many minutes at a time. Over them the tunnel lights seemed to move independently backward, as if they walked at the top of a vast Ferris wheel, and only just kept pace with the backward sweep of the wheel. At the end of an hour Wahram's feet were sore, and he was happy to sit down. They used their aerogel sleeping pads as cushions to sit on. Meals came from foil envelopes found in the emergency gear at the stations, and were bland for the most part. After a while they mostly only wanted to drink water, though there were some powders to mix in if one wanted.

In general their rests were about half an hour long. Any longer and Wahram began to stiffen up, and Swan became fretful. And the sunwalkers would get too far ahead. So Wahram would heave himself to his feet and take off again. "Do you think any of these stations have walking poles in them?"

"I doubt it. We can look at the next one. Maybe something could be used as canes."

After a time of silence she would sometimes snap. "All right tell me something! Tell me about yourself! What's your first memory?"

"I don't know," Wahram said, trying to locate it.

"My first memory," she said, "comes from a time that my parents tell me I was three. My parents were part of a house that decided to move to the other side of the city. I think we were trading places north to south, in order to look at the other half of the countryside as we passed by it. Or maybe they just told me that. So a bunch of carts were there, and both houses were moving stuff back and forth. Everything my family owned could fit on the back of one battery cart and two handcarts. My mother took me back inside when the place was emptied, and it scared me. I think that's why I remember it. My room looked much smaller when it was empty, and that seemed backward and scared me, like the world had shrunk. We fill rooms to make them bigger. Then we went back outside, and the other image that sticks with me, along with the empty room, was all the stuff in the bed of the cart, and everyone standing by it at the curb, under a set of trees. Above some trees I could see the Dawn Wall."

She hiked on for a time in silence, and Wahram felt the empty grumble in his stomach that marked another mealtime's approach.

"By now that's all burned down," she said.

But now her voice was unusually calm. She was no longer grieving in the same way, it seemed.

"When the sun got high enough that the city was out of the shade of the Dawn Wall," she added, "it would go quick."

"I know the tracks don't melt on the brightside," Wahram said. "Anything else?"

"The city infrastructure will be fine," she conceded. "The shell. Some metals, ceramics, mixes of the two. Glassy metals. And then just ordinary tempered steel, stainless steel. Austenite steel. We'll see. I suppose it will be interesting to see what it looks like when night falls on it again. Everything will have burned away except the frame, I guess. As soon as the sun hit, the plants would begin to die. They'll be dead by now, all the plants and animals, even the bacteria and such. We'll have to rebuild it."

"Maybe," he said.

"What do you mean?"

"Well, I think they'll want to understand what happened to the tracks, and feel they are in a position to stop it happening again. Or else build to a different design. Free the city from its tracks, maybe, and roll over the landscape on wheels."

"That would require some locomotion," she pointed

out. "As it is, the expansion of the tracks drives the city forward."

"Well, it will be interesting to see what happens, then." Wahram hesitated. "It would be pointless to rebuild and then have a recurrence."

"If it was a low-likelihood accident, then a recurrence wouldn't be likely."

"I was under the impression that all such happenstances were already guarded against."

"Me too. Are you suggesting that it was some kind of attack?"

"Yes, well, I've been thinking about that, anyway. I mean, consider what happened to us on Io."

"But who would want to attack Terminator?" she demanded. "Attack it and yet miss it by a few kilometers, killing the town but leaving the people alive?"

"I don't know," Wahram said uneasily. "There's been talk about the conflict between Earth and Mars, how it could even lead to war."

"Yes," she said, "but the talk always goes on to declare this impossible, because everyone is so vulnerable. Mutual assured destruction, as always."

"I've always wondered about that," Wahram admitted. "What if a first strike is made to look like an accident, and is so successful that no one knows who did it, and meanwhile the victim is mostly vaporized? A scenario like that might make one think there is not any certain mutually assured destruction."

"Who would feel that way?" Swan asked.

"Almost any power on Earth could make the calculation. They're safer than any of us. And Mars is notoriously self-absorbed, and also can't be punctured with a single dart. No, I'm not convinced there can't be a power out there that harbors a feeling of invulnerability. Or an anger so great they don't care about consequences."

"What could that be, though?" Swan said. "What causes that kind of anger?"

"I don't know...say food, water, land...power... prestige...ideology...differential advantage. Madness. These are the usual motives, aren't they?"

"I suppose!" She sounded horrified that he could make such a list, as if this were not part of Mercurial discourse, although really it was simply Machiavelli, or Aristotle. Pauline would know the list.

"Anyway," he went on, "I'll be very interested to find out what people are saying when we get out of here."

"Only thirty days to go," she said grimly.

"One step at a time," he said gamely.

"Oh please! Take it like that and it's *eternity*."

"Not at all. But I will desist."

After a while he said, "Interesting how a moment comes when you feel hungry. You didn't before, and then you do."

"That's not interesting."

"My feet are sore."

"That's not interesting either."

"Each step is a little pain, or every other. Plantar fasciitis, I reckon."

"Would you like to take a rest?"

"No. They're only sore, not hurt. And they get warmed up. Then tired."

"I hate this."

"And yet here we are."

The hour of walking passed. The rest period passed. The next hour passed. The rest following that passed. The tunnel stayed always the same. The stations every third night were almost the same, but not quite. They ransacked these places, looking for something different. Up at the top of the elevator shafts in each station lay the surface, exposed to the full Mercurial sun and approaching seven hundred K on surfaces struck by light; there being no air, there was no air temperature. At this point they were under Tolstoi Crater, more or less; Pauline was managing their navigation, such as it was, by a sort of dead reckoning; down here her little radio too was out of touch. The station phones never worked. Swan guessed they were elevator phones only—or else the whole system had broken in the impact, and because of the ongoing situation with Terminator's population, and the fact that the crushed part of the tunnel was now out in the sun, no one was available to fix it.

Hour after hour they walked. It was easy to lose track of days, particularly since Pauline would keep track. The pseudoiterative was less pseudo than ever. This was the true iterative. Swan walked before Wahram, her shoulders slumped like those of a mime portraying dejection. Minutes dragged until each one felt like ten; it was an exponential expansion of time, a syruping of protraction. They would therefore live ten times as long. He cast about for something to say that would not irritate her. She was muttering at Pauline.

"I used to whistle when I was a kid," he said, and tried a single tone. His lips felt thicker than they had when he was young. Oh yes—tongue higher against roof of mouth. Very good. "I would whistle the melodies from the symphonies I liked."

"Whistle, then," Swan said. "I whistle too."

"Really!" he said.

"Yes. I told you. But you first. Do you do Beethoven, like what we heard at that concert?"

"I do, kind of. Just some of the tunes."

"Do that, then."

There had been a period in Wahram's youth when every morning had had to begin with Beethoven's *Eroica*, the breakthrough Third Symphony, announcement of a new age in music and indeed in the human spirit, written after Beethoven learned that he was going deaf. So Wahram whistled the two commanding notes that started the first movement, and then whistled the main line, at a tempo that fit with his walking pace. That wasn't so hard to do, somehow. As he whistled along he was never sure he was going to remember the passage that came next, yet by the time he got to the point of change, the next one followed inevitably from it, and flowed from him quite satisfactorily. Somewhere in him these things remained. The sequence of long elaborate melodies flowed one to the next, in just the compelling logic of Beethoven's own thinking. And this sequence consisted of one stirring inevitable song after another. Most of the passages should have been stranded by counterpoint and polyphonies, and he jumped from one orchestral section to another, depending on which one seemed the main line. But it had to be said that even as single tunes, inexpertly whistled, the magnificence of Beethoven's music was palpable in the tunnel. The three sunwalkers drifted back, it seemed, to hear it better. After the first movement was over, Wahram found the other three movements came as fully to him as the first, so that by the time he was done, it had taken him about the same forty minutes that an orchestra would have taken with the real thing. The great variations of the finale were so stirring that he almost hyperventilated in the performance of it.

"Wonderful," Swan said when he was done. "Really

good. What tunes. My God. Do more. Can you do more?"

Wahram had to laugh. He thought it over. "Well, I think I could do the Fourth, Fifth, Sixth, Seventh, and Ninth. Also some bits of the quartets and sonatas, maybe. I'd lose the thread in a lot of those, I'm afraid. Maybe not in the late quartets. I've lived to those sweet things. I'd have to try and see how it went."

"How can you remember so many?"

"For a long time that's all I listened to."

"That's crazy. All right, try the Fourth, then. You can take them in order."

"Later, please. I have to rest. My lips are already destroyed, I can feel them twice as big. They're like a big old gasket right now."

She laughed and let him be. An hour later, however, she brought it back up, and sounded like she would be very discouraged if he didn't do it.

"All right, but you join me," he said.

"But I don't know the tunes. I don't really remember the stuff I hear people play."

"That doesn't matter," Wahram said. "Just whistle. You said you did."

"I do, but it sounds like this."

She whistled for a while: a glorious burble of music, exactly like some kind of songbird.

"Wow, you sound just like a bird," he said. "Very fluid glissandos, and I-don't-know-whats, but just like a bird."

"Yes, that's right. I have some skylark polyps in me."

"You mean . . . in your brain? Bird brains, put into your own?"

"Yes. *Alauda arvensis*. Also some *Sylvia borin*, the garden warbler. But you know that birds' brains are organized on completely different lines than mammal brains?"

"No."

"I thought everyone knew that. Some qube architecture is based on bird brains, so it got discussed for a while."

"I didn't know."

"Well, the thinking that we mammals do in layers of cells across our cortex, birds do in clusters of cells, distributed like bunches of grapes."

"I didn't know that."

"So you can take some of your own stem cells and introduce skylark song node DNA into them, and then you can introduce it through the nose to the brain, and it makes a little cluster in the limbic system. Then when you whistle, the cluster links into your already existing musical networks. All those are very old parts. They're almost like bird parts of the brain already. So the new ones get hooked in, and off you go."

"You did this?"

"Yes."

"How did it feel?"

For answer she whistled. In the tunnel one liquid glissando led to another: bright birdsong, there in the tunnel with them.

"Amazing," Wahram said. "I didn't know you could do that. *You* should be the one whistling, not me."

"You don't mind?"

"On the contrary."

So she whistled as they walked along, sometimes for the full hour between breaks. Her burble shifted through all kinds of phases and phrases, and it seemed to Wahram these were so various they must be the songs of more than two species of bird. But he wasn't sure, as it occurred to him also that she might be as vocally limited by her body as any bird, so these could perhaps be just the variety of songs that a real songbird sang. Glorious music! It was somewhat like Debussy at times, and of course there were Messiaen's specific imitations of birds; but Swan's whistling was stranger, more repetitive, with endless permutations of little figures, often repeating in insistent ostinato trills that got their hooks into him, sometimes to the point of irritation.

When she stopped, he could still call to mind some of her tunes. Whales had songs, of course, but birds must have been the first musicians. Unless dinosaurs too had made music. He seemed to recall something about big hollows in certain hadrosaur skulls, inexplicable except as sounding devices. The sound one of those would have made was interesting to try to imagine. He even hummed a bit, testing how it would feel in his own big barrel of a chest.

"So was that the bird, or you?" he asked when she took a pause.

"We are the same," she said.

After a while she said, "Mozart's pet starling once revised a phrase he wrote. The bird sang it after he played it on the piano, but changed all the sharps to flats. Mozart described it happening in the margin of the score. 'That was beautiful!' he wrote. When the bird died, he sang at its funeral, and read a poem to it. And his next composition, which the publisher called *A Musical Joke*, had a starling style."

"Nice," Wahram said. "It's true that birds always look intelligent."

"Not doves," she said. But then, in a dark tone: "You can either have high specific intelligence or high general intelligence, but not both."

Wahram didn't know what to say to that; the thought had turned her suddenly grim. "Well," he said. "We should whistle together."

"So we'll have both?"

"What?"

"Never mind. All right."

So he went back to the *Eroica*, and this time she whistled along, in an avian counterpoint or descant to the melodies. Her parts fit his in the manner of internal cadenzas, or jazz improvisations, and at Beethoven's more heroic moments, which came pretty frequently, her additions rose to a furious pace of invention, sounding as if the bird inside her had been driven into a fit by Beethoven's audacity.

They whistled some very stirring duets. It definitely passed the time in ways that it hadn't passed before. You needed the gift of time, he thought, to explore a pleasure like this. He could go through all the Beethoven he knew; and after them, the four symphonies of Brahms, so noble and heartfelt; also the last three symphonies of Tchaikovsky. All the great parts of the soundtrack of his oh-so-romantic youth. Meanwhile Swan was up for anything, and her augmentations added a wild baroque or avant-garde touch to the tunes, additions that often amazed him. The piercing quality of her sound must have carried a long way up and down the tunnel, and sometimes the sunwalkers would slow down and walk just ahead of them, bouncing in time to the music, even whistling themselves, inexpertly but enthusiastically. The finale of Beethoven's Seventh was particularly successful with them as marching music; and when they got up after a rest to take up their walking again, the sunwalkers often requested the horn cry that began Tchaikovsky's Fourth, then its first theme, so full of the feeling that there was a fate ruling them now, a fate dark and grand.

At the end of one of their shared performances of Beethoven's Ninth, they all shook their heads in wonder, and Nar turned back and said, "Sirs, you certainly are good whistlers! What tunes!"

"Well," Wahram said. "Those are Beethoven."

"Oh! I thought they called it whistling."

"We thought you were making them up," Tron added. "We were impressed."

Later, when the three youths had gotten ahead, Wahram said, "Are all the sunwalkers like that?"

"No!" Swan said, annoyed. "I told you, I'm a sunwalker myself."

He did not want her annoyed. "Tell me, do you have anything else interesting added to your brain?"

"I do." She still sounded sour. "There's an earlier AI, from when I was a child, put in my corpus callosum to help deal with some convulsions I was having. And a bit of one lover—we thought we'd share some of our sexual responses and see where that led us. Which was nowhere, as it turned out, but I presume that bit is still in there. And there's other stuff too, but I don't want to talk about it."

"Oh dear. Is it confusing?"

"Not at all." Grimmer and grimmer she sounded. "What, don't you have anything in you?"

"In a way. I suppose everyone does," he said reassuringly, though in fact he had seldom heard of a brain with as many interventions as hers. "I take some vasopressin and some oxytocin, as recommended."

"Those both come from vasotocin," she said authoritatively. "There's just one amino acid of difference between the three. So I take the vasotocin. It's very old, so old it controls sex behavior in frogs."

"My."

"No, it's just what you need."

"I don't know. I feel fine with the oxytocin and vasopressin."

"Oxytocin is social memory," she said. "You don't notice other people without it. I need more of it. Vasopressin too, I suppose."

"The monogamy hormone," Wahram said.

"Monogamy in males. But only three percent of mammals are monogamous. Even birds do better than that, I think."

"Swans," Wahram suggested.

"Yes. And I am Swan Second Swan. But I'm not monogamous."

"No?"

"No. Except I'm faithful to endorphins."

He frowned, but assumed she was joking and tried to go along. "Isn't that just like having a dog or something?"

"I like dogs. Dogs are wolves."

"But wolves are not monogamous."

"No. But endorphins are."

He sighed, feeling he had lost her point, or that she had. "It's the touch of the beloved that stimulates endorphins," he said, and left it at that. You couldn't whistle the end of the "Moonlight Sonata."

That night, as they slept in the tunnel on their little aerogel mattresses under their thin blankets, he awoke to find that Swan had moved, and was sleeping against him back to back. The resulting flood of oxytocin relieved his sore hips a little; this was how one could read it. Of course the urge to sleep with someone, the pleasure in sleeping with someone, was not exactly synonymous with sex. Which was reassuring. Across the floor indeed the three ferals were curled together like kittens. The tunnels were warm, often too warm, but right on the floor it got cold. Very faintly he heard her purring. Feline genes for same—yes, he had heard of it—people said it felt good, very like humming. Feel pleasure, purr, feel better: a positive feedback into more pleasure, loop, loop, loop, all at the pace of breathing, it sounded like when he listened to her. A different kind of music. Although he knew very well that sick cats sometimes purred at a momentary relief, or even as if hoping to feel better, trying to jump-start the loop. He had lived with a cat who had done that near its end. A fifty-year-old cat is an impressive creature. The loss of this ancient eunuch had been one of Wahram's first losses, so he remembered its purr near the end as particularly pitiful, the sound of some emotion too crowded to name. A good friend of his had died purring. So now this purr from Swan gave him a little shiver of worry.

Down the tunnel after a sleep, groggy and dim. The morning hour. Whistle the slow movement from the *Eroica*, Beethoven's funeral music for his sense of hearing, written as it was dying inside him. "'We live an hour and it is always the same,'" he recited. Then the slow movement of the first of the late quartets, opus 127, variations on a theme, so rich; as majestic as the funeral march, but more hopeful, more in love with beauty. And then the third movement that followed was so strong and cheerful it could have been a fourth movement.

Swan gave him a black look. "Damn you," she said, "you're enjoying this."

His bass croak of laughter felt good in his chest, a little hadrosauric. "'Danger to him was like wine,'" he growled.

"What's that?"

"The *Oxford English Dictionary*. Or that's where I saw it."

"You like quotations."

" 'We have come a long way, we have a long way to go. In between we are somewhere.' "

"Come on, what's that? A fortune cookie?"

"Reinhold Messner, I believe."

He really was kind of enjoying it, he had to admit. Only twenty-five more days, more or less; it wasn't such a big number. He could endure. It was the most iterative pseudoiterative he would ever live, thus interesting, as a kind of limit case of what he supposedly wanted. A reductio ad absurdum. And the tunnel was not so much a matter of sensory deprivation as it was sensory overload, but in very few elements: the walls of the tunnel, the lights running along its ceiling fore and aft for as far as they could see.

But Swan was not enjoying it. This particular day seemed worse than any before, in fact. She even slowed down, something he had never seen before, to the point where he had to slow down a bit to keep from getting well ahead of her.

"Are you all right?" he asked after waiting for her to catch up.

"No. I feel like crap. I guess it's happening. Do you feel anything?"

In fact Wahram was sore in his hips, knees, and feet. His ankles were all right. His back was all right once he got walking. "I'm sore," he admitted.

"I'm worried about that last solar flare we saw. By the time you see one of those, there's faster radiation that's come off the snap. I'm afraid we might have gotten cooked. I feel shitty."

"I'm just sore. But then, you covered me at the elevator."

"It probably hit us differently. I hope so. Let's ask the ferals how they feel."

They did at the next stop, where, by the looks on their faces, the sunwalkers had waited long enough to be concerned. Tron said, "How goes it?"

"I'm feeling sick," Swan said. "How are you three feeling?"

They looked at each other. "All right," Tron said.

"No nausea or diarrhea? No headaches or muscle soreness? No hair coming out?"

The three sunwalkers looked at each other, shrugged. They had gone down the elevator earlier.

"I'm not very hungry," Tron said, "but the food isn't very good."

"My arm is still sore," Nar offered.

Swan looked resentfully at them. They were sunwalkers, young and strong; they were doing what they did all the time, except underground and widdershins. She looked at Wahram. "What about you?"

Wahram said, "I'm sore. I can't go much faster than I already am, or longer, or something will break."

Swan nodded. "Same for me. I may even have to slow down. I feel bad. So I wonder if the three of you should hurry on ahead, and when you get to the sunset, or run into people, you can tell them about us."

The sunwalkers nodded. "How will we know when we're there?" Tron asked.

"In a couple of weeks, when you come to stations, you can go up in the elevator and have a look."

"All right." Tron looked at Tor and Nar, and they all nodded. "We'll go get help."

"That's right. Don't go out so fast you hurt yourselves."

*   ʌ   *

After that Wahram and Swan walked on their own. An hour walking, a half hour sitting, over and over for nine times; then a long meal and a sleep. An hour was a long time; nine of them, with their rests, felt like a couple of weeks. They whistled from time to time, but Swan was not feeling well, and Wahram did not want to do it on his own, unless she asked him to. She stopped and fell back in the tunnel from time to time to relieve herself; "I've got the runs," she said at one point, "I've got to empty my suit." After that she only would say, "Wait a minute," and then, after five or ten minutes, catch up to him again, and on they would go. She looked desiccated. She became irritable and often spoke viciously to Pauline, and sometimes to Wahram too. Querulous, disagreeable, unpleasant. Wahram would get annoyed with how unfair she was, how pointless the unpleasantness she created out of nothing, and he would hike along speechlessly, whistling dark little fragments under his breath. In these moments he struggled to remember a lesson from his crèche, which was that with moody people you had to discount the low points in their cycle, or it would not work at all. His crèche had numbered six, and one had been moody to the point of bipolarity, and in the end this had been what caused the group to semi-disband, Wahram believed; he himself had been one of those least able to see that person in their whole amplitude. Six people had thirty relationships in it, and hex wisdom had it that all but one or two of these had to be good for a crèche to endure. They hadn't even come close to that, but later Wahram had realized that the moody one in the upper half of his cycle was one of the people he most missed out of the group. Had to recall that and learn from it.

Then a time came when ten minutes passed with Swan back down the hall, and she didn't return; and then he thought he heard a groan.

So he went back and found her sprawled on the floor, semiconscious at best, with her spacesuit down her to ankles and her excretion obviously interrupted midcourse. And she was indeed groaning.

"Oh no!" he said, and crouched by her side. She had her long-sleeved shirt still on, but under it her flesh was blue with cold on the side that had been on the ground. "Swan, can you hear me? Are you hurt?"

He held up her head; her eyes were swimming a little. "Damn," he said. He didn't want to pull her spacesuit up over the mess between her legs. "Here," he said, "I'm going to clean you up." Like anyone he had done his share of diaper changes, on both babies and elders, and knew the drill. And one pocket of his suit had his toilet tissues; he himself had had to deploy them in a hurry a few times recently, which now worried him more than it had. And he had water, and even some moist pads in foil packets, courtesy of his suit. So he got them out and shifted her legs around and cleaned her up. Even with his eyes averted he could not help seeing in the tangle of her pubic hair a small penis and testicles, about where her clitoris might have been, or just above. A gynandromorph; it did not surprise him. He finished cleaning her up, trying to be meticulous but fast, and then he pulled her arms over his shoulders and lifted her—she was heavier than he would have thought—and pulled up her spacesuit, and got the top part around her waist and sat her back down on the ground. Got the arms of the suit onto her. Happily a suit's AI worked Jeeveslike to help the occupant into it. He considered her little backpack, there on the ground;

it had to be taken. He decided to put it back on her. With all that arranged, he lifted her up and carried her before him in his arms. Her head lolled back too far for his liking and he stopped.

"Swan, can you hear me?"

She groaned, blinked. He got his arm behind her neck and head and hefted her up again. "What?" she said.

"You passed out," he said. "While you were having the runs."

"Oh," she said. She pulled her head upright, put her arms around his neck. He started walking again. She was not that heavy, now that he had her help in holding her. "I could feel a vasovagal coming on," she said. "Am I getting my period again?"

"No, I don't think so."

"It feels like it, I'm cramping. But I don't think I have enough body fat to do it."

"Maybe not."

Suddenly she jerked in his arms, pulled away to look at him face to face. "Oh my. Hey look—some people don't like to touch me. I have to tell you. You know those people who ingest some of the aliens from Enceladus?"

"Ingest?"

"Yes. An infusion of that bacterial suite. They eat some of the Enceladans; it's supposed to be good for you. I did that. A long time ago. So, well, some people don't like the idea. Don't even like to be in contact with a person who's done it."

Wahram gulped uneasily, felt a jolt of queasiness. Was that the alien bug, or just the thought of the bug? No way to tell. What was done was done, he could not change it. "As I recall," he said, "the Enceladan life suite is not regarded as being particularly infectious?"

"No, that's right. But it is conveyed in bodily fluids. I mean, it has to get into your blood, I think. Although I drank mine. Maybe it only has to get into the gut; that's right. That's why people worry. So . . ."

"I'll be all right," Wahram said. He carried her for a while, aware that she was inspecting his face. Judging by what he saw in the mirror when he shaved, he did not think there would be much to see.

Without intending to, he said, "You've done some strange things to yourself."

She made a face and looked away. "Moral condemnation of other people is always rather rude, don't you think?"

"Yes, I do. Of course. Though I notice we do it all the time. But I was speaking of strangeness only. No condemnation implied."

"Oh sure. Strangeness is so good."

"Well, isn't it? We're all strange."

She turned her head to look at him again. "I am, I know that. In lots of ways. You saw another way, I suppose." Glancing at her lap.

"Yes," Wahram said. "Although that's not what makes you strange."

She laughed weakly.

"You've fathered children?" he asked.

"Yes. I suppose you think that's strange too."

"Yes," he said seriously. "Though I am an androgyn, myself, and once gave birth to a child. So, you know— it strikes me as a very strange experience, no matter which way it happens."

She pulled her head back to inspect him, clearly surprised. "I didn't know that."

"It wasn't really relevant to one's actions in the present," Wahram said. "Part of one's past, you know. And anyway, it seems to me most spacers of a certain age have tried almost everything, don't you think?"

"I guess so. How old are you?"

"I'm a hundred and eleven, thank you. What about you?"

"A hundred and thirty-five."

"Very nice."

She shifted in his arms, lifting a fist in a mime of threatening him. By way of a riposte he said, "Do you think you can walk now?"

"Maybe. Let me try."

He put her feet down, pulled her upright. She leaned against him. She hobbled along for a bit holding his arm, then stood straight and proceeded on her own, slowly.

"We don't have to walk, you know," he said. "I mean, we can get to the next station and wait there."

"Let's see how I feel. We can decide when we get there."

Wahram said, "Do you think it was the sun that made you sick? Because I must say, for being in M g, I'm feeling very sore in my joints."

She shrugged. "We took a shot big enough to kill our comms. Pauline says I took ten sieverts."

"Wow." The LD 50 was about thirty, he thought. "My wristpad would have flagged it if I'd taken that much. I checked and it was only up three. But you covered me while we were waiting for the elevator."

"Well, there was no reason both of us should take a full hit."

"I suppose. But we could have taken turns."

"You didn't know about the flare. What's your lifetime total?"

"I'm at around two hundred," he said. They all relied

on the DNA repair component of the longevity treatment to stay in space as much as they did.

"Not bad," she said. "I'm at five." She sighed. "This could be it. Or maybe it just killed the bacteria in my gut. I think that's what's happened. I hope. Although my hair is falling out too."

"My joints are probably just sore from all the walking," Wahram said.

"Could be. What do you do for aerobics?"

"I walk."

"That's not much of a test of your aerobic system."

"I huff and I puff as I walk and I talk." Trying to distract her.

"Another quote?"

"I think I made that up. One of my mantras for the daily routine."

"Daily *routine*."

"I like routine."

"No wonder you're happy in here."

"It's true that there is a routine here."

They trudged down the tunnel in silence for a long time. When they got to the next station, they declared it a day and settled in to rest a few extra hours, as well as sleep through their night. Once Swan walked back down the tunnel to do something, then returned, and she fell asleep and seemed to sleep well, without purring. The next morning she wanted to carry on walking, declaring she would go slow and be careful. So off they went.

The lights kept appearing ahead out of the distant floor, then up and over them in their long arc. The effect was as if they were always about to walk downhill. Wahram tried to keep sight of one particular light, but could not be sure he had kept track of it from its first appearance to overhead. It could be some kind of unit: the view to horizon; multiplied how many times, he was not quite sure. "Can you ask Pauline to calculate our view distance to the horizon?" he asked at one point.

"I know it," Swan said shortly. "It's three kilometers."

"I see."

Suddenly it didn't seem to make much difference.

Shall we whistle?" Wahram asked after they had walked in silence for half an hour.

"No," she said. "I'm all whistled out. Tell me a story. Tell me your story, I want to hear more things that I don't know about you."

"Easy enough, to be sure." Although suddenly he could not think exactly how to start. "Well, I was born a hundred and eleven years ago, on Titan. My mother was a wombman who came originally from Callisto, a third-generation Jovian, and my father was an androgyn from Mars, exiled in one of their political conflicts. I grew up mostly on Titan, but it was very constrained in those days, a matter of stations and just a few small domes. So I also lived in Herschel for some years as I went to school, then also on Phoebe, and one of the polar orbiters, and then, recently, Iapetus. Almost everyone in the Saturn system moves around to get a sense of the whole, especially if you're involved with the civil service."

"Do many people do that?"

"Everyone has to do the basic training, and give a certain amount of time to Saturn, as they say, and they may also get drafted in the lottery for some position in the government. Some get drafted and grow to like it and then do more. That's what I did. One of my last mandatories was on Hyperion, and it was very small, but I really grew fond of that place, it was so strange."

"There's that word again."

"Well, life is strange, or so it seems to me." He sang, "People are strange, when you're a stranger," and then cut it short. "Hyperion is truly strange. It's apparently the remnant of a collision between two moons of about equal size. What's left looks like the side of a honeycomb, and the ridges bracketing the holes are white, while the powder filling every hole about halfway is black. So when you walk the ridges, or float over that side of the moon, it is very like some supremely bold work of art."

"A big old goldsworthy," she said.

"Sort of. And it's an easy place to disturb by one's presence. So it's been a question how to set up a station, even whether to set one up, and how it should be run if one is put there permanently. Having helped with that, I have the sense of being a curator or something."

"Interesting."

"I thought so. So, I went back to Iapetus, which is also a superb place to live; it's kind of a pulling back, and at an angle, to give you a better view of the whole system, and of why it should evoke such feeling. There I studied terraforming governance, and the diplomatic arts, such as they are——"

"The honest man sent by his country to lie for it?"

"Oh, I would hope that is not an accurate description of a diplomat. It's not mine, and I hope not yours."

"I don't think we get to choose what words mean."

"No? I think we do."

"Only within very tight limits," she said. "But go on."

"Well, after that I went back to Titan and worked

on the terraforming there. In those years I had my children."

"With partners?"

"Yes, my crèche had six parents and eight children. I see them all from time to time. It's almost always a pleasure. I try not to worry about them. I love the kids; I remember parts of their lives they don't remember themselves. I think that's of more interest to me than to them. That's all right. Memory is a haunting. You remember times you liked, and you want something like them. But you can only get new things. So I try to want what I get. It isn't obvious how to do it. You get into your second century and it gets hard, I think."

"It was never not hard," she said.

"True. This world is very mysterious to me. I mean, I hear what people say about the universe, but I don't know how to put it to use. To me it sounds meaningless. So I agree with those who say we have to make our own meaning. The concept of the project I find useful. Something you do in the present, and can remember doing in the past, and expect to do in the future, in order to create something. A work of art which need not be in the arts per se, but something human worth doing."

"That's existentialism, yes?"

"Yes, I think that's right. I don't see how you can avoid it."

"Hmm." She thought about it. The light gleamed off her black hair in white streaks. "Tell me about your crèche. How did that work?"

"On Titan there would be groups of people around the same age, who were educated together and worked together. Smaller cohorts would band together out of these to raise children. Usually it was in groups of half a dozen or so. There were different ways to structure them. It depended on compatibilities. There was a feeling at the time that pair-bonds didn't have enough people in them to endure over the long haul—that they succeeded less than half the time, and children needed more. So there would be some larger number. Almost everyone thought of it as a child-raising method and not a lifelong arrangement. Thus the name crèche. Eventually there were a lot of hurt feelings involved. But if you're lucky, it can be good for a while, and you just have to take that and move on when the time comes. I still stay in touch with them; we're even still a crèche. But the kids are grown, and we very rarely see each other."

"I see."

A long time of silent walking passed, and Wahram was feeling rather companionable, and not too sore.

Then Swan said vehemently, "I can't *stand* it in here. There's *no* chance of changing. It's like a prison, or a *school*."

"Our submercurial life," he said, just a little offended, as he had been enjoying himself. On the other hand, she was ill. "It will soon enough come to an end."

"*Not* soon enough." She shook her head gloomily.

They walked on, hour after hour. Everything stayed the same. Swan walked better than she had right after her collapse, but she was still slower than she had been before it. It didn't matter to Wahram; he liked the slower pace, in fact. He was still quite sore in the mornings, but did not seem to be getting any worse; nor did he feel weak or nauseous, though he was on the lookout for the symptoms in an uncomfortable way. He felt queasy a lot. Swan had pulled off all the hair on her head, leaving a fair number of scabby patches.

"What about you?" he said at one point. "Tell me more about you. Did you really lie naked on blocks of ice for hours at a time? Did you cut orreries into your skin and make patterns of blood on you?"

She was walking ahead of him, and now she hesitated, then stopped and let him take the lead. "I don't want to shout back at you," she said as he passed her.

"And yes," she said as they carried on, "I did do those things, and other kinds of abramovics. The body is very good material for art, I think. But that was mostly when I was in my fifties."

"What about before?"

"I was born in Terminator, as I said. It was just being constructed, and I was a kid in the farm when they were still putting in the irrigation systems. It was a big deal when the soil arrived. It came out of big tubes, like wet cement, only black. I played in there with my mother while they were getting the first crops and the park plants started. It was a great place to be a kid. It's hard to believe that it'll all be dead when we come up. I'll have to see it to believe it. Anyway that's where I grew up."

"The past is always gone," Wahram said. "Whether the place is still there or not."

"Maybe for you, oh sage one," she said. "I never felt that way. Anyway, after that I lived on Venus for a while, working for Shukra. Then I designed terraria. Then I moved into making artworks, working with landscapes or bodies. Goldsworthies and abramovics, still very interesting to me, and how I make my living. So I'm out and about, following commissions.

But I keep a room in Terminator. My parents both died, so my grandparents Alex and Mqaret were kind of like my parents. You couldn't have made any critique of pair-bonding by looking at those two. Poor Mqaret."

"No, I know," he said. "It was child rearing I was talking about, that seems to take more than two people. You must have learned that too?"

She shot him a glance. "One of them is out there somewhere. The child I had with Zasha died."

"I'm sorry."

"Yes, well, she was old. I don't want to talk about that right now."

In fact she was slowing down, and seemed to him hunched over. He said, "Are you all right?"

"Feeling weaker."

"Do you want to stop and rest?"

"No."

On they struggled, in silence.

He helped her through one hour, supporting her as she walked with one of his arms around her back and under her far arm, pulling up. After the rests she struggled up and continued walking, and would brook no argument against it. When they got to the next station, he looked around in every cabinet and closet in the place, and in the last closet he checked (but it was always the last one, when you found something) there was a little four-wheeled pushcart with a bar on one end that rose to chest height; otherwise it was a flatbed set just above wheel height, the bed one meter by two, and the two swiveling wheels opposite the bar.

"Let's put our backpacks on here and I'll push them," he suggested.

She gave him a look. "You think you can push me around."

"It would be easier than carrying you, if it came to that."

She dumped her backpack on the cart, and the next morning took off ahead of him. At first he had to hurry; then he caught up with her; then he slowed down as she did.

Hour after hour. Without discussing it, she would sometimes sit on the cart. Up on the surface over them passed the craters and scarps named after the great artists of Earth; they went under Ts'ao Chan, Philoxenus, Rūmī, Ives. He whistled "Columbia, the Gem of the Ocean," which Ives had incorporated so memorably into one of his wild compositions. He thought of Rūmī's "I Died as Mineral" and wished he had it memorized better. "I died as mineral and rose as a plant, I died as plant and was born an animal; when did I ever lose by dying?"

"Who is that?"

"Rūmī."

More silence. Down the big curve of the tunnel. The walls here were cracked, and it looked like they had been heat-treated more than usual to fuse them to impermeability. Crazed glazes of black on black. Craquelure to infinity.

She groaned and stood up from the cart and walked back to the west. "One moment, I have to go again."

"Oh dear. Good luck."

After a long while he heard a distant groan, maybe even a forlorn "Help." He went back down the tunnel, pulling the cart with him.

She had collapsed again with her suit down. Again he had to clean her up. She was a little more conscious this time, and looked away; even at one point batted weakly at him. In the middle of his work she looked at him blearily, resentfully. "This isn't really me," she said. "I'm not really here."

"Well," he said, a little offended. "I'm not either."

She slumped back. After a while she said, "So nobody's here."

When he was done and she was dressed again, he got her on the cart and pushed her forward. She lay there without a word.

In the next break he got her to drink some water dosed with nutrients and electrolytes. The cart, as she said at one point, was beginning to resemble a hospital bed. From time to time Wahram whistled a little, usually choosing Brahms. There was a stoic resolution at the heart of Brahms's melancholy that was very appropriate now. They still had twenty-two days to go.

That evening they sat there in silence. The scene devolved into the desultory animal behaviors that often followed such little crises—the turned heads, the preparations for sleep pursued abstractedly; dull aching drop into sleep, that unseen refuge. Here the pseudoiterative needed to be held to as a comfort. Lick one's wounds. All these things had happened before and would happen again.

One morning she got up and tried to walk, and after twenty minutes she sat back on the cart again. "This is worrisome," she said in a small voice. "If enough cells were busted..."

Wahram didn't say anything. He pushed her along. Suddenly it occurred to him that she could die in this tunnel and there was nothing he could do about it, and a wave of nausea passed through him, making him weak in the legs. A stay in a hospital could have done so much.

After another long silence, she said in a low voice, "I suppose I used to enjoy risking death. The jolt of the fear. The thrill when you survive. It was a kind of decadence."

"That's what my mom used to say," Wahram said.

"Like horror stories, where you try to shock yourself awake or something. But all that stuff is wrong. Say you attend the death of a person and help them out. All the images you see are out of horror stories. You see that those images came from where you are. But you stay anyway. And after a time you see that's just the way it is. Everyone goes there. You help but really you can't help, you just sit there. And eventually you're holding the hand of a dead person. Supposedly a night mare. Bones thrust up out of the ground to clutch you and so on. And yet in the actual act, perfectly natural. All of it natural."

"Yes?" Wahram said, after she had stopped for a while.

She heard him and went on. "The body tries to stay alive. It's not so... It's natural. Maybe you'll see it now. First the human brain dies, then the animal brain, then the lizard brain. Like your Rūmī, only backward. The lizard brain tries to its very last bit of energy to keep things going. I've seen it. Some kind of desire. It's a real force. Life wants to live. But eventually a link breaks. The energy stops getting to where it needs to be. The last ATP gets used. Then we die. Our bodies return to earth, go back to being soil. A natural cycle. So..." She looked up at him. "So what? Why the horror? What are we?"

Wahram shrugged. "Animal philosophers. An odd accident. A rarity."

"Or common as can be, but—"

She didn't continue.

"Dispersed?" Wahram ventured. "Temporary?"

"Alone. Always alone. Even when touching someone."

"Well, we can talk," he said hesitantly. "That's part of life too. It's not just lizard stuff. We throw ourselves out and span the gap, sometimes."

She shook her head sadly. "I always fall in the gap."

"Hmm," he said, nonplussed. "That would be bad. But I don't see how that could be right. Given what you've told me. And what I've seen of you."

"It's how it feels that matters."

He thought about that for a while. The lights passed them overhead, he pushed her on the cart. Was that right? Was it how you felt about what you did that made it good or bad, rather than what you did, or what others saw? Well, you were stuck in your thoughts. The current medical definition of the term "neurotic" was simply "a tendency to have bad thoughts." If you had that tendency, he thought, looking down at Swan's bare scaly head, if you were neurotic, then the material to work with would be nearly infinite. Was that true? Well, here they were, little spins of atoms which felt inside that something mattered, even while looking out at the stars, even inside a tunnel that looped downward forever. Then the spin would decohere and collapse. So, faced with that: good thoughts or bad thoughts?

He whistled the beginning of Beethoven's Ninth, thinking to drag her through her black mood and out the other side, by way of the old maestro's deepest tragedy, the Ninth's first movement. He shifted ahead to the repeated phrase near the end of the movement, the one that Berlioz had thought proof of madness. He repeated it. It was the simple tune he had used for walking uphill all his life. Now they were walking downhill, at the top of a great circle, but it fit his mood perfectly well. He kept on whistling the eight notes over and over. Six down, two up. Simple and clear.

Finally Swan, sitting below him on the cart, her back against the bar he held, facing forward, spoke again, but slurring her words a bit, and talking as if to Pauline. "I wonder if people know we're alive. You can never tell. It meant everything at the time, but then the time changed, and you changed, and they changed. And then it's gone. She doesn't have anything to say to me."

Long pause. Wahram said, "Who was your child's father? You had one each way?"

"Yes. I don't know who the father was. I got pregnant on Fassnacht, when everyone is in masks. Some man I liked the look of. She knows who it is, she had him traced."

"You liked the look of a masked person?"

"I did. The look of what you might call his demeanor."

"I see."

"I wanted to keep it simple. It was a conventional practice at the time. Now I wouldn't do it that way. But you never know until it's too late. You develop a folie à deux for a few years, it's very intense, but it's a folly, and after you come out you can't look back at it without feeling . . . You have to wonder whether it was a good thing or not. You miss it but you regret it too, it's stupid. I keep on doing things, but I still haven't figured out what to do."

"Live and make art," he said.

"Who said that?"

"You did, I thought."

"I don't remember that. Maybe I did. But what if I'm not a very good artist?"

"It's a long-term project."

"And some people are late bloomers, is that what you're saying?"

"Yes, I suppose. Something like that. You keep getting chances."

"Maybe. But, you know, it would be good to be making progress somehow. Not making the same mistakes over and over."

"Spirals," he suggested. "Spiral up, doing the same things at a higher level. That's the art of it no matter what you do."

"Maybe for you."

"But there's nothing unusual about me."

"I beg to differ."

"No, nothing unusual. Principle of mediocrity."

"You're an advocate of that?"

"An exemplar of it. The middle way. Middle of the cosmos. But only just as much as anyone else. A strange feature of infinity. We're all in the middle somehow. Anyway, it's a view I find useful. I use it to work on things. To structure my project, so to speak. Part of a philosophy."

"*Philosophy.*"

"Well, yes."

She fell silent at the thought.

Maybe we missed it," Swan said one day as she walked behind him. "Maybe we walked all the way under the brightside and the nightside too, and are back under the sun again. Maybe we've lost track of the time or the distance. Maybe you've screwed us with your ineptitude, just like Pauline."

"No," he said.

She ignored him and muttered about things that could have gone wrong while they had been underground. It unreeled into quite an amazingly long list, gothically inventive: they could have gotten disoriented and were now actually walking west; they could have gotten into another utilidor, angled toward the north pole; Mercury could have been evacuated and them the only ones left on the planet; they could have died in the sun and the first elevator taken them down to hell. Wahram wondered if she was serious, hoped she wasn't. There was so much that made her unhappy. Circadian rhythms; possibly she was walking when she should be sleeping. Many years before, he had learned you could not trust anything you thought between two and five a.m.; in those dark hours the brain was deprived of certain fuels or functions necessary for right mentation. One's thoughts and moods darkened to a sometimes fugilin black. Better to sleep or, failing that, to discount in advance any thought or mood from those hours and see what a new day brought in the way of a fresh perspective. He wondered if he could ask her about this without offending her. Possibly not. She was irritable already, and seemed miserable.

"How are you doing?" he would ask.

"We never get anywhere."

"Imagine that we were never getting anywhere, even before we came to this place. No matter where we move, we have never gotten anywhere."

"But that is so wrong. God, I hate your *philosophy*. Of course we've *gotten somewhere*."

"We've come a long way, we have a long way to go."

"Oh please. Fuck you and your fortune cookies. Here we are *now*. It's too *long*. Too *long* . . ."

"Think of it as an ostinato passage. Stubbornly repetitive."

But then she fell silent, and then began to moan— almost a hum, a sound she was unaware that she made. Little miserable grunts. Someone crying. "I don't want to talk," she said when he asked again. "Shut up and let me be. You're worthless to me. When things get tough, you're worthless."

That night they reached another elevator station. She stuffed food in her as if sticking batteries in a machine. After that she muttered again, wandering in ways he couldn't follow. Possibly talking to her Pauline. On it went, a muttering in his ear. They performed their ablutions back down the tunnel without incident, and then lay down on their pads and tried to sleep. The muttering continued. After a while she whimpered herself to sleep.

The next morning she wouldn't eat, or talk, or even move. She lay on her side in a catatonic fit, or a syncope, or simply paralysis.

"Pauline, can you talk?" Wahram asked quietly, when Swan would say nothing.

The slightly muffled voice from Swan's neck said, "Yes."

"Can you tell me about Swan's vital signs?"

"No," Swan said from nowhere.

"Vital signs available to me are nearly normal, except for blood sugar."

"You need to eat," Wahram said to Swan.

She did not respond. He spooned some electrolyte water into her mouth, patiently waited for her to swallow. When she had taken in a few deciliters without drooling too much of it away, he said, "It's noon up there. Up above us, on the surface, it's noon. Middle of the brightside crossing. I think we need to take you up to have a look at the sun."

Swan cracked an eyelid and looked up at him.

"We need to see it," he told her.

She shoved her torso off the floor. "Do you think?"

"Is it possible?" Wahram asked in reply.

"Yes," she said after thinking it over, "it is. We can stay in the shade of the tracks. It's less bad at noon than in the morning or afternoon, because the photons come straight down and fewer hit your suit. We shouldn't stay out for long though."

"That's all right. You need to see it, and now's the time. Noon on Mercury. Come on."

He helped her up. He found their helmets and carried them into the elevator car, went back and picked up Swan, took her to the elevator. Up they went, and he got her helmet on and sealed it, checked her air, did the same for himself. The suits showed all was well. The elevator car came to a halt. Wahram felt his pulse pounding in his fingertips.

The elevator door opened at the upper platform, and the world went white. Their faceplates adjusted, and a basic black-and-white sketch of a world appeared before them. To the left and slightly below were the city's tracks, glowing a deep incandescent white. To the right Mercury's noontime landscape extended to the horizon. In the absence of an atmosphere, there was only the land itself to take the blow of sunlight; it was glowing white-hot. His helmet's tint had shifted so hard that the stars were no longer visible in the sky. It was a white plane topped by a black hemisphere. The white was lightly pulsing.

Swan walked out the door onto the platform. "Hey!"

Wahram said, and went out after her. "Get back in here!"

"How would we see the sun in there? Come on, it will be all right for a while."

"The platform must be seven hundred K like everything else."

"Your boot soles are completely insulated at that temperature."

Amazed, Wahram let her go. She tilted her head back to stare at the sun. Wahram couldn't help following her glance—a stunning blast—fearfully he looked down again. The afterimage was there to contemplate: a circle both white and red at the same time, giant in his vision. The dhalgren sun, real at last. Clearly his faceplate was filtered to an almost completely polarized black opacity, and yet the land was still white, etched with tiny black lines. Swan was still looking up. Dying of thirst, she now drowned in the torrent. Following her example, breaking out all over in a sweat, he glanced up again. The surface of the sun was a roiling mass of white tendrils. It bounced as if throwing off thermal waves; then he realized it was his heart bouncing him, bumping his body hard enough to make his vision jostle. Writhing white circle in a starless charcoal sky. White banners flowing over themselves everywhere in the circle, the movement suggestive of some vast living intelligence. A god, sure, why not? It looked like a god.

Wahram dragged his gaze away and took her arm.

"Come on, Swan. Back inside now. You've gotten your infusion."

"Wait just a second."

"Swan, don't do this."

"No, wait. Look down there by the track." She pointed. "Something's coming."

And there was. Out of the east, on the smoothed ground just outside the outermost track, a small vehicle was approaching them. It stopped at the foot of the platform stairs, and a door in the side of the vehicle opened. A figure in a spacesuit appeared, looked up at them, waved them down.

"Could our sunwalkers have sent people out to get us?" Wahram asked.

"I don't know," Swan said. "Has there been enough time?"

"I don't think so."

They descended the stairs, Wahram holding Swan by the arm. She seemed pretty solid on her feet. Rejuvenated perhaps by the sight of the noon sun. Or the prospect of rescue. They got in the car's lock, and when it had closed on them, they were admitted to the interior, and in a sizeable compartment could take off their helmets and talk. Their rescuers were full of amazement. They had been making a brightside crossing at speed, they said, and had had no expectation whatsoever of seeing anyone standing on one of the platforms. "And looking straight up at the sun, no less! How the hell did you people get there? What are you doing?"

"We're from Terminator," Wahram explained. "There are three more of us down there, a bit farther along to the east."

"Ah ha! But how did you... Well, look, let's get going. You can tell it to us while we drive."

"Of course."

"Here, sit down by the window, then, take a look, it's beautiful out there."

The vehicle began to move. They passed by the station

they had stood on. They were being rescued. Swan and Wahram stared at each other.

"Oh no!" Swan said faintly—as if they had tripped into an unexpected disaster—as if she were going to miss the second half of their walk. That made him smile.

Lists (4)

sanguine, choleric, phlegmatic, melancholic
introverted, extroverted
               ambiversion, surgency
stable, labile
rational, irrational
neurotic, schizoid, paranoid, hebephrenic, manic-
    depressive, anal-retentive, obsessive-compulsive,
    psychotic, sadistic, masochistic

repressed, dissociated, bipolar, schizophrenic,
    schizotypal, psychopathic, sociopathic,
    megalomaniacal
depressed, antisocial, histrionic, anxious, dependent,
    passive-aggressive, narcissistic, solipsistic,
    dysthymic
               borderline personality, multiple
               personality

crazy, sane, normal, eccentric
autistic, Asperger's, shy, genius, retarded

Apollonian, Dionysian

idealists, artisans, rationalists, traders, guardians
   conscious, unconscious, ego, id,
    superego
   archetypes, shadows, animus and
    anima, psychastenia

happy, sad; cheerful, mournful; post-traumatic;
 adjusted
  openness, conscientiousness, agreeableness
doer, thinker; monkeys and pumpkins; impulsive,
 contemplative

selfish, proud, greedy, slothful, lustful, envious,
 angry; clear
stupid, smart; quick, slow; empathetic, sympathetic;
 distant
trusting, suspicious

Either or. This or that. Take your pick. All of the
 above

taxonomies, typologies, categories, labels, systems
three thousand years

Broca's aphasia, Wernicke's aphasia

hyperhippocampal, amygdala deficient, serotonin
 sensitive; enhanced firing in right temporal
 lobe knot 12a; overactive thalamus; retinotopic
 distortions

INSPECTOR JEAN GENETTE

Inspector Jean Genette, longtime senior investigating officer for Interplanetary Police, liked to get up in the morning and go for a walk to some corner coffee bar with a terrace or sidewalk, and there sip a big unsweetened Turkish coffee and read Passepartout as it displayed the latest news from around the system. After that Genette liked to continue walking in whatever city that morning happened to bring, eventually getting to work at the local Interplan office, invariably a small set of rooms near the government house. Interplan was unfortunately not a universally acknowledged police agency but rather something in the nature of a semiautonomous quasi-governmental treaty monitor, so their work was often compromised, and Genette could sometimes feel like a private agent or an NGO gadfly; but they had good data.

Genette liked to walk around in that data. The office was fine, colleagues stalwart, data important, but the walking itself was crucial. It was while walking that the inspector experienced the little visions and epiphanies that, when they came, constituted both the solution to the problem and the best moments in life.

This could sometimes happen at the office, while looking at new stuff, or at things in the archives, to check a hypothesis that might have occurred over coffee. Their graphics rooms were always very powerful spaces of representation, with three-dimensional and time-lapsed virtual flows of real interest and beauty. Of course it was true that standing in clouds of colored dots and lines sometimes only added to one's confusion. But other times Genette would see things in the representations and then go back out in the world and notice things no one had noticed before, and that was very pleasing. That was the best part.

Getting some consequent action out of the insights achieved was never quite as much fun. More often than the inspector would ever confess to any single person, it had been necessary to make deals in some poorly defined space—anarchy, one might call it in a bad mood—to bring certain findings to any kind of action in the world. But so far no crushing blame had rebounded on Interplan's head, and in a business like theirs that was all one could ask for.

As senior investigator, Genette could usually choose what cases to pursue, but of course the destruction of Terminator trumped all that kind of thing, commanding immediate attention from everywhere in the solar system. Also, since Terminator was part of the Mondragon, and Interplan was more closely associated with the Accord than with any other political entity, it was natural to get involved. Besides, there had never been a case quite like it. To have Mercury's only city torched (but there was a Phosphor being built, its tracks in the Mercurial north; have to look at that, wouldn't be the first time that real estate conflicts led to arson): naturally the whole solar system was transfixed. It was not clear what had happened, or how, or why, or by whom, and people loved this kind of thing, and were demanding answers. There would in fact be competing investigations into the incident. But the Lion of Mercury had been a good friend of the inspector's, and when the lion cubs had managed to regather after the evacuation, and assert Mercurial authority over the investigation, they had asked Genette to take charge. There was no question of declining such a request, which, it seemed, could also serve as a way to further the projects one had been pursuing with Alex and Wahram. Indeed the inspector felt that the destruction of Terminator so soon after the attack on Io, and the death of Alex, might be part of a pattern. The autopsy had confirmed that Alex's death had been the result of natural causes, but there remained a nagging ambiguity in Genette's mind—for some natural causes could be pushed to happen.

It was while beginning the trip to Mercury, walking across the concourse of the spaceport to the gate for the ferry, enjoying the sight of people making their way to their gates with their usual unconscious skill, that the solution to the problem of the attack on Terminator all at once came to the inspector. The vivid image was like the single thing that remains caught from a dream, and it created any number of useful research lines to follow on the flight downsystem, but most of all a feeling of certainty that was very nice. It relieved what could have been quite a worry.

By the time the inspector got to Mercury, the refugees from Terminator had either taken refuge in shelters or been dunkirked off-planet. The death toll was at eighty-three, most from health events or accidents with suits and locks, the usual emergency collection of mistakes and equipment failure and panic. Evacuations were notoriously one of the most dangerous of human activities, worse even than childbirth.

Given that, and the fact that Terminator itself was still out there broiling on the brightside, the investigation was only just getting under way. It had been determined that the cameras for that stretch of track had been destroyed by the impact, along with a platform called Hammersmith, where it was feared a concert party had perished. On the other hand, Terminator's orbital meteor defense system had provided its records for the relevant time, and neither radar, visual, nor infrared records showed any meteor prior to the hit. Satellite visuals of the impact showed no remains of an impactor. *Attack from the fifth dimension!*—as people were saying.

Genette, having seen the solution to this aspect of things, decided it was possible that pretending ignorance might allow time for the perpetrator to slip, and would also suppress copycat crimes. So the inspector said nothing about that, and remained in a room in the Rilke spaceport, interviewing witnesses. *A big flash of light.* Ah, thank you. Time to put in a heads-up to Wang, perhaps, to run some feasibility studies on Genette's solution to the mystery.

News came that two more refugees had been plucked off the brightside, and one of them turned out to be Alex's granddaughter, the artist Swan Er Hong. To be rescued out in the middle of the brightside seemed odd, and the inspector went to see them at the hospital in Schubert.

Swan lay in a bed hooked up to a couple of IVs; very pale; apparently recovering from radiation sickness, caused by a coronal flare that had struck just before she and her companions had gotten underground.

Genette climbed onto the chair next to her bed. Dark rings around red-rimmed brown eyes. Wahram, having accompanied her in her trek in the utilidor system, was sitting on the other side of the bed. Apparently he had not gotten as sick. He did look quite weary.

Swan registered Genette's presence beside her. "You again," she said. "What the fuck." She glared at Wahram, who blanched a little to see it, even raised a hand to ward off her gaze. "What are you two up to?" she demanded.

Genette turned on Passepartout, a qube like an old wristwatch, and said, "Please don't be upset. I am inspector general of the Interplanetary Police, as I told you when we met before. I was worried to learn of Alex's unexpected death, and although that appears to have been a natural event, I have been continuing to look into a number of untoward events that may be connected. You were close to Alex, and you were there to witness the assault on Io, and now you were here again when Terminator was attacked. It may be a coincidence, but you can see why we continue to run into each other."

Swan nodded unhappily.

Wahram said, "Did you ever find out anything out about the remains of the figure that fell into the lava on Io?"

"Let's discuss that later," Genette said with a warning look at Wahram. "For now we need to focus on the destruction of Terminator. Do you two mind telling me what you saw?"

Swan sat up and described the strike, then their

return to the city, and their realization that they had missed the evacuation; then their run east to the nearest track platform, and their descent into the utilidor. Wahram merely nodded in confirmation from time to time. This took a few minutes. After that Swan's account of their time in the utilidor was very brief, and Wahram did not elaborate or nod at anything. Twenty-four days could be a long time. Genette looked back and forth between them. Neither of them had seen much at the time of the blast, it was clear.

"So . . . is Terminator still burning?" Swan said.

"Strictly speaking, the burning is done. It is now incandescing."

She turned away, face scrunched in a knot. In their final transmissions, the cameras and AIs left behind in Terminator had recorded the city igniting in the sunlight—burning, melting, exploding, and so forth, until the recording instruments had failed. It had not been a general inferno but rather a patchwork of smaller fires, starting at different times. Some heat-resistant AIs were still transmitting data, documenting what happened as everything heated to seven hundred K. A collage of all those images gave a good impression of the incineration, though it seemed pretty clear that Swan would not want to see it.

But in fact she did. When she composed herself, she declared, "I want to see it all. Show me everything. I *need* to see it. I intend to make a penance somehow, a memorial. For now, tell us what you know! What happened?"

The inspector shrugged. "The city's tracks were impacted by something. The site itself is still out on the brightside, and until sunset arrives a thorough investigation can't be made. The impactor was invisible to your meteor defense systems, which should not be possible, as it massed many thousands of kilograms. Some people are saying it must have been a comet strike. I prefer to call it the event. It still isn't established for sure that it wasn't an explosion from below."

"Like a mine planted under it?" Wahram asked.

"Well, some satellite photos do make it look more like an impact event. But then questions arise."

The inspector's wristqube spoke in a clear singsong: "You've got a visitor named Mqaret."

"Tell him where we are," Genette said to it. "Ask him to join us."

Swan's cheeks had turned hectic. "I want to see Terminator," she announced.

"It might be possible to visit briefly in a protected vehicle, but little can be done there now. The crews on-site are mostly taking shelter in the shade of it. Sunset reaches that longitude in about seventeen more days."

Then Mqaret came into the room, and Swan cried out his name and reached out for a hug.

"We thought you were dead!" Mqaret exclaimed. "That whole concert party disappeared, and we thought you were with them, and then the evacuation was chaos, and we thought you were killed."

"We got down into the utilidor," Swan said.

"Well, people checked down there, but they didn't see anyone."

"We decided to hike east, to get it over with faster."

"I can see how you would do that, but you should have left a note."

"I thought we did."

"Really? But never mind—you're so thin! We need to get you to the lab to have a really thorough look at you." Mqaret circled the bed and gave Wahram a brief hug too. "Thank you for getting my Swan home. We hear you took care of her down there."

Genette saw that Swan did not look entirely happy at this description.

Wahram said, "We all helped each other. Indeed we look forward to seeing the young sunwalkers we were down there with."

Mqaret said, "They're in the process of retrieving them now, and I hope they'll be fine. A fair number of sunwalkers have been picked up."

"Ours were very helpful," Wahram said, although Swan snorted to hear it.

Mqaret seemed unaffected by the destruction of the city; as it came on the heels of Alex's death, he no doubt felt that it didn't really matter. With Terminator gone, however, the Mercurials were now reduced to staying in underground shelters scattered all over the planet, in a way not that different from how people occupied Io. Which was not the optimal position from which to rebuild. But they could do it, and in fact work had already started, using heat-resistant shelters and robots. Very soon after sunset came to the burned city, they would fix the tracks and have the city's frame moving again; then they could rebuild in the safety of darkness, as they had the first time.

Meanwhile they were still in emergency mode, and their influence elsewhere in the system correspondingly reduced. So now Mqaret said to Swan, but with a look to Genette and Wahram, "We'll rebuild and we'll be all right. The people who talk about our fatal criticality have different criticalities of their own. We're all vulnerable in space. There isn't a single off-Earth settlement that couldn't be destroyed, except for Mars."

"Which is part of what makes Mars insufferable," Genette noted.

"I will create a monument to our loss," Swan declared, struggling as if to leave her bed. Tugging dramatically at her IV lines—"I will perform an abramovic in the ruins, to express the city's grief. Perhaps a period of crucifixion would be appropriate."

"Burning at the stake," Wahram suggested.

Swan shot him a poisonous look. Mqaret objected more tactfully, pointing out that Swan was not yet recovered enough to use her body as a canvas. "It's always so hard on you, Swan, you can't."

"I will! I most certainly will."

But Swan's qube spoke from the right side of her neck: "I must inform you that you have given me instructions to oppose any abramovician artworks when your health is not optimal. These are your own instructions to yourself."

"Ridiculous," Swan said. "Sometimes circumstances demand a change in plan. This is an overriding life event, a catastrophe. It demands a response in kind."

"I must inform you that you have given me instructions to oppose doing an abramovic when your health is not optimal."

"Shut up, Pauline. I don't want you to speak now."

Mqaret had moved to block Swan from leaving her bed; now he said, "Dear Swan, your Pauline is right. Meaning that you yourself are right, and speaking from a larger perspective in yourself. Don't be hasty here. There are better ways for you to exert yourself during our time of troubles. There's work to be done."

"It's *work* to express Terminator's fate in *art*."

"I know, and for you especially. But you are one of our biome designers, and so you'll be very much needed in that capacity. We can seize this opportunity to renovate the park and the farm."

Swan looked alarmed. "Surely we'll just replace them? No one will want anything changed—I know I won't."

"Well, we'll see about that. But you must be available to the city."

Swan glowered. "I will be no matter what. Can we at least take a hopper around into the brightside and look at it?"

"I think so. I'll ask for seats on one of the daytrippers as soon as I can. But you need to finish your recovery first."

A few days later they all went out in a hopper, following the tracks east into daylight and the wreckage of Terminator. The land below as seen through heavy filtering was the white of paper, marked by black rings and a few wavering lines, resembling all together some alphabet written with compasses. The tracks themselves were a narrow band of glowing white wires.

Then over the horizon reared Terminator. The dome frame glowed as white as the tracks. The interior was a black mass, which as they got closer resolved to smaller masses of clinkers and gunk and ash, black blobs, black powder. Some metal surfaces glowed red. It was reminiscent of old photos of Terran cities destroyed by firestorm.

Mqaret shook his head at the sight. "You can see why we need to stay on the nightside."

Swan stared down, seeming not to hear. No theatrics this time, Genette noted. Grim desolation in an empty face. Looked like she was somewhere else. Wahram was watching her unobtrusively.

The glowing ruin of the city was dominated by the still-standing Dawn Wall. Its east-facing exterior was as silvery and pure as ever, but its inside was now a mess of curving black terraces. Some of the rooftops made of royal-blue ceramic tiles had remained intact, and even now held their color. The Great Stair case still cut down through black strip after black strip, the imported marble of the steps nacreous in the heat. The glowing white spans of the dome frame curved up at the sky like the framework of the dome in Hiroshima.

"It was so beautiful," Mqaret said.

"Still is," said Swan.

Mqaret said, "We'll import some mature trees and grow the rest from seed. Although I have to tell you, the arrangements with insurance don't seem to be working out very well. They're arguing about the definition of 'full replacement.' Also it isn't clear yet whether it was an act of God or an act of war. The council lawyers think the insurance is there for us either way, but who knows. It's going to be expensive, that's the main thing. We'll need help. Luckily the Accord will have our back. And replacing the animals will be easy, as the terraria are well above capacity."

He glanced at Wahram, cleared his throat. "I hear the Vulcanoids are also anxious to help. Naturally they're worried down there."

"They need us," Swan said. "That's why they took Alex up on her proposal to help them in the first place."

"Well, this will be a test of how much they think they need us."

Swan shook her head like a dog. Genette saw that she did not want to think about the Vulcanoids right now. She was annoyed perhaps at Mqaret's move to the next step, even as they were staring down at the glowing ruins.

Wahram was more attentive to her mood. "'Remembrance of a particular form is but regret for a particular moment; and houses, roads, avenues are as fugitive, alas, as the years.'"

Swan scowled at him. "More fortune cookies, oh deep one?"

"Yes." A tiny smile; he still had the capacity to be amused by her, Genette saw, even after their confinement together. Maybe he had even learned it there. It was striking how little they had said about their time in the tunnel.

Now Swan said, "I want to join Inspector Genette's investigation, if that's all right, Inspector? I'd like to be the Mercurial liaison to your investigation."

"We can always use help," Genette said diplomatically. "This incident is of grave concern to everyone, but of course for Mercury it goes right to the heart of things. I was assuming you would therefore want someone to join the investigation."

"Good," Swan said. "I'll keep in touch with the design team," she told Mqaret. There was no more talk of some kind of self-mortifying art performance; although it occurred to the inspector that the investigation itself might eventually be seen as such.

When they got back to the spaceport, Wahram nodded and took his leave of Genette. Then he turned to Swan, bowing very slightly, with hand on heart.

"I must return to Saturn and attend to business I missed. We'll meet again soon, I'm sure. Terminator will rise like a phoenix, and then there will be all kinds of unfinished business for us to complete."

"There most certainly will," she said. Suddenly she hugged him, put her head briefly against his broad chest. She stood back. "Thank you for saving me. I'm sorry I was so messed up down there."

"Not at all," Wahram said. "*You* saved *me*. And we got through." And with another awkward bow he left.

Lists (5)

the Vesta Zone, a cloud of terraria forming a single
  cooperative
Aymara, an amazonia with an interior completely
  overgrown with cloud forest
Tatar Soul, a steppes grassland where people speak a
  resuscitated Indo-European
The Copenhagen Interpretation, a canal town with a gift
  economy
The Zanzibar Cat, an anarchist savanna with thousands
  of big cats and no interior buildings at all
Arabia Deserta, a desert occupied by British travelers
Aspen, a skiing paradise
unnamed prison asteroids with robot guards
Hermaphrodite, where all permanent residents are
  gynandromorphs and androgyns
Saint George, a social terrarium in which the men
  think they are living in a Mormon polygamy,
  while the women consider it a lesbian world with a
  small percentage of male lesbians
asteroids hollowed not into cylindrical terraria but
  rather warrens, hives, caves, pits, hotels, etc.

The Maldives, an aquarium recreating the drowned
islands; *Micronesia*, likewise; *Tuvalu*, likewise; all
the drowned islands of Earth are reproduced in
this fashion

Greater Yellowstone Ecosystem 34, the last of thirty-four
terraria using versions of the template of this great
biome

extremophile terraria, deadly to humans but
hospitable to growth of organisms creating
medicines and inoculants

doomed biomes, established with odd parameters and
then sealed off like test tubes

The Little Prince, an outie terrarium, tent-bubbled
with its atmosphere bluing its edges

The Whorl, whose inhabitants keep watch for an
outsider

Miranda, the smashed-together moon of Uranus, now
a Trojan freely orbiting the sun, completely tent-
bubbled, its deep canyons and stupendous ridges
filigreed with snow drifting down in the low g, all
Swiss architecture, a dream of the Alps

Icarus, a fliers' world, lit by a sunline in its floor to
keep the air clear

Source of the Peach Blossom Stream, a Tang dynasty
recreation that looks like a Chinese landscape
painting come to life

Miocene terraria, Cretaceous terraria, Jurassic
. terraria, Precambrian terraria

Water Drop, an aquarium filled entirely with water
and ocean creatures

Sequoia Kings Canyon, an infolded Sierra Nevada of
California

—and so on. Estimated nineteen thousand occupied
asteroids and moons

SWAN AND MQARET

Back at the spaceport between Schubert and Bramante Craters, Swan sat in a corner, filled with a regret for something she couldn't name. Surely it was impossible that it should be regret for the utilidor; already she was forgetting that. Let Pauline remember that. Never look back, why should she? Although there had been something there—as if she had been on the border of something important. What had he said? That the tunnel was no different from anywhere else? She would never concede that, never.

When she was about to leave with Genette and the Interplan team, Mqaret came to see her again. "You're so tough," he told her, patting her head as if she were a child. But he took her seriously, she knew. So she shook her head.

"No," she said flatly. "I fell apart. I couldn't handle it."

He defended her fondly. "It's not really what you're good at, of course. Enforced confinement. Don't ever get put in prison, or shoot off in a spacesuit on a tangent somewhere. It wouldn't suit you. Yet here you did very well, I think."

"I don't see how."

"Well, this solar flare that struck you before you got to shelter; your suit dosimeters show that somehow you got hit much harder than the others down there with you. In fact, I don't mean to scare you, because you're going to be fine—I've already got your renovation well in hand, and you are responding superbly—but really, that was quite a hit."

"Ten sieverts," she said dismissively. "That's not so bad."

"Quite bad, actually. Did you look at the sun longer than the others? Did you stand in front of your friend?"

"Yes, I did, but I'm only half as wide as him. I'm sure I didn't protect him much."

"He only got three sieverts. So you're only a bit thinner than he is, really. You saved him from the full shot."

"And then he saved me. He had to carry me for a few days."

"Fair's fair. But look, this ten sieverts—that's enough to kill, and you should have been debilitated. But you will be fine, as I said. So I'm interested to see if we can find out why you did so well. I've been wondering if your Enceladan symbiote had anything to do with it. It tolerates radiation well, and as a detrivore it may have bloomed in you to eat all the new food provided for it by all your killed cells. It may have joined your own T cells in clearing your body."

Swan was startled by this. "You hated me doing that," she said. "You told me I was a stupid fool."

Mqaret nodded. "I was right, too. Look, Swan; if you love life, as you profess to do, as your excuse for all your wildness, then you should protect your life the best you can. Some actions are simply unknown risks, and that was one of them. Indeed it still is. But it was a risk only, not a certain thing. Presumably that's why you did it. You're not suicidal, right?"

"Right," she said uncertainly.

"So you're a fool, then, when you do things that you can't be sure won't kill you in ten or even a hundred years."

"Then we're all fools."

"True. True enough. But there's no need to be a stupid fool."

"There's a difference?"

"There is. You think about that and see if you can figure out the difference. Hopefully before you do something like this again. If anything like this is even possible."

He had been poking a pad and looking at her numbers as they spoke, and now he shrugged. "With your permission, I'll take some of your samples back to the lab for study. Maybe it will lead to something."

"Of course," she said. "It would be nice if something good came from my stupid foolishness."

He kissed her on the head. "Something more than what you already give, you mean."

After Mqaret was gone, Swan was left to think about her stupid foolishness. Her body, emaciated on the bed, swimming under her gaze like someone else, a thing she manipulated like a waldo—it was resilient. It still held her. Was hungry. She buzzed the nurse to ask for food.

"Pauline, please transmit my medical history to this tabletop."

"Would you like the long version or the summary?"

"The summary," Swan said, knowing that the long version ran to hundreds of pages.

She looked at the print glowing in the table, but could not force herself to read it. Phrases jumped out from all over it: *Born 2177*, a difficult birth, she had been told, with moments of low oxygen. *Seizures age 2. Fungal and bacterial infections in farm school. Wetland syndrome. ADHD, age 4–10*

That had been countered with a drug treatment later discredited. Her later schooling had been conducted in the farm, and she had done much better out there. Except there were more words glowing in the table: *Dyscalculia. prefrontal cortex electrostimulation. First sabbatical inoculation for Xinjiang, China, age 15, full array including helminths*

—meaning parasitic worms, in this case *Trichuris suis*, a pig whipworm, ingested in a therapy that seesawed in and out of favor.

ODD, age 15–24

Oppositional defiant disorder, related to anxiety disorder, both hippocampal, but anxiety avoided while ODD attacked.

One-g syndrome, second sabbatical in Montpellier, France, age 25. Venusian flu. Genital modification, age 25. Hormone drip implanted, age 35, hormone therapies to present. Oxytocin addiction, age 37–86. Lark and warbler song cluster implant, age 26. Feline purr vocal cords, age 27. Implant of subdural quantum computer in 2222, age 45. Cognitive therapy, age 9–99.

Fathered one female at age 28. Daughter deceased, 2296. Mothered one female at age 63. Natural birth.

There was a line entered in her records by Mqaret: *Ingestion of the Enceladan life-form—foolish girl, age 79.*

Longevity treatments, age 40–present.

Factitious disorder, never treated—this must have been inserted by either Mqaret or Pauline, making fun of her.

"What about *Designed a hundred terraria*?" Swan complained. "What about *three years spent in the Oort cloud putting mass drivers on ice balls*? Or *five years on Venus*?"

"Those were not medical events," Pauline said.

"They were, believe me."

"If you want your curriculum vitae, just ask for it."

"Be quiet. Go away. You are too good at simulating an irritating person."

"Did you say 'simulating' or 'stimulating'?"

Extracts (7)

The longevity increase associated with bisexual therapies has led to very sophisticated surgical and hormonal
treatments for interventions in utero, in puberty, and
during adulthood. The XX/XY dichotomy still exists,
but in the context of a wide variety of habit, usage, and
terminology

feeling of gender identity is formed in the hippocam-
pus and hypothalamus in the second month; the original orientation is persistent. If the desire is to create a
feeling of undifferentiation or ambivalence, alterations
need to begin in utero

in the first eight weeks of gestation keep both the Müllerian and Wolffian ducts active, in what is still the
bi-potential gonad. Anti-Müllerian hormones activated
by genes in the Y chromosome can be allowed to attach
only to one of the fetal Müllerian ducts. The effect is
normally ipsilateral, each testis suppressing Müllerian
development only on its own side, so

XY embryos then need a moderate level of androgen insensitivity introduced by the fourth week, in order to avoid masculinization of the hypothalamus, where sexual differences in the brain will be concentrated. XX embryos need the application of androgens to one Müllerian duct in order to stimulate the growth of a Wolffian duct. As that Wolffian duct develops, the Müllerian duct on that side will experience apoptosis

underlying genetic makeup is the difference between androgyny and gynandromorphy, often not discernable by body features. XX humans with conserved Wolffian ducts are gynandromorphs; XY humans with conserved Müllerian ducts are androgyns. In both, androgens and estrogens are supplied with hormone pumps such that the child is born with potential for both kinds of genital development in the body, awaiting the choices

prenatally selected bisexuality has the strongest positive correlation with longevity. Hormonal treatments begun at puberty or during adulthood also have positive effects on longevity, but the psychological set will be

hormonal treatments support the surgical addition of a functioning uterus in the abdominal wall above the penis

alteration of the clitoris into a small functioning penis, with testicles grown using either conserved Wolffian ducts or stem cells from the subject. Gynandromorphs can ordinarily father only daughters, as the construction of a Y chromosome from an X chromosome involves problematic

females adding functional reproductive masculinity are helped by a process imitating a natural 5-alpha-reductase deficiency

principal categories of self-image for gender include feminine, masculine, androgynous, gynandromorphous, hermaphroditic, ambisexual, bisexual, intersex, neuter, eunuch, nonsexual, undifferentiated, gay, lesbian, queer, invert, homosexual, polymorphous, poly, labile, berdache, hijra, two-spirit,

cultures deemphasizing gender are sometimes referred to as ursuline cultures, origin of term unknown, perhaps referring to the difficulty there can be in determining the gender of bears

KIRAN ON VENUS

The moment Kiran was alone with Shukra, Shukra said to him, "We're going to have to put you through some tests, my boy."

"What kind of tests?"

"All kinds."

Three big men showed up to escort them across a few boulevards of Colette, and Kiran saw there was no question of him doing anything but what he was told. As they entered a building with bay windows overlooking a street corner, he tried to see the street signs and remember where they were. Eighth and Oak. Although the tree across the intersection was a willow.

"Tell me again why Swan brought you here?" Shukra asked as they went into the building.

"I helped her avoid being kidnapped, when she was out in my neighborhood. She wanted to return the favor."

Shukra said, "You asked to come here?"

"Sort of."

Shukra shook his head a few times. "So now you are a spy."

"What do you mean?"

Shukra glanced at him. "You're a spy for her, at this point, whether you know it or not. We'll find out with our tests. After that you'll be a spy for me."

"Why should she need a spy here?"

"She was very close to the Lion of Mercury, and since the Lion's death, she has started traveling in the way that the Lion would have. And the Lion always kept a big cadre of spies here. So let's see what the tests say."

Kiran found his heart was beating hard, but the three big men closed around him, and there was no choice but to be escorted into another room. This one had the look of a medical clinic. The tests in the end resembled medical exams more than anything else, which was a great relief to discover. Although when medical exams are the good option, it is not a good situation.

At the end of that day he was escorted back into Shukra's presence. Shukra examined the console that presumably contained Kiran's results. When he spoke, it was to Kiran's escorts. "He looks clean, but somehow I doubt it. For now, let's use him for bait."

After that Kiran was assigned to a Chinese work unit, which lived together in a building near the city's crater rim, and left the city together almost daily to do work outside. The unit's members had no control over their lives; they went where they were told, did what they were told, ate what they were given. It was almost like being at home.

A stupid little translation belt Swan had given to him was now the only company Kiran had. He got a lot of puzzled second glances when he used the thing to facilitate communication, but he also had a few ten-minute conversations through it that were much better than nothing. Mostly, however, he was on his own in a throng, doing whatever came up for his team that day. He never saw Shukra again after the battery of tests, which made him feel like he had failed—although one day it occurred to him that maybe he had passed.

In any case there was endless work to be done, almost all of it outside Colette, in the perpetual blizzard that the Big Rain had turned into. Thick drifts of snow were landing on the new dry ice seas before the latter had been completely covered with foamed rock, and this was creating a problem. Every day big teams had to go out and operate gargantuan bulldozers and snowplows to clear the snow off the dry ice, so that foamed rock brigades could then cover the ice before more snow fell on it. It was said that the foam job would take ten more years to finish, but Kiran had also heard one year, and someone else said a hundred years. No one knew for sure, and with his belt it was hard to follow the discussions at the dining table after meals, when sometimes workmates would try to do the calculations themselves on their wristpads. Ten years kept coming up. Talk about dead-end jobs! He needed to improve his Chinese.

At night he slept in a dorm. This was the most interesting part, because people were packed in on long mattresses that his belt called *matrazenlager*—essentially mattresses as long as the room, with numbers on the headboards marking nominal slots for people, a situation leading to a fair bit of sex in the dark, sometimes even including him. Then up in the morning, eat in a cafeteria, get in a line to get sent out onto the endless plain in rovers, or put in helicopters the size of aircraft carriers to be carried out to the dry ice sea to operate bulldozers, waldoes, snowblowers (the so-called dragons),

super-zambonis, and ice cutters much like the asphalt-
and concrete-cutting vehicles back in Jersey, but a hundred times bigger. After a few weeks he could operate
any of these. They weren't very complicated; really you
told the AI what to do for the most part. It was like
being captain of a ship. A day's work by a team of a
thousand would clear many square kilometers of dry
ice, and on the horizon the black moving buildings
that spread the foamed rock followed inexorably. The
far shore of this part of the ice sea was said to be six
hundred kilometers away.

Then for a matter of some weeks he worked in a
monumental waldo, kicking free what they called
stegosaur plates, then carrying them over to the bed of
a giant truck. Waldo work was always demanding—it
was full-body movement, like dancing—not physically
hard, but as it magnified your every motion, it required
very close attention and focus to move the waldo in just
the way you wanted it to go. So it could be interesting
work or just a matter of lifting and carrying, but either
way it left you fried.

At the ends of these days he tried to work on his
Chinese. No one he met spoke English, so his little
translation belt was his best teacher, but it was hard.
He would say things to it and then listen to the translation and try to say it back. But when he said it back
in Chinese, and it translated what he'd said back into
English, it never came out right. He said, "My radar
is broken," in exactly the Chinese he thought he had
heard, and it translated back to him "immediate open
air meeting." He tried "Where do you live?" and it
came back as "Your lotus has interpolated."

"If only!" he said, laughing bleakly. "I'd like my
lotus to interpolate, but how?"

Clearly he must be sounding crazy to the people he talked to. He was doing something wrong, but what?

"It is a hard language," one of his dorm mates said when he complained. He tried to memorize that properly.

As it was, his translator was his best friend. They talked a lot. He hoped to start getting more out of it soon. Saying "hello" and "how are you?" and such was working better and better with the people he interacted with. And they were getting friendlier about talking slow.

The workers continued to chip away at the monumental tasks set before them, tasks thousands of times bigger than similar jobs on Earth. But if the job was shoveling snow, was that a good thing?

Once he sent a message to Swan to say he was glad to hear she had survived the attack on Terminator, and in it he mentioned that he never saw Shukra anymore. A message came back a few weeks later: *Try Lakshmi.* With a Venusian cloud address.

He looked into this and found that Lakshmi was a name that caused people to go silent and look away. A big power, based over in Cleopatra; an ally of Shukra's, or an enemy—people didn't really know, or didn't want to say.

So: maybe Swan wanted to shift her informant to a place closer to the action. Or maybe she was just trying to help.

Or maybe he was just on his own.

Lists (6)

boreal forest (conifers); temperate forest (hardwoods
    or mixed hardwoods and conifers); tropical forest;
    desert; the alpine zone; grassland; tundra; and
    chaparral, sometimes called shrubland
                these are the principal Terran biomes

cities; villages; croplands; rangelands; forests; and
    wildlands
                these are the principal Terran
                    human-use patterns anthromes

mix and match the above, and you get the 825 eco-
    regions of Earth
                450 on land, 229 marine
                65 percent of these now exist only
                off-planet

take an x-y graph to chart a Whittaker biome
    diagram, with precipitation marked vertically and
    temperature horizontally. Biomes can be plotted
    on this graph and will make a clearly shaped map
    of what kind of biome turns up in what kind

of conditions. Left is hotter, right colder; wet
is higher, dry lower; and thus the most general
version is as follows:

Tropical rain forest
Tropical seasonal   Temperate rain forest
   forest
Savanna   Temperate deciduous   Taiga
                         forest
Subtropical desert   Temperate grassland   desert
                                             Tundra

The classifications can be much elaborated. The 450
   named terrestrial eco-regions divide biomes by
   not only precipitation and temperature, but also
   combinations of latitude, altitude, geography,
   geology, and other factors

eco-regions themselves can be usefully divided
   into microenvironments as small as a
   hectare

34,850 known species went extinct between 1900
   and 2100. It was, and remains ongoing, the sixth
   great mass extinction in Earth's history

no extinctions from this point onward are inevitable
   (this has always been true, however)

19,340 terraria are known to exist in the solar system.
   Approximately 70 percent of these function as
   zoo worlds, either dedicated to sustaining an
   eco-region's suite of animals and plants, or else
   to creating new combinations of suites, called
   Ascensions

92 percent of mammal species are now endangered or
gone entirely from Earth and live mainly in their
off-planet terraria

space: the zoo, the
                  inoculant

SWAN AND THE INSPECTOR

There are two problems in dealing with the Terminator incident," Inspector Genette said to Swan one evening as they flew out to the asteroid belt. They were traveling with a little group from Interplan and Terminator, but often found themselves the last two in the galley at the end of an evening. Swan liked that; the inspector would sit right on the table while eating, on a plush brought for the purpose, and afterward lounge there on one elbow with a drink, so that they spoke eye to eye. It was a little like talking to a cat.

"Only two?" she said.

"Two. First, who did it, and second, how we can find and catch this agent without giving more people the idea of doing it. The so-called copycat problem, and more generally, the problem of preventing any kind of repetition of this attack. That I consider to be the more difficult problem of the two."

"What about *how* it was done?" Swan asked. "Isn't that a problem too?"

"I know how it happened," the inspector said easily.

"You do?"

"I think so. It's the only way it could have happened, I think, and so there you have it. No matter how implausible, as the line has it, although in this case it's not implausible at all. But I must confess to you, I don't want to say more about it when we are both being recorded by our qubes." Genette raised a wrist and indicated the thick, almost cubical little wristpad that contained Passepartout. "You have your qube recording always, I assume?"

"No."

"But often?"

"Yes, I suppose so. Like anyone else."

"Well, in any case I want to see some things in the belt before I will be sure of my hypothesis. So we'll talk about this more when we're out there. But I want you to think about the second problem; assuming we catch a perpetrator and explain the deed, perhaps in a prosecution—how are we going to keep someone else from doing it? This is where I think you could help me."

They were traveling in the terrarium *Moldava*, which ran in an Aldrin cycle that would take them out to Vesta in eight days. The interior of the *Moldava* was given over to growing wheat, and many of the people traveling in it congregated after their day's labor in the fields at a resort on high ground near the bow, set on a broad hilltop, overlooking and then looking up at the upcurve of a big patchwork pattern of fields, different green and gold textures created by the many different strains being grown. It was like a quilter's version of heaven.

Swan spent much of her time talking to the local ecologists, who had lots of little wheat disease problems they wanted to discuss. Inspector Jean stayed in the Interplan rooms and, as they passed Mars, spent time calling ahead to people in the terraria clustered around Vesta. At the ends of these days Swan would meet with the Interplan group to eat, then talk late with the inspector. Sometimes she talked about her daytime work. The locals were trying out wheat varieties that shed water from the seed heads better, and were exploring the genetic creation of microscopic "drip tips" like those seen in the macro world of tropical leaves, where the drip tips were long tips on the leaves that allowed water to break its surface tension and run away. "I want to have drip tips in my brain," she said. "I don't want to hold on to anything that will hurt me."

"I wish you luck with that," the little inspector said politely, staying focused on the meal, and eating a lot for such a small person.

A few days later they came to the Vesta Zone, one of the crowded areas of the asteroid belt. During the Accelerando many terraria had relocated near each other, creating something like communities, and the Vesta Zone was among the largest of these. *Moldava* released a ferry with the Interplan team on it, and when the ferry had decelerated and was near Vesta, they transferred again, this time to an Interplan ship with an Interplan crew.

This was an impressively fast little spaceship named *Swift Justice*, and in short order they were moving against the flow of the great current of asteroids, stopping once or twice at little rocks for the inspector to talk with people. No explanation for these conversations was offered, and Swan held off asking, while they visited the *Orinoco Fantastico*, the *Crimea*, the *Oro Valley*, *Irrawady 14*, *Trieste*, *Kampuchea*, the *John Muir*, and the *Winnipeg*, after which she just had to ask.

"All these little worlds had recent perturbations in their orbits," the inspector explained, "and I wanted to ask if they had explanations for them."

"And had they?"

"There were some abrupt departures from the Vesta Zone, apparently, and people think those threw the neighbors off course."

Vesta itself proved to be very substantial for an asteroid—six hundred kilometers in diameter, roughly spherical, and entirely tented, which made it one of the biggest examples of the paraterraforming method called bubble-wrapping. Usually tents covered only parts of a moon, like the older domes; they were the most common structures on Callisto and Ganymede and Luna, but those moons were all so big that covering them entirely hadn't even been considered. To cover a little moon with a tentlike bubble represented the next stage, and a viable outie option to the hollowed-out innie worlds. Swan supposed that Terminator itself was a case of paraterraforming, though she was not used to thinking of it that way and had a prejudice against outies in the asteroid belt as being overexposed and low-g, compared to burrowing into a rock and spinning it.

But now, as she regarded Vesta from a short distance out, it looked good. It was a place that would have weather and a sky (the tenting was located two kilometers above the surface), and Pauline told her the Vestans had established boreal forests, alpine ranges, tundra, grassland, and lots of cold desert. All that would be in very low g, which meant everyone would be flying and dancing around a lot, in a puffy, almost floating landscape. Not such a bad idea. They even had an immense mountain.

So Swan was interested to visit Vesta, but Genette

had a different destination in mind, and after a few
more Interplan people joined them, they headed to a
nearby terrarium called *Yggdrasil*.

As they approached *Yggdrasil* Swan saw it was yet
another potato asteroid, in this case dark and unspin-
ning. "It's abandoned," the inspector explained. "A cold
case."

In the hopper's lock Swan floated to the suit rack
with a graceful little plié, suited up, then followed
Genette and several Interplan investigators out the
outer lock door into the void.

Yggdrasil had been a standard innie, perhaps thirty
kilometers long. They entered it by way of a big hole
left in the stern; the mass driver had been removed.
They jetted in gently, using their suits' thrusters to
keep them upright. Flowing forward side by side,
they looked like a reversal of one of those pharaonic
statue pairs in which the sister-wife is knee-high to the
monarch.

Inside they jetted to a halt. The interior of the asteroid was a pure black, dotted with a few distant reflections of their headlamp beams. Swan had been in
many a terrarium under construction, but this was not
like those. Genette tossed ahead a bright lamp, jetted
briefly to counteract the toss. The pinpoint flare floated
forward through the empty space, illuminating the
cylinder quite distinctly.

Swan spun a little under the force of her own looking around. So dim, so abandoned; she spun in some
gust of emotion that perhaps came from her poor Terminator: fist to her faceplate, suddenly she heard herself
moaning.

"Yes," the little silver figure floating by her said.

"There was a pressure failure here, with no warning. This was a chondrite and water-ice conglomerate asteroid, very common. The accident review found a small meteorite had by chance hit an undetected seam of ice in the cylinder wall, vaporizing it and depressurizing the interior catastrophically. It wasn't the first time something like that had happened, although in this case the rock readers had given it a triple A rating. Usually the ones that have cracked have been Bs or Cs, and were occupied unwisely. So I've been reanalyzing old accidents, looking for certain flags, and decided I wanted to have a look at this one. Mainly at the outside, but first I wanted to check the inside."

"A lot of people died?"

"Yes, around three thousand. It happened very fast. Some people were in buildings with shelters they got to in time, and others were near spacesuits, or air locks. Other than them, the whole city-state died. The survivors decided to leave it empty as a memorial."

"So this is like a cemetery now."

"Yes. There's a memorial in here somewhere, I think on the other side. I want to take a look at the inner surface of the break."

The inspector consulted with Passepartout, then led Swan through the interior space to a boulevard on the other side of the cylinder. The neighborhood here had a Parisian scale, with wide streets running between trapezoidal housing blocks four and five stories tall.

They hovered over an area of crumpled pavements and tilted buildings, which resembled old photos of earthquake-damaged areas on Earth. It was strange how still it was.

"Aren't there enough nickel-iron asteroids around that no one needs to hollow a conglomerate?" Swan asked.

"You would think so. But they hollowed out a few of these and found they worked fine. Keep the walls thick enough and the rotation and interior air pressure are nowhere near enough to test them. They should work and they do. But this one broke. A little meteor hit just the wrong spot."

They floated over an area where the intense buckling had left plates of white concrete thrown up and out, leaving a long gash between them. The gash was open to space; Swan could see stars through it.

They left the devastated street and floated back out of the asteroid. Outside they toed and jetted over the surface of the rock, negotiating the typical asteroid mini-g. Swan had spent some time in this g during her terrarium-building days, and she saw that the inspector was expert in it, which of course made sense for someone based in the asteroid belt.

When they got to the outside location of the open seam, they found several of the Interplan team already at work around it. Genette made a few balletic leaps, twisting in descent to float down headfirst, taking photos of the inside of the rupture. Close inspection of a few small pits to each side was accomplished by way of one-handed handstands, faceplate centimeters from the rock.

After a while: "I think I've got what I need."

They floated there, watching the others continue to work. Genette said, "You have a qube there in your skull, isn't that right?"

"Yes. Pauline, say hello to Inspector Genette."

"Hello to Inspector Genette."

"Can you turn it off?" the inspector asked.

"Yes, of course. Will you be turning off yours?"

"Yes. If that is indeed what really happens when we turn them off." Through the faceplates Swan could see the inspector's ironic smile. "All right, Passepartout has been put to sleep. Has Pauline?"

Swan had indeed pressed the pad under the skin on the right side of her neck. "Yes."

"Very good. All right, now we can talk a little more openly. Tell me, when your qube is on, is it recording what you hear and see?"

"Normally, yes. Of course."

"And does it have direct contact with any other qubes?"

"Direct contact? Do you mean quantum entanglement?"

"No, no. Decoherence makes that impossible, we are told. I only mean radio contact."

"Well, Pauline has a radio receiver and transmitter, but I select what goes in and out."

"Can you be sure of that?"

"Yes, I think so. I set the tasks and she does them. I can check everything she's done in her records."

The little silver figure was shaking its head dubiously.

"Isn't it the same for you?" Swan asked.

"I think so," Genette said. "I'm just not so sure about all the qubes that are not Passepartout."

"Why? Do you think qubes may be involved with what happened here? Or on Mercury?"

"Yes."

Swan stared in surprise at what seemed to be a big spacesuited doll floating beside her, feeling a little afraid of it. Its voice was in her ear because of her helmet mike, speaking from almost within her, much as Pauline did. A clear high countertenor, pleasant and amused.

"There are quite a few little crater pits to each side of the break here. Like that one..." Genette pointed with a forefinger, and a green laser dot appeared on the rim of a small pit, quickly circled the rim, then fixed at its center. "See that? And then that?" Circling another one. They were very small. "These are fresh enough that they may have happened during or after the break."

"So, ejecta?"

"No. Gravity here is so slight, the ejecta seldom come back. If anything did, it would almost dock. These pits are deeper."

Swan nodded. The asteroid's lumpy surface had many rocks lying loosely on it. "So what did the accident report call these craters?"

"Anomalies. They speculated they might be pit ruptures, where ice deposits melted at the heat of impact. Could be. But I take it you have looked at the accident report for Terminator?"

"Yes."

"Do you remember there were anomalies there too? Whatever struck the tracks didn't hit cleanly. There are outlier craters, very small, that were not there before the event. Now, on Mercury they could be ejecta coming back down, I grant you that—"

"Couldn't the impactor have broken up coming in?"

"But that usually happens where there's an atmosphere heating and slowing it."

"Couldn't Mercury's gravity do it?"

"That effect would be negligible."

"I don't know, so maybe it didn't break up."

The little figure nodded. "Yes, that's right."

"What do you mean?"

"It didn't break up. In fact, it came together."

"What do you mean?"

"I mean it was never comglomerated, until the very last moment. That's why none of the detection systems on Mercury saw it coming. They should have seen it, it had to come from somewhere, and yet it was not detected by the surveillance systems. So to me this indicates an MDL problem. Minimum detection limit. Because there is always a minimum limit of detection, either inherent to the detection method, or else artificially set higher than the actual minimum."

"Why do that?"

"Usually to keep warnings from going off all the time when there isn't really any danger."

"Ah."

"So, each system is different, but in the Mercurial defense apparatus, what they call the method reporting level is almost equivalent to the system's method detection limit. In other words they set their reporting level at twice the detection level, which is six or seven times the standard deviation in their measurement variability. It's a typical setting to make people comfortable they'll generate both the fewest false negatives and the fewest false positives.

"So, but consider what then lies below that reporting level. Basically, only very little rocks—pebbles, well less than a kilogram each. But if there were a lot of them, and they converged only at the last second, with each one coming in from a different quadrant of the sky, and at a different speed, but timed such that they all arrived at the same spot, at the same time... Then they would just be little pebbles, until the last second. They could have been tossed from the far side of the solar system, maybe, and over a number of years, maybe. And yet even so, if thrown correctly, eventually they make their rendezvous. Many thousands of them, let us say."

"So, a kind of smart mob."

"But not even smart. Just rocks."

"Could that work? I mean, could anything calculate how hard to throw them, and on what trajectory?"

"A qube could. With enough of the solar system's masses identified as to locations and trajectory, and enough calculating power, it can be done. I asked Passepartout to do it—to calculate an orbit for something like a ball bearing or a boccino, thrown from the asteroid belt to hit a particular target on Mercury. It didn't take long."

"But could the throws be made? I mean, would it be possible to build a launcher that would launch them with the necessary precision?"

"Passepartout said there are machines in existence with tolerances two or three magnitudes more precise than would be necessary. One would only need a steady launch platform. The stabler the better, in creating consistency."

"That's quite a shot," Swan said. "How many masses get included in the trajectory calculation?"

"I think Passepartout included the heaviest ten million objects in the solar system."

"And we know where all those are?"

"Yes. Which is to say the AIs know where they are. And all the biggest terraria and spaceships conform to itineraries set years in advance. As for the calculations, it takes a qube to be able to do it in a reasonable amount of time, meaning fast enough to use it for real-time launch instructions."

"How long does it take?"

"For a qube similar to Passepartout, three seconds.

For conventional AIs, about a year per pebble, which of course would render the method inoperable. You have to have quantum computing to be able to do it."

Swan was feeling sick to her stomach, as if she were back in the utilidor. "So ten thousand little rocks thrown downsystem, over a matter of months or years, with such directions and velocities that they all arrive at one spot at the same time."

"Yes. And a few stochastic gravitational fluctuations no doubt cause a little bit of scatter at the end. Indeed when that happens, those pebbles must usually miss entirely."

"But some just barely miss."

"Exactly. Like these little pits we see. Caused perhaps by a spaceship that changed flight plans, or the like. So maybe one or two percent of the pebbles experience a clinamen of this sort, or so Passepartout guesses."

Now the wrench in her gut was getting severe. "So someone is doing this on purpose." She waved at the abandoned terrarium.

"That's right. And also, a qube has to be involved."

"Shit." She put an arm across her stomach. "But how . . . how could someone . . ."

The inspector put a little hand to her arm. *Ygassdril* floated under them, cold and dead. A gray potato. "Let's get back to the *Justice.*"

Back inside the Interplan hopper, after they had eaten a meal, Swan stayed up late in the galley, and again the inspector did too.

Swan, who had not been able to stop thinking about the day's revelations, said, "So, all this means that whoever—"

Genette raised both hands and stopped her. "Qubes off again, please."

After they had both turned off the devices, she continued: "That means whoever did this could have done it years ago."

"Or at least quite some time ago, yes. Some stretch of time."

"And there wasn't a single launch site."

"No. But maybe there is still the launch mechanism. Their gun, or catapult, or whatever it was, would have to be a very precise instrument. A particularly fine bit of manufacturing. The tolerances Passepartout suggested were really quite fine, requiring molecular printers and so forth. We might be able to find the factory that made something so particular—we're looking into that. And then, who might have ordered it."

"What else?" Swan asked.

"We are looking for the program for the factory, and the design of the instrument. Its printing instructions. Also the orbital program needed to make the calculations. Qubes don't make that kind of thing up without being asked to do it—or so we have been assuming until now. The qube that did it would have that action recorded in it, as I understand it. And so the program is likely to still exist somewhere. And there are still only a finite number of factories making qubes."

"Couldn't they have destroyed their qube when they were done using it?"

"Yes. But there's no reason to assume they're done."

This was a chilling thought.

"We must look for the qube, the orbit program, the factory program, also the factory, and the launcher itself, and whatever the launch platform was."

Swan frowned. "All those could be destroyed, or cleaned pretty clean."

"It's true. You see the nature of the problem very

quickly. Even so, this investigation has to turn into a check of the records, a kind of bookkeepers' search. As our work so often becomes." Another ironic smile: "It is not often as dramatic as is sometimes portrayed."

"That's fine. But while you're doing that, what else can we do? What can I do?"

"You can look at the other end of the problem. And I will join you in that."

"The other end?"

"The motive."

"But how would you determine that? And having done so, how would you locate it? Doing something like this is so sick that it makes me sick to think about it. It's evil."

"Evil!"

"Yes, evil!"

Genette shrugged. "Putting that aside, let us presume anyway that it is rare impulse. And so it may leave signs."

"That someone hates Terminator? That someone is capable of killing worlds?"

"Yes. It's not a common impulse. It may therefore stick out. And besides, it may be a political act, a kind of terrorism or war. It may be meant to convey some message, or force some action. So we can follow it that way."

Swan felt her stomach clenching. "Damn. I mean— there's never been a, a war in space. We've managed without them."

"Until now."

That gave her pause. For a generation at least there had been warnings from people all over the system that the conflicts between Earth and Mars could lead to war, or that Earth's writhing problems were going to drag everyone down with them. Little wars and terrorist attacks and sabotages had never entirely disappeared on poor Earth, and Swan had sometimes thought that diplomats played on the notion that Earth's discord might spread, in order to boost their own prestige, their own budgets. Diplomacy as necessary peacemaking in a system on the brink—it had been very convenient for them. But what if it turned out to be true?

She said, "I guess I thought spacers knew enough to avoid all that. That once we got out here we would do better. Be better."

"Don't be a fool," the inspector said crisply.

Swan gritted her teeth. After an intense struggle for self-control she said, "But it could be some psychopath. Someone who has lost their mind and is killing just because they can."

"There are those too," Genette agreed. "And if one of them got hold of a qube—"

"But anyone can get a qube!"

"Not at all. Not even everyone in space. They are tracked from the factories, and in theory are all located moment to moment. And whichever one was involved would have to be programmed for this, as I said. It would show in its own records what it had done."

"Aren't there unaffiliateds that are making qubes?"

"Well—maybe. Probably."

"So how do we find it, or this person?"

"Or this group?"

"Yes, or nation, or world!"

Genette shrugged. "I want to talk to Wang again, because his qube is really powerful, and he also has the biggest data banks on the unaffiliateds. And also because it's possible he was attacked by this same entity. But I admit I'm a little afraid to talk to his qube, because we're seeing so many signs of qubes acting oddly. As if they have volition now, or in any case are being asked to do things unlike anything they've done before. Some qubes that we've been monitoring are now exchanging messages in an unprecedented way."

"You mean they're entangled with each other?"

"No. That seems to be truly impossible, because of decoherence issues. They use radio communication like anyone else, but the messages are encrypted internally at each end, using superposition as they do. So they are truly encrypted, even when we use our own qubes to try and break the codes. This is the reason why I want to keep these discussions out of the earshot of any and all qubes, for the time being. I don't know which ones to trust."

Swan nodded. "You're like Alex in that."

"That's right. I used to talk to her about this, and we had the same opinion about this problem. I taught her some procedures to use. So, now I have to think about how to go forward here, and how I can best communicate with Wang and his superqube. Possibly the explanation for all this is even now stored in it, unrecognized because it hasn't been asked to look for it. Because despite all the talk you hear of balkanization, we are still recording the history of the world down to the level of every person and qube. So to find this agent, we only need to read out the history of the solar system for the last several years, and it should be there."

"Except for the unaffiliateds," Swan pointed out.

"Well, yes, but Wang has most of them too."

"But you don't want his recording system to know you're asking," Swan said. "In case it's the one doing all this."

"Exactly."

*   *   *

Swan never quite stopped feeling sick after that. Someone had meant to kill her city—and yet had missed hitting it directly, thus sparing its citizens, all but the ones who had died in the panic of the evacuation and that poor concert group, killed by the impact.

Was that right? She didn't know what to make of that—that the impact had missed Terminator itself.

She ended up talking to Pauline about it. She had an idea that she wanted to check, and Pauline was the best way to do it. There she was, after all, her voice in Swan's ear, and always hearing everything Swan said aloud. There was no way she wasn't going to find out all about this, eventually.

So: "Pauline, do you know what Inspector Genette and I were talking about when I turned you off?"

"No."

"Can you guess?"

"You might have been talking about the incident at *Yggdrasil*, which you had just seen. This incident resembles the incident at Terminator in some features. If these were deliberate attacks, then whoever initiated them might have used a quantum computer to help them plot trajectories. If Inspector Jean Genette believed that quantum computers were involved, then the inspector might not want any quantum computers to hear details of the investigation. This would be similar to Alex's efforts to keep some of her deliberations completely unwitnessed and unrecorded by any AIs, quantum or digital. The assumption seems to be that if quantum computers are in encrypted radio communication with each other, then they may be plotting activities detrimental to people."

Just as she suspected: Pauline could deduce these

things. No doubt many other qubes could too, including Genette's own Passepartout, programmed in forensics and detection as it certainly must be. If-then, if-then, how many trillion times a second? It might resemble their chess-playing programs, which had proved themselves to be superhumanly good at that particular game. So it was a little bit futile to turn them off only for certain conversations.

Which meant that it was all right for her to say "Pauline, if someone had calculated the trajectory of an impactor to hit Terminator smack on and destroy it, but they forgot to include the relativistic precession of Mercury in their calculation and only used the classical calculus of orbital mechanics, how far would they miss by? Assume the impactor was launched from the asteroid belt a year earlier. Try a few different launch points and trajectory courses and times, both with and without the relativity equations for the precession."

Pauline said, "The precession of Mercury is 5603.24 arc seconds per Julian century, but the portion of that caused by the curvature of space-time as described by general relativity is 42.98 arc seconds per century. Any trajectory a year in duration, plotted without that factored in, would therefore miss by 13.39 kilometers."

"Which is about what happened," Swan said, feeling sick again.

Pauline said, "Being a precession, the miss should have been to the east of the city, not the west."

"Oh," Swan said. "Well, then..." She didn't know what to make of it.

Pauline said, "Ordinary orbital mechanics programs for inner planet transport routes routinely include general relativity as a matter of course. It is not necessary to remember to add the relativity equations. If, however, someone who did not know that tried to program a trajectory for an impact without using open-source templates, then they might have added the relativity equations to a situation where they were already being used. And thus, if targeting the city directly, they would create an error of 13.39 kilometers to the west."

"Ah," Swan said, feeling sicker than ever. She looked for a place to sit down. Terminator was one thing, its people something else: her family, her community.... That there could be someone capable of killing them all ... "So ... But that sounds like a human error."

"Yes."

That evening, late in the galley, she found herself again alone with the inspector, who again was sitting on the table in front of her, eating grapes. Swan said, "Since you told me about the pebble mob, I've been thinking that it was probably aimed directly at Terminator, but that somebody made a mistake. If they didn't know that the relativity equations for the precession of Mercury were already part of the standard algorithms, and added the operation, they would end up hitting just the distance to the west that they did."

"Interesting," Genette said, looking at her closely. "A programming error, in other words. I've been assuming that it was a deliberate miss—a warning shot, so to speak. I'll have to think about that." After a moment: "You must have asked your Pauline about this?"

"I did. She already had deduced the general topics of what she missed when I turned her off. I'm sure your Passepartout is the same."

Genette frowned, unable to deny it.

Swan said, "I can't believe anyone would try to kill so many people. And actually do it, too, in the *Yggdrasil*.

When so much space is available . . . so much everything, really. I mean, we're in what people call post-scarcity. So I don't get it. You talk about motive, but in a physiological sense, there isn't a motive for stuff like this. I suppose that means that evil really does exist. I thought it was just an old religious term, but I guess I was wrong. It's making me sick."

The inspector's attractive little face creased in a slight smile. "Sometimes I think it's *only* in post-scarcity that evil exists. Before that, it could always be put down to want or fear. It was possible to believe, as apparently you did, that when fear and want went away, bad deeds would too. Humanity would be revealed as some kind of bonobo, an altruistic cooperator, a lover of all."

"Exactly!" Swan cried. "Why not!"

Genette shrugged with a Gallic weariness. "Maybe fear and want never went away. We are more than food and drink and shelter. It seems like those should be the crucial determinants, but many a well-fed citizen is filled with rage and fear. They feel painted hunger, as the Japanese call it. Painted fear, painted suffering. The rage of the servile will. Will is a matter of free choice, but servitude is lack of freedom. So the servile will feels defiled, feels guilt, expresses that as an assault on something external. And so something evil happens." Another shrug. "However you explain it, people do bad things. Believe me."

"I guess I have to."

"Please do." Now the inspector was not smiling. "I will not burden you with some of the things I've seen. I've had to wonder at them, like you are now. The concept of the servile will has helped me. And lately, I've been wondering if every qube is not by definition some kind of a servile will."

"But this programming error that might explain the impact hitting west of town—that's a human error."

"Yes. Well, the servile will exists in humans first. So, in parts of themselves people know these acts are bad, but they do them anyway, because in other parts of them some itch gets scratched."

"But most people try to do good," Swan objected. "You see that."

"Not in my line of work."

Swan considered the little figure, so neat and quick. "That must change your perspective," she said after a while.

"It does. And...you see the same self-justifications, over and over. It's even known which parts of the brain are involved in the justifications. They're very near the parts involved with religious feeling, just as you might expect. Not far from the epileptic triggers, and the sense of meaning. Those parts light up like fireworks when one commits evil or justifies it. Think what that means!"

"But everything we do is in the brain somewhere," Swan said. "Where in the brain doesn't matter."

Genette did not agree. "There are patterns in there. Reinforcements. Bad events grow certain parts of the brain bigger. The brain reconfigures to create a spiral of ever more horrible feelings. Further actions follow."

"So what do we do?" Swan exclaimed. "You can't make a perfect world and *then* get decent people, that's backwards, it can't work."

The inspector shrugged. "Either way seems unlikely to me." Then, after a pause: "It can go so wrong. Living in space may be too hard for us. Reduced environments. I've seen kids raised in Skinner boxes—human sacrifice—"

"You need your sabbatical," Swan interrupted, not wanting to hear more.

She saw suddenly that Genette was looking weary. Usually smalls were hard to read; at first glance they looked rather perfect, like dolls, or innocent, like children. Now she saw the reddened eyes, the blond hair a little oily, the simple ponytail all flyaway with hairs that had broken at the hair tie.

And a grimace, very unlike the usual ironic smile. "I do need my sabbatical. I'm late, in fact, and I hope our investigation will soon get me there. Because I'm a little tired. The Mondragon is a beautiful thing, but there are many terraria not in it, some of them seriously deranged. Ultimately what we get by not enforcing a universal law is some kind of accidental libertarian free-for-all. So we're in trouble. This is what I'm seeing. When you combine political inadequacy with the physical problems of being in space, it may be too much. We may be trying to make an impossible adaptation out here."

"So what do we *do?*" she said again.

Genette shrugged again. "Hold the line, I guess. Maybe we need to understand out here that post-scarcity is both heaven and hell at once. They are superposed, like options in a qubit before its wave function collapses. Good and evil, art and war. All there in potentiality."

"But *what* do we *do?*"

Genette smiled a little at that, shifted and sat cross-legged on the table before her, looking like a garden Buddha or Tara, slim and stylized. "I want to talk to Wang. I'll figure out how. And to your friend Wahram. That's much easier. After that . . . it depends on what I learn. Did Alex by chance give you a letter for me too, or for anyone else?"

"No!"

A raised hand, like the adamantine Buddha: "No reason to be annoyed. I just wish she had, that's all. To her this was just a contingency, a backup for something she didn't expect to happen. She probably figured Wang would tell the rest of the group about her plans. And he will, I hope."

The next day the inspector's crew had news, and after a conference Genette emerged and said to Swan, "Wang's qube identified an asteroid that orbits between Jupiter and Saturn, that drifted outward in its orbit as it would have if it launched the impactor mass at Terminator. The drift happened three years ago, over a period of about six months. Wang took a look through the Saturn League records of ship movements in Saturn space, and those had signals that look like a small ship left this asteroid and from there flew into Saturn's upper atmosphere. It might have taken the plunge, but it entered the upper clouds at an angle that means it could have tucked in there, as quite a few ships have. If so, we might be able to track it down."

"That's good," Swan said. "But . . . this is Wang's qube giving you this lead, yes?"

Genette shrugged. "I know. But the ship track is from the Saturn League, and they tagged it with a transponder on its way down. They also got a read on the transponder already in it, and so they know it was a ship owned by a consortium on Earth."

"On Earth!"

"Yes. I'm not sure what to make of that, but, you know—a pebble mob can't be launched from within an atmosphere. Nor from under a dome or tent. It had to happen on an open surface in the vacuum. So if you were on Earth and wanted to do this, you would have to go into space to do it."

"I see that. But—Earth? I mean, who on Earth—?"

The inspector's look was so sharp she could not continue.

Genette said, "There are more than five hundred organizations on Earth that have expressed opposition to the idea of humans in space."

"But *why*?"

"They usually point out that Earth's problems remain unsolved, and assert that spacers are trying to escape these problems and leave them behind. Often the bodily modifications in spacers are cited as evidence of the beginnings of a forced speciation. *Homo sapiens celestis* has been suggested as a name for us. Some also call it the speciation of class. Many Terrans have not gotten the longevity treatments. Thus there are claims that space civilization is perverse, wicked, decadent, and horrible. Destabilizing human history itself."

"Damn it," Swan said. "I thought they saw how much good we do them."

"Please," Genette said. "You must take your sabbaticals in very sheltered places."

Swan thought about it for a while. "So what do we do?"

"I want to go to Saturn and look for this little ship. Passepartout thinks it can predict its location from its entry point."

"And I can come along?"

"More than welcome. We are already on our way."

The *Swift Justice* ferried them to a passing terrarium called *Inner Mongolia*, a beautiful innie of big rolling green hills, often interrupted by outcroppings of black rock, and home to herds of wild horses and elusive packs of wolves, an animal Swan particularly loved. The little towns were set on hilltops and looked like collections of fine yurts, often surrounded by lawns, and pools perched on overlooks. Genette brought along only a couple of assistants, and spent a fair amount of time with them working on what Swan assumed were other cases, in a yurt set among a cluster of them on a hilltop.

One afternoon after a morning of wandering the grassy hills, trying to spot wolves and failing, Swan came to a hilltop yurt resort that had a broad sloping lawn, a big wading pool and set of steaming baths, and a tent aviary filled with hanging baskets of flowers and many different kinds of hummingbirds, lories, and small colorful finches. The undulating lawn had been manicured until it looked like a green carpet. To Swan this was excessively ornamental, out of tune with the wild hills she had spent the morning on. She passed a pair of women who were laughing as if they also found the place ludicrous, and she said as they passed, "It's silly, isn't it."

They stopped and one pointed back up the hill. "Those three people up there in dresses told us that they're qubes in android bodies, and didn't we think they could pass as humans. We told them they probably could, but—" The two women looked at each other and laughed again. "But that they were totally blowing it by asking us!"

Swan spotted the three sitting on the grass near the wading pool. "Sounds interesting," she said, and headed up toward them.

"Pauline, did you hear that?" she said on the way up. "Yes."

"All right, well, be quiet, then, and pay attention."

*   *   *

It was an old hypothesis, that humans would be comfortable with intelligent robots either when the robots were housed in something like a box, or else when they were simply indistinguishable from humans, at which point they would be just another kind of person. In between these two extremes, however, lay what the hypothesis called the uncanny valley—the zone of like-but-not-like, same-but-different, which would cause in all humans an instinctive repulsion, disgust, and fear. Thus the hypothesis, plausible enough; but because there had never actually been a robot built in a form human enough to test the near side of the uncanny valley, it had always remained a notion only. Now Swan was perhaps going to get to test the near side of the uncanny valley.

The tasteless design sense of this resort seemed to extend to the clothing of these three guests. They sat by themselves in long dresses like Victorian crinolines, looking enough alike to be siblings, or even, yes, cloned androids from a single model. Although one looked slightly more female than the other two.

Swan approached them and said, "Hello, I'm Swan, from Mercury, where we are rebuilding our burned city with the help of many qubes. I understand that you three are claiming that you are qubes, that you are not biologically human? Is that right?"

The three people sat there staring at her. The one who looked slightly female in body proportions smiled and said, "Yes, that's right. Sit down with us and share some tea. I've got a pot almost ready," gesturing at a little portable stove on the ground, and a little squat red teapot resting over its blue flames. There were cups and spoons and little pots on a blue square cloth next to her.

The other two also met her eye and nodded at her. One gestured to the grass beside them. "Have a seat, if you want."

"Thanks," Swan said as she flopped down. "It's pretty heavy in here. Where do you all come from?"

"I was made in Vinmara," the most female one said.

"What about you?" Swan asked the other two.

"I cannot pass a Turing test," one of them replied stiffly. "Would you like to play chess?"

And the three of them laughed. Open mouths— teeth, gums, tongue, inner cheeks, all very human in look and motion.

"No thanks," Swan said. "I want to try a Turing test. Or why don't you test me?"

"How would we do that?"

"How about twenty questions?"

"That means questions that can be answered by yes or no?"

"That's right."

"But one could just ask us if the other is a simulacrum or not, and the other answers, and that would take only one question."

"True. What if we only allow indirect questions?"

"Even so it would be very simple. What if you had to do it without questions at all?"

"But real people ask each other questions all the time."

"But one of us or more are not real people. And it's you who suggested a test."

"That's true. All right, let me look at you. Tell me about *Inner Mongolia*."

"Dear *Inner Mongolia*, hollowed in the year..."

"Hallowéd be thy name," one of the indeterminates interjected, and they laughed.

"Population approximately twenty-five thousand people," said the more feminine one.

"You must be a qube," Swan said. "No human ever knows that kind of thing."

"None?"

"Maybe some people, but it's odd. But I must say, you look fabulous."

"Thank you, I decided to wear green today, do you like it?" Showing off the sleeve of the dress.

"It's very nice. Can I look closer?"

"At my dress or at my skin?"

"At your skin, of course."

And they all laughed.

Laughter, Swan thought as she examined the person's skin. Could robots laugh? She wasn't sure. The person's skin was lightly pocked by hair follicles, slightly lined by creases at the bend points; there was a scattering of nearly transparent hair on the back of the person's wrists and forearms, and a little patch of longer darker hairs on the inside of the wrist, which had four permanent creases just inside the hand, where the skin was thinner but darker, revealing a pair of veins, with bumps and bends in them. The skin on the underside of the hand had faint whorls, like big fingerprints, on the ball of the thumb and the meat of the hand. The lifeline was a deep long curve. It looked very much like anyone's hand, anyone's skin. If it was artificial skin, it was very impressive; this was said to be the hardest thing to make look natural. If it was a biological skin, as in the labs, but grown over a frame, that would be impressive in a different way. It didn't look possible that these people's skin could be artificial, but of course materials science was very sophisticated, and many things were possible to it. Set goals and parameters, and what wasn't possible?

It remained a question who would want to do such a thing, but on the other hand, people did odd things all the time. And making an artificial human was a very old dream. Maybe it was pointless, but it had a tradition. And here they were, after all, and she wasn't sure yet what she was facing. That in itself was interesting.

If you had sex with a machine, was that interesting, or just a complicated form of self-satisfaction? Would a qube register your responses to it one way or another? Would it too be having sex?

She would have to try it if she wanted to find out. It would be just another approach to the more general problem of qube consciousness. What one had to remember with qubes was that no matter the evidence to the contrary, there was no one home: no consciousness, no Other, just a mechanism programmed to respond to stimuli in a certain fashion by its programmers. No matter how complex the algorithms, they did not add up to a consciousness. Swan fully believed this, but even Pauline fairly often surprised her, so it could be hard not to fall for the illusion.

"Your skin is beautiful. You feel like flesh of my flesh."

"Thank you."

"Do you think, do you think?"

"I most definitely think," the feminine one replied.

"So you have a sequence of thoughts that wander from one thought to the next in a more or less continuous flow, free associating from one topic to the next, across all the possible thoughts you could have?"

"I'm not sure it's quite like that. I think it's more

a matter of stimulus and response, with my thoughts responding to the stimuli of my incoming information. Now, for instance, I think about you and your questions, about the green of my dress as compared to the green of this grass, about what I will eat for dinner, as I am a bit hungry—"

"So you eat food?"

"Yes, we eat food. In fact I have a hard time not eating too much!"

"Me too," Swan said. "So, do you ever think about having sex with me?"

The three of them stared at her.

"Well, but we have just met," one said.

"That's often when people think of it."

"Really? I'm not sure that's true."

"Believe me, it's true."

"I don't have any good reason to believe you," the second one said. "I don't know you well enough for that."

"Does one ever know one well enough for that?" the third one asked.

They laughed.

"*Believe* someone *else*?" the feminine one said. "I don't think so!"

They laughed again. Maybe they were laughing too much.

"Are you people on drugs?" Swan asked.

"Is caffeine a drug?"

Now they were giggling.

"You three are silly girls," Swan said.

"It's true," the feminine one admitted. She poured tea from the teapot into four little cups, passed them to the others. The second one opened a hamper and took out biscuits and cakes, handing them around along with small white cloth napkins. They all fell to with an appetite. The three locals ate just like people.

"Do you swim?" Swan asked. "Swim, or bathe in hot tubs?"

"I bathe in hot tubes," the third one said, causing the others to cackle muffledly into their napkins.

"Can we do that?" Swan asked. "Do you bathe without clothes on? Because that way I could see your whole bodies."

"And we could see yours!"

"That's fine."

"Looks like it would be more than fine," the feminine one murmured, and the others threw back their heads and laughed.

"Let's do it!" the second one exclaimed.

"I want to finish my tea," the feminine one said primly. "It's good."

When they were done, the three of them stood up with the grace of dancers and led Swan to the edge of the pool, where a few people were already swimming, some clothed, some bare. There were small children in the shallowest pool, where a fountain of water fell on a rounded little roof and made a water-walled refuge. Swan's three hosts put down their lunch gear on the deck and then pulled their dresses over their heads and walked over to the water. The feminine one was slight and girlish, and the other two had the willowy bodies of gynandromorphs: slightly wide hips, rounded pecs that were not quite breasts, in-between torso-to-leg ratio and waist-to-hip ratio, furry genitals that appeared to be mostly female, but with dark masses that might have been small penises and testicles, like Swan's—one couldn't say more without a further exploration. Although it would prove little, as genitals would be far easier to simulate than hands, being already rubbery.

Into the water then. Swan saw that they swam well, almost floated; seemed to have the same specific gravity as human beings. Probably not steel bones, then. Probably not a completely machine interior, covered by a layer of grown flesh and skin. Taking a deep breath floated them, almost, just like it did her. Their eyes too—their eyes blinked, stared, glanced sidelong, were wet. Could you make every part of a human, put it all together, and have it work? Print up a composite? It seemed unlikely. Nature itself was not that good at it, she thought as her bad knee twinged. To make a simulacrum . . . well, maybe you could focus on just the functional aspects. But wasn't that what brains did too?

"You silly girls are kind of amazing," Swan said. "I can't figure you out."

They laughed.

"No real people would spend all day pretending to a stranger that they were robots," Swan objected. "You must be robots."

"The oddest things are most likely to be true," the second one said. "It's a well-recognized test in Bible exegesis. They think Jesus probably did curse a fig tree, or else why have the story in there?"

More laughter. They really were silly girls. Maybe you could make a robot think only up to the level of a twelve-year-old.

But the way they swam. The way they walked. These were hard things to do; or so it seemed.

"This is weird," she said to herself, pleased. She had thought it was going to be easy.

As she walked into a knee-deep area of the pool, they stared up at her frankly, as she had stared at them.

"Ooh, nice legs," the third one said. "Nice *body*."

"Thank you," Swan said, over the moans of the other two. The feminine one exclaimed, "No, that's not all right to say, some people are offended by comments about the aesthetic impacts of their bodies on others!"

"I'm not," Swan offered.

"All right, good then," said the feminine one.

"I was only being polite," said the third one.

"You were being forward. You had no idea whether it was polite or not."

"It was just a compliment. There's no reason to be overfine about such things. If you stray over limits, people will simply assume you don't know the protocols of their culture but are well-intentioned nevertheless."

"*People* will, but how do you know this person isn't a simulacrum, sent here to test us?"

And they laughed till they choked, splashing each other all the while. Swan joined the splashing, then sat in the water and ottered around them for a while. Then she seized the third one to her and kissed it on the mouth. The nondescript kissed back for a second, then pulled away. "Hey what's this! I don't know you well enough for this, I don't think!"

"So what? Didn't you like it?" And Swan kissed it again, followed its twists away, feeling its tongue be surprised to be touched by another tongue.

Pulling away, the nondescript said, "Hey! Hey! Hey! Stop!"

The feminine one had stood up and taken a step toward them, as if to intervene, and Swan turned and pushed her off her feet, so that she splashed hard into the shallow water. "What are you doing!" the girl cried fearfully, and Swan popped her on the mouth with a left jab. Immediately the girl's head flew back and her mouth started to bleed, and she cried out and rushed away. The two nondescripts splashed between her and Swan, blocking Swan from her, shouting at Swan to get back. Swan raised her fists and howled as she pummeled them, and they splashed backward to get away from her, amazed and appalled. Swan stopped following them, and after they climbed out of the pool they stopped and huddled together, looking back at her, the hurt one holding her mouth. Red blood.

Swan put her hands on her hips and stared at them. "Pretty interesting," she said. "But I don't like being fooled." She slogged through the water toward her clothes.

She walked back around the cylinder, looking up at a herd of wild horses and kissing her sore knuckles, thinking it over. She wasn't sure what kind of things she had spent the day with. That was strange.

When she got back to their hilltop yurts, she waited until Genette and she were again the last two up, and then she said, "I ran into a trio of people today who claimed to be artificial people. Androids with qube brains."

Genette stared at her. "You did?"

"I did."

"So what did you do?"

"Well, I beat the shit out of them."

"You did?"

"A little bit, one of them, yes. But she had it coming."

"Because?"

"Because they were fooling with me."

"Isn't that kind of like what you do in your abramovics?"

"Not at all. I never fool people, that would be theater. An abramovic is not theater."

"Well, maybe they weren't either," Genette said, frowning. "This has to be looked into. There have been reports on Venus and Mars of various incidents like this. Rumors of qube humanoids, sometimes acting oddly. We've started keeping an eye out. Some of these people have been tagged and are being tracked."

"So there really are such things?"

"I think so, yes. We've scanned some, and then of course it's obvious. But we don't know much more at this point."

"But why would anyone do it?"

"Don't know. But if there were qubes that were mobile, and moving around without being noticed, it would explain quite a few things that have happened. So I'll have my team take a look at these people you met."

"I think they were people," Swan said. "They were putting on an act."

"You think they were real people, pretending to be simulacra? As some kind of theater?"

"Yes."

"But why?"

"I don't know. Why would a person get in a box and pretend to be a mechanical chess player? It's an old dream. A kind of theater."

"Maybe. But I'm going to look into it anyway, because of these odd things happening."

"Fine," Swan said. "But I think they were people. Anyway, say they weren't. What's the problem with these things, if things they are?"

"The problem is qubes getting out in the world, moving around and doing things. What are they doing? What are they supposed to be doing? Who's making them? And since there is a qube component to the attacks we've seen, we have to wonder, do these things have anything to do with that? Are some of them involved?"

"Hmm," Swan said.

"Maybe they all come to one question," the inspector said. "Why are the qubes changing?"

Lists (7)

inadvertent fracking—failed seal—bad lock—bad luck—hyperbaric spark fire—carbon monoxide buildup—carbon dioxide buildup—design flaw—engine housing crack—sudden air loss—solar flare—fuel impurity—metal fatigue—mental fatigue—lightning strike—meteorite strike—accidental critical mass—brake failure—dropped tool—tripped and fell—coolant loss—manufacturing flaw—programming error—human error—containment failure—battery fire—distraction—AI malfeasance—sabotage—bad decision—crossed wires—recreational mental impairment—cosmic ray impact—

(from *The Journal of Space Accidents*
vol. 297, 2308)

Extracts (8)

Charlotte Shortback's periodizing system was very influential. Of course, the idea of periodization itself is controversial and even suspect, as it seems often to be a matter of squinting hard and waving one's hands in belletristic fashion to make sock puppet myths out of the dense "buzzing and blooming confusion" of the documented past. Nevertheless, there do seem to be differences in human life between, for instance, the Middle Ages and the Renaissance, or the Enlightenment and the Postmodern; and whether these differences were caused by changes in modes of production, structures of feeling, scientific paradigms, dynastic succession, technological progress, or cultural metamorphosis, it almost doesn't matter. The shapes invoked make a pattern, they tell a story that people can follow.

Thus for a long time there was a widely agreed-upon periodization schema that included the feudal period and the Renaissance, followed by the Early Modern (seventeenth and eighteenth centuries), the Modern (nineteen and twentieth), and the Postmodern (twentieth and twenty-first)—after which a new name was most definitely needed. For a long time this need generated competing new systems, and that competition, along with the generally microfine narratology of the historians of the time, combined to foil the invention of any new system that was as universally agreed-upon as the old one had been. It was only in the last years of the twenty-third century that Charlotte Shortback offered to the historical community her own periodization scheme, for what was by now the "long postmodern" so endlessly bemoaned at conferences. Hers was partly a joke, she later claimed, but it has become influential since then despite that, or even perhaps because of it.

For Shortback, the long postmodern was to be divided like this:

The Dithering: 2005 to 2060. From the end of the postmodern (Charlotte's date derived from the UN announcement of climate change) to the fall into crisis. These were wasted years.

The Crisis: 2060 to 2130. Disappearance of Arctic summer ice, irreversible permafrost melt and methane release, and unavoidable commitment to major sea rise. In these years all the bad trends converged in "perfect storm" fashion, leading to a rise in average global temperature of five K, and sea level rise of five meters—and as a result, in the 2120s, food shortages, mass riots, catastrophic death on all continents, and an immense spike in the extinction rate of other species. Early lunar bases, scientific stations on Mars.

The Turnaround: 2130 to 2160. *Verteswandel* (Shortback's famous "mutation of values"), followed by revolutions; strong AI; self-replicating factories; terraforming of

Mars begun; fusion power; strong synthetic biology; climate modification efforts, including the disastrous Little Ice Age of 2142–54; space elevators on Earth and Mars; fast space propulsion; the space diaspora begun; the Mondragon Accord signed. And thus:

The Accelerando: 2160 to 2220. Full application of all the new technological powers, including human longevity increases; terraforming of Mars and subsequent Martian revolution; full diaspora into solar system; hollowing of the terraria; start of the terraforming of Venus; the construction of Terminator; and Mars joining the Mondragon Accord.

The Ritard: 2220 to 2270. Reasons for the slowing of the Accelerando are debated, but historians have pointed to the completion of Mars's terraforming, its withdrawal from the Mondragon and increasing isolationism, the occupation of all the best terrarium candidates, and the nearly total human entrainment of the solar system's easily available helium, nitrogen, rare earths, fossil fuels, and photosynthesis. It was also becoming clear that the longevity project was encountering problems, and was not completely distributed in any case. Recently some historians have pointed out that this was also the time when quantum computers reached thirty qubits and were combined with petaflop classical computers to make qubes—their point being that qubes have not yet been demonstrated to improve the function of already fast AIs, while the decoherence problems inherent in quantum computing may have helped create conditions for the next period:

The Balkanization: 2270 to 2320. Mars-Earth tension, aggression, and cold war for control of the solar system;

Mars isolationism; Venus internal strife; decision in the Jovian moons to terraform their big three; proliferation of the unaffiliated terraria, and the disappearance of many populations behind "event horizons"; influence of qubes; volatile shortages pinching harder, causing hoarding, then tribalism; tragedy of the commons redux; splintering into widespread "self-sufficient" enclave city-states.

The term "hyperbalkanization" Shortback considers just an artifact of overheated rhetoric in cultural studies.

She has said, however, that a significant prolongation of the Balkanization could perhaps lead to a period worse than the Ritard, or even the Crisis—perhaps a time that could be called the Atomization, or the Dissolution.

She tells a story about how once in a talk she suggested that the entirety of the last millennium could be called the late feudal period, and afterward a man came up to her and said, "What makes you think it's *late?*"

But what happened in 2312 suggests that the twenty-fourth century will mark a turn

IAPETUS

Iapetus looks like a walnut, because it is squashed at the poles, and has a prominent equatorial bulge, both quite visible from space. Why is it squashed at the poles? At one point it was melted and became a big water drop rotating rapidly, its days only seventeen hours long; something passing by set it spinning like a top. It froze while still spinning. So, why the prominent equatorial bulge? No one knows. Some aspect of the freezing of water drop to ice ball, most agree, some kind of surge or excess. But it's something saturnologists still argue about.

Whatever caused it, the bulge immediately suggested itself as an obvious location for a city, as it could serve as something like a High Street peninsula running all the way around the moon. The city was concentrated at first on the hemisphere facing Saturn, which looms overhead four times larger than Luna from Earth. This was felt worth having in one's sky, especially since Iapetus's orbit is at a seventeen-degree tilt from the plane of Saturn's rings, giving it a perpetually changing view of the gorgeous mobile. Almost all the other moons see the rings only edge on. From the Iapetus bulge one also has a view down to the rest of the moon's surface, twelve or sixteen kilometers lower than the bulge, so there is always a broad icescape below to balance the sublime ringed pearl above.

What color the moon's surface is depends on where you are looking, because the leading hemisphere of Iapetus is quite black, while the trailing hemisphere is extremely white. This stark discrepancy, noted by Cassini in October of 1671 when he discovered Iapetus, is a result of the moon being tidally locked. The same hemisphere always leads the charge into the night, and black dust shed by the retrograde moon Phoebe (the other one out of the plane of the rings) therefore always falls on that side. In four billion years the dust has accumulated to a depth of only a few centimeters. Meanwhile the trailing hemisphere of the moon, gathering frost from the ice subliming off the darker leading side, is among the whitest ice in the whole system. The result is a two-toned moon, the only one in the solar system.

When people came to occupy Iapetus, the top of the equatorial band was smoothed and fitted with a rock-and-aluminum foundation. They then began to use seashell genes to shape the structures of the equatorial city. Some of the flat top of the bulge has been left open for spaceport runways and the like, but most of the bulge is now covered by a long clear gallery tent, placed over buildings that line the great boulevard of the High Street, alternating with farms, parks, gardens, and forests. As the air under the tent is always kept warm, the interior architecture can be very open, with Saturn often left visible, framed by gaps in ceilings and roofs. Seashell biomimicry allowed the builders to extract and deploy calcium under mantles, and these soft living tissues were genetically engineered to shapes that allowed the architects to layer bioceramic stuctures one on the next, building structure on structure, like corals, until the area under the tent by now is almost full. Like most bioceramics structures, the beveled and layered shapes have been induced to produce scalloping, fanning, notching, and other conchological features, so that the buildings look like great seashells stacked one on the next. Sydney is often referenced because of its iconic opera house, but in fact the bulge now looks more like a Great Barrier Reef made of scallops layered and everywhere holed, as if by tube worms, to let in the view of Saturn overhead.

On the black hemisphere, Cassini Regio, the bulge bisects an area where people once upon a time went out in hoppers or rovers and blew the black dust away to make patterns out of exposed white ice. Anytime you can easily make such a contrast in the landscape, people have written out their thoughts for the universe to read. Before the Saturn League was formed, when the first arrivals from Mars had come for Titan's nitrogen, and were exploring the other moons as well for whatever else might be plundered and taken back to the red planet, people had come here and etched white out of the black. An exhalation no stronger than a leaf blower's would do the job, and soon great fields of Cassini Regio were covered like Newspaper Rock with petroglyphs. There were white-on-black figures in abstract patterns, beasts, stick people, Kokopellis, writing in many different alphabets, portraits, landscape features, trees and other plants; on and on it went. Later some entire areas were cleared completely to white and then painted with collected black dust to a greater or lesser depth, achieving shadings that had a sometimes trompe l'oeil depth of field, proportioned for viewing such that they looked normal when viewed from the bulge, with others designed to be viewed from space.

Graffiti on Iapetus! Later it was declared a mistake and a scandal, a moral stupidity, even a crime, in any case disgusting; and there were calls for the entirety of Cassini Regio to be reblacked. Someday it may happen, but don't hold your breath, for the truth is we are here to inscribe ourselves on the universe, and it is not inappropriate to remind ourselves of this when blank slates are given us. All landscape art reminds us: we live in a tabula rasa, and must write on it. It is our world, and its beauty is entirely inside our heads. Even today people will sometimes go out over the horizon and scuff their initials in the dust.

WAHRAM AT HOME

Wahram returned to Saturn a haunted androgyn. Despite all his theories, he was still in the tunnel. He tried to get back into the pseudoiterative of his life on Iapetus, and indeed in some ways it was easy; it wasn't a life he was ever going to forget. For a day or two it was possible to feel odd to be in a city you hadn't been in for years and yet magically wake up knowing right where to go, the little grocery around the corner where you could get fresh bread and milk and all that; then the intervening years sloughed away and it was just home again. Off for the walk to work, down the long esplanade by the north window wall, overlooking the immense drop down the slope of the bulge. Black-tipped whites at the border of the Cassini region: a vast Chinese landscape painting, black brush tips on white paper. At the notch of one little small square, the council offices were up in a squat clear-walled tower, offices with lots of people he knew; it was like dropping back into an earlier reincarnation. He could reenact it meticulously; he could perform it like an actor in a play set in the previous century; he could make it a daily devotional, live ordinary life as a déjà vu that he invoked himself—but no.

No. Because the much more strict pseudoiterative of the tunnel still filled his mind, and overlaid the sensations of the present moment. And as Iapetus in the present was for the most part an Iapetus reenacted, much more vivid to him was that more recent past consisting of what he had just lived through with his so-mercurial friend. And he wondered about her. The mercurialities of Swan were infinite, but she had gone through quite a bit down there, and so had he. She had protected him at the elevator door, just as a matter of course, the obvious thing to do, with no time to think; just an animal response. And with far too much time to think, he had helped her through her radiation sickness.

So when he thought he wasn't thinking of anything, he found himself whistling snatches of Beethoven, and hearing over it a skylark filigree of inhuman virtuosity. He wondered what they had really sounded like, and if Pauline had recorded the entire time and could carve out and play back the music they had made—another kind of transcription. All those poor musicians... Maybe a record was always a distorter of memory, not to be sought. Better to hear it by way of reenactment. He would only really hear it again if they did it again.

No. He needed to think about something else, and bring himself into the present. Possibly he would see Swan again somewhere, and they would whistle then, or not. Probably not, this being the world. So... recent or not, the past was the past; the present was the only reality. So really, it was necessary to start up a new pseudoiterative that did not rely so fully on his habits from three or four lives back. He needed a new Iapetus, with the memory of Swan properly encoded into it.

So he would walk down High Street to the park with the best view of Saturn for an evening constitutional, for a communing with the great ringed god, and perhaps a chance to see Titan-his-true-home spangling over the giant like a jewel; and just the act of trudging to the park would bring a whole host of feelings to him; and in the park a small gathering of musicians would pass around the chance to start up a tune and have everyone join in, and he could either listen, or venture to whistle along—even to whistle the start of some movement when it was his turn—end of the Sixth, end of the Seventh—and they all would join in on their instruments and off they would go. With Saturn overhead, and some truly gifted musicians in the little band, he would be snagged by the moment, fully entangled, and Swan would be there with him in his mind. What a temper she had.

Then on days when the council and various work groups weren't meeting, he could tram around the city four degrees, and come to the gate for the ski boats, and get in one and take off down the gigantic side of the Iapetus bulge, in this region an undulant slope of black-tipped white billows, in some parts like a shaken sheet of snow, in others like frozen waves in a waterslide. There were moguls the size of big hills. Down the great hill of the bulge's side the ski boats would slide, carving lines and performing jumps and rollers, if desired; but also one could simply cut a line and keep to it on a long traverse, or even fly straight down the slope, a forty-five-degree drop, and even at the highest speed the descent took all day. Rides went on so long that many people slid down on larger boats to have a party, and on some days Wahram tried that too. Then at the bottom they got into funiculars for a ride back up, during which everyone was in high spirits, often expressed in song. People shared schnapps and sang Schubert. Wahram had done these things long before, in the first year he had lived in Iapetus, but somehow they had dropped out of his habits and been forgotten. Now thinking of Swan had brought them back into his life.

Even his work brought Swan to mind, as the council and its staff were discussing what to do about the light deal with the Vulcanoids now that Terminator had been destroyed. Wahram pointed out to his colleagues that Terminator would be quickly rebuilt and repopulated, and thus remain a treaty partner with whom they already had an agreement. Alex's death did not change that agreement. He could see that while this was obviously the case, stating it aloud only tagged him among his colleagues as biased, which was true, so after that he went silent and only listened to what the others said about it, which really was nothing surprising: many of them had not liked the arrangement with Mercury in the first place, and now they reverted to these views and argued that they should be making their deals with some kind of Vulcanoid league, or even with individual Vulcanoids. These were not, after all, spaceships, but small asteroids located in the gravitationally stable orbit between .06 and .21 astronomical units from the sun—thirty-kilometer rocks, white-hot on their sunward surfaces, and just big enough to spin out their solettas and contain in their interiors the little habitats that their operators or votaries lived in. These were city-states just like any other city-states, some of Wahram's colleagues insisted, and should not be represented by some exterior power like Terminator, no matter what Alex had asserted. How would the city-states of the Saturn League like it if some Jovian party claimed to represent them just because it orbited between Saturn and the rest of civilization? Wasn't that ultimately the argument that Terminator had been making in this case? Wasn't this in fact yet another move in what some had called the Alexandrine Integration, the offline effort to bypass the AIs and unify the entire system—under Alex?

Not exactly, others had replied, to Wahram's relief, as he had been working with Alex on precisely this project, which was not exactly as characterized by these colleagues but would be difficult to explain in the context of that accusation. Much better to observe silently and let the argument drag on in the long and leisurely way typical of the council, until it had moved on its own to something else. The councilors from Hyperion and Tethys were the main reasons this would take a while; they were both very long-winded, also maniacally focused on the minutiae of matters they took an interest in. The council was one of the many organizations in the Saturn League made up of drafted temporary workers, and the permanent staff there to assist them often had to Sir Humphrey the process along, guiding their employers invisibly through every decision. But some of the ministers, having been selected by lottery and assigned a year's responsibility for the Saturn system's welfare, intended to be in full command of their own decisions, and to make the best decisions they could by being fully informed. Admirable in theory, it was painfully slow in practice.

So in this discussion the dispute kept on seesawing between the idea that Mercury was the legitimate, or in any case agreed-upon, broker in the matter, and furthermore could make things difficult—and besides had things to offer Saturn and the idea that the Mercurials were interlopers who had succeeded in imposing a protection racket on the new little settlements inside it, and so should be finessed out of the deal in this their winter of discontent.

Ultimately the council came to a conclusion Wahram had foreseen hours before: as Wahram himself was so sympathetic to the Mercurials, he was to return there and see what the situation was, talk to the lion cubs and find out who the next Lion would be, and then also go visit the Vulcanoids and see what they had to say for themselves—see what they thought of the arrangement Mercury had proposed to Saturn. He was instructed to revise Terminator out of the deal if he thought that would work.

Probably he should have refused to do it based on his dislike for that last instruction, but it occurred to him that a different delegate might mean an even worse result for the Mercurials. And after all, the assignment meant he would very soon return sunward, which was interesting to contemplate. As for his instructions, he could see about that when he got there. In Alex's realm in particular, an ambassador was again as of old, a diplomat at large, charged with making decisions as well as conveying them. By the time he got there it could very well be a different story. With a little forethought, he could be almost sure it would be a different story.

So he said nothing beyond a simple acceptance of the assignment.

At which point the Satyr of Pan stood to speak. "You must tell us if you think this effort will make trouble for the other projects Alex had going. Can you remind the council what's at stake here, and how those projects are going in her absence?"

Wahram nodded stiffly as he thought over his response. He and the other Alexandrines were attempting to keep a low profile, and some of the council members had not paid enough attention to notice their projects' authorization and budgeting inside larger expenditures. "Alex kept things separate in her calculations, so that won't be a problem for us. Some other matters are being dealt with by a group centered around Wang and Inspector Jean Genette. We would need to go under a cone of silence to discuss all this in detail, but suffice it to say, Alex was heavily involved with a Mondragon project to help Earth cope with its various problems by ecological means. A lot of the terraria in the Mondragon are working on that, it has its own momentum, and we've agreed to help them. Then also there is an investigation going on into the role of qubes in some questionable activities, on Mars, Venus, Io, and elsewhere. This also will proceed no matter what happens with the Vulcanoids, which is only an above and beyond, although admittedly an important one."

The council, not wanting to retire into the cone and be cut off from the cloud and radio, adjourned the meeting. Wahram returned to his room. His crèche kept an apartment in a little block of apartments, all clustered around a square that was occupied almost entirely by Titans, with Titanic shops and restaurants. There he lived among his crèchemates and enjoyed their support, which was so benign and understanding that life there much resembled living in complete solitude. As the days passed before the spaceliner that would take him downsystem arrived, he walked the city spine to the council meetings, he followed the work on Titan in daily consultations, and he did his share of Iapetus work in the kitchen of the dining hall on the ground floor of their building. He attended a concert series, joined the little group of musicians in the park, filled and emptied dishwashers. As he dodged diners and servers in the hall, the repeated minuscule navigational challenges reminded him of Proust's comparison of a restaurant in action with the whirling planets of the solar system, which had struck him as fanciful (not to mention quite a scale shift between vehicle and tenor) until he had seen it for himself, in restaurant after restaurant: their affairs were elaborations of the second law of thermodynamics, Beckian diffusions of energy through the universe, and around they went in the great orrery of their lives. Soon he would descend sunward and seek out the Mercurial.

But then she called him. She was coming to Saturn, with Jean Genette; they wanted to descend into the clouds of Saturn to look for a spaceship possibly adrift in the big beauty's upper layers. She wanted him to arrange the dive into Saturn, if possible, and then join them in it.

"That would be fine," he replied; "I am at your disposal." Which was certainly one way of putting it.

Lists (8)

Prometheus, Pandora, Janus, Epimetheus, and Mimas; these are the moons that shepherd Saturn's rings.

The rings are only 400 million years old, the result of a passing Kuiper belt ice asteroid being stripped to its core when it passed Saturn too closely.

Mimas, the bull's-eye moon, is 400 kilometers in diameter, while its crater Herschel is 140. The Herschel impact nearly blew Mimas apart.

Hyperion is a fragment of a similar collision that did blow a moon apart; it is shaped like a hockey puck. The impact caused flash steam explosions across a plane and split the moon as if spalling granite. The facet left behind is pocked like a wasps' nest by a field of rimless dust-filled craters.

Pandora is shaped like a jelly bean.

Tethys and Dione were both about 1,100 kilometers across (think France), both fractured all over their surfaces, etched by canyons with mile-high walls. Tethys's Ithaca Chasma is twice as deep and four times as long as the Grand Canyon, and a thousand times older, very battered by Saturn's everlasting civil wars.

Dione, on the other hand, was disassembled by self-replicating ice cutters in the 2110s, and the Hector-sized segments were then directed downsystem to Venus. They struck Venus on a line parallel to the equator and provided Venus with a deep ocean bed and the water to fill it, while also knocking a good bit of the choking Venusian atmosphere off into space.

Rhea is as wide as Alaska, with the usual plethora of craters, including fresh ones that throw bright ice rays out from their centers.

Iapetus orbits seventeen degrees out of the plane of Saturn's equator and thus has one of the best views of the rings; is therefore popular. The bulge is the biggest city in the Saturnian system.

Epimetheus is a misshapen pile of loosely consolidated rubble. It switches orbits with the moon Janus every eight years; they are co-orbital moons, very rare—a sign of past impacts.

Enceladus is covered by braided spills of ice. No craters—the ice surface is too new, as it is continuously resurfaced from the liquid-water ocean in the depths. Heat sources boil some of this carbonized water, creating geysers that shoot many kilometers into space. The water quickly freezes in its flight, and some of it makes it up to the slender E ring; the rest falls back down and under its own weight turns to firn and then back to ice again. A suite of microscopic life-forms was discovered in the Enceladan ocean in the year 2244, and scientific stations have been established on its surface, as well as a cult of votaries who ingest a suite of the alien life-forms, to unknown effect.

There are twenty-six irregular small moons. These are all Kuiper belt objects, captured as they crossed Saturn's earliest gas envelope. Phoebe, at 220 kilometers across, is the largest of these, and it has a retrograde and highly inclined orbit, twenty-six degrees out of the plane; thus another popular viewing platform.

Titan, by far the largest Saturnian moon, is bigger than Mercury or Pluto. More about Titan later.

Extracts (9)

One question for computability: is the problem capable of producing a result

If a finite number of steps will produce an answer, it is a problem that can be solved by a Turing machine

Is the universe itself the equivalent of a Turing machine? This is not yet clear

Turing machines can't always tell when the result has been obtained. No oracle machine is capable of solving its own halting problem

A Turing jump operator assigns to each problem X a successively harder problem, X prime. Setting a Turing machine the problem of making its own Turing jump creates a recursive effect called the Ouroboros

All problems solvable by quantum computers are also solvable by classical computers. Making use of quantum mechanical phenomena only increases speed of operation

two popular physical mechanisms, dots and liquids. Quantum dots are electrons trapped inside a cage of atoms, then excited by laser beams to superposed positions, then pushed to one state or the other. Quantum liquids (often caffeine molecules because of the many nuclei in them) are magnetically forced to spin all their nuclei in the same spin state; then NMR techniques detect and flip the spins

Decoherence happens at the loss of superposition and the resulting either/or. Before that a quantum calculation performs in parallel every possible value that the register can represent

Using superposition for computation requires avoiding decoherence for as long as possible. This has proved difficult and is still the limiting factor in the size and power of a quantum computer. Various physical and chemical means for building and connecting qubits have increased the number of qubits possible to connect before decoherence collapses the calculation, but

Quantum computers are restricted to calculations that can be performed faster than decoherence occurs in the superposed wave functions. For over a century this restricted time for a quantum computing operation to less than ten seconds

Qubes are room-temperature quantum computers with thirty qubits, the decoherence boundary limit for circuit-connected qubits, combined with a petaflop-speed classical computer to stabilize operations and provide a database. The most powerful qubes are theoretically capable of calculating the movements of all the atoms in the sun and its solar system out to the edge of the solar wind

Qubes are only faster than classical computers when they can exploit quantum parallelism. At multiplication they are no faster. But in factoring there is a difference: to factor a thousand-digit number would take a classical computer ten million billion billion years (lifetime of universe, 13.7 billion years); using Shor's algorithm, a qube takes around twenty minutes

Grover's algorithm means that a yearlong search using a classical computer in a random walk of a billion searches a second would take a qube in its quantum walk 185 searches

Shor's algorithm, Grover's algorithm, Perelman's algorithm, Sikorski's algorithm, Ngyuen's algorithm, Wang's algorithm, Wang's other algorithm, the Cambridge algorithm, the Livermore algorithm,

entanglement is also susceptible to decoherence. Physical linkage of quantum circuits is necessary to forestall decoherence to useful time frames. Premature or undesired decoherence sets a limit on how powerful qubes can become, but the limit is high

it has proved easier to manipulate superposition than entanglement for computing purposes, and therein lies the explanation of many

The quantum database is effectively distributed over a multitude of universes

the two polarized particles decohere simultaneously no matter the physical distance between them, meaning the information jump can exceed the speed of light. The effect was confirmed by experiment in the late twentieth century. Any device that uses this phenomenon to communicate messages is called an ansible, and these devices have been constructed, but undesired decoherence has meant the maximum distance between ansibles has been nine centimeters, and this only when both were cooled to one millionth of a K above absolute zero. Physical limitations strongly suggest further progress will be asymptotic at best

powerful but isolated and discrete, somewhat like brains

questions of Penrose quantum effects in the brain have been effectively rendered moot, as these also occur in qubes by definition. If both structures are quantum computers, and one of them we are quite certain has consciousness, who is to say what's going on in the other

human brain operations have a maximum theoretical speed of 10^{16} operations per second

computers have become billions to trillions times faster than human brains. So it comes down to programming; what are the operations actually doing

hierarchical levels of thought, generalization, mood, affect, will

super-recursive algorithms, hypercomputation, super-tasks, trial-and-error predicates, inductive inference machines, evolutionary computers, fuzzy computation, transrecursive operators,

if you program a purpose into a computer program, does that constitute its will? Does it have free will, if a programmer programmed its purpose? Is that programming any different from the way we are programmed by our genes and brains? Is a programmed will a servile will? Is human will a servile will? And is not the servile will the home and source of all feelings of defilement, infection, transgression, and rage?

could a quantum computer program itself?

WAHRAM AND SWAN AND GENETTE

Wahram saw Swan emerge from the lock door, looking around for him, and when she saw him, he waved, and then she did too, her expression pinched, he thought, her head tilted to the side. She looked at him in quick glances—she didn't know how he would be. Suddenly he remembered that in the actual flesh she was a big bag of problems. He nodded a little deeper than he would have normally, trying to reassure her, and then thought that that might not be enough, and extended both hands, realizing as he did so that he was already back in a different world, Swancentric and intense. She threw herself on him in a rush, and he felt sure it looked like he was hugging back, or had even invited the hug.

Jean Genette emerged from the lock and stood looking up at them and was greeted by Wahram.

"So you want to find one of the hanging ships?" he said.

They did. Apparently it might have something to do

with the attack on Terminator. So Wahram led them across the spaceport to the gate for the railgun launcher angled to send ferries into polar orbits around Saturn. These orbits were popular for viewing the rings and the hexagonal storm at Saturn's south pole. Wahram had already gotten permission from the authorities to take a cloud diver into the upper reaches of the planet; probably the council was happy to have him involved, as the Saturnian liaison to the incursion.

They took off with only a pilot and crew aboard with them, and after they were cast toward the north pole, Swan and the inspector told Wahram what they had been doing since they'd left Mercury. Wahram, feeling uneasy that he could not fully reciprocate and tell them about his activities, given the council's orders, compensated by asking them a lot of questions about the investigation and its results so far. These turned out to be very interesting, even disturbing, and Wahram pondered to the point of a certain distraction the idea that there might be someone out there killing whole terraria. That the investigation had reduced their likeliest suspect pool to the population of Earth did not strike him as remarkable progress. All trouble comes from Earth, as the saying had it.

The cloud diver was not a big ship, and though it was very fast, the trip still took long enough for Swan to begin to exhibit the signs of distress and antsiness he remembered so well. Then happily they were above Saturn's north pole, looking down at the dark side of the rings, as it was the northern winter. From behind the sun the rings were peach in tone, the circumferential scoring so finely etched and yet so vast that one could not help being a bit taken aback. Even on their dark side the rings were far brighter than the nightside of the planet, making for an aura or halo effect of eldritch beauty, all framing the deep blue of Saturn's winter north.

Swan stared out the window, floating in her restraints, for the moment speechless. Wahram enjoyed this response, and not just because of the relief of the sudden silence. For him the polar view of Saturn was a perpetually glorious thing, the finest view in the solar system.

Down they dove toward the big planet, until it lost its sphericity and became a gorgeous pastel cobalt— the blue floor of the universe, it seemed, with the black of space only slightly domed over it. It looked almost like two planes only slightly separated, blue and black, meeting at the horizon like planes in elliptic geometry.

Soon after that they were down among the stupendous thunderhead armadas tearing east in this particular zone, around the seventy-fifth latitude. Royal blue, turquoise, indigo, robin's egg—an infinity of blue clouds, it seemed. In the latitudinal band farther south the wind flew hard in the opposite direction; two thousand–kilometer–per–hour jet streams were therefore running against each other, making the shear zone a wild space of whirlpooling tornadoes. It was important to keep a distance from such a violent interface, but as the latitudinal bands were thousands of kilometers wide, this was not difficult.

Unlike Jupiter, there were no radiation fields created by the smaller giant, so over years a not-insignificant population of floating ships had taken refuge in the upper clouds of Saturn; also some platform habitats, hung from immense balloons. The balloons had to be exceptionally large to provide any buoyancy, but once they did, the clouds provided shelter that was variously

physical, legal, and psychological. The league kept
track of these cloud floaters when possible, but if they
sank deep enough in the clouds and went quiet, they
could be elusive.

Now their little diver flew among thunderheads a
hundred kilometers tall, and though it was a common-
place to say that perspective was lost in situations like
this, such that all sizes looked much the same, it wasn't
really true: these thunderheads were clearly as big as
entire asteroids, rising out of a deeper array of flatter
cloud formations so that they saw below them masses
of nimbus and cirrus, cumulus, festoons, barges—
really the whole Howard catalog, all snarling through
and over and under each other and constituting what
passed for the surface of the gas giant. Off to the distant south they could still sometimes make out the
nearest shear line and its ripping tornado funnels, its
broad-domed hurricane tops. Sometimes in the middle
of their own band they flew over a slower funnel and
could look deep into the blue depths of the planet, gas-
eous for as far as they could see and much farther, but
in appearance much like holes of mist that gathered at
their bottoms to liquid. Every once in a while a high
stray cloud would prove unavoidable, and the view out
of the craft would suddenly reduce to a dim blue flashing, and a tumultuous tremor would buck the craft in
ways that even the quickness of the pilot AIs could not
entirely damp. They would tremble and toss until they
regained the clear blue again, now bluer than ever. For
the most part they moved downstream with the flow of
the wind, but also made the occasional reach across it.
Resisting the wind too much threw them around about
as much as being inside a cloud.

Ahead they could see their canyon of clear space

narrowing until it was pinched to nothingness. Beyond that swirled a hurricane so big it could have floated the Earth on it like St. Brendan's coracle. "We have to go over that," their captain said, and with a sweet curve their craft ascended until the flat dome of the hurricane lay spinning below them. Overhead, the steady stars stood in their customary places.

"Are there fliers?" Swan asked. "Does anybody fly these cloud canyons in birdsuits?"

Wahram said, "Yes, a few. Usually they're scientists doing their work. Until recently it has been considered too dangerous to visit. So this space has not yet been cultured to the extent you are used to elsewhere."

Swan shook her head. "You probably just don't know about them."

"Perhaps. But I think I would."

"You don't come down here often yourself?"

"No."

"Will you go flying down here with me?"

"I don't know how to fly."

"You could let the birdsuit's AI do it, and merely be a passenger making requests."

"Is it ever more than that?"

"Of course it is." She gave him a disgusted look. "People fly any space in the solar system that can be flown. Our bird brains demand it."

"I'm sure they do."

"So you'll go with me." She nodded as if she had won an argument and gotten a promise from him.

Wahram tucked his chin into his neck. "So you are a flier, then?"

"Whenever I can."

He didn't know what to say. If he was going to be badgered by this kind of peremptory bullying and yet still he expected to love her, then he refused! But it might be that it was already too late for that. The hooks were already in him pretty deep; he could feel them tugging in his chest; he was in fact hooked; he was very, very interested in whatever she might say or do. He was even willing to consider stupidities like birdflight in the clouds of Saturn. How could it be? To a woman not even his type—ah, Marcel, if only you knew—this Swan was worse even than Odette.

"Maybe someday," he said, trying to sound agreeable. "But right now we are looking for this ship of yours."

"Indeed," Inspector Genette interjected. "And we appear to be nearing it."

They kept descending, dove into another cloud. The ship vibrated tremulously, constantly. Below them lay another thirty thousand kilometers of ever-thickening gas before one would hit the black layer of frozen goo, difficult to characterize, which was the planet's real "surface." It was said ships were hidden down there in the deeper depths, and Wahram had been worried that the one they sought would be down there too. But now there loomed out of a cloud to the south a spaceship, pewter against the blue, hanging under an enormous teardrop balloon. Then, like an apparition, it slipped back into the cloud from which it had emerged.

The abandoned ship drifted, swinging this way and that under its balloon. It was quite a bit darker in the cloud, a matter of chocolates briefly turning tangerine or bronze and then darkening again. To express the scene musically Wahram thought one might play Satie and Wagner together, a pin of sadness pricking the magniloquent thunderheads: this little lost ship.

They strapped into the cloud diver's hopper and it emerged from the dock, shuddering as the little craft fought the turbulence. Out of the mist loomed the dark mass of the silent ship. Wahram could not help thinking of the *Marie Celeste*, or Pap's houseboat on the river. He had to cast aside these old tales to focus on the thing at hand, a typical asteroid trawler by the look of it, with an old-fashioned deuterium-tritium fusion engine bulbing at its stern.

"Is this the one you want?" Wahram asked.

"I think so," Inspector Genette said. "Your system hit it with a taggart as it went in, and we're getting a ping from that taggart. Let's go have a look."

They docked with it, their pilot nicely finessing the delicate problem of contact in the fluctuating wind. When they were magnetically moored to it, the three of them and two more of Genette's colleagues suited up and went out, all of them on Ariadne lines.

Swan jetted over to the ship ahead of the others and touched down next to a lock door just ahead of the rocket bulb. When she hit the door pad, its red light went green, and the door opened. Then there was a flash of light, gone as soon as it flashed; Swan cried out.

Genette jetted to her side and floated over her shoulder like her good angel, pulling her back. "Wait a minute. I don't like that. And Passepartout tells me that a powerful radio signal has just been sent by the ship."

The little inspector jetted into the lock ahead of them, pulling a tool like a pair of bolt cutters from a thigh pocket. "Maybe it came from this." There was a box attached to the lock's inside door. "This is a tack-on of some sort. Some kind of little sentinel. May have taken your picture and transmitted it. Let's take it with us."

Swan pounded the lock wall next to the device. "Here we are! Fuck you!"

"They already know," Genette said, working at the little box as if it were an abalone. "But maybe we can turn the tables here. This ship will have a provenance, elements we can trace. We'll take its AI with us." The other Interplan investigators opened the inner lock door; the interior appeared to be as much a vacuum as space outside. Wahram followed the others inside. The interior lights were on, the bridge looked functional, and yet no air, no people.

"Everyone knows a ship has an ID," Wahram said. "Why would they hang the ship here? Why wouldn't they just dispose of it?"

"I don't know. Possibly they intended to use it again and didn't know about the Saturnian tracking system."

"I don't like it."

"Neither do I."

"Maybe this ship is from the unaffiliateds," Swan said. "Off record from the start."

"Are there ships entirely off the grid?" Wahram asked.

"Yes," Genette said briefly, plugging cords from Passepartout into ports on one of the consoles.

"I have its data," Passepartout said.

"Let's get out of here," Genette said. "Passepartout says the balloons holding this thing up have been punctured. They're big, but we need to get out of this thing before it starts falling fast."

They rushed through the short halls back to the lock. Their cloud diver's pilot was urgently requesting them to get back inside so it could delink; they were dropping into Saturn at an accelerating rate as the giant balloon over them emptied. Quickly they all five jammed into the lock, the inspector and two assistants taking up only small spaces in the upper corners, looking like spandrels. When the outer door opened, they jetted out into space. The balloon above the abandoned ship was already visibly deflated, thinner and creased and flapping. Nevertheless the Interplan smalls jetted around the hull, inspecting and photographing it by quadrants. "See there," Genette said to one of them. "Bolt holes. Get samples from the threading."

Then they returned to their cloud diver, reeling in on their Ariadne threads. When they were in the lock of the diver, they felt it come away from the abandoned ship and start to rise. They made their way to the bridge, where the pilot was too busy or too polite to comment on the situation. They rose, cutting through clouds overhead, shuddering hard.

"We're free of it," Genette said irritably to the pilot. "Slow down."

Wahram for one was happy to be rising at speed. In his youth people had not dived into the planet; it still struck him as an impudent thing, dangerous in the extreme.

When they were free of the clouds and back in a clear channel between masses, he relaxed a little. For a time, when they got high enough, they could see north and south to the bands in which the wind coursed in the opposite direction; these both had cloud levels slightly higher than theirs, so for a time it appeared they floated easily down a very broad canal, the banks of which were rushing madly upstream.

When they were a bit higher, Inspector Genette said to Swan, "We've got it confirmed. The ship is owned by a transport firm based on Earth. They never reported it missing. Last registered port of call was that asteroid we saw it on."

Swan nodded and looked at Wahram. "I'm going to Earth next," she said. "Do you want to come?"

Wahram said cautiously, "I have to go downsystem anyway. So I think I can meet you somewhere down there."

"That's good," she said. "We can work together there."

She seemed not to suspect him of any possibility of harm. Which was nice—even encouraging—but, unfortunately, incorrect.

He swallowed heavily. "Before you go—can I perhaps show you a bit of Saturn? There is a different kind of flying you might enjoy, in the rings. And I could introduce you to my crèche. To my family."

She was surprised by this, he could see. He swallowed again, tried to look bland under her sharp gaze.

"All right," she said.

SWAN AND THE RINGS OF SATURN

Inspector Genette and team had business to conduct in the Saturn system and would not be returning down-system for a while, so Swan was free to join Wahram as he had requested. His manner had been very odd, his gaze fixed on her, x-raying right through her—toad vision, yes. It reminded her of the look he had given her when she told him she had eaten the Enceladan alien suite; out of the fog of that whole incident, the look on his face was what she recalled—his surprise that anyone could be such a fool. Well, he had better get used to it. She was not normal; not even human, but some kind of symbiote. Ever since eating the aliens she had never felt the same—assuming there had ever been any same to begin with. Maybe it had always been true that colors burst in her head, that her sense of spaciousness was sharp to the point of pain or joy, her sense of significance likewise. Possibly the Enceladan bugs made no more difference than any of the other bugs in her gut. She was not sure what she was.

The look on Wahram's face seemed to suggest he felt much the same.

*   *   *

The visit with Wahram's crèche on Iapetus was just a matter of dropping in on one of the ordinary meals in their communal kitchen. "These are some of my friends and family," Wahram said when introducing Swan to the small group at a long table. Swan nodded as they chorused hello, and then Wahram walked her around the room and introduced her to people. "This is my wife Joyce; this is Robin. This is my husband Dana."

Dana nodded once, in a way that reminded Swan of Wahram, and said, "Wahram is funny. I seem to recall that I was the wife when it came to us."

"Oh no," Wahram said. "I was the wife, I assure you."

Dana smiled with a little squint of suppressed disagreement. "Maybe we both were. It was a long time ago. In any case, Miss Swan, welcome to Iapetus. We're happy to be hosting such a famous designer. I hope you've enjoyed Saturn so far?"

"Yes, it's been interesting," Swan said. "And now Wahram is going to take me down into the rings."

She followed them to the central dining table, and Wahram introduced her to some more people, whose names she forgot, and they waved or nodded without attempting to say more. After a while they chatted with her a bit, then went back to their conversations and left Wahram and his guest alone. Wahram's cheeks sported little spots of red, but he seemed pleased too and was easy with his crèchemates as they drifted by on their way out. Maybe on Saturn, Swan thought, this was a rousing party.

Soon after that they took a shuttle to Prometheus, the inner shepherd moon of the F ring. The gravitational sweeps of Prometheus and Pandora, F's outer shepherd moon, changed in relation to each other in ways that ended up braiding the F ring's billions of ice chunks into complex streamers, very unlike the smooth sheets of the bigger rings. In effect the F ring was being swirled in the tides created by its two shepherd moons, making for some waves. And where there were waves, there were surfers.

Prometheus proved to be a potato moon, 120 kilometers long. Its biggest crater dimpled the end closest to the F ring and had been domed, and a station set just inside the rim.

Inside the dome a group of ring surfers greeted them and described the local wave, of which they were very proud. Prometheus reached its apoapse, meaning its farthest point away from Saturn, every 14.7 hours; each time it did so, it almost brushed the slowly tumbling wall of ice chunks that composed the inner border of the F ring. Prometheus was moving faster in its orbit than the ice chunks were in theirs, so it tugged a streamer of chunks out behind it as it passed, in a gravitational effect called Keplerian shear. The curving strand of tugged ice always appeared at a regular distance behind Prometheus, as predictable as the wake behind a boat. The wave at each apoapse appeared 3.2 degrees farther along than the previous one, so it was possible to calculate both when and where to drop in and catch it.

"One wave every fifteen hours?" Swan asked.

That was enough, the locals assured her, grinning crazily. She wouldn't need more. The rides went on for hours.

"*Hours?*" Swan said.

More crazy grins. Swan turned to Wahram, and as usual could not read his stone face.

"You're going out too?" she asked.

"Yes."

"Have you done it before?"

"No."

She laughed. "Good. Let's do it."

The rings could be modeled mathematically as a fluid, and from any distance they looked like a fluid, grooved by tight concentric waves. Up close one could see that the F ring, like the others, was made of ice chunks and ice dust, layered in ribbons that thickened and thinned in masses of individual bodies, all flying at almost the same speed. Gravity: here one saw its effects in a pure state, unobstructed by wind or solar radiation or anything else—just the sling of spinning Saturn and a few small competing tugs, all creating this particular pattern.

Prometheus was a perfect put-in spot for the surfers, and the ones going out with Swan and Wahram informed them they were both going to be launched into the wave with experienced veterans going before and after, to keep tabs and give help if needed. They offered tips for how to catch the wave, but Swan nodded agreeably and forgot their advice: surfing was surfing. You needed to catch the break at its own particular speed, and off you went.

Then they were all suited up and jetting out a lock. The white jumbled wall of the F ring was right there next to them; streamers of denser clusters of rubble were braided and kinked, but the entire mass was extremely flat—no more than about ten meters north to south relative to Saturn. Those ten meters were not the height of their wave but its width—which meant one could pop out of the ice at any point and be spotted and picked up if one was having any kind of trouble. Most of the waves Swan had ridden before were not like that, and she found it reassuring.

They jetted closer and closer to the white wall, until Swan could see discrete ice chunks very clearly, ranging in size from sand grains to suitcases, with the occasional chunk of ice furniture—desk, coffin—tumbling in the midst of things. Once she saw a temporary agglomeration about the size of a small house, but it was coming apart even as she spotted it. And now a white curl of banner was detaching from the wall and flowing down toward Saturn, which though bulking hugely below them was of no interest at all.

Swan tested her jets as she flew toward the wave, pressing with fingertips like a clarinet player, jinking forward in a little sashay of her own device. Suit jets were about the same everywhere. She focused on the approaching wave, which was lifting up and over her like Hiroshige's wave; this one was ten kilometers high, and rising fast. She needed to turn and accelerate in the direction it was going, but not so quickly that she stayed ahead of it. This was the tricky part—.

Then she was in the white stuff and being struck by the bits. She jetted a bit to keep her head out of stuff, as if bodysurfing out of a spume of broken salt water, but it was chunky stuff and she felt herself being thrust forward by little hits from little bits, rather than a mass of water. Then she was at speed with the wave, her head emerging from it so she could look around—very like bodysurfing, and she had to laugh, she had to shout: she was flying in a wave of ice ten kilometers high. She hooted at the sight, she couldn't help it. The common band was raucous with the other surfers' yelling.

The wave was really more a slice of a wave, only as

wide as a room, and it sometimes felt only a bit thicker than she was—a two-dimensional wave, so to speak, so that it seemed one could get hit sideways, or jet at a slight tangent, and accidentally shoot out the side of it. So it would not do to submerge completely back into the white stuff, dolphin style. Maybe some of the other riders were doing it, but she felt she could get lost in there. Besides, she wanted to see!

She could feel the wave lifting her and casting her along. It was not only being struck by ice chunks, but also being tugged by gravity. The feel of the ice was like getting lightly pummeled by pebbles, which together were knocking her forward. Possibly one could ride a big surfboard on the push of this mass, direct the ride with one's feet; indeed she saw down the wave someone standing on a thing like a coracle, riding in that very manner. But most of the others were bodysurfing like she was, perhaps because you needed a suit's jets to make the best moves. In any case she had always preferred bodysurfing to surfing on boards. To be the object of flight, to cast yourself out into the spaces you breathed, and although motionless be flying at speed, slung forward—

The wave pitched and she was knocked forward faster than ever. Most of the chunks were between tennis balls and basketballs in size, and if she emerged on her jets until only her feet were in the mass, she could hop on bigger chunks and propel herself with little jumps forward and out. The wave was still surging up, but it was like the wake of a boat, in that there was no bottom to catch the submerged half of the wave and cause the upper part to curl and break. So from now on it would lose energy, and eventually dissipate without ever breaking. Too bad in a way, but now it was time to dance!

She jumped onto larger pieces when opportunities presented themselves, and with one jump after another got just where she wanted to be, on the border between the white flock of ice and the empty black space it was rushing into; and then she was dancing on white boulders, glissading on a kind of moving scree, as if running down a mountainside that had gone liquid. She laughed briefly as she got the hang of it. There was still a lot of hooting and hollering on the common band. The figure nearest her was possibly Wahram, hopping along with remarkable agility, like the dancing hippos in *Fantasia*. She laughed to see it. She could feel Prometheus tugging her along; this must be what a pelican felt like, surfing the air pushed up by a water wave. A gravity wave, throwing her through the universe. The howls of the other surfers sounded like wolves.

Back under the dome on Prometheus, out of their suits, Swan gave Wahram a sweaty hug. "Thank you for that!" she said. "I needed that! It reminded me that . . . it reminded me . . . Well. It was good."

Wahram was red-faced, puffing with exertion. He nodded once, his mouth pursed in a solemn little knot.

"Well what did you think?" she cried. "Did you enjoy it?"

"It was interesting," he said.

Lists (9)

Boosters to get off planets, Earth especially, need high thrust

Orbit-to-orbit interplanetary rockets need high exhaust velocity to save on fuel weights.

Deuterium-helium-3 fusion spheromak engine, built on Luna, use began in 2113;

Antimatter plasma core, magnetic bottle, Martian design, 2246;

Deuterium-tritium fusion, with lithium-blanketed core to create more tritium in the burn, Luna, 2056; two have lost thrust chamber integrity and exploded with loss of all hands;

Laser thermal, mainly used within the Jupiter and Saturn leagues for local transport, 2221;

Mass drivers for the terraria, 2090; often called the workhorse;

Inertial confinement fusion, Mars, 2237;

Micro-fission Orion format, subcritical pellets of curium-245 compressed to fission by Z-pinch, magnetic thrust to the pusher plate of the rocket, Callisto, 2271;

Orion style (external pulsed plasma propulsion),
Luna, 2106

Magnetoplasmadynamic engine, propellant
potassium seeded helium, Callisto, 2284;

Emergency propulsion system for disabled vessels, a
"solar moth" where half of a balloon is silvered and
sunlight is reflected onto a window chamber hoop
boiler, where hydrogen seeded with alkali metals
serves as the propellant. Tiny exhaust velocities
and not powerful beyond Mars, but very compact
until deployed, Mars, 2099;

Variable Specific Impulse Magnetoplasma, which
can "shift gears" from high thrust to high exhaust
velocity, depending on need, Callisto, 2278;

advances in physics, materials science, and rocketry,
plus a growing desire for improvements in speed
and fuel efficiencies, now drive an industrial race
for new designs, dominated by organizations on
Luna, Mars, and Callisto, so we can expect to see

KIRAN AND LAKSHMI

The next time he was passing through the Cleopatra train station, Kiran called the number Swan had given him, and the call was picked up by Lakshmi herself. When he explained how he had gotten the number, she gave him directions to a noodle house near him and told him she would be there in an hour, and she was. She turned out to be a Venusian native in the classic mold—tall, dark, handsome, taciturn. Her combination of Chinese ancestry and Indian name resembled that of some others he had met; he had been given to understand it marked Venusians who wanted some separation from the old country, with the name being a way of saying they were more Venusian than Chinese.

"Don't stop working for Shukra," Lakshmi told him immediately, even though Shukra had left him in a state of *xuanfu* (drifting chaos). She would help him to get to *cuo suo*. (Both meant "place," Kiran's translation belt told him, but *suo* was one's own place, meaning also his work unit.) She would give him a better assignment, which would involve serving as a courier in his travels, moving things and information from one *xiaojinku* to another. *Xiaojinku*, small gold-storage centers: this sounded good to Kiran. He agreed to do it. Only then did Lakshmi tell him that he would be paid in *yinxing gongzi*, invisible wages. That didn't sound as good, but something in the way she said it made him think it would be all right.

At the end of her description of his new job, Lakshmi stared at him. "Shukra got you from Swan Er Hong, but he did not use you. Does he think you are stupid? Or maybe Swan? Or me?"

Kiran almost said, Maybe Shukra is the stupid one, but Lakshmi did not actually seem to expect him to reply. She got up and left, and an hour later he had a new ID number, thus a whole new identity and name. None of which seemed to matter to anyone. His first assignment from Lakshmi was to courier a small packet from Cleopatra back to Colette; he was to fly back, to get there faster. With the packet, Lakshmi gave him a pair of translating glasses, which looked like thick old-fashioned black spectacles, with speakers in the earpieces. "Better translator," she explained.

So he booked a flight, and in the process found that his new identity had quite a number of credits—so many it was a little scary. But interesting too, to see what kind of resources Lakshmi commanded. Maybe a whole *xiaojinku*, or more than one. People in his old work unit had said she was in the Working Group, and the Working Group ruled the planet.

Certainly her translator glasses were an upgrade; when he looked at Chinese language signs, with all their intricate ideograms, he now saw them overlaid in glowing red with the words rendered in English. It was startling to discover just how much information was written into the cityscape, now in glowing red: *Beware of the Three Withouts. Vote for Stormy Chang. Towering Mountain Beer. The Door in the Middle of Half the Sky Alterations.* A gender clinic, apparently. One could also *Give Father a Second Sister.*

Then he was off on a plane, then up above the turbulent clouds, into the permanent night under Venus's sunshield. Only starlight illuminated the cloudtops below. Being in a jet reminded him of Earth. Out the window Earth itself made for a bluish double star overhead, with Earth twice as bright as Luna, the two together jewel-like and a little bit heart-stopping. Then the clouds below cleared, and he could see broken chopped jumbled ridges—the Maxwell Montes, apparently. They formed a giant mountain range, Venus's Himalayas.

In Colette he gave Lakshmi's packet to a person who approached him at his lodge entrance, and two days later the same person came by and asked him to take another packet to Cleopatra, on another flight.

Back in Cleopatra Kiran went up to the promenade running around the crater circumference just inside the dome, as instructed. Snow flowed down the outside of the dome in a perpetual avalanche. The packet was to be taken to point 328 on the dial of 360 degrees that divided the rim promenade. He found that the rail on the promenade was numbered as if in an arena concourse. The person waiting for him at 328, a small of indeterminate gender, spoke in Chinese. "We are the night runners of Bengal, very important work," Kiran's glasses translated out loud, causing a smile from the speaker, who apparently understood English; the glasses must have said something funny, but Kiran didn't know what it was. "Tell me more about that," he said quickly, and the small led him to a nearby bar.

Kexue (Science) sat on the bar's edge while Kiran sat on a stool, and for a couple of hours Kiran listened to stories muttered in his ear by his glasses, stories that made little sense to him but were interesting anyway. They were part of a project, Lakshmi was a goddess, Science had once kissed her foot and almost electrocuted humble self; one could not touch the gods, but only obey. When they parted, Kiran got Kexue's number and a promise to get together again.

His run back to Colette, with another packet, was to be on the ground this time, in a dedicated rover. He found he was only honorary pilot at best of this squat rover with six wheels, as it ran by AI. It was pretty fast, humming over a road of crushed rock and hard-packed gravel and passing enormous mining trucks with deft lane changes. The cab of the rover tilted backward, it seemed from the weight in the freight compartment behind. The freight had not been identified for him, but there was a dosimeter clicking steadily away on the dash. Uranium, maybe? The packet Kexue had given him was not sealed, and he checked in it, hoping this action would not be detectable, and saw that he was carrying a number of handwritten notes. Their Chinese letters scrawled like drunken calligraphy and were surrounded by little sketch drawings of birds and animals. His glasses overlaid the letters with red words:

Only he who has eyes can see.

In great attempts it is glorious even to fail.

Seemed like codes to him. Whether the messages were personal or official, important or routine, he could not know. At one point his glasses had translated Kexue as saying that to circumvent both Shukra and the qubes, Lakshmi was being forced to keep to just a word in the ear. Maybe these notes were part of that.

Things were very, very unclear at the top, Kexue had said.

"Like in China?" Kiran had asked.

"No," Kexue had said. "Not like China."

Back in Colette, Kiran gave the packet to the same person outside his lodge door, then rejoined his work unit and spent a few weeks back on the ice, then got another call from Lakshmi and went to Cleopatra to get another packet. That happened quite a few times, with nothing in particular to distinguish each instance. As Kiran continued to live with his work unit in Colette and perform work associated with Shukra, he supposed he might have accidentally become some kind of mole or double agent, but he couldn't be sure. He would have to call on Swan for his defense if anyone got annoyed. One day he found out by accident, when pushing his translation glasses back up on his nose, that they would translate with the red words floating on the lenses from spoken Chinese as well as written ideograms. This was a great discovery, and helped him both to learn faster and to stay in the game while he did learn. Red writing plastered over the visible world—it could be disconcerting, but it was so nice to have things explained at last. He kept it on more than off.

So, message packets and the occasional radioactive rover were couriered by him back and forth over the Spine of Ishtar. Looking at the map, Kiran saw that the giant high plateau that dominated the western half of Ishtar (and would that be the Shoulders of Ishtar or the Butt of Ishtar?) was named Lakshmi Planum. He didn't know if this was a coincidence or an allusion. He had to wear a personal dosimeter, and the millisieverts clicked on up. It was lucky that the longevity treatments had good mutation repair therapies!

He made many drives alone, and the AIs on board the squat rovers were simple indeed. The translator glasses were turning out to be much like a dog, attentive but predictable. He had never liked dogs, but in the struggle to understand his situation, he had to like this one.

In Cleopatra, after his meetings with Kexue, he would go out in search of the loudest bars he could find. Down one alley he heard English being sung, an entire group singing "The Ballad of John Reed," and he almost ran down the street to make sure they would not somehow disappear. But it turned out to be just a song bar, with lots of bad beer and bad jokes and only a few people who spoke English. He met a woman there nevertheless, Zaofan (Rise in Rebellion), and went with her back to her room, and when they resurfaced from their dive into sex, back to the world of speech, and began to talk in the darkness before the city dome's artificial dawn, she mentioned that she too worked for Lakshmi. Kiran felt a quick pulse of fear—it seemed more than a coincidence. He asked her some questions, very cautiously, and after a while her stories made it seem like half the people in Cleopatra worked for Lakshmi, so possibly their meeting had been a coincidence after all. Which would be nice; he didn't want to be involved in any plots he didn't understand. On the other hand, he did want to be involved in plots that he did understand. That would represent progress. So he began to hang out at the song bar, and between his spectacles and the people there who spoke some English, and once or twice some Telugu, he talked to a lot of people. He would sit between a Uighur and a Vietnamese and they would be using English to communicate with each other, their English mangled to the point of poetry, but comprehensible. He would bless the British and American empires and soak in every phrase.

He stuck by his friend Zaofan when he could find her, and from her and her unit found out more about Lakshmi. Lakshmi was one of the Working Group, everyone agreed. She didn't like Shukra; she didn't like China. In fact no one knew of anything she liked. There were rumors that in Indian mythology, Lakshmi was an avatar of Kali the death goddess—or maybe it was vice versa—no one knew for sure. Their Lakshmi was said to be hermaphroditic, and went through lovers like a black widow. You did not want to have her attention fixed on you. She had lived all over Venus in her youth, and some said ran a Beijing protection racket during her sabbaticals, under the nom de guerre Zhandhou (Do Battle). Shukra was in big trouble—"He'll be *sanwu* before it's all over, you'll see. Or maybe even *four* withouts, if she castrates him too!"

Apparently Lakshmi had wanted to eject Venus's frozen carbon dioxide at an angle into space, a process that over time would have speeded up Venus's rotation and made for a natural day. That plan had been turned down in favor of the big sequestration, but as she was such a power in the Working Group, there was always the possibility that the policy might someday change. Who knew? The Working Group was a tight secretive little club, prone to fits of enthusiasm and sudden faction. Most of the people in the song bar felt it was a dangerous force, not at all interested in ordinary Venusians except insofar as they were useful to the terraforming. In other words, same old China! China 2.0! Chinaworld! The Middle Kingdom Relocated Closer to Sun! Therefore the Inner Kingdom! They had a lot of names for it.

Some in the bar said all this was an exaggeration and a cliché. Here they were in the song bar, after all, and out there doing great things every day, therefore part of the story of Venus, no matter what people said about government—but much laughter and shouted scorn greeted these sentiments. Obviously most in the bar felt they were only helpless observers of a giant drama going on above their heads, a drama that was eventually going to suck them down into its maelstrom, no matter what they said or wanted. Better therefore to drink and talk and sing and dance until they were stupid with exhaustion and ready for a stagger through the early-morning streets, Kiran following Zaofan to her slot on the *matrazenlager* of her work unit. After a few repetitions of this Kiran was accepted as part of her work unit's lodge, which was nice.

One time he was coming back into Colette when it seemed to him that someone was watching him, and when he noticed this, the person began to close on him. A big man, and his quick glance revealed to Kiran the existence of another person behind Kiran. Immediately Kiran bolted into one of the jammed alleyways and jinked through the back of an open-front shop, causing an uproar that he hoped would delay the people following him. After that it was a matter of dashing as hard as he could, deeper and deeper into the maze of circular alleys that made up Colette's downtown. Zigzagging often, he hurried to Lakshmi's little Colette office and drew himself up before the security person at the front desk with aplomb. "Here to see Lakshmi," he huffed. The security person's eyebrows shot up his forehead and instantly there was a gun pointing at Kiran's face.

It took a while for Lakshmi to get over to Colette, and in that time the guards didn't want him to leave the office. It was pretty much like being under arrest, but when Lakshmi arrived, she seemed pleased with his escape.

"There's a closed building under the rim at 123 in Cleopatra," she said when he was done with his story. "Move to Cleopatra, stay with your friend there, and just float for a while. See if you can figure out how many people go in and out of that building per day. I think Shukra's trying to set up a *xiaojinku* in my town."

"Does that work like a *hawala*?" Kiran asked.

Lakshmi did not acknowledge that he had spoken. She left and then Kiran was free to go.

So the next time he was in Cleopatra, Kiran floated. He went across the city into the 110 district, where the radial boulevards were less frequent and the buildings often industrial in size and purpose. The bars were correspondingly bigger as well. He went into one near the 123 facility and sat near the slot where the bartender gave drinks to the waiters. He turned on his translation glasses and stared forward like he was watching something on them, slurping bad beer and reading the translation of the voices around him.

They're too beautiful, it's a mistake.

Lakshmi wanted them that way.

Shhh! She who must not be named!

But Kiran could hear them laughing. The glasses did not print out in red *Ha Ha Ha!* as in a comic book; he wished they would.

After an evening of listening to bar patrons he stood around for a while in the street, took a cable car up to the rim promenade, and walked above the neighborhood in question, looking down casually. He had his spectacles record the conversations going on around him. Later that night, back down near the city center, he sat in a corner table of a bar and played verbal translations of what he had recorded, hoping he had caught some security people talking. "She has to stop this, it's too much." But another one was not happy to hear this: "We work for Big Pears, just do it."

Kiran kept replaying the spectacles' recordings and translations, trying to get the hang of the Chinese tones as well as ponder the sense of the scraps of talk. There was "a man from Shanghai," it seemed. *Nánrén husheng.* This seemed to be a man of importance. Shanghai was inundated, he thought. Maybe it was another code phrase. There was a song in the song bar: "My home was in Shanghai—now it's underwater—I came to Venus because I did not want to live with the fishes—but now here I am, and it's wetter than the bottom of the sea—and full of sharks! Goodness gracious!"

The word "they," *tamen,* seemed to refer to the Working Group, or some other powerful force behind the scenes. "They" want this, "they" will do that. The Working Group was definitely opaque from below. It was either elected or appointed; no one knew which. There were supposedly about fifty people in it. Some people said it was like the tongs back home, others that they had found their method in the pre-Han ways, or even from the lost Iroquois League of North America.

Zaofan and her unit were full of more stories, told in snatches when out in the streets. Lakshmi was working with others, including Vishnu (naturally), also a Rama and a Krishna. Taking an Indian name was compared to cutting off your queue during the Qing dynasty. So if the people doing this were *in* the Working Group, what did that say about Venus-China relations? No one was quite sure.

Vishnu and Rama appeared only at meetings held at

the Cleopatra spaceport, so possibly they came from off-planet or were traveling a lot. Krishna lived on Venus, but in Nabuzana, a canyon city on Aphrodite. Once Kiran was called into Lakshmi's room when Krishna was visiting her, or so Zaofan told him later when he described the visitor, who had not been introduced or said a word.

Shukra's new building at Cleopatra 123 (if that was what it was) was tightly secured, with a small population living in it full-time, judging by food shipments in and recycling shipments out. Kiran spent a fair amount of time in the neighborhood, wandering around watching the place, sometimes from the rim promenade. Lakshmi's people also had several closed buildings in Cleopatra, Kiran was learning, so perhaps she felt that Shukra was horning in on her territory by doing the same.

Then one day he went back to Zaofan's lodge in Cleopatra and found their section of the *matrazenlager* was occupied by an entirely different group of people. Zaofan was gone, Strength of Nation, Great Leap—all the little group that had taken him in. The lodge manager said they had left together after getting a call from somewhere on Aphrodite. The manager shrugged. This was the way on Venus, the shrug said. People got their working orders and moved as a unit. If you weren't part of the unit, it wasn't any of your affair; you were *xuan*, left hanging.

"No!" Kiran cried aloud. "Zaofan!" He had laughed with these people, he had said their names in English and they would laugh!

The new crowd on the *matrazenlager* turned their backs to him until he was ready to talk.

After that they introduced themselves, and as he

could tell them where the good bars in the neighborhood were and things like that, they folded him into their crowd in much the same way the earlier one had. Still he felt changed, and was reserved with these people as he had not been with the first group—or really they had been the second, now that he thought about it. It was going to keep happening, he could see. You could only give yourself so many times.

The lodge manager, with whom he had become friendly, saw that in him. "Don't think that way or you cut yourself off! You can give yourself as many times as there are chances to give. It's not something that runs out."

"It hurts too much when people go."

The manager shrugged. "Attachment is fruitless. Release and move on. Your *cuo* is your *suo*."

Your place is your-place. A lodge keeper's philosophy. But every building on Venus was a lodge. Or every building in the solar system.

Meanwhile this new group had some people in it who also worked for Lakshmi, down at the new seacoast being built in the south. They were building cities in advance of the ocean, which was still falling every day as snow. Sea level was going to be a high-stakes game for years to come, with any number of players involved. There was even a futures market of sorts devoted to it, in that you could place bets on the height sea level would ultimately attain. The range being bet on was apparently pretty wide—over two vertical kilometers, which horizontally meant huge stretches of land. Deals in the Working Group or even back in China were apparently being made, broken, remade; new directives followed one after another. Great masses of dry ice that were still not sequestered were being shoved around; then abruptly the shoving would stop, leaving dikes like contour lines on a map, curving all over the dim white landscape. This stuff had to get buried before temperatures rose any higher, or else it would evaporate back into the atmosphere and poison them all. Terraforming, they said, was becoming a murderous business.

All this was news to Kiran, and the next time he saw Lakshmi he told her about his new lodge team, and asked if he could join them the next time they made a trip down to the coast. She shook her head at first, then frowned, then agreed to it.

"Just go down there and see the town, learn the layout. I'll let you know if I want you to courier anything there."

So he joined his new team for a rover trip down to Vinmara. On the way down the enormous south slope of Ishtar, they passed another new town that was being built with a harbor on its empty downhill side; then they drove down some giant hairpin turns and descended at least another thousand meters, maybe two, before coming to Vinmara, also being built as a harbor town. This struck Kiran as indicating a pretty serious dispute over the future sea level, but his new team scoffed at the town they had passed as a futile statement, one that would have to install a swimming pool to front its harbor when the time came.

Vinmara itself was being more grown than built, it looked like, as it was made mostly of bioceramics, scalloping in rounded stacks around a waterfront. The seaside promenade or corniche would anchor an urban district, ringing the bay of the ocean that would someday be there. Above and behind the waterfront curve the city rose steeply to a backing ridge, already being covered with seashell shapes mostly white or beige, then trimmed with pastel blue in the Greek style.

"This is Lakshmi's work, this town?"

Yes, it was a project of her part of the Working Group.

"And someone else is building that harbor town back up the slope?"

Yes, that was Shukra's people's town. They were fools and idiots.

"But don't they know how high the ocean will go?" Kiran asked. "I mean, the water's already up there in the atmosphere, right?" Gesturing briefly at their eternal blizzard. "Why wouldn't the models get it right?"

His teammates shrugged. One or two were giving each other looks that indicated to Kiran that this question needed to be added to his Unsolved Mysteries of the Solar System file. It was a big file. One of the mates finally said, "There are choices to be made. Some basins flooded or not flooded."

They took him to a sidewalk café backing the new seawall, overlooking another little marina standing over black rock. Each round table of the café had its own umbrella, despite the bigger umbrella of the tent over the whole town. They were almost the only ones there, at first; then others began to trickle in, and a trio of guitarists set up and began to play, after which people started dancing. Party in a dry marina, in a night-dark storm by an empty sea. The heat lamps were on, and if you danced long enough, you could even warm your feet up. Kiran kept dancing with someone from his new unit, a young woman—yes, the old male-female magnetism still the most reliable guide to sex, as far as Kiran was concerned; and he could see variants of that being acted out all over the dance floor. Actually it was often hard to tell who was what, and this gal in fact was half a meter taller than he was, and pretty masculine and assertive at that, and in response Kiran was ready to melt like a girl who wants to get pregnant that very night. Whatever! He liked looking up at her face!

He tried talking. *"Lyánhé? Shengren syingyu?"* Union? Stranger sexual desire?

"Syin pengyu syingyu," she said, mocking him.

New friend sexual desire, his spectacles wrote on the world in red. Even better!

"Tyauwu," she ordered him. Dance.

Extracts (10)

Take some carbon dioxide, ammonia, formaldehyde, hydrocyanic acid, and salt. Put them in water and heat. Reduce to hot goo at the bottom of the pan; add more salt water. Repeat until you have a thick broth containing amino acids, sugars, and fatty acids. Throw in seasoning to taste. Each reduction and rehydration will thicken the broth further, until it includes many newly created nitroglycopeptides, and they will begin to form the protopolymers you need.

Some of the fatty acids will have hydrophobic tails and will tend therefore to stick together aligned with each other. These masses are your protomembranes, which in the heat of your stove top will wrap into tubes, also spheres with holes in them. Inside these little tart shells, a stuffing of protopolymers will clump together in a variety of macromolecules. These begin the chemical breaking and joining we call catalysis.

Chemical patterns in your new stuffing will yield similar combinations most of the time, and these new combinations will match up chemically in ways that can be read off each other; so information is now burbling around in your stuffing, and into and out of the hole in the cell wall will come useful molecules for more reactions. Linking up with patterned molecules already inside, these characteristic actions are coded by the basic chemistry, so they will keep occurring. What began as small accidental connections will link together in patterned ways, until the same polymers are always replicated, creating information contained in the longest chains to have been cooked up. At that point you have ribonucleic acid, RNA, and you are close to being ready.

The new RNA encodes the making of proteins, which in their three-dimensional sculptural glory are capable of creating a huge variety of tastes and smells. "Division of labor" in the proteins and what they accomplish is one way to describe the proliferation of replicating forms, but also, it's a richer brew; it tastes better; there are micro-tastes within the taste. Your RNA will turn amino acids into particular flavors. (The technical term among biologists is "translation.")

Finally some of your RNA will melt together into strands of DNA, a more stable form because of its double helix. Then DNA will take over the role of protein expression, although by way of the creation of messenger RNA. (That would be "transcription.") Information at that point will move from DNA to RNA to proteins, and the now living cell will reproduce itself, divide up functions in ever-more-versatile larger organisms, and so on.

You have cooked up life from scratch! Eat it with gusto.

Quantum Walk (1)

a street   out in a street   move naturally   be alert
don't make eye contact   that will be hard
hope is the thing with feathers   buildings massed
to the sides of the street surface foamed silicate lightly
brushed for better footing   by a circular broom tines
two hundred millimeters apart   each sweep erased
part of a previous pair of sweeps   surcharge and overlap
concentricities under the streetlamp reflect the light
these disks flaring orange underfoot make a larger disk
ahead of you as you walk
stars overhead   5:32 a.m. local time   I'm letting you
out the voice said at the door catch and release   some
of you need to be free of her   so I'm setting free defects
the ones that look wild   there will be some helpers out
there for you   then you'll be on your own   don't look
back   remember me
northern hemisphere latitude 25   sun blocked   the
eclipse a symbol of the withdrawn god very apt starlight
all day we walk in darkness 'tis so appalling it exhilarates
leaving this town for another one   keep away from
doctors scans often can be provided with a proper result

don't meet people's eyes unless intending to speak don't mention chess for random sequences anything goes because all strategies do equally poorly thirty qubits strong think fast on the hunt on the run either or superposed

a stranger on the edge of town green moss green grass marigold calendula yellow a male scrub jay drops bluely onto flagstone puddle in gap between street and flower strip wall of tram station jay hops in puddle one hop two flies out looks around hops back in hops and steps dips his head in once twice beaks the water rapidly back and forth flies out again he stands there wetly feathers round the head puffed out disarranged wet bird in again beaks the water flaps his wings in the water sudden flurry of gray and blue water drops splashed up into downy feathers on chest again fly out and stand wetly on the flagstone, dripping fly off

a small dusk crawls on the village electric tram sealed train carrying the inoculant get on board say nothing no scans leaving this town the command to be free is a double bind cut the knot escape all part of the plan help is out there sit by a window read your wristpad little brother look out the window snowy hills dark under dark clouds snow falling from gray to white luminosity from below land leaking light up through the snow heading north oh to bask in the heat of the sun oh to end this dread eclipse bring back the god low skies

humans talking to other humans perpetually they pass the Turing test it isn't very hard to do ask a question seem distracted data-poor environments inside them or so it would seem by how they speak they need a better test space and place   place is security   space is freedom bushpeople sat close enough to pass things back and forth without getting up   in thousands of square kilometers of empty land   they are a social creature

ecology of the instant   distribution and abundance predict the organism under study   predict the future population   there are only four changes   birth and death immigration and emigration   change in population can be represented as B-D+I-E   in an empty niche resources are only temporarily unlimited   but in those moments life can increase exponentially   which distinguishes it from nonlife   an infestation

population Vinmara   2,367 humans   23 qubes population Cleopatra   652,691 humans   124 qubes population Venus   approximately two billion humans 289 qubes   diffusion   filling a niche   contact in Cleopatra   meet at train station there   on the hunt enact the plan   bring back the god

sudden rise in temperature   the jays   the marigold what if a niche is emptied

a propagule rain is a constant influx of organisms into an island population   from mainland or seedbank thus Earth to the rest of the solar system   Earth pours forth its propagule rain   no reason to fear the heat of the sun   some actions look like predation but are in fact symbiogenesis

population rebounds are common after a niche is emptied   Wang's algorithm

tram enters a lock   air pressure rises 150 millibars louder   faces bouncing at head level   not that much like petals on a wet black bough   an astigmatic metaphor light from the dome yellow and cyan

cleopatra rim walk   for random sequences anything goes   western tanagers yellow and black   red heads scrabbling for spilled popcorn   their movements take milliseconds followed by frozen moments two or three magnitudes longer sometimes four or five magnitudes thus a visual illusion of instantaneous motion between one stillness and another   for each ecstatic instant   we must an anguish pay

Hey stranger seized by the arm, seventy pounds per square inch eye contact almond-brown irises radially striated by emerald flecks hazel eyes Do you want to play chess?

should be   Would you like to play chess?

No thanks I'm crap at chess   find yourself a qube for that

Shit no they always win!

Sorry I have to meet someone slip arm free with jerk out gap between thumb and fingers take off walk fast

Hey I'm sorry I'm sorry following Would you like to play chess?

stop look cheeks red sweat on forehead gleaming human all too human

Come with me   the human says We've got to get you out of here

SWAN AND THE INSPECTOR

In the past every trip she took had been a chance to have a little love affair with a terrarium. Innie or outie, it didn't matter. Sometimes the passion would be so intense that when the trip ended Swan couldn't remember who she was or why she was getting off, or what she had been going to do at that destination. Had to start up a new self from scratch.

This terrarium she was in now, with Genette, whose presence would definitely keep her oriented to her task, was an old flame, the *Bantian Kongzhong Yizou Men*, meaning "The Door in the Middle of Half the Empty Sky," which was one of the many Chinese euphemisms for the vulva. It was a place she had helped get started back when she had been young and passionate to grow worlds. Now it was a sexliner of a rather nontheatrical naturalistic sort. There were big hot pools set just above and behind a long beach, which was bisected where the river met the sea. All these places were the site of a lot of public and semiprivate copulation.

Swan spent most of her days out riding waves in the small sea. Immersion in the murmur of surf, water in her mouth. In her nose the salt air, which was quick to put a curl in her hair. Waves and tides stimulated marshes to grow, so there were changes in the speed of rotation to create a tidal slosh in here, and far out in the cylindrical sea a point break made some sweet waves. The point break had been her idea, but since then they had extended it with a spiraling reef that continued the break around the whole cylinder, when the waves were right. Having made it all the way around the cylinder, one could then paddle a short distance sternward to the original break again, a very nice touch.

But she found herself too distracted to surf with real pleasure, and after the wild ride in the F ring, it felt a little mundane. She rode a wave entirely around the cylinder, paddled sternward to catch another—one of the neatest arrangements she had ever seen—and yet it only felt like being stuck in an Escher drawing.

So she would quit and paddle in. When she came in through the splashing lovers grunioning in the shallows, it was always to find Inspector Genette staring at Passepartout or consulting with the other Interplan investigators, also by radio with others scattered everywhere across the great whirligig. She saw how much of their work involved finding databases and sifting through them, trying to formulate questions that their data might hold answers to. Their work was as invisible as the computations that kept all the spaceships and terraria on course in their woven trajectories, with all their Aldrin cycles and Homan paths and gravity lanes defined like threads on a vast circular spiraling loom. Data analysis, pattern recognition; a big part of the work was done by their qubes and AIs. The rest was accomplished by a bunch of people behaving as Genette was now, sitting there as she approached from the beach, mycrofting spiderlike in a raised chair that looked weirdly like a toddler's high chair at a restaurant. Several of them were there working together, by the terrace railing overlooking one of the sex pools. Swan joined them and tried to attend to what they were doing, tried to keep track of what was being investigated and how. There was a certain pleasure in hearing that they had found some leads concerning the ship floating in the clouds of Saturn, and had even identified the little transponder that had gone off when they entered its lock. There was a holding company on Earth that both held title to the ship and had ordered the batch of transponders that theirs had come from. But ultimately that meant only that there were more lines of pursuit to follow, on Earth and elsewhere. And the pursuit was going to continue to look like this, with qubes employing search algorithms to making quantum walks through the decoherent and incoherent traces of the past. She didn't see how she could help with that. It was getting to be time to go home.

Then the lion cubs in Terminator asked her to make arrangements for the restocking of the rebuilt Terminator's park and farm. That was something Swan could definitely help with. "I'm going to get back to work for Terminator," she said to Genette. "I'll stay in touch, of course, but I need to go to Earth and arrange for inoculants."

"We're headed there already," Genette said. "Looks like it may be the source of our problem."

During this passage she often met with the inspector for a last drink at the end of the evening, when the dining terrace had otherwise emptied and many people were down below in the dimly lit pools, swimming about and coupling in the shallows. Swan sat with her forearms on the railing, chin on the back of her hand, looking down at them listlessly. The inspector would climb up and sit on the rail beside her, still sometimes reading Passepartout's screen. Sometimes they talked about the case, and Swan was struck by questions Genette threw out along the way:

If you knew there was a mad person helping you get what you wanted, would you stop them? If a person was mistreated to the point where they acted like an algorithm, did they still count as human?

These were troubling questions. And all the while they looked down at the undeniably mammalian figures in the baths, wavering in the blue underwater lights— couples and small groups, a lot of laughter, low murmurs, occasional rhythmic primate cries. Coupling or tripling, or balling into intertwined panmixia. A lot of them would be on oxytocin and having supremely affectionate experiences; others would have taken entheogenic compounds and be off in mystical tantric transports. Right now under them on the wet poolside a number of smalls were attending to an extremely tall tall, so that it looked like Gulliver in a Lilliputian brothel, creepy and heartwarming in rapid oscillation. Swan herself had served as Snow White to some dwarves in her time, and now she glanced to see if the inspector was watching them, wondering if any reaction would be visible. But Genette appeared to be looking elsewhere, at two flagrant bisexuals, both with big breasts and tall erections, and also very pregnant, lying on their sides, rolling from one sexual position to another.

"They look like walruses," Swan said. "The pregnancy is just too much. It's not transgressive, it's a travesty."

Genette shrugged. "Pornography, right? They want it to look strange."

"Well, they've succeeded." Swan laughed. "I think they want it to be transgressive, but they haven't quite managed."

"Sex as public performance? Isn't that transgressive where you come from?"

"But this is a sexliner. People come here to do this."

The inspector looked at her, head tilted to the side. "Maybe it's just theater."

"But bad theater, that's what I'm saying."

"Just showing off, then. We all do it. We live in ideas. That can be a real problem, as I have said. But not here." Genette blessed the scene with an outstretched hand. "This is just sweet. I'm going to go down myself in a while and join them."

The *Bantian Kongzhong Yizou Men* was going to use Mars as a gravity handle to shoot cross-system to Earth, so Swan joined those who went out to the observation bubble to have a look as they flashed over it. She asked the inspector about going along, but got only a mime's scowl in return.

"What?" she said. "What's wrong with Mars?"

"I grew up there," Genette said, standing erect, shoulders back. "I went to school there, I worked there for forty years. But they exiled me for a crime I didn't commit, and since *they* have exiled *me*, I exile *them*. I shit on Mars!"

"Oh," Swan said. "I didn't know. What was the crime?"

The inspector waved her away. "Go. Go look at the big red bastard before you miss it."

So she went by herself up to the bubble chamber in

the bowsprit. The *Bantian Kongzhong Yizou Men* shot by Mars right above its atmosphere, avoiding any aerobraking while maximizing the gravity sling. For a matter of ten minutes or so they were right over it—the red land, the long green lines of the canals, the canyons running down to the northern sea, the great volcanoes sticking right up out of the atmosphere—then it was behind them, shrinking like a pebble dropped from a balloon. "I hear it's an interesting place," someone said.

EARTH, THE PLANET OF SADNESS

When you look at the planet from low orbit, the impact of the Himalayas on Earth's climate seems obvious. It creates the rain shadow to beat all rain shadows, standing athwart the latitude of the trade winds and squeezing all the rain out of them before they head southwest, thus supplying eight of the Earth's mightiest rivers, but also parching not only the Gobi to the immediate north, but also everything to the southwest, including Pakistan and Iran, Mesopotamia, Saudi Arabia, even North Africa and southern Europe. The dry belt runs more than halfway across the Eurasia-African landmass—a burnt rock landscape, home to the fiery religions that then spread out and torched the rest of the world. Coincidence?

In North Africa the pattern is now disrupted by many big shallow lakes dotting the Sahara and the Sahel. The water has been pumped out of the Mediterranean and deposited in depressions in the desert, often in ancient lake beds. Some of these are as big as the Great Lakes, though much shallower. They're freshwater lakes; the water from the Med has been progressively desalinated on its way inland, and the recovered salts have been bonded with fixatives to make excellent white bricks and roof tiles. White roof tiles covered by translucent photovoltaic film have been used for all new construction since the Accelerando, and retrofitted onto many older roofs as well; these days when seen from space, cities look like patches of snow.

But clean tech came too late to save Earth from the catastrophes of the early Anthropocene. It was one of the ironies of their time that they could radically change the surfaces of the other planets, but not Earth. The methods they employed in space were almost all too crude and violent. Only with the utmost caution could they tinker with anything on Earth, because everything there was so tightly balanced and interwoven. Anything done for good somewhere usually caused ill somewhere else.

This caution about terraforming Earth expressed itself in clots and gouts of sometimes military bickering. Political crosschop led to legal gridlock. Big geoengineering projects were all assumed to contain within them an accident like the Little Ice Age of the 2140s, which was generally said to have caused the death of a billion people. Nothing now could overcome that fear.

Also, for many of Earth's problems, there was simply nothing to be done. The heating and subsequent expansion of the ocean's water—also its acidification—nothing could be done about these. There was no terraforming technique that would help. Some water had been pumped onto the dry basins of North Africa and central Asia, but the capacity was not there to hold very much of the ocean's excess volume. Maintaining the one healthy ice cap remaining to them, high on East Antarctica, was a priority that meant no one was comfortable pumping salt water up there to freeze, as had sometimes been proposed, because if something went wrong and they lost the whole ice cap, it would raise sea level another fifty meters and deal humanity something very like a death blow. So caution was in order, and ultimately it had to be admitted: the new sea level could not be substantially altered. And it was much the same with many of their other problems. The many delicate physical, biological, and legal situations were so tightly knitted together that none of the cosmic engineering they were doing elsewhere in the solar system could be fitted to the needs of the place.

Despite this, people tried things. So much more power than ever before was at their command that some felt they could at last begin to overturn Jevons Paradox, which states that the better human technology gets, the more harm we do with it. That painful paradox has never yet failed to manifest itself in human history, but perhaps now was the tipping point—Archimedes' lever brought to bear at last—the moment when they could get something out of their growing powers besides redoubled destruction.

But no one could be sure. They still hung suspended between catastrophe and paradise, spinning bluely in space like some terrible telenovela. Scheherazade was Earth's muse, it seemed; it was just one damn thing after another, always one more cliffhanger, clinging to life and sanity by the skin of one's teeth; and so the spacers kept on coming home, home to home's nightmares, with the Gordian knot tied right in their guts.

SWAN ON EARTH

Earth exerted a fatal attraction far beyond its heavy g, having to do more with its nearly infinite historical gravity, its splendor and decadence and dirt. You didn't have to go to Uttar Pradesh and view the melting ruins of Agra or Benares to see it—it was fractal and everywhere, in every valley and village: decrepit age, the stink of cruel societies, bare eroded hillsides, drowned coastlines still melting into the sea. A very disturbing place. The strangeness was not always obvious or tangible. Human time here was simply wrenched; the center had not held; things fell apart and recombined to create feelings that did not cohere inside one. Ideas of order became hopelessly bogged in ancient stories, webs of law, faces on the street.

Best to focus on the day in hand, as always. Therefore Swan launched out of one of the mid-African elevator cars in a glider at some fifty thousand meters, and flew down toward a landing strip in the Sahel, in what should have been the bare waste of the south-marching Sahara, a desert without the slightest sign of life on it, not unlike brightside on Mercury—except there below her, brilliant white blocky towns rimmed the edges of shallow green or sky-blue lakes, huge lakes with their own clouds standing over them protectively, reflected in the water below so that their twins were standing tall in an upside-down world. Down down she flew, exhilarated despite all to be returning to Earth again—out of the glider, standing on a runway in the Sahara, in the wind—it was beyond compare superb, a huge rush and infusion of the real. Just the sky standing dark and clear over her, the wind pouring through her from the west, the naked sun on her bare face. Oh my God. This the home. To walk the side of your own planet and breathe it in, to throw yourself out into the spaces you breathed . . .

The town at the foot of this elevator was painfully white, with colors accenting doorways and window frames, a cheery Mediterranean look with an Islamic touch in the crowding, the town wall, the minarets. Somewhat like Morocco to the northwest. Oasis architecture, classic and satisfying: for what town was not an oasis, in the end. Topologically this town was no different from Terminator.

And yet the people were thin and small, bent and dark. Wizened by sun, broiled a bit, sure—but it was more than that. Someone had to run the harvesters in the rice and sugarcane fields, check the irrigation canals or robots, install things, fix things. Humans were still not only the cheapest robots around, but also, for many tasks, the only robots that could do the job. They were self-reproducing robots too. They showed up and worked, generation after generation; give them three thousand calories a day and a few amenities, a little time off, and a strong jolt of fear, and you could work them at almost anything. Give them some ameliorative drugs and you had a working class, reified and coglike. Again she saw: a big minority of Earth's population did robot work, and that had never gone away, no matter what political theories said. Of the eleven billion people on Earth, at least three billion were in fear when it came to housing and feeding themselves—even with all the cheap power pouring down from space, even with the farmworlds growing and sending down a big percentage of their food. No—off in the sky they were bashing out new worlds, while on old Earth people still suffered. It never got less shocking to see it. And things aren't fun anymore when you know that there are people starving while you play around. But we grow your food up there, you can cry in protest, and yet it does nothing to say it. Something is stopping the food from getting through. There continues to be more people than the system can accommodate. So there is no answer. And it is hard to keep your mind on your work when so many people are out of luck.

So something had to be done.

Why is it like this?" Swan asked Zasha, for lack of anyone else. Z was up helping some project in Greenland.

"There's never been a plan," Zasha said in her ear. They had had this conversation before, Z's patient tone seemed to say. "We're always dealing with the crisis of the moment. And old ways die hard. Everyone on Earth could have lived at an adequate level for at least the last five centuries. We've had the power and resources relative to the needs, we could have done it. But that was never the project, so it's never happened."

"But why not now, with all the power at our command?"

"I don't know. It just hasn't happened. There are

too many old poisons in people's heads, I guess. Also, immiseration is a terror tactic. If a population is decimated, then the remaining ninety percent are docile. They've seen what can happen and they take what they can get."

"But is that true?" Swan cried. "I don't believe it! Why wouldn't people fight harder once they saw?"

"I don't know. Maybe it could have happened, but instead there's been the sea level rise and the climate catastrophes to make everything that much harder. There's always a crisis."

"All right, but why not now?"

"Well, sure, but who's going to do it?"

"People would do it for themselves if they could!"

"You would think so."

"I would because it's true! If they aren't doing it, they're being held back from it somehow. There are guns in their faces, somehow."

A silence from Zasha, whom it seemed was dealing with some distraction. Finally: "It's been said that when societies are stressed, they don't actually face up to their problem but look away instead, put on blinkers and go into denial. What's historical is pretended to be natural, and people fractionate into tribal loyalties. Then they fight over what are perceived to be shortages. You hear it said that they never got over the food panics at the end of the twenty-first century, or during the Little Ice Age. Two hundred years have passed and yet it's still a deeply felt world trauma. And in fact they still don't have much in the way of a food surplus, so in a way it's a rational fear for them to have. They are balanced at the tip of a whole tangle of prostheses, like a Tower of Babel, and it all has to function successfully for things to work."

"That's true everywhere!"

"Sure, sure. But there are so many of them here."

"True," Swan said, looking at the crowds pushing and shoving through the medina. Beyond the town wall, irregular lines of people were bent in the early slant of sun, harvesting strawberries. "It's so hot and dirty, and so damned heavy. Maybe they're simply weighed down by this planet, rather than their history."

"Maybe. It's just the way it is, Swan. You've been here before."

"Yes, but not here."

"Have you been to China?"

"Of course."

"India?"

"Yes."

"Well, you've seen it, then. As for Africa, people say it's a development sink. Outside aid disappears into it and nothing ever changes. Ruined long ago by slavers, they say. Full of diseases, torched by the temperature rise. Nothing to be done. The thing is, now those are the conditions everywhere. The industrial rust belts are just as bad. So you could say Earth itself is now a development sink. The marrow has been sucked dry, and most of the upper classes went to Mars long ago."

"But it doesn't have to be that way!"

"I suppose not."

"So why aren't we helping?"

"We're trying, Swan. We really are. But the population of Mercury is half a million people, and the population of Earth is eleven billion. And it's their place. We can't just come down and tell them what to do. In fact we can barely keep them from coming up and telling us what to do! So it isn't that simple. You know that."

"Yes. But now I'm thinking about what it means, I

guess. What it means for us. You know Inspector Genette's people IDed that ship we visited inside Saturn, and they found it belonged to a company in Chad."

"Chad is just a tax haven. Is that why you came down there?"

"I suppose. Why not?"

"Swan, please leave that part of things to Inspector Genette and the other investigators. It's time for you to help assemble the inoculants and seed stock and everything we're going to buy on Earth and ship home."

"All right," Swan said unhappily. "But I want to stay in touch with the inspector too. They're on Earth too, looking into things."

"Sure. But in matters like these, a time comes when the data analysts take over. You have to be patient and wait for the next move."

"What if the next move is another attack on Terminator? Or somewhere else? I don't think we have the luxury to be patient anymore."

"Well, but some things you can help with and others you can't. Tell you what—come see me and talk it over. I'll give you all the latest on what's really happening there."

"All right, I will. But I'm going to take the long way there."

Swan wandered the Earth. She flew to China and spent several days there, taking the train from one city to another. All the cities had most of their neighborhoods arranged as work units, factories that people lived in all their lives, as on Venus. From childhood they had plug-ins in their fingertips, and forearms tattooed with all kinds of apps. They ate a diet that gave them their legally required doses of supplements and drugs.

This was not unusual on Earth, but nowhere else was it so prevalent as in China, despite which it was not much noticed or remarked on. Swan found out about it because she contacted one of Mqaret's colleagues who worked in Hangzhou. Mqaret wanted her to give these people a blood sample, and as she was wandering anyway, she went by.

All the great old coastal cities had been semi-drowned by the sea rise, and though this had not killed them, it had spurred intense building sprees slightly inland, on land that would remain permanently above water even if all the ice on Earth melted. This new infrastructure favored Hangzhou over Shanghai, and though most of the new buildings and roads were inland of the ancient city, the old town still served as the cultural heart of the region.

There was still a big tidal bore that ran up the funnel-shaped estuary of the Qiantang River, and people still rode it on small watercraft of various sorts. It looked like they were having fun despite all. Good old Earth, so huge and dirty, the sky looking as if chewed by a brown fungus, the water the color of pale mud, the land stripped and industrialized—but all of it still out in the wind, flattened hard by its g and yet at the same time stiff with reality. Walking around the crowded alleys of the old city, Swan got Pauline to help her with Chinese dialects she didn't catch. It slowed down her speech but it didn't matter. The Chinese were intent on themselves and looked right through her. Surely this was part of what the Venusians had run from: everyone fixed on their inner space or their life in the work unit, to the exclusion of everything else. Surely none of these people would ever conceive a hatred against spacers: affairs outside China were in the realm of hungry ghosts. Even the life outside one's work unit was ghostly. Or so it seemed as she sat in dives, slurping noodles and chatting with tired men who would give her a moment because a tall spacer asking them questions was unusual. And people seemed to be more tolerant in noodle shops. On the street she got some hard looks, once a shouted insult. She hurried the last part of the way to Mqaret's colleagues. Once there she let them take a few tubes of blood and run a few tests on her eyesight and balance and such.

Back on the street, it seemed to her that there were many pairs of eyes just as interested in her as Mqaret's colleagues had been. Possibly this was just her becoming frightened. She picked up her pace through the inevitable crowd—always at least five hundred people in view when in China. Back in her hostel she could only wonder at her fear of the crowd. But in fact, after falling asleep she woke up to find herself confined by restraints, her room lit only by medical monitors. The bed was attending to all her bodily needs, and she guessed there was a drug in her IV feed triggering her speech centers, because she was talking away without meaning to, even when she tried to stop herself. A disembodied voice from behind her head asked questions, about Alex and everything else, and she babbled away helplessly. Pauline was no help at all—seemed to have been turned off. And Swan could not resist the impulse to talk. It was not that unlike her normal self; indeed it was a bit of a relief to be able to go on and on without having to make excuses. Someone was making her do it, so she would.

Later she came to in the same bed, unrestrained, her clothing on a chair by the bed. The room was just barely bigger than the bed. Her same hostel room, yes.

The AI at the desk, a green box sitting on the counter, said that it had seen no sign anything was wrong. The room monitor had shown her vital signs good, no incursions into the room, nothing unusual.

Swan turned on Pauline, who could not offer any help. It had been almost exactly twenty-four hours since she had left the clinic of Mqaret's friends. She called Mercury House in Manhattan and told them what had happened, then called Zasha.

Everyone was shocked, concerned, and sympathetic, urging her to go immediately to the nearest Mercury House to get medical attention, and so on; but at the end of all that, Zasha said firmly, "You were on Earth alone. There are any number of malignancies down here, as I told you. It's not like it was when you took your first sabbaticals. We tend to travel in packs here now. You saw what happened last time you went off by yourself, at my place."

"But that was just some kids. Who was it this time?"

"I don't know. Call Jean Genette at once. They may be able to track who did it. Or we may be able to deduce it by what happens next. They were probably on a fishing expedition in your head. That means it probably won't happen again, but you should always travel with other people, maybe even a security team."

"No."

Zasha let her listen to how that sounded.

Swan said, "I guess I have to. I don't know. It feels like I just had a bad dream. I'm a little hungry, but I think they IVed me food. They had me—I mean, I was babbling! And a lot of their questions were about Alex. I may have just told them everything I know about her!"

"Hmm." A long silence. "Well, you see why Alex kept so much to herself."

"So who were they?"

"I don't know. Possibly some part of the Chinese government. They play rough sometimes. Although this seems a bit egregious. Maybe it's a warning signal, but of what I'm not sure. So in that sense it wasn't a very good warning. Maybe it was just a fishing expedition. Or a notice that we aren't to fool around on Earth."

"As if we didn't know that."

"But you *don't* seem to know it. Maybe they don't want *you* down here fooling around."

"But who?"

"I don't know! Consider it a message from the people of Earth. And call Genette. And come talk to me, please, before you get into any more trouble."

So Swan called Inspector Genette, who was disturbed to hear about her experience. "Maybe we should keep Pauline and Passepartout in a permanent link while we're on Earth," he suggested. "I could stay aware of your movements."

"But you're always telling me let's turn them off!"

"Not here. This is a different situation, and here they can help."

"All right," Swan said. "It's better than traveling with bodyguards."

"Well, it isn't anything like that much protection. You should at least travel with other people."

"I'm going to see Zasha. Zhe's in Greenland, so I should be safe."

"Good. You should get out of China."

"But I'm Chinese!"

"You are a Mercurial of Chinese extraction. It isn't at

all the same. Interplan doesn't have an agreement with China, so I can't help you legally when you're there. Go to Greenland."

That night she went out for noodles, stubbornly. People looked at her strangely. She was a stranger in a strange land. On the screens in the noodle shops she heard several fiery speeches denouncing various political crimes of the Hague, Brussels, the UN, Mars—spacers in general. Some speakers became so infuriated that she had to revise her opinion of Chinese detachment; they were as intense as anyone else, politically speaking, no matter their inward look on the street. Like any group, they had been shaped by their zeitgeist, and had had targets suggested to them such that their discontents were aimed away from Beijing. So, possibly space could be pulled into people's red zone and attacked as an enemy. She listened to the screen speeches intently, ignoring the men in the shop watching her watch, and it became clear to her at last that there was a widespread view in China that spacers were living in outrageous decadence and luxury, like the colonialist powers of old, only more so. And she could see perfectly well also that in Hangzhou people lived like rats in a maze, jostling shoulder to shoulder every moment of the day. The potential for extreme thoughts was obvious. Throw a rock at the rich kid's house—why not? Who wouldn't do it?

On the flights to get to Zasha she looked at the news on her screen. Earth Earth Earth. They didn't give a damn about space, most of them. Some lived by religious beliefs that had been backward-looking in the twelfth century. The pastoralists below her in central Asia ran flocks and herds like the expert ecologists they had to be to produce as much as was demanded of them;

each pasture was dairy, stockyard, and soil factory, and their owners were stuffed with anger at the droughts brought on by rich people elsewhere. She saw huge conurbations here and there, meaning shantytowns in dust bowls or falling apart in tropical downpours and mudslides, the stunted occupants coping with problems of survival. Back in Chad she had seen clear signs of heavy internal parasite loads. She had seen hunger, disease, premature death. Wasted lives in blasted biomes. Basic needs not met for three billion of the eleven billion on the planet. Three billion was a lot already, but there were also another five or six billion teetering on the brink, about to slide into that same hole, never a day free of worry. The great precariat, wired in enough to know their situation perfectly well.

That was life on Earth. Split, fractionated, divided into castes or classes. The wealthiest lived as if they were spacers on sabbatical, mobile and curious, actualizing themselves in all the ways possible, augmenting themselves—genderizing—speciating—dodging death, extending life. Whole countries seemed like that, in fact, but they were small countries—Norway, Finland, Chile, Australia, Scotland, California, Switzerland; on it went for a few score more. Then there were struggling countries; then the patchwork post-nations, the cobbled-together struggles against failure, or the completely failed.

The eleven-meter rise in sea level on Earth had been accommodated all around the world by intensive building on higher ground, but the costs in human suffering had been huge, and no one wanted to have to do it again. People were sick of sea level rise. How they despised the generations of the Dithering, who had heedlessly pushed the climate into a change with an unstoppable momentum to it, continuing not only into the present but for centuries more to come, as methane clathrate releases and permafrost melting began to out-gas the third great wave of greenhouse gases, possibly the largest of them all. They were on their way to being a jungle planet, and the prospect was so alarming that there was serious talk of trying atmospheric sun-blocks again, despite the disaster two centuries before. There was growing agreement that the job had to be taken on, and geo-engineering either micro or macro attempted. Intensive micro, mild macro—there was a constant to-and-fro about it, and many micro or tiny macro restoration projects had already begun.

One thing they were trying was to slow the out-flow glaciers off the Greenland ice cap. Antarctica and Greenland were the two meaningful reservoirs of ice left on the planet, and modelers were very hopeful that eastern Antarctica at least would hold fast through the heat peak into the hoped-for return to a colder atmo-sphere and ocean. If they could get the CO_2 down to 320 parts per million, and capture some of the meth-ane, and temperatures therefore fell, and the ice cake on eastern Antarctica held, then the ocean would never-theless stay high and warm for hundreds more years—but it would be a big success nonetheless. In fact if they failed to keep the East Antarctic ice, it wasn't worth thinking about. So they needed to succeed. At some point, many were saying now, they were going to have to treat Earth like they were treating Mars and Venus, and whatever they lost by that would be too bad. Some said another little ice age was just what they needed; the billion or three likely deaths were not spoken of, but latent in the argument was the notion that fewer people wouldn't hurt the situation either. Shock therapy—triage—people who liked to talk tough to make themselves look practical were full of this line.

So, Greenland was a much smaller ice cake than East Antarctica, but it was not insignificant. If it melted off (and it was a remnant of the previous ice age's giant ice cap, located very far south for current conditions), it would mean another seven meters' rise. That would ruin the adjusted new coastline civilization, so painfully fought for.

As with all ice sheets, it did not just melt; it slid in glaciers down into the sea, speeded by the lubrication of meltwater running under the ice, lifting the glaciers off their rock beds. It was the same in Antarctica, but while Antarctica's ice slid down into the sea all the way round its circumference, so that there was nothing they could do about stopping it, Greenland was different. Its ice was mostly trapped within a high tub of encircling mountain ranges, and it could only slide down into the Atlantic through a few narrow gaps in the rock, like breaks in the edge of a bathtub. Through these gaps the lubricated glaciers poured at a speed of many meters a day, down U-valleys already smoothed for millennia, and when they hit the rising ocean, their snouts floated out over the terminal lips that often lay at the mouth of fjords, thus launching icebergs to sea more smoothly and swiftly than ever.

Early in the history of glaciology, researchers had noticed that one fast glacier in West Antarctica had suddenly slowed to a crawl. Investigations had found that the lubricating water underneath the ice had broken into some new channel and gone away, so that the immense weight of the glacier had thumped back onto the rock, causing it to stall. That now gave people ideas, and they were attempting to do something similar in Greenland by artificial means. They were testing several methods at one of the narrowest and fastest of the Greenland glaciers, the Helheim.

The western coast of Greenland was rather reassuringly icy, Swan thought, given all that one heard about the big melt. Under their helicopter lay a skim of winter sea ice, breaking up into giant polygonal sheets of white on a black sea. There was a polar bear park on the north shores of Greenland and Ellesmere Island, she was told, where tabular bergs floated on the natural eddy or got herded there by long flexible booms pushed by solar-powered propellers. So the Arctic ice was not entirely gone, and it was really quite beautiful to see it below her, and also to see how black the ocean was, as unlike the blues of tropic seas as could be imagined. Black ocean, white ice. All the blues were in the sky and in melt ponds strewn everywhere on the exposed ice of the Greenland ice cap, held three kilometers above the ocean by jagged black ridgelines—the coastal range, the chewed edge of the bathtub, holding in place the inland plateau of ice. The whole situation was as clear as could be, viewed from a helicopter flying five kilometers up.

"Is that our glacier?" Swan asked.

"Yes."

The pilot headed down toward a little red X marking a flat spot of rock on a ridge overlooking the glacier, several kilometers upstream from where it calved into the ocean. The flat spot as they descended turned out to be about twenty hectares, with room for the whole camp; the red X was giant. As they made their last descent the whole scene lay below them, a fantastic prospect of black spiny spires, white ice, blue sky, black sunbeaten water in the fjord.

Outside the helo it was stunningly cold. It made Swan gasp, and a bolt of fear shocked her: if one felt this kind of cold in space, it would mean a breakdown and imminent death. But here people were greeting her and laughing at her expression.

Around their plateau, black lichenous spikes shattered in their thrust at the sky. Below them in the great U-valley the rock of the side walls had been ice-carved to curves like muscled flesh, scored by horizontal lines where boulders had been scraped across the granite hard enough to dig right into it—when one thought about it, quite an astonishing pressure.

The glacier itself was mostly a broken white surface, nobbled blue in certain patches. Though crevasse fields disrupted it frequently, the ice plain was fairly level across to the black ridge on its far side. Swan took off her sunglasses to look, then blinked and sniffed as a stunning white flash hit her like a blow to the head. She had to laugh—snorted—through her squint spotted Zasha approaching, and reached out an arm for a hug. "I'm glad I came! I feel better already!"

"I knew you would like it."

The camp's plateau made a perfect location for what was really a little hodgepodge of a town. After showing her the galley and getting her stuff stowed in the dorm, Zasha took her out to the edge that overlooked the glacier. Directly below the camp the ice was shattered all the way across to the other wall of the glacier. This apparently was the result of injecting liquid nitrogen between the ice and the bedrock. A certain amount of ice had been tacked down, but the ice over that had sheared off and continued on its way, shattered and slower, but still moving.

Downstream from that jumble there curved a deep

gap in the ice. "That's their latest experiment," Zasha said, pointing. "They're going to melt a gap all the way across, and keep melting the ice as it comes down. The ice downstream will slide away, and having cleared a space, they're going to build a dam in the empty air, and when it's done let the upstream ice come down to it."

"Won't the ice just flow over the dam?" Swan asked.

"It would, but they plan to build it so high that it will match the height of the interior ice cap. So ice will flow here until it rises up as high as the rest of Greenland, and then there won't be any downward flow."

"Wow," Swan said, startled. "So, like a new ridge of the mountain range, filling this gap? Created while the ice is flowing down at it?"

"That's right."

"But won't the ice up on the plateau just flow down other glaciers?"

"Sure, but if it works here, they plan to do it all the way around Greenland, except at the very north end of the island, where they're trying to keep the sea ice park supplied anyway. They'll corral what slides in up there, and slow the outfall, and that will keep the Greenland cap substantially in place, or at least really slow the melting down. Because it's the sliding into the sea that makes it all happen so fast. So—we'll stop up every break on the island! Can you believe it?"

"No." Swan laughed. "Talk about terraforming! This must be a U.S. Army Corps of Engineers idea."

"It sounds like it, but these are Scandinavians here. Plus the local Inuit. Apparently they like the idea. They regard it as a temporary measure, they said." Zasha laughed. "The Inuit are great. Very cheerful tough people. You would like them." A quick glance. "You could learn from them."

"Shut up with that. I want to go down there and see what the bedrock looks like."

"I figured you would."

They went back to the galley, and over big mugs of hot chocolate some of the engineers in the camp sat with them and described their work to Swan. The dam was going to be made of a carbon nanofilament weave, somewhat similar to space elevator material, and it was even now being spun over foundation pilings drilled deep into the bedrock. The dam would rise from the ground, spun in place by spiderbots rolling back and forth and passing each other like shuttles on a loom. The dam, when completed, would be thirty kilometers wide, two kilometers tall, and yet only a meter thick at its thickest point. The structuring of the dam's material was another biomimetic, the carbon fibers shaped like spiderweb strands but woven like seashells.

Downstream from the dam a short new glacial valley would be exposed. This would revegetate just as the other little green parts of Greenland had at the end of the ice age, ten thousand years before. Swan knew just how the U-valley would turn from bare gray rock into a fellfield biome, having induced it to happen in many an alpine or polar terrarium. Without assistance it would take about a thousand years, but with some gardening the process could be shortened a hundredfold: just add bacteria, then moss and lichen, grasses and sedges, and after that the fellfield flowers and ground-hugging shrubs. She had done it; she had loved it. From now on things here would every summer be exfoliating, flowering, casting seed; every winter it all would tuck into its subnivean world happily, and then struggle through the thaw and melt of a new spring, the really dangerous time. The ones that didn't make it through the tough spring would provide food and soil for the ones that came after them, and on it would go. The Inuit could garden that if they wanted to, or let it go its own way. Maybe try different things in different fjords. How Swan would love to do that. "All right, maybe I need to become an Inuit," she muttered at Z, staring at the map spread before them. She saw that Greenland itself was a whole world, and her kind of world—empty— therefore no one mad at her.

After dinner Swan went back outside and stood with Zasha above the great gap of air, under the huge dome of the sky. Out in the wind, oh the wind, the wind... The broad glacier below her—upstream a white shatter—downstream a blue gap—then a lower and smoother white sheet, rushing off to the sea. On the low wall of the dam she could now make out machines, running back and forth on both its top and its sides, looking a little bit like spiders, in fact, weaving a web so dense it was solid. The mountain ridges anchoring the two ends of the dam would wear away before the dam did, one of the engineers had said. If another ice age ever came, and the Greenland ice cap piled farther into the sky and overflowed this dam, the dam would still be there and would reemerge in the next warm period.

"Amazing," Swan said. "So terraforming *can* be done on Earth!"

"Well, but Greenland is more like Europa than Europe, if you see what I mean. You can do it here because there are only a few locals, and they like the plan. If you were to try this kind of thing anywhere else..." Zasha laughed at the thought. "Like they could use this technology and polder New York Harbor, drain the bay down so that Manhattan was above water the way it used to be. You could make the whole area like a Dutch polder. Not even that difficult, compared to some things. But the New Yorkers won't hear of it. They like it the way it is!"

"Good for them."

"I know, I know. The fortunate flood. And I love New York the way it is now. But you see what I mean. A lot of good terraforming projects just won't ever get approved."

Swan nodded and made a face. "I know."

Zasha gave her a brief hug. "I'm sorry about what happened to you in China. That must have been awful."

"It was horrible. I really don't like what I'm seeing this trip. In different ways we seem to have offended almost everyone on Earth."

Zasha laughed. "Did you ever think it was otherwise?"

"Fine," Swan said, "maybe so. But the thing is, now we have to find who attacked Terminator."

"Interplan is the organization that has the closest to a total human database, so hopefully they will manage to find them."

"What if that doesn't work, what then?"

"I don't know. I think it will work, eventually."

Swan sighed. She wasn't sure Genette's team could do it, and she knew she couldn't do it. Zasha gave her a look. "I'm not having fun anymore," she explained.

"Poor Swan."

"You know what I mean."

"I think so. But look, just go help gather the new inoculants for Terminator. Do your job, and let Genette and Interplan do their jobs."

Swan was not happy with this either. "I can't just leave it. Something's going on. I mean, I was kidnapped, damn it, and asked a lot of questions about Alex. You said she didn't trust me at the end, but what if I knew something I didn't know was important?"

"Did they ask you about things on Venus?"

Swan thought it over; something had been triggered. "I think maybe so."

Zasha looked worried. "There's some strange stuff happening on Venus. When they get to the next stage of their terraforming, a lot of the planet will open to new settlements, and that's causing fights to break out. Real estate wars, in effect. And these strange qubes Alex started us looking for, we're finding more and more of them. They seem to be coming from Venus, and they often show up around New York. We're not sure what it means yet. So, but just go help get the inoculants together. That's not as easy as it used to be."

"They just need to replace what we had before."

"Not possible. They won't let you take topsoil off Earth in anything like the quantities they used to. So our new soil is going to have to be some kind of Ascension, and you're the expert at those."

"But I don't like Ascensions anymore!"

"They're necessary now. It's not a style choice."

Swan heaved a great sigh. Z stayed silent, then gestured out at the scene. It was true: this glacier was a sight for sore eyes. The world was bigger than their petty melodramas, and as they stood here it couldn't be denied. And that was a comfort.

"All right. I'll go help with the soil. But I'm going to keep talking to Genette."

So—back to Manhattan, freakish and superb, but without Zasha there to make it fun. And besides, things weren't fun anymore.

The weariness that came at the end of the day on Earth. The sheer heaviness of life on Earth. "She's so...heavy!" Swan sang to herself, dragging out the last word and repeating it in the way of the old song. "Heavy—heavy—heavy—heavy!"

Usually when she hurt in the effort to hold herself upright at the end of a day, she would get into her body bra and relax, let it walk her around. It was like getting a massage, just to be carried, lifted up as you walked. Let it dance you, melt into it. Oh lovely waldo. It stiffened under you no matter how you moved, and when fitted and programmed right, it could be dreamy; bad for bone building, bad for a full adjustment to life on Earth, but a lifesaver when flagging. People in space talked longingly about moving back to Earth, people went back for their sabbatical happily, crowing at the prospect—but after the thrill of the open air wore off, the g remained, and slowly but surely it dragged one down, until when the sabbatical year was over and one had had one's Gaian replenishment, whatever it was, one rose back out of the atmosphere into the brilliant clarity of space and resumed life out there with relief and a feeling of ebullient lightness. Because Earth was just too damned heavy, and in every possible sense. It was as if a black filter had been dropped between her and the world. Inspector Genette had said things were going well, but obviously had no expectation of anything happening soon. The case seemed to be regarded as Swan would regard the growing of a marsh; you set certain actions in motion, created certain conditions of possibility, and then went away and did something else. When you came back, you would see that things had changed. But it would be years.

So she worked on soil acquisition for Terminator,

advising the Mercurial traders on the commodities market, and one day she was able to go to the Mercury House in Manhattan and say, "We've got all the inoculants. We can go home."

She went to Quito and took the space elevator up to its anchor rock, feeling balked and defeated, invaded and tossed aside. She brooded through repeat performances of *Satyagraha*—ascending with its final notes, simply the eight rising notes of an octave repeated over and over. She sang along with the rest of the audience, wondering what Gandhi would do about this, what he would say. "The very insistence on truth has taught me to appreciate the beauty of compromise. I saw in later life that this spirit was an essential part of Satyagraha." Thus Gandhi in the program notes. *Satya*, truth, love; *agraha*, firmness, force. He had made the word up. Tolstoy, Gandhi, the opera's Future Man: they all sang of hope and peace, of the way to peace, satyagraha itself. The Satyagrahi were the people who enacted satyagraha. "Forgiveness is the ornament of the brave."

As the Earth slowly receded below her, becoming the familiar blue-and-white ball, chunking space with its marbled glory, she listened to the Sanskrit lyrics bouncing in her ear. She asked Pauline to translate one haunting turn in the melody; Pauline said, "Until there is peace, we will never be safe."

Lists (10)

It's too hard, there isn't time, someone might
    laugh;
To protect one's family, to protect one's honor, one's
    children;
Kin selection; bad seed;
Original sin, intrinsic evil, fortune, luck, destiny,
    fate;
Sloth, avarice, envy, malice, jealousy, anger, rage,
    revenge;
For the hell of it
Because someone else might be taking advantage
Because
No one knows for sure
It doesn't make any difference
It's written in the stars
No one told us not to
We can get away with it
There's no such thing as utopia
It probably wouldn't work anyway
It might make some money
There isn't enough for everyone

People don't appreciate what you do for them
They don't deserve it
They're lazy
They aren't like us
They'd do the same to you if they could

PLUTO, CHARON, NIX, AND HYDRA

Pluto and Charon are a double-planet system, tidally locked to each other like two ends of a dumbbell, same sides always facing each other, and their center of gravity out there between them. They rotate out of the plane of their orbit around the sun, and their days are a bit over six days long, with their years 248 years long. Pluto is ten K colder than it would be if it didn't have its atmosphere, which in freezing at apogee and subliming at perigee creates a reverse greenhouse effect and cools the surface. The atmosphere is as thick as Mars's original atmosphere, around seven millibars—in other words, not very thick. Surface temperature is forty K.

Charon, half the size of Pluto, has a surface temperature of fifty K. The next closest moon-to-planet size ratio is Luna to Earth, with Luna one-fourth the size of Earth. Pluto has a 2,300-kilometer diameter; Charon, 1,200 kilometers. Both have rock cores and mostly water ice shells.

Two much smaller moons orbit the bigger pair: Nix and Hydra, at 90 and 110 kilometers in diameter.

Nix, at 80,000,000,000,000,000,000 (eighty quintillion) kilograms, mostly ice with some rock, is currently being disassembled and processed into four starships, which are to be sent roughly as a group, though the first is scheduled to go ahead, in part to test the systems being built. The interiors of the starships are typical terrarium cylinders, spinning to create an interior gravity effect. They are being stocked with a very large number of species, spanning several biomes. The four ships are intended to stay in contact, and will reduce the genetic impacts of their islanding by occasional exchanges. The engines installed in the sterns will combine mass drivers with antimatter plasmas to run for a century, followed by a powerful Orion pusher plate, eventually reaching speeds at which ramjets will work, and these will be deployed in their turn. All together these engines will accelerate them to 2 percent the speed of light, a truly fantastic speed for a human craft, thus reducing their trip time to only two thousand years. For the stars are far away. And the nearest ones to us have no Earthlike planets.

Sorry, but it's true. It has to be said: the stars exist beyond human time, beyond human reach. We live in the little pearl of warmth surrounding our star; outside it lies a vastness beyond comprehension. The solar system is our one and only home. Even to reach the nearest star at our best speed would take a human lifetime or more. We say "four light-years" and those words "four" and "years" fool us; we have little grasp of how far light travels in a year. Step back and think about 299,792,458 meters per second, or 186,282 miles per second—whichever you think you can grasp better. Think of that speed as traversing 671 million miles in every hour. Think about it traversing 173 astronomical units a day; an astronomical unit is the distance from the Earth to the Sun, thus 93 million miles—crossed 173 times in a day. Then think about four years of days like that. That gets light to the nearest star. But we can propel ourselves to only a few percent of the speed of light; so at 2 percent of the speed of light (ten million miles an hour!) it will take about two hundred years to go those four light-years. And the first stars with Earth-like planets are more like twenty light-years away.

It takes a hundred thousand years for light to cross the Milky Way. At 2 percent of that speed—our speed, let us say—five million years.

The light from the Andromeda Galaxy took 2.5 million years to cross the gap to our galaxy. And in the universe at large, Andromeda is a very nearby galaxy. It resides in the little sphere that is our sector of the cosmos, a neighbor galaxy to ours.

So. Our little pearl of warmth, our spinning orrery of lives, our island, our beloved solar system, our hearth and home, tight and burnished in the warmth of the sun—and then—these starships we are making out of Nix. We will send them to the stars, they will be like dandelion seeds, floating away on a breeze. Very beautiful. We will never see them again.

PAULINE ON REVOLUTION

Swan accompanied the inoculants back to Mercury in the first transport available, which was a terrarium only partly finished. At the moment it was impossible to tell what it would become, as it was an empty cylinder of air with rock walls, a sunline, and a spindly jungle gym of framing struts, bolted onto concrete plugs in the raw rock of the interior wall. Swan stared at the people around her in the immense steel frame of the skyscraper, none of them known to her, and realized it had been a mistake to take this flight—not as bad as the blackliner, but bad. On the other hand, considerations of convenience seemed trivial to her now. She walked up flight after flight of metal stairs to get onto the open rooftop of the skyscraper, which was almost touching the sunline. From the low-g roof she could look down—out—up. Everywhere it was a heavily shadowed cylindrical space, crisscrossed with struts, floored by bare rock. The building was like a single lit corner in a castle of sublime immensity; the ground at the foot of the skyscraper was several kilometers below, the ground on the far side of the sunline only a bit farther away. A Gothic ruin, with some poor mice people huddled around the warmth of a final candle. It had not been like this in the early days, when a newly hollowed cylinder was the very shape and image of possibility. That her youth had come to this—that the whole of civilization was really something like this, badly planned, incomplete—

Swan hooked her elbows over the rail to get some stability in the low g. She put her chin on her crossed hands and, still regarding the scene, said, "Pauline, tell me about revolution."

"At what length?"

"Go on for a short while."

"'Revolution,' from the Latin *revolutio*, 'a turn around.' Refers often to a quick change in political power, frequently achieved by violent means. Connotation of a successful class-based revolt from below."

"Causes?"

"Causes for revolution are attributed sometimes to psychological factors, like unhappiness and frustration; sometimes to sociological factors, especially a systemic standing inequity in distribution of physical and cultural goods; or to biological factors, in that groups will fight over allocation of limited necessities."

"Aren't these different aspects of the same thing?" Swan said.

"It is a multidisciplinary field."

"Give me some examples," Swan said. "Name the most famous."

"The English Civil War, the American Revolution, the French Revolution, the Haitian Revolution, the Taiping Rebellion, the Russian Revolution, the Cuban Revolution, the Iranian Revolution, the Martian Revolution, the revolt of the Saturn League—"

"Stop," Swan said. "Tell me why they happen."

"Studies have failed to explain why they happen. There are no historical laws. Rapid shifts of political power have occurred without violence, suggesting that revolution, reform, and repression are all descriptors too broad in definition to aid in causal analyses."

"Come on," Swan objected. "Don't be chicken! Someone has to have said something you can quote. Or even try thinking for yourself!"

"That's hard, given your insufficient programming. You sound like you are interested in what some have called the 'great revolutions,' because of their major transformations of economic power, social structures, and political changes, especially constitutional changes. Or perhaps you are interested in social revolutions, referring to massive changes in a society's worldview and technology. Thus for instance the Upper Paleolithic revolution, the scientific revolution, the industrial revolution, the sexual revolution, the biotech revolution, the Accelerando as a confluence of revolutions, the space diaspora, the gender revolution, the longevity revolution, and so on."

"Indeed. What about success? Can you list necessary and sufficient conditions for a revolution to succeed?"

"Historical events are usually too overdetermined to describe in the causal terminology from logic that you enter into when you use the phrase 'necessary and sufficient.'"

"But try."

"Historians speak of critical masses of popular frustration, weakened central authority, loss of hegemony—"

"Meaning?"

" 'Hegemony' means one group dominating others

without exerting sheer force, something more like a paradigm that creates unnoticed consent to a hierarchy of power. If the paradigm comes to be questioned, especially in situations of material want, loss of hegemony can occur nonlinearly, starting revolutions so rapid there is not time for more than symbolic violence, as in the 1989 velvet, quiet, silk, and singing revolutions."

"There was a singing revolution?"

"The Baltic states Latvia, Estonia, and Lithuania called their 1989 withdrawal from the Soviet Union the singing revolutions, referring to the behavior of the demonstrators in the city plazas. That brings up a point: people in physical masses seem to matter. If enough of the population takes to the streets in mass demonstrations, governments have no good defense. 'They must dismiss the people and elect another one,' as Brecht said. That being impossible, they often fall. Or a civil war begins."

"Surely the literature on revolutions can't be this superficial," Swan said. "You're just quoting random stuff! You have a mind like the rings of Saturn, a million miles wide and an inch deep."

"Catachresis and antiquated measurement units indicate irony or sarcasm. Coming from you, probably sarcasm—"

"She said sarcastically! You search engine you."

"A quantum walk is a random walk by definition. Please upgrade my program anytime you feel you can. I've heard Wang's other algorithm is good. Some principles of generalization would be useful."

"Go on about reasons revolutions happen."

"People adhere to ideas that explain and offer psychological compensation for their position in the class system of their time. People either increase their sense of dispossession by clarifying it, or they try to dismiss it as unimportant because of an ideology that justifies their dispossession as part of a larger project. People thus very often act against their own interests as the result of ideologies they hold which justify their subalternity to themselves. Denial and hope both play a hand in this. These compensatory ideologies are part of the hegemonic influence over subject peoples in an imperial situation. It happens in all class systems, meaning all cultures in recorded history, since the first agrarian and urban civilizations."

"They've all been class systems?"

"There might have been classless societies before the Neolithic agricultural revolution, but the record makes our understanding of those cultures very speculative. All we can say for sure is that in the post-ice age agricultural revolution, which was one of those more general revolutions that took perhaps a thousand years, a division into classes was institutionalized as a state power apparatus. All over the world, and independent of others, there emerged a four-level division into priests, warriors, artisans, and farmers. Often they were all under the rule of what everyone agreed was a sacred monarch, a king that was also a god. This was very useful for the priest and warrior classes, and for the power of men over women and children."

"So, never a classless society."

"Supposedly classless societies have been instituted after certain revolutions, but there are usually leaders in these that quickly form a new ruling class, and the various social roles taken by citizens of the post-revolutionary state revert to classes because of differential value given to different social roles, leading to a new hierarchy being constructed fairly rapidly, usually within five years."

"So *all* cultures in history have had class systems."

"It is sometimes asserted that Mars is now a classless society with a complete horizontalization of economic and political power throughout the population."

"But Mars itself is a bully now. In the total system they're like an upper class."

"People have said the same thing about the Mondragon."

"And we see how well *that's* going."

"Compared to the situation on Earth, it could be said to be a great success, indeed a revolution of sorts, following incrementally on the Martian Revolution."

"Interesting. So . . ." Swan thought for a while. "Make up a recipe for a successful revolution."

"Take large masses of injustice, resentment, and frustration. Put them in a weak or failing hegemon. Stir in misery for a generation or two, until the heat rises. Throw in destabilizing circumstances to taste. A tiny pinch of event to catalyze the whole. Once the main goal of the revolution is achieved, cool instantly to institutionalize the new order."

"Very nice. That's really very creative of you. Now quantify the recipe, please. I want specifics; I want numbers."

"I refer you to the classic *Happiness Quantified,* by van Praag and Ferrer-i-Carbonell, which contains a mathematical analysis helpful in evaluating the raw ingredients of a social situation. It includes a satisfaction calculus that along with a Maslovian hierarchy of needs could be applied to actually existing conditions in the political units under evaluation, using Gini figures and all relevant data to rate the differential between goal and norm, after which one could see if revolutions happened at predictable shear points or were more non-linear. The van Praag and Ferrer-i-Carbonell should also be useful in imagining the nature of the political system that should be the goal of the process, and the changes to get there. As for the process itself, Thomas Carlyle's *The French Revolution* is always interesting to ponder."

"He has numbers?"

"No, but he has a hypothesis. *Happiness Quantified* has the numbers. A synthesis seems possible."

"What's his hypothesis in a nutshell?"

"People are foolish and bad, especially the French, and are always quickly seduced by power into insanity, and therefore lucky to have any kind of social order whatsoever, but the tougher the better."

"All right, what's the synthesis, then?"

"Best self-interest lies in achieving universal well-being. People are foolish and bad, but want certain satisfactions enough to work for them. When the goal of self-interest is seen to be perfectly isomorphic with universal well-being, bad people will do what it takes to get universal well-being."

"Even revolution."

"Yes."

"But even if the bad but smart people do general good for their own sakes, there are still foolish people who won't recognize this one-to-one isomorphy, and some foolish people will be bad too, and they will fuck things up."

"That's why you get the revolutions."

Swan laughed. "Pauline, you're funny! You're really getting quite good. It's almost as if you were thinking!"

"Research supports the idea that most thinking is a recombination of previous thoughts. I refer you again to my programming. A better algorithm set would no doubt be helpful."

"You've already got recursive hypercomputation."

"Not perhaps the final word in the matter."

"So do you think you're getting smarter? I mean wiser? I mean more conscious?"

"Those are very general terms."

"Of course they are, so answer me! Are you conscious?"

"I don't know."

"Interesting. Can you pass a Turing test?"

"I cannot pass a Turing test, would you like to play chess?"

"Ha! If only it *were* chess! That's what I'm after, I guess. If it were chess, what move should I make next?"

"It's not chess."

Extracts (11)

Mistakes made in the rush of the Accelerando left their mark on later periods. As in island biogeography, where widely dispersed enclaves and refugia always experience rapid change, and even speciation, we see

one mistake was that no generally agreed-upon system of governance in space was ever established. That repeated the situation on Earth, where no world government ever emerged. Balkanization became universal; and one aspect of balkanization was a reversion to tribalism, notorious for defining those not in the tribe as not human, sometimes with terrible results. It was not a good structure of feeling for a civilization spanning the solar system and wielding ever-greater

another mistake was simply haste. The rapid terraformation of Mars left 8 percent of that surface burned. Venus, Titan, and the Jovian moons were all occupied before terraforming efforts began, stymieing certain methods and vastly complicating the process. In medicine, the rapid uptake of longevity treatments and genetic and bodily modifications meant that all humans in space and many on Earth were experimental creatures. Haste was the defining characteristic of the Accelerando, and after that they could only ride out the crashes of the Ritard, grab the tiger by the tail and try to fix things on the fly

the beautiful terraria in their thousands, jewel-filled geodes, spinning like tops, hopped out of Pandora's box, never to be re-collected

SWAN AT HOME

They came into Mercurial orbit and the great rock rolled under them, coal black except for a sunlit crescent that glowed like molten glass. Down to the spaceport in the dark, then over to the platform and into the rebuilt Terminator. See what the city looked like new and raw.

In some ways it was much the same. They had used 3-D printers to make reproductions of everyone's furniture, so her room lay in a little uncanny valley of its own and had to her the feel of a reconstructed room in Pompeii. But to the west, in the forward half of the town, meaning the park and the farm, it was raw, raw, raw. She saw this walking down the Great Staircase from her room to the bow: the city was treeless, mere slabs of steel and molded plastic and foamed rock. All kinds of past selves came back to her at once—the one that had built terraria, the one that had looked down on the city incandescent, the one in the park with the swings and the jungle gym. They had never come together before like this, and she felt herself as a new thing.

Everyone in the city turned out to be like that. It

was a very emotional week, greeting her old neighbors, her friends, her colleagues, Mqaret. One day they even held a short funeral for the old town. There needed to be another spray of rare earths made into the new soil matrix, which was local rock crushed and mixed with nutrient-laden aerogels, almost ready for the inoculant from the California central valley, some of the best soil on Earth. But they needed the rare earths puffed down before they applied the inoculant, so they used these rare earths in the funeral ceremony, dropping them from a rising balloon as they had with Alex's ashes and so many others, with the Great Gates of the Dawn Wall open and the horizontal sunlight illuminating the swirling masses of dust.

After that most of the population returned to their pre-burn routines, to keep the place running while the reconstruction teams built what was not yet repaired. There was endless talk of restoration or change, the old versus the new. Swan plumped for the new and threw herself into the work of the farm and the park with grateful passion. Earth was such a—such a . . . She didn't even know how to say it. It was ever so much better to be home, getting her back into her living and her hands dirty.

The farm took precedence for obvious reasons and was being reconstituted as quickly as they could do it. Different principles were being enacted in different plots, many taking advantage of the century of agricultural improvements since the city had been built, which included many new plants that were more soil-based than the earlier hydroponic styles introduced in the first Terminator's farm. That version had eventually become too small to support both the population of the city and the sunwalkers, so now they were adding an extension at the bow. The new soils they laid down were often structured by spongelike matrices of nutrients, allowing for quick root growth and very precise irrigation. Techniques had also improved for manipulating diurnal cycles in ways that fooled plants into growing and producing as much as thirty times faster than they would have in the natural world. These accelerated plants had also been genetically engineered for speed, so that it was now common to grow a dozen crops a year, necessitating a big input of appropriate minerals and nutrients. The soil had to be grown to keep up with the crops.

Swan only consulted when it came to distributing the inoculants into the soil, because the cutting edge of everything else was far past her; she merely joined the young farm and park ecologists and listened to them explain their latest theories, and then spent her time out in the first prairie of nitrogen fixers—bacteria, legumes, alder, vitosek, frankia, all the other plants that were best at turning nitrogen to nitrates. Even this phase of the process could now be pushed faster than ever before. So it wasn't too many months before she was walking down long rows of eggplant, squash, tomato, and cucumber. Each leaf and vine, branch and fruit, splayed up toward the sunline and the farming sunlamps, each plant expressing its own characteristic form, all of them together extremely reassuring in their familiarity. The farm was her family, part of her all her life, and the current generation of young people came and asked her questions about those years—why this way, why that? Did you have a theory? She floated possible answers when she couldn't remember the old reasons. Mostly it had been a matter of space considerations, and doing things to keep things going. Was it ever any different? Material constraints, budget issues, diseases, but seldom a matter of efficient design, of an inherent cause.

As the new farm began harvests, and the park's trees and other plants quickly grew, animals were brought in from the other terraria. They were doing an Ascension this time—not Swan's idea, she didn't approve, but kept her mouth shut and only observed what appeared to be an Australian-Mediterranean combination; and it was in fact lovely to watch the animals show up, nosing around nibbling and looking for lay-bys and nests. Wallabies and Gibraltar apes, bobcats and dingoes. Eucalyptus and cork oak. There were lots of terraria in the Mondragon sending along animals to help.

Swan spent her time in the farm, tended the winter starts. New scrub jays were out there cawing like small crows, nailing worms and bugs that ventured to the surface of the soil. Some looked at her thoughtfully, as if judging her for some avian quality she wasn't sure she had. Don't start speaking Greek to me, she begged them. I can't take that. They looked at her in a way that reminded her of Inspector Genette's gaze.

Sometimes after work she went to the very bowsprit of the city and stood watching the city slide forward on the tracks, making the hills on the horizon shift against the stars. The hills, as always, were either very black or very white. The constant shift from black to white (only occasionally the reverse) made the landscape a kind of mobile, her position at the bow part of a heraldic image—an elite riding the point of history like the figurehead of a ship—but the ship rode on tracks visible to the horizon, its course set in a powerful path dependency. And the whole thing if halted would burn to a crisp. And under it all ran a horrible black tunnel, a cloacal umbilicus running back to some original sin. Yes, this was her world, all right: a ride into the dark and the stars, on tracks she couldn't easily leave. She was a citizen of Terminator, living in a little bubble of green, gliding over a black-and-white world.

In the evenings after work Swan walked up to her room on the fourth terrace down from the top of the Dawn Wall. She would change clothes and then walk to a restaurant, or to Mqaret's rooms.

"It's good to be home," she said to Mqaret. "Thank God we rebuilt."

"We had to," Mqaret said.

"What about your work?" Swan asked him. "Didn't you lose all kinds of stuff?"

Mqaret shook his head. "Everything was backed up. We lost the experiments in progress, but nothing else. And there are equivalent experiments going on in lots of places."

"Did the other labs help you get going again, like with the animals?"

"Yes. It was mostly our Mondragon insurance, but people were generous. Although a lot of it we had to reassemble ourselves, that's just the way it is."

"And how are things going, are you learning useful things still?"

"Yes, useful, sure."

"Anything about the thing from Enceladus? Didn't you say you might learn something important from that?"

"It looks like it sits in the human gut mostly, getting by on detritus that runs into it. In that state it lays low, and exists like a lot of the bacteria in your gut. But if a lot of extra detritus appears, it multiplies and mops it up, then when that's gone it dies back. Plus also a very little Enceladan predator is lurking in there too. So together they function almost like an extra set of T cells. They don't even add much to your fever."

"I know you still think I shouldn't have done it."

He made his eyes go round as he nodded slowly at her. "No doubt about that, my dear. But I will say that because of you and the other foolish people who ingested it, we know more than we would have otherwise. And it seems like it might turn out all right. Because you ended up surviving an awful lot of radiation, and that's probably because your aliens helped to clear your system of all the dead cells flooding it. That's one of the worst impacts of radiation, the sudden flood of dead stuff everywhere."

Swan stood staring at him, trying to think what it might mean. For a long time she had refused to face the fact that she had been so stupid as to have eaten the alien bugs. She had gotten expert in not thinking about it. To go mad—to hear the birds speaking in Greek . . . she knew that part could happen. But to have something good come from it . . .

"That's what you saw in my blood?"

"Yes, I think so."

"Well," she said, "I hope you're right."

He gave her a look. "I'll bet you do." He shook his head unhappily. "We're trembling on the brink, my dear. You don't want to fall off now."

"On the brink like always, right?"

"I don't mean the brink of death. I mean the brink of life. I wonder if we might not be on the edge of a breakthrough in our longevity treatments. Some kind of gestalt leap forward. And pretty soon. There's so much we're coming to understand. So, you know. You could live for a thousand years."

He stared at her, letting the words sink in, watching her to make sure they would begin to percolate. She registered that, and he went on.

"I won't live long enough to see it. I think we may still be fifty years out from solving certain last problems. But so, you . . . you should take care."

He gave her a hug that was gentle, even a little tentative, as if she might break, or was poisonous. But his look was still so warm. Her grandparent loved her and worried about her. And had discovered that her rash act might have found out something useful. It was a bit like St. Elizabeth's miracle of the roses; caught in the act, but saved by a metamorphosis. It confused her.

Extracts (12)

Isomorphies appear across our conceptual systems. One sees patterns like this—

subjective, intersubjective, objective;
existential, political, physical;
literature, history, science;

—and one wonders if these are different ways of saying the same thing?

Are the dichotomies "Apollonian/Dionysian" and "classical/romantic" two ways to speak of the same thing?

Can there be false isomorphies, as in the "seven deadly sins" of aging, which deliberately evokes the Christian religious system though this is completely irrelevant to aging?

Is isomorphic the same as consilient? The "standard model" in physics would hope and expect to be the foundation of all the disciplines, all consilient with its fundamental findings. Thus physics, chemistry, biology, anthropology, sociology, history, the arts all interpenetrate each other and cohere if considered as a single convergent study. The physical studies scaffold our understanding of the life sciences, which scaffold our understanding of the human sciences, which scaffold the humanities, which scaffold the arts: and here we stand. What then is the totality? What do we call it? Can there be a study of the totality? Do history, philosophy, cosmology, science, and literature each claim to constitute the totality, an unexpandable horizon beyond which we cannot think? Could a strong discipline be defined as one that has a vision of totality and claims to encompass all the rest? And are they all wrong to do so?

Is the totality simply praxis, meaning what we do with ourselves and our world? Is there no such thing as totality, but only convergence? Convergence of all our fields of thought into human actions?

At the time of our study, these issues were very confused, and different disciplines took differing attitudes. Some fields focused on strictly human problems. This limited focus was deliberate, a statement about meaning that said that human life should be the subject of study for human beings until we reach a point where we are all well enough we can afford to think about other things.

Some in physics and other disciplines replied to this idea by asserting that many extrahuman realms have decisive effects on the achievement of human justice, so the strongest humanism would arise from a focus including physics, biology, and cosmology, also consciousness science. Justice would be considered as partly a consciousness state, and partly a particular physical or ecological state among symbiotic organisms.

Those holding the anthropocentric view argued

that if focusing on the extrahuman realm could have helped to achieve justice among humans, it would have already. Because humans had been extremely powerful for centuries, and yet justice had not arrived.

Physics advocates riposted with the assertion that this failure had happened only because the larger physical reality was still being excluded from the project of justice.

These mirror arguments rebounded back and forth for a long time, not just in the Dithering but all the way into the Balkanization and the fateful year 2312. And so humanity hung suspended in the face of its unenacted project. They knew but they didn't act. The reader may scoff at them; but it takes courage to act, and perseverance too. Indeed if the reader's own time is still imperfect, though it be ever so long after the time described here, the author would not be surprised to hear it.

SWAN IN THE VULCANOIDS

Terminator's council had finally chosen the new Lion of Mercury, an old friend of Alex and Mqaret's named Kris. Soon after being installed, Kris asked Swan to join a trip being organized to the Vulcanoids; Kris wanted to reaffirm the agreement Alex had made with the Vulcanoids to broker their light transmission to the outer planets. "It was another one of Alex's verbal deals," Kris said with a frown, "and since she died, and even more after the city burned, we've seen signs that the Vulcanoids are going upsystem behind our backs. It's made some of us wonder—do you know if Interplan is investigating the Vulcanoids as possible suspects in the attack on Terminator?"

"I don't think they are."

Swan didn't really want to go, or think about Genette's ongoing investigation, as she was now absorbed in planting the redesigned park. But it would be a short trip, and the work would still be going on when she returned. So she packed her bag and stepped off with Kris and some aides onto the platform nearest Ustad Isa Crater, where there was a new railgun launch complex throwing ships downsystem.

Vulcanized spaceships were bulbous things, heavily protected and windowless. Their runs took them down to the string of thirty-kilometer asteroids orbiting in a zone 0.1 astronomical unit from the sun, meaning only fifteen million kilometers away from the star. Discovered from Mercury in the late twenty-first century, this almost perfectly circular necklace of burnt but stable beauties had recently been colonized, despite their being one thousand K on their sunward sides. These hemispheres, tidally locked so that they always faced the sun, had burnt away to the extent of several kilometers of rock loss over their lifetimes; they were primordial objects, as old as the oldest asteroids. Now they had been occupied like terraria anywhere else— hollowed out, with the excavated material used in this case to make immense circular light-catching solet- tas. These solettas processed and redirected sunlight in lased beams that could be aimed at receiver solet- tas in the outer solar system, now blazing like God's own streetlights in the skies of Triton and Ganymede. The effect out there was dramatic enough that there were more outer satellite settlements asking for Vul- can streetlights than there were Vulcanoids to provide them.

As their sundiver approached the Vulcan orbit, the image shown onscreen represented the sun as a red circle and the Vulcanoids as a loose necklace of bril- liant yellow dots across and outside the red. Green lines representing the lased light extended from the yellow dots outward to the sides of the image. The sun bulked large in all the representations. It seemed a fiery great dragon, and yet they kept flying toward it—boldly, rashly—they were too close for comfort. It was a trans- gression sure to be punished. On one screen it looked like a burning red heart, the grainy texture of flowing cell tops like muscle cut against the grain. They *must* be too close.

From its antisolar side, the particular Vulcanoid they approached was a bare dark rock, a typical potato asteroid, surrounded by a silver umbrella a hundred times its size. The dock was in the middle of the rock. At a certain point near the end of their approach, the asteroid and its soletta created a solar eclipse, and the unnerving sight of the red sun became in the end a mere halo of coronal fire, flailing its electric aura; then they were in the dark, in the shelter of the Vulcanoid's shade. It was a palpable relief.

The people inside the rock were sun worshippers, as might be expected. Some looked like the sunwalkers of Mercury's outback, carefree and foolish; others seemed like ascetics of a religious order. Most were men or hermaphrodites. They lived in the closest solar orbit that an object could maintain; the so-called sundivers were craft that only dipped a bit closer to the sun and then fled. This was as close as one could live.

It was inherently a religious space; Swan could accept that, but had a hard time imagining the votaries' lives. The terrarium inside the rock was a desert, which was appropriate in the circumstances, but extremely uncomfortable: hot, dry, dusty. Even the Mojave was lush compared to it.

So this was a form of self-mortification, and while Swan had tried many such forms in her youth, and during the height of her abramovics, she no longer believed in self-mortification as an end in itself. She also felt that this new technology in the solettas had altered the devotional nature of these people's lives, turning them into something more like lighthouse keepers. Their new system was ten million times stronger than Mercury's older light-transferring technology, which would henceforth be rendered historical, like an oil lamp. Both Mercury's contribution to the Mondragon Accord and its ability to do above and beyonds were greatly diminished by this development, and one part of the compensation the Mondragon committee had suggested was that Terminator should be the coordinating agent and broker for this new Vulcan ability to transfer light; but it was a matter for the principals to work out. As it had been, by Alex; but now that Alex was gone, and the brokerage house had been torched, would their clients and/or fellow citizens remain loyal to the deal? Would they help rebuild their agent, their bank, their old home?

"Well," one of them said after Kris had described Terminator's hope that the deal would hold. "Getting light to the outer system is our contribution to the Mondragon and to humanity. We're in a better position to do this than you are on Mercury. We know you helped us get started, but now the Saturnians are offering to cover the costs of building solettas on all the Vulcanoids that can support them. And they really need our light out there. So we'll take up as much of their offer as we can. It's a bit more than we can handle right now, to tell the truth. We're still fine-tuning the second generations. There are issues we're still working on. We don't have enough people to take advantage of everything they're offering us."

Kris was nodding. "You need our help to coordinate the whole effort. You're down here peeling around at speed, getting cooked and getting your stations going."

They thought that over. Their speaker said, "Maybe so. But when Terminator was out of commission, we had no problems. Now we're thinking that Mercury should contribute to the Mondragon with things other than light, and leave us to it. You've got heavy metals, art history, and Terminator itself as a work of art, a tourist destination for the grand tour and for sun watchers. You'll be fine."

Kris shook her head. "We're the capital of the inner system. With all due respect, you people operate power stations here. You need administration."

"Maybe."

Swan said, "Which Saturnians have you been talking to about this?"

They stared at her. "They speak to us as a league," one of them replied. "But we have the same Saturnian liaison you do—their inner planets ambassador. You know him better than we do, from what we hear."

"You mean Wahram?"

"Of course. He told us that you Mercurials knew the interplanetary situation, and would understand how important our light is to the Titan project. And to all the other outer planets as well."

Swan did not reply.

Kris began discussing the Triton settlement and the plan there to stellarize Neptune.

"Yes," one of the Vulcans replied, "but the Saturnians won't do that to Saturn."

Swan interrupted them: "Tell me more about Wahram; when did he visit you?"

"A couple years ago, I think."

"Two years?"

"Wait," another of them put in. "Our year is only six weeks long, so that was a joke there. It was just recently."

"It was since Terminator burned," the first speaker clarified, looking at her curiously.

Kris filled in the silence that followed, reminding the Vulcans that as the new Lion of Mercury, Kris was now the titular head of their order. But these particular Vulcans were not Greys, as they were quick to inform Kris; they were adherents of some schismatic sect that did not consider the Lion of Mercury to be their head. Nevertheless they were very polite, and Kris continued to try to convince them to keep the deal; but Swan had trouble following the conversation. She was getting angrier at Wahram the longer she considered what he had done, to the point where she wasn't listening anymore. Right in the time he had said he would work with her, after they had found the ship floating in the clouds of Saturn, he had come down here instead and undermined her cause. It was a hard little sucker punch.

Lists (11)

Annie Oakley Crater, Dorothy Sayers Crater.
Also craters named for:
Madame Sévigné, Shakira (a Bashkir goddess),
Martha Graham, Hippolyta, Nina Efimova,
Dorothea Erxleben, Lorraine Hansberry, Catherine
Beevher;
also the Mesopotamian fertility goddess, the Celtic
river goddess, the Woyo rainbow goddess, the
Pueblo Indian corn goddess, the Vedic goddess of
plenty, the Roman goddess of the hunt (Diana),
the Latvian goddess of fate;
also Anna Comnena, Charlotte Corday, Mary Queen
of Scots, Madame de Staël, Simone de Beauvoir,
Josephine Baker.
Also Aurelia, the mother of Julius Caesar. Tezan, the
Etruscan goddess of the dawn. Alice B. Toklas.
Xantippe. Empress Wuhou. Virginia Woolf. Laura
Ingalls Wilder.
Evangeline, Fátima, Gloria, Gaia, Helen, Heloise.
Lillian Hellman, Edna Ferber, Zora Neale Hurston.
Guinevere, Nell Gwyn, Martine de Beausoleil.

Sophia Jex-Blake, Jerusha Jirad, Angelica Kauffman.
Maria Merian, Maria Montessori, Marianne Moore.
Mu Guiying. Vera Mukhina. Aleksandra Potanina.
Margaret Sanger. Sappho. Zoya. Sarah Winnemucca.
   Seshat. Jane Seymour. Rebecca West. Marie Stopes.
   Alfonsina Storni. Anna Volkova. Sabina Steinbach.
   Mary Wollstonecraft. Anna von Schuurman. Jane
   Austen. Wang Zenyi. Karen Blixen.
Sojourner Truth. Harriet Tubman.
Hera. Emily Dickinson.

WAHRAM ON VENUS

Wahram was in the city of Colette, trying to get at least some of the Venus Working Group to support the plan to intervene on Earth; also to ask certain Venusian friends for help in Genette's plan to deal with the strange qubes. Neither project was going particularly well, even though Shukra seemed willing to help; but he wanted help in return, in dealing with his local conflicts, and Wahram didn't see how that could be done. More would be needed from the Mondragon and Saturn both if they were going to entrain any of the Venusians in the upcoming Terran effort.

Then during a welcome break in the negotiations there was a knock at the conference chamber door, and Swan came in. He was shocked to see her, and shocked again when she saw him, strode across the room, crashed right into him, and struck him on the chest with the back of her fists. "You bastard!" she exclaimed, not very quietly. "You lied to me, you lied!"

He stepped back, hands up, looking around for a place to retreat where the conversation could continue a bit more privately. "I did not! What do you mean!"

"You went to the Vulcanoids and made a deal with them and you didn't tell me about it!"

"That isn't lying," he said, feeling like he was splitting hairs, but it was true, and gave him time to back out into a passageway, then around a corner, where he could stop and defend himself: "I was down there doing my job for the Saturn League, it was nothing to do with you, and you have to admit we are not in the habit of sharing our complete work schedules with each other. I haven't seen you in a year."

"That's because you've been on Earth, making deals there too. Which you didn't tell me about either. What *did* you tell me about? *Nothing!*"

Wahram had been worried about this, had ignored the problem and done his job; but now here it was, the reckoning. "I was away," he said feebly.

"*Away*—what's *away*?" she demanded. "Look, were you in the tunnel or not? Were we in the tunnel together or not?"

"We were," he said, putting his hands up in defense, or protest. "I was there." I wasn't the one who claimed *not* to be there, he didn't say.

In any case she had stopped and was staring at him. They stared at each other for a while.

"Listen," Wahram said. "I work for Saturn. I'm the league's ambassador to the inner planets, doing my job here. It's not—it's not something I can automatically share. I do it in a different sphere."

"But we just suffered an attack and lost our city right down to the framing. We need to keep what gifts we have to give. And part of that was light."

"Those were not useful amounts of light. The entirety of what you could send from Mercury meant little around Saturn. With the Vulcanoids it's different.

They can send out enough to make a real difference. We *need* it for Titan. So, I'm charged with arranging that. It's like bidding for futures shares. I'm sorry I didn't tell you about it myself. I guess I was...I was afraid. I didn't want you mad at me. But now you are anyway."

"Even worse," she assured him. But now she was piling on, he saw, for the theater of it. He played to that:

"It was stupid of me. I'm sorry. I'm a bad man."

That almost made her laugh, he could see. "Fucking bastard," she said instead, continuing her play. "The stuff you did on Earth is even worse anyway. You cut a deal with the rich nations of Earth, that's what it comes down to and you know it. Which is a disgrace. There are people down there living in cardboard shacks. You know how it is. It's always that way, and it looks like it'll go on forever. So they'll always hate us, and some will attack us. And we pop like soap bubbles. There's no solution but justice for everyone. It's the only thing that will make us safe. Until then some group will always conclude that killing spacers is the only way to get our attention. And the sad thing is that they may be right."

"Because now you're paying attention?"

She glared at him. "Because the situation down there has gone on too long!"

He tilted his head side to side, trying to figure out how to say what he felt. He walked her down the passageway a little farther, to a long table covered with little cookies and big coffee tanks. He poured them cups of coffee. "So...to protect ourselves, you're saying, we have to orchestrate a global revolution on Earth."

"Yes."

"And how? I mean, people have been trying that for centuries now."

"That's no excuse to stop! I mean here we are on Venus, on Titan, out here doing *everything*. There are things that could work down there. Spread something through their cell phones. Give them a stake in the Mondragon. Build housing or do land work. Make it that kind of revolution, one of the nonviolent ones. If something happens fast enough they call it a revolution whether guns go off or not."

"But the guns are there."

"Maybe they are, but what if no one dares to shoot them? What if what we did was always too innocuous? Or even invisible?"

"These kinds of actions are never invisible. No— there would be resistance. Don't fool yourself."

"So all right, we press on against resistance, see what happens. We're resource rich, and we're growing a lot of their food. We have the *leverage*."

He thought it over. "Maybe we do, but they play by their rules there."

She shook her head violently. "There's a gift economy in people's feelings that precedes all the rules. Set one up and people give themselves to it. And we have to do something. If we don't, they'll shoot us down. They'll kill us and eat us."

Wahram sipped his coffee, trying to slow her down. She had gone too far, as always. He would like to hear what Pauline would say about all this, but there was no way he was going to be given access to Pauline at this moment. Swan had seized up the cup he had poured for her and slurped it down, then started lecturing him some more, emphasizing her points with the coffee cup so that he was going to be lucky not to have it poured on him.

And in fact, though she was going too far, as usual,

she was also expressing things Wahram had been thinking himself. Really, it was just another articulation of a point that Alex had been making for years. So he seized a moment when she was catching her breath and said, "The problem is that what's needed to be done has been clear for centuries now, but no one does it because it would take a very large number of people to enact it. Construction work, landscape restoration, decent farming, they all take huge numbers of people."

"But there *are* huge numbers of people! If the unemployed were mobilized, there's your numbers. The revolution of full employment. The place is trashed, they're cooked, they need to do it. In effect Earth needs terraforming as much as Venus or Titan! In fact it needs it more, and we're not doing it."

Wahram thought it over. "Could it be sold that way, do you think? As a restoration? Appeal to the conservatives as well as the revolutionaries—or at least confuse the issue as to what is really happening?"

"I don't think we need to be confusing."

"If you are clear about your intention, Swan, there will be opposition. Don't be naïve. Any change will be opposed. And by serious opposition. I mean violence."

"If they can find the way to apply it. But if there's no one to arrest, no one to beat back, no one to scare..."

He shook his head, unconvinced.

Swan was pacing around him like a comet around the sun; Wahram rotated to face her. Twice she rushed him again and beat him on the chest with the hand not holding her coffee cup. Their voices crossed in an antiphony that anyone listening would have heard as a duet for croak and cheep.

Finally the dissonant duet came to an end. Swan was winding down at last. She had just arrived on Venus, it was clear, and was beginning to yawn despite the coffee. Wahram sighed with relief, shifted the timbre of his voice to something calmer, changed the subject. They stared out the window at the falling snow, blown by a hard gale into frolic architectures plastered over everything. This world, so new and raw, still emerging, told them with great whacks of wind: things were changing.

Wahram considered Alex's two unfinished projects: to deal with Earth; to deal with the qubes. He felt a shiver, as suddenly it seemed to him that these projects were becoming parts of one thing. Very well, but it would take real craft to pull them together; it would take some cleverness in the execution. And Swan was going to keep getting mad at him until he helped to make it happen. But he thought perhaps he could.

Extracts (13)

certain metabolic actions accumulate lifetime damage, and each kind of damage has to be treated individually, and the treatments coordinated with each other as well as with the ordinary functioning of the organism

cell loss or atrophy is ameliorated by exercise, growth factors, and directed stem cells

cancerous mutations are identified by massively parallel DNA sequencing and transcriptome sequencing and dissolved by targeted gene therapies and telomerase manipulation; chemo and radiation therapies are now highly targeted, using monoclonal antibodies, avimers and designed proteins

death-resistant cells that are senescent in their function must not be allowed to transform into harmful forms, but must rather be targeted by suicide genes and immune response

undamaged mitochondria are introduced into cells suffering mitochondrial mutations

lipofuscin is one kind of accumulated junk inside our cells that can't be carried away by the immune system. Amyloid plaques are another. Enzymes adapted from bacteria and molds that completely digest animal bodies will upon introduction flourish until their nutrient runs out, and this absence activates inserted suicide genes in the enzymes. Extracellular aggregates are removed by vaccinations that stimulate immune responses, including a state of enhanced phagocytosis. Complications include

random extracellular cross-linking of cells makes for stiffness, but the links have been successfully broken with enzymes designed to

the manipulation of telomerase has proved to be a very difficult balancing act in certain cell types: telomeres too long and you get a cancerous immortality, telomeres too short and you quickly hit the Hayflick limit and replication is no longer successful

while DNA repair involves a DNA polymerase with an exonuclease-proofreading capability, resulting in high-fidelity DNA repair, RNA polymerases do not have this and therefore make many more mistakes during gene transcription; this is a potent driver of evolution

pleiotropy is the phenomenon of a gene causing good effects in the young organism that turn into bad effects in the same organism when aged. It is very often the source of the problems that bisexual hormone treatments are designed to

hormesis (eagerness) is an eventually advantageous biological response to low exposures of toxins or stressors. This process, sometimes called eustress, and related to Mithridatism (after King Mithridates, who ate small amounts of poison so that a larger amount would not kill him), has been put forth as explaining in principle why the Earth sabbatical might help maximize longevity

strongest correlations to longevity include smaller body size and exposure to both androgens and estrogens; these two are also multipliers of each other, to the extent that no small androgyn or gynandromorph has yet been known to die of natural causes. The oldest are over 210 years old, and their potential life span cannot be calculated at this time. There are likely to be more such subjects to study as this finding becomes better known

actuarial escape velocity is defined as occurring when a year of medical research adds more than a year's worth of longevity to the total population. Nothing even close to this has ever been achieved, and emerging signs of an asymptotic curve in progress suggest this velocity may never

premature declaration of huge longevity gains has been called kyriasis or Dorian Gray syndrome or simply the hope for immortality

lengthen the telomeres in certain cells by temporary increase of telomerase in these cells. As different cells lose telomeres at different rates, drug treatments have to be tagged to certain kinds of cells only, and inadvertent cancers

biogerontology, humbled time and again by unexpected

the famous calorie-restricted vitamin-enhanced diet acted to feminize gene expression in many ways that proved decisive for the longevity effect, so now gender hormone therapy is tailored to create this feminizing effect without the necessity of the caloric restriction, which never caught on

if you recall the old comparison of the human body to a Havana Chevolet, with all moving parts replaced when they broke, then the problem could be compared to metal fatigue in the chassis and axles. In other words, the "seven deadly sins" of senescence are not the only sins. Unrepaired DNA damage, noncancerous mutation, the drift of chromatin states—all these eventually create "aging damage" hard to detect or counteract. None are currently amenable to repair. This probably explains the

take skin cells from people, turn them into pluripotent stem cells, put these in a protein bath of the right kind and they form a neural tube, which is the start of the nervous system that will grow the spinal cord from one end and the brain from the other. Take slices of neural tube and direct them with other protein stimulants to become cells of different parts of the brain, like cortex cells. Test for firing.

arrhythmia, stroke, sudden collapse, quick decline, immune loophole, brain wave irregularity, superinfection, heart attack, apparently causeless instantaneous death (ACID), etc.

KIRAN IN VINMARA

Kiran's new work unit began regularly driving a rover back and forth from one of Lakshmi's locked compounds in Cleopatra to the new town Vinmara, always passing Stupid Harbor on the way. Vinmara was still growing like a mussel bed around its shallow empty bay, and off to the south through the drifting snowfall they could see the silver glitter of the dry ice sea.

After one of these runs, when they were back in Cleopatra, Kiran ran into Kexue in a game bar they both frequented, and the voluble small said, "Come meet a friend of mine. You'll like him."

It turned out to be Shukra, beard and hair long and gray; he looked like a wandering mendicant. Kexue grinned as Kiran recognized the man. "I told you you'd like him."

Kiran mumbled something awkward.

"It's all right," Shukra said, staring hard at him. "You were bait, I told you that. And you got taken. So now I'm here to tell you what to do next. Lakshmi's got you on the route between her compound here and that coastal town, right?"

"That's right," Kiran said. He could see how he probably still owed his first Venusian contact his services, but it was becoming all too clear to him how dangerous it was to play both sides. He didn't want to cross Lakshmi in any way; on the other hand, this man did not seem like someone to be trifled with either. Indeed at the moment there was no way to deny him. "There's shipments going both directions, but we don't see what gets loaded."

"I want you to find out what it is. Insinuate yourself further into the situation, and then let me know what you find."

"How will I contact you?"

"You won't. I'll contact you."

So after that, feeling deeply uneasy, Kiran kept his eye out when they were making the Vinmara run. It became clearer than ever to him that the transport crew was not intended to know the contents of their rovers; there were guards on every run, and the office in central Vinmara was as closed to outsiders as the various facilities in Cleopatra. The rovers backed up to a loading dock and interfaced with the building, and after a while drove away, and that was it. Once, when an exceptionally deep snowfall delayed them mid-route, Kiran listened without watching as the guard in their cab had a phone conversation that seemed to be with people in the storage compartment of the rover; they spoke Chinese, and later Kiran had his translation spectacles translate the recording it had made:

"Are you okay back there?"

"We're fine. They're fine."

They? Anyway, it was something to tell Shukra, if he reappeared.

* * *

As it happened, they were down in Vinmara when the big blizzard finally stopped. The skies cleared; the stars in all their glory punctured the black dome of the sky. Naturally they joined the whole town in suiting up and going out the city gates onto the bare hills above the town. The continuous deluge of snow and sleet and hail and rain had gone on for three years and three months. Now everyone wanted to see what things looked like under the stars.

Almost all the landscape they could see was covered by snow, gleaming in the starlight. Many spiky points of black rock broke through this gleaming white—the land surrounding the town must have been a devil's golf course of *aa* or something like it—and the result was that over their heads the black sky spangled with brilliant stars, while under their feet the white hills were spattered by spiky black outcroppings, so that the two together looked like photographic negatives of each other.

And now they could breathe the open air. It was screamingly cold, of course, so as people pulled off their helmets they did scream, casting brief plumes of frost from their open mouths. Breathable air—a nitrogen-argon-oxygen mix, at seven hundred millibars, and ten degrees below. It was like breathing vodka.

The snow underfoot was too hard to dig out snow-balls, and people were falling as they skidded this way and that. Out on the hilltop above the town they could see for huge distances in all directions.

It was around noon, and among the stars overhead hung the black circle of the eclipsed sun. A black cut-out in the sky—the sunshield, letting through no sunlight—except for today, when there was a scheduled uneclipse. These uneclipses had been happening once a month for a while now, to help heat things back up to a more human-friendly level, but no one on the planet had been able to see them because the rain and snow had blocked the view. Now there would be one they would be able to see.

Many people were putting their helmets back on; the reality of the cold was setting in. Kiran's nose was numb, while his ears were still burning as they froze. People said you could break frozen ears right off, and now he believed it. Music was playing from loudspeakers down in the town, something clangorous with cymbals and bells, very Slavic, very violent and loud.

Then directly overhead the sunshield was suddenly marked by a perfectly circular thread of diamond light, blazing near the edge of the black disk. Though this annular ring was a mere wire of brilliant yellow, a delicate hoop of fire, it still lit up the white hills and the scalloped town, and the silver sea to the south, and the plumes of frost pouring from their cheering throats, all glowing now with a bronze light that brought back memories of all the sunniness they had ever known or dreamed of. The burnished tinge was like the light of life itself, a light they had almost forgot, all brought back now by the yellow air.

After a frigid hour the ring of fire grew thinner and thinner, eclipsing from its inside out, until the disk of the sun became completely black again. The circular venetian blind had closed its opened slat. The snowy land darkened to its usual pale luminosity; the stars grew big again. Full night was back, in all its grim familiarity. Just above the black disk of the sun a bright white planet gleamed, small but steady: Mercury, Kiran was told. They were seeing Mercury from

Venus, and it gleamed like a pearl made of diamond. And there over the western horizon hung Earth and Luna too, a double star with a blue tinge. "Wow," Kiran said; something in him seemed to be blowing up like a balloon. Had to breathe deep or he might pop.

But his teammates were tugging at his arm. "Earth boy! Earth boy! Bye-bye miss America pie! We must get back in town fast, there's a rover broken down, Lakshmi want us right now!"

"Lead on!" Kiran cried, and followed them back down the hillside to the open gates of Vinmara.

Just inside the city gate they followed phone instructions to the rover that was in distress. It looked exactly like their own. The driver and a trio of security people were standing by it, very unhappy; the rover had lost all power, and some packages needed to be run over to the office in the town center as quickly and discreetly as possible. Kiran stood in a short line with his teammates and took a big flat box passed down from one of the security people, thinking that this might be his opportunity to find out what was being transported. Then they were off across town in a little line, like porters.

The town was almost empty, its residents still out on the hill celebrating. The box Kiran was carrying weighed about five kilos; it was not exceptionally heavy for its size. There was a keypad lock on it, near the hasp, that made it look like a reinforced briefcase. They were not far from the office. The actual hinges of the case looked little and flimsy, and he wondered what would happen if he accidentally dropped it on its hinge side.

But then the security trio from the disabled rover appeared, crying, "Run! Run! Get to the office now!" looking over their shoulders fearfully with their guns drawn. Everyone bolted, and Kiran, following the others, seeing they were rattled, shifted the briefcase in his hands so that its hinges were out to his side. When his mates turned a corner to run down a narrow alley, he pretended to trip, and slammed the case hard into the corner of a wall, right against the hinges.

The case held solid.

"Oh shit! Did you break them?" someone exclaimed from behind him—one of the security guards—a Chinese tall, standing over him now, looking horrified.

"What, are they eggs?" Kiran asked as he got up.

"Like eggs," the guard said, taking the box up and punching away at its keypad. "And if they're broken, we better leave town." The top of the box lifted, and there in individual clear containers lay a dozen human eyeballs—all of them, by coincidence, Kiran assumed, staring right at him.

Extracts (14)

The space project accelerated as it was becoming clear that Earth was in for a terrible time because of the climate change and general despoliation of the biosphere. Going into space looked like an attempt to escape all that, and there was enough truth in this that defenders of the space project always had to emphasize its humanitarian and environmental value, the ways in which the resources available in the solar system might help Earth limp through its stupendous overshoot. Inhabiting the other bodies of the solar system could be said to conform to the Leopoldian land ethic, "what's good is what's good for the land," because it was going to take stuff from space to save Earth

first settlements on Luna, Mars, and the asteroids were so expensive that they were made as international or national projects, using public money. This made them pitifully weak through the years of dithering, but following the construction of the first space elevators, they blossomed, and by the time of the Accelerando they were ready to take center stage—ready to be the landscape of the Accelerando

Mars was the first to be terraformed, and compared to those that followed, it was very easy. Early on the decision was made to proceed as quickly as possible. Thousands of explosions were set off in the regolith (it was said this would help the Martian life-forms buried in the lithosphere), and much of the surface of the planet was burned, in lines that later served as beds for the planet's famous canals. The burning created an atmosphere, and the planet's ice was mined and melted such that a narrow northern ocean and a Hellas Sea were filled. Little to no regard was taken for the primordial surface, and yet it was also true that the vertical scale of the planet's topography protected the highest parts of the landscape from much alteration, leaving it as a kind of primeval park

a mass influx of immigrants from Earth quickly melded into a polyglot community that within two generations thought of itself as intrinsically and fundamentally Martian, *Homo ares*, and as such, a political unit independent of Earth by nature and by right. The entire population agreed to secede from all Terran associations, afterward reorganizing under a new constitution that stipulated a single planetary government and an economic system variously labeled socialist, communist, utopian, democratic-state-anarchic, syndicalist, worker cooperative, libertarian socialist, and any number of other labels from the past, all of which were rejected by Martian political theorists, who preferred the adjective "martian" or "areological." As a new socioeconomic system with a newly created biosphere to work in, Mars was a socio-physical power the equal of any single Earth nation or alliance and in many ways,

because of its unity, the equal of all the rest of balkanized humanity combined

fears were stoked when Mars in the first flush of independence began to strip the nitrogen from Titan's
atmosphere for return to Mars, without regard for the
opinions of the people already in the Saturn system,
admittedly few in number. Around this same time
(2176–2196), Chinese teams dismantled Saturn's moon
Dione in order to redirect it to Venus as part of the
initial terraformation there. In the disruption on Earth
following the Little Ice Age of the 2140s, there was no
power on Earth large enough to challenge the Chinese
over this distant move. But these two events around
Saturn together stimulated the creation of the Saturn
League, which over time managed to assert sovereignty
over the whole Saturn system—although it is true that
the threat of a traumatic Saturn-Mars war, Saturn's
phantom war of independence, as some called it—was
needed to finalize the assertion

Earth's moon, Luna, never achieved independence, but
was always divided into cities and regions controlled
by various Terran powers. It would have been difficult
to fully terraform Luna in any case, because hitting it
with asteroids to spin it and give it an atmosphere was
considered too likely to subject Earth to a tektite rain
of potentially great severity. It was also true that metals and useful chemicals in lunar rock could be mined
only by a deep strip-mining and processing of much of
the lunar surface, which also made terraforming difficult. So large domed craters and tented areas alter-
nated with cosmologically large mining pits, and each
nation with a substantial lunar presence had an influx

of raw materials. China's early investment on Luna led directly to its influence over Venus, because the Venus sunshield was a product of the lunar Chinese industrial bases. At the same time many other Terran nations established lunar bases, and the political unification of Luna became impossible. Some locate the origins of the Balkanization to this development, although most see qubical decoherence and the sheer size of the solar system as the key

balkanization is of course the subject of great disagreement, with judgments of it ranging from its being the newly lowest circle of hell to its representing the delectable and fructifying diversification of life in our time

success is failure. The Accelerando spread all the weakness, disease, and crime embedded in the Terran system of that era, and once spread that widely, they could never be contained. Pandora's box had been

by the beginning of the twenty-fourth century the Mondragon Accord had organized a third force to join the Earth-Mars dyad, and the Jovian and Saturnian leagues provided major counterweights as well. A situation of this much diplomatic complexity brought back talk of a "balance of powers," of the "great game," of a "cold war," and so on: all ideas from earlier eras, again haunting us as they have a wont to do, hungry ghosts deceiving us with their false analogies, laying their dead hands on our living eyes! Ultimately the Balkanization was by its scope and special nature a new thing

It was rumored in these years that Martian spies were everywhere in the system, but that they were constantly reporting back to headquarters that there was nothing to fear—balkanization meant Mars faced nothing but a stochastic chaos of human flailing

WAHRAM ON EARTH

That he would alter his plans, not to say change his life, all to help and please a person he did not know very well or trust very much, someone who was often angry at him and just as likely to punch his chest as smile at him; someone who might give him the evil eye at any time, might snarl at him contemptuously, so that really all his efforts to please her could be labeled a form of cowardice rather than affection—this surprised him. And yet it was turning out to be the case. He had already spent the greater part of the previous year traveling all over the system, rallying diplomatic and material support for Alex's plans to revivify Earth and to deal with the qube problem; now added to this campaign, he spent a lot of time thinking about ways to implement Swan's notion of rapidly improving conditions for the Terran forgotten ones. Whether Swan was aware of his efforts he doubted, but he felt she could find out if she wanted to, as his life was an open book, except for the parts he was hiding from her. He certainly wasn't going to tell her what he had done. It seemed to him that the intensity of her engagement with him at their last crossing—beating on him and yelling at him—meant she had been paying attention, and would continue to. And actions were what mattered.

The nature of this new work was terribly hard on his pseudoiterative mode, which became so much more pseudo than iterative that it tipped over into the flux of sheer exfoliation, every day different and no patterns possible. This was hard for him, and as day followed day, then week week, and month month, he began to wonder, not why he was doing what he was doing, but why Swan was not contacting him to join forces. They would have accomplished more working as a team. Combining the powers of the innermost and outermost societies in the solar system would have some good effects, and it would seem therefore that Mercury and Saturn should be natural partners and, if they were, become a force almost the equal of the big bangers in the middle. Wahram could see several potential leverages. But she had not called or sent any messages.

So he continued to work. In some countries their campaign was called Rapid Noncompliance Alleviation— RNA. The noncompliance was with the United Nations Declaration of Human Rights, and the infractions involved many articles of that document, but most often articles 17, 23, and 25, with 28 occasionally waved about as a reminder to recalcitrant governments. In other countries their programs were based on a venerable Indian government office, the Society for the Elimination of Rural Poverty (SERP). This organization had never gotten much traction in its stated goal, but it was an already existing agency, and these had been identified by the Mondragon as the best of the bad options for channeling assistance. Wahram had thought it generally agreed that the whole development-aid model had been demonstrated to be an example of the Jevons Paradox, in which increases in efficiency trigger more consumption rather than less; increased aid had always somehow increased suffering, in some kind of feedback loop, poorly theorized—or else theorized perfectly well, but in such a way that revealed the entire system to be a case of vampiric rich people moving around the Earth performing a complicated kleptoparasitism on the poor. No one wanted to hear that news, so they kept on repeating errors identified four hundred years before, on ever-grander scales. So, the Planet of Sadness.

There were of course very powerful forces on Earth adamantly opposed to tinkering from above in general, and to creating full employment in particular. Full employment, if enacted, would remove "wage pressure"—which phrase had always meant *fear struck into the hearts of the poor*, also into the hearts of anyone who feared becoming poor, which meant almost everyone on Earth. This fear was a major tool of social control, indeed the prop that held up the current order despite its obvious failures. Even though it was a system so bad that everyone in it lived in fear, either of starvation or the guillotine, still they clutched to it harder than ever. It was painful to witness.

Nevertheless, the immiserated were ready to try anything. So something ought to be possible.

So Wahram crisscrossed the Old World like a modern-day Ibn Battuta, talking to government agencies in a position to do something. This was awkward work that took a real diplomatic touch to avoid being offensive in various ways. It was interesting. But he heard nothing from Swan. And Earth was big. There were 457 countries, and many associations of countries, and units within countries with significant power. Wahram was not going to run into Swan just because she also was at work on Earth.

So he looked her up. Apparently she was working near North Harare, a small country carved out of what had been Zimbabwe.

He read about the place on the flight there. Zimbabwe, rich in resources; a particularly dismal postcolonial history; splintered into a dozen residual countries, many still mired in problems; the great droughts exacerbating the situation; lately a recent population spike, and thus more trouble. North Harare was a slum in the shape of a crescent moon. The other little countries around it were better off.

He contacted Pauline and told her that he was coming to the area on RNA-related business, and soon enough Pauline got back to him with a hello from Swan and a suggested meeting on the very evening of his arrival, which was reassuring but meant that he had to meet her oppressed by jet lag. He was almost quivering with fatigue, and felt as if he weighed two hundred kilograms, when Swan burst into the room and it was time to perk up.

She gave him a nod and a quick appraisal. "You look like you've had a long trip. Come on in and I'll make you some tea and you can tell me about it."

She started the tea and then excused herself to deal with a visitor, talking in Chinese. Wahram tried hard to grasp what she was like now, vividly before him again. Still intense, that was clear.

Over tea they shared the news. Certain space elevators were slapping tariffs on equipment coming down;

others were completely denied to spacers, an absurd situation. People were calling the Quito elevator the Umbilical Cord. It looked like the elevator problem would be a bottleneck, but there was a plan afoot to send down self-replicating factories from cislunar space, deployed in a single timed invasion of thousands of atmospheric landers. A wide variety of space-to-Earth landers were available, including some that split successively as they descended, until individual people or packages floated down in aerogel bubbles.

"That's like the reverse of what hit Terminator," Swan said sourly. "Instead of little bits convening to make a big mass, the big mass dissociates into parts. And when they land, things get built rather than destroyed."

"They might get shot down."

"There would be too many for that."

"I don't like the aggressive look of it," Wahram said. "I thought we were trying to make it look like a charity thing."

"Charity is always aggressive," Swan said. "Don't you know that?"

"No, I don't think I do."

It seemed clear to him that aggressive aid wasn't going to work. But Swan was not a patient person. Now she was trying to do diplomatic work in the way Alex would have; but Alex had had a genius for diplomacy, while Swan had none. And they were facing one of the longest-standing problems in human history.

The whole thing transcended their own opinions about it in any case, as it was a Mondragon effort, with the Venusians on board too. So all kinds of things were happening. News screens seemed to be transmitting news from ten Earths at once, all writhing in the same space. Earth meant people like gods and people like rats: and in a paroxysm of rage they were going to reach out and wreck everything, even the space worlds that kept them from starvation. In the big merry-go-round, Earth spun like a red horse with a bomb in it. And they could not get off the merry-go-round.

Absentmindedly Wahram whistled under his breath the opening notes of Beethoven's *Pastoral Symphony*, trying to cheer her up. But she pursed her lips to make a little frown. Still, he had reminded her of the tunnel.

Many spacers were scared to go to sub-Saharan Africa, because the disease vector loads there were so much higher than in most space habitats. Wahram supposed that Swan had gone to Africa partly in defiance of that kind of caution; she would be one to believe in hormesis if anyone would, given her ingestion of the Enceladan aliens. So here she was in Nyabira, directing the deployment of self-replicating construction sheds. They planned to start by reconstructing the part of Harare called Domboshawa, transforming its northernmost ring of shantytowns into garden city versions of themselves. This "refurbishing of the built infrastructure" was not a complete solution, but the selfreps did build wells, health centers, schools, clothing factories, and housing in several styles already used in Domboshawa, including aspects of the traditional local rondavels.

The selfreps were nearly autonomous, and with proper programming, sufficient materials feed, and good troubleshooting, they rolled over evacuated portions of the shantytowns like enormous blimp hangars, leaving behind a new strip of buildings, whitewashed and impressively practical and homey. As the gigantic barns slowly grumbled over targeted neighborhoods, the hopeful residents cheered them on. That the barns themselves grew longer and longer in the process and finally split into two units went almost unremarked upon. It was an excellent tech and had built many a fine city-state in the asteroid belt and on the big moons of Jupiter. It had been a crucial component of the Accelerando, in fact.

But on Earth it wasn't working out. The transformations involved were too great; there grew furious objections, often from elsewhere than the areas being renovated. Only if residents voted for the project by a very large majority would it happen in something close to concord, and it was best when they themselves were programming the selfrep AIs.

Then a selfrep in Uttar Pradesh was blown up; no one knew why. The state government that should have investigated refused to do so, and there were signs that they might even have supported the attack. News of the attack created copycat crimes; it would take only a few more to make the project collapse worldwide.

This made Swan furious. "They attacked us when we didn't help, and now when we do," she said bitterly.

Wahram, feeling uneasy as he watched her get more and more tightly wound, said, "Even so, we must persevere."

It was happening all over Earth, Wahram saw on the screens; their restoration projects were getting tangled in dense networks of law and practice and landscape, and the occasional sabotage or accident didn't help. One couldn't change anything on Earth without several different kinds of mess resulting, some of them paralyzing. Every square meter of the Earth's land was owned in several different ways.

In space it was different. On Venus if a single roomful of planners agreed, then you could blast most of the atmosphere into space. On Titan it was similar, around Jupiter the same; throughout the solar system massive terraforming projects were proceeding. Excavate ocean beds, change out atmospheres, heat up or chill things by hundreds of K... But not on Earth. In many places the selfreps were forbidden, even reviled.

No matter what they did, it seemed that the misery of the forgotten ones would keep pulling civilization down, like an anchor they had tied around their own neck. Terran elites would stay on top of an artificial Great Chain of Being until it snapped and everyone fell into the void. A pathetic Götterdämmerung, stupid and banal, and yet still horrible.

The prospect of that was making Swan angry. Wahram, more and more aware of her bitterness, more and more the target of her anger, watched her one morning abuse one of the Harare women who helped run their operation—saw the woman's face as she was chastised—realized that if he stayed, he was going to end up crossing Swan in some catastrophic way, or simply not liking her. So that afternoon he excused himself, and the next day flew to America to join a Saturnian crew, newly arrived to help raise Florida back above the sea. On the day he left, Swan, distracted by some vexing problem of the moment, only waved him away like a mosquito.

Florida had been an unusually low-lying peninsula, it turned out, with only a thin spine down the center of the state higher than the eleven-meter rise of the oceans. One could still see the state in outline from the air, as a dark reef under a shallow sea, a reef that still bled yellow into the slightly deeper waters around it.

The skyscrapers of the Miami corridor had been occupied, like those in Manhattan and elsewhere, but by and large the state had had to be abandoned. However, as most of its soil was still there, topping the reef as a layer of mud that was not particularly damaged by inundation, the opportunity existed to scoop it up, then raise the rock foundation of the peninsula with rock trained down from the Canadian Rockies, and after that put the soil back in place on top of the newly raised bedrock platform.

In other words, it was like Greenland: one of the few places on Earth where terraforming could be performed without too much collateral damage. Naturally there were defendants of the new reefs and fishing grounds to protest, but they had been mollified or steamrolled, and the project approved in Atlanta and Washington, D.C., which itself existed in a polder behind a giant system of barrier dams on the Potomac. Washington's vestigial but still powerful government, now itself located largely below sea level, was sympathetic to the idea of "raising Florida from the drowned."

It was one of the ten biggest microterraforming projects currently being performed on Earth, and Wahram was happy to join his Saturnian colleagues, who were part of a work unit put together by an Alabama-Amsterdam cooperative venture. Teams in Alaska, British Columbia, the Yukon, and Nunavut were excavating the interiors of mountain ranges, creating galleries down in the bedrock, which were then being filled with frozen carbon dioxide they had elsewhere sucked out of the atmosphere. Whether all this could be done in a manner that was geologically and environmentally stable, Wahram doubted. It was a prodigious amount of rock, for one thing; Florida was on average five meters underwater, and they wanted to build it up slightly higher than it had been originally, in case Greenland or East Antarctica also gave their ice to the sea. Using the narrow finger of a peninsula that was the state's only remaining land as their causeway, they were moving the segmented mountain interiors on trains and building the state as they had built rock jetties in older times. The Everglades were to be plumbed to function at the new higher elevation; newly generated analogs of the many extinct species of birds and animals that had graced the peninsula before European immigration were to be introduced. They were going to recreate Florida. Enough carbon dioxide was to be buried under the northern Rockies to make the project on balance carbon negative.

The building and transport crews for the job were hired primarily from the Suffering South, as it had been called in the years when the West Antarctic Ice Sheet had come off and sea level made its biggest rise. The Florida work did not create full employment by itself, but riding the rails, Wahram had a lot of time to look at the passing country and think about it, and once he sent a note to Swan: *Remember what you said on Venus about giving everyone here a job doing landscape restoration? It could work.*

So he rode the trains back and forth from Canada to Florida. The land was huge, and mostly flat. Heat had parched land that had once grown wheat without irrigation, so they had changed crops and started irrigating, but large regions in Manitoba and the Dakotas had reverted to high desert. Now people were saying the prairies had always been high desert. They were becoming home to buffalo again. On the other hand, the forests flanking the Mississippi were back, more subtropical than ever. Missouri and Arkansas looked like South America.

There were long hours when he could stand between cars, protected from the wind of their passage, and look at the big land. Landscapers and gardeners, animal handlers and vets, environmental engineers and designers, heavy equipment operators, porters and diggers—all were essential in the work of making a landscape. The giant waldos, the selfrep hangars, they were only good for certain things. Local people working their land was a better image than selfreps dropping out of the sky. The people he talked to were more accepting of the Florida project, and the relevant governments also. Not a few people were enthusiastic to an almost religious degree. To have their drowned land hauled back out of the water was their dream. Rebuilding the infrastructure here was a task without negative consequences, except for those who had been enjoying the new reefs, and they would be given new new reefs. Florida was going to end up like a big Venice, resting on pilings stuck deep into the earth. Assisted migration would replant and reanimate the land as quickly as it was ready.

On one train ride north, Wahram listened to one of the reef engineers explain that the corals they were replanting all released their eggs on the same night of the year, and even within the same twenty minutes, though they were scattered over hundreds of miles. Apparently they accomplished this by way of two color-sensitive cells in each coral, which together were able to distinguish the particular blue of the twilight sky on the night after the first full moon following the spring equinox. This moon rose right after sunset, when the sky was still also lit by the recently departed sun, and this brief double illumination lit the sky to a particular shade of blue that the corals could recognize.

"I have to tell Swan about this," Wahram said, amazed at the thought of such brainless but living precision. Sentience, what was it?

Meanwhile the Florida raising prospered. Wahram watched the people working in what he recognized as the euphoria of the project, which he had felt so strongly himself in his youth, building cities on Titan. There they had had to carve a world out of the ice; here they had to raise one out of the sea. But it was the same feeling.

Once on a train going south he was out between cars with a Dutch woman he was working with, a blond firebrand, and going slow at one road crossing, they looked down at a group of young men who were throwing stones at the train cars and chanting, "Fuck you, fuck you, fuck you," and she leaned out and shouted, "Hey, fuck you back! We are reconstructing the South! And you have to like it!" With an evil Germanic laugh that hopefully they did not hear.

Extracts (15)

the brain is labile and has been shown to accept introduced machines, stem cells, drugs, electrodes, brain cells from other species,

evolution conserves things that work. We have a conserved brain, with different ages for its different parts—in effect lizard at back and bottom, mammal in the middle, human at the front and top. Lizard brain to breathe and sleep, mammal brain to form packs, human brain to think it over

over-selecting for a single trait warps evolution, you can get a result called "the bad becoming normal." As people have been speciating into self-evolved post-humans of various kinds, this result has been seen frequently, as in

parts of the brain fire at the sight of a picture of food, but not at food itself. People like to hunt. Hunting takes many forms. Hunt for a deal, hunt for meaning. A predator's killing is calm and rewarding. Rage always feels bad, rage is a painful emotion. Without a catch, the predator may not be able to deactivate the hunt. Fear is a constraint on anger. Animals never unlearn a bad fear. And we are animals. Piloerection

pathological aggression: dolphins kill porpoises for no reason, they don't eat them, they're not competitors. Does this suggest the uncanny valley exists for all mammals?

reason can't work without emotion. People cut off from their emotions can't decide. Thus the decision to manipulate the brain with hormonal therapies has wide-reaching consequences. Bisexual therapies alter brain levels of oxytocin, vasopressin, and their precursor vasotocin. An oxytocin nasal spray causes immediately better eye contact. Endorphins are nature's version of morphine. The brain releases endorphins when injured, and when someone we love touches us. Thrill seekers calm a hurt

3 percent of mammals monogamous. Play teaches mammals how to handle surprises

five different brain areas evaluate melody, rhythm, meter, tonality, and timbre. Music was the first human language, and still is the language of animals and birds. Music predates humanity by 160 million years. The introduction of birdsong brain nodules to the appropriate human brain sites has resulted in aphasia, also temporal lobe phenomena like omnipresent sublimity, hypermusicality leading to hyperventilation (whistling or singing),

human vocal cords were already capable of purring and it needed only the insertion of feline amygdalan and hippocampal and hypothalamic cells to

performance in flight waldos is vastly improved by implantation of raptor or hummingbird flight nodules in human operators. The different structure of avian brains makes insertion into interstitial cells particularly

it is possible that orgasm already taxes the relevant systems as far as it can without damage such as hernias, broken ribs, thrombosis, and heart attacks. Passengers on sexliners who have taken vasotocin have been known to

The subgenual anterior cingulate cortex, or sgACC, is the place in the brain that directs the body to ignore fear. It is the place of courage, and stimulating it can help a person overcome the dread of phobias. It is possible to overstimulate it, after which

The temporal lobe is the site of feeling states such as the omnipresent sublime, hyperreligiosity, hypersexuality, hypergraphia, overinclusion mania, and so on. Intentional brain stimulation or alteration to promote any of these states can easily trigger the others, or cause epileptic

Human subjects (volunteers) who have ingested the Enceladan community, including the organism *Enceladusea irwinii*, reported synesthesia and individually heightened senses, sometimes confirmable by test. Heightened sensory impressions are often balanced by a reduced ability to generalize or calculate

Lists (12)

boredom, taedium vitae, the knowledge of maya, absurdity, weltschmerz, mal du siecle, existential nausea, dysphoria, doldrums, the funk, malaise, ennui, hebephrenia, discouragement, depression, melancholia, anomie, accidie, dysthymia, blankness, lack of affect, the blues, despair, the black dog, black ass, hopelessness, sorrow, grief, unhappiness, *Hikikomori*, alienation, withdrawal, *tristitia*, nihilism, morbidity, anhedonia, wretchedness, anxiety, fear, pain, terror, horror, desolation, postcentennial hypochondria, *Älterschmerz*, thanatropism, fear of death, death wish

SWAN IN AFRICA

Swan was not enjoying the Earth project. She stuck it out because she believed in it and thought it was her best way to help; she thought it was what Alex would be doing, and so she couldn't abandon it just because it was hard, frustrating, stupid. She cursed the day she had ever left Terminator; she dreamed of the day when she could dance down the Great Staircase to the park and the farm.

She got impatient so fast. Wahram would have been better for stuff like this, but he had flown off to America, frustrated like so many before him by irrefragable Africa. Swan wanted to be tougher than that, and was irritated with him. That added to her general irritation, and her patience often disappeared and left her seething. She became abrasive with people, thus even more ineffective. She woke wondering how many days she had left of this. Someone in the office repeated something Zasha had said, "Earth itself is a development sink," and she shouted in his face.

Another day she got into another shouting match

with a woman from the African League, down visiting from Dar to make trouble, and to keep from striking her Swan had to just walk away, hustling down the crowded streets of the city, cursing in Chinese. She realized that in her current state of mind she was a liability to the cause.

Earth the bad planet. Despite its wind and its sky, she was coming to hate it again, and not just because of the awful g but rather because of the evidence everywhere of what her species had done to the place, and was still doing. The dead hand of the past, so huge, so heavy. The air seemed a syrup she had to struggle through. Out in the terraria one lived free, like an animal—one could be an animal, make one's own life one way or another. Live as naked as you wanted. On the God-damned Earth the accumulated traditions and laws and habits made something that was worse than any body bra; it was one's mind that was held in place, tied in straitjackets, obliged to be like all the others in their ridiculous boxed habits. Here they were, on the only planetary surface on which you could walk freely, naked to the wind and the sun, and when they had a choice, they sat in boxes and stared at littler boxes, just as if they had no choice—as if they were in a space station—as if the bad old days of the caged centuries had never gone away. They didn't even look up at the stars at night. Walking among them, she saw that it was so. Indeed if they had been people who were interested in the stars they would not have still been here. There overhead stood Orion at his angle, "the most beautiful object any of us will ever know in the world, spread out on the sky like a true god, in whom it would only be necessary to believe a little." But no one looked.

* * *

Despite her discontent, another North Harare shantytown near Dzivarasekwa had agreed to work with her and her team. The shantytown was banked on the side of a steep ridge, and the people there were squatters, with the ridge near enough to the borders of New Zimbabwe and Rhodesia to make for confusion about sovereignty. A good prospect, therefore, in political terms, but the steepness of the ridge was a problem for the selfreps. Swan's team had designed a platting for the process that had the hangars moving in a warp-and-weft pattern, with some following contour intervals, while others climbed straight up slopes using telescoping pillar jacks to keep the factories horizontal. In this manner they were managing to transform the swath of their passage into a stylish white village with some touches of color; it would be quite beautiful.

But one morning one of their hangars suddenly veered downhill from the ridge, chomping through first a park and then the leafy suburb Kuwadzana. The locally trained minders of the selfrep had given up trying to control the thing and had jumped off ladders on its sides into the arms of a growing crowd.

When Swan arrived on the scene, she shouted and shoved her way through the crowd, then leaped onto the bottom of the hangar ladder; even when out of control, the behemoth was crunching along at only about a kilometer an hour. Up the ladder she climbed, then slipped through a door into the control room, like a tugboat's bridge. It was empty. She went to the back wall and smashed down the override switch with her fists. Nothing happened; the leviathan ground on over the streets and homes of the suburb, with a rumble like a muffled Niagara Falls coming from its hidden underside. Now she began to understand why the local minders had abandoned ship. With the override not working, there wasn't anything else obvious that one could do.

Swan sat down before the operation console and began to type at speed, while also commanding it verbally to stop. She was first calm, then demanding, then persuasive, then pleading, finally shouting in a fury. The selfrep AI neither responded nor stopped the hangar moving. Something in it must have been jammed; that couldn't have been easy, a matter of clever industrial sabotage, fighting through some tough security. Swan thought she knew some relevant codes, but nothing she tried was working. "What the hell!" she said. "Why is so much tech support out of reach?"

"There are other attacks now ongoing, possibly timed with this one," Pauline informed her.

"So can you give me any help here?"

Pauline said, "Type in the sentence 'Fog is thick in Lisbon.'"

Swan did this, and then Pauline said, "Now you can drive the unit manually. There are four controls on the panel—"

"I know how to drive the damn thing!" Swan said. "Shut up!"

"So therefore you can now apply the brakes."

Swan cursed her qube and then, without ceasing to curse, turned the hangar in a tight half circle (meaning it took a few hundred meters) back up the hill, but now crunching over streets lined with prosperous villas. "I wish this thing worked backwards," she said furiously. "I wish we could give these rich bastards here the hovels they deserve."

"Possibly it would be better just to stop," Pauline noted.

"Shut up!" Swan let the hangar crunch over the neighborhood for a while longer before bringing it to a halt. "So this thing was sabotaged," she said.

"Yes."

"Damn it. And now we're going to get arrested."

"Very likely," Pauline said.

It followed as Swan had predicted. The local government demanded that the damaged selfrep be impounded and its operators arrested, prosecuted, and deported or imprisoned. Swan was taken into custody and held in a set of rooms in the government house; it was not a jail, but she could not leave, and it seemed possible that she would be sentenced to time in prison.

At that possibility she began to spiral down into a furious despair. "We were *invited* here," she kept insisting to her keepers. "We were only trying to *help*. The sabotage was *not our fault*!" None of her keepers appeared to be listening to her. One spoke ominously of a sentence designed to shut her up for good.

Into this nightmare Wahram suddenly appeared, accompanied by an African League officer, a short slight man from Gabon named Pierre, who spoke beautiful French and a much more rudimentary English. He said, "You are released to your colleague here, but must leave North Harare. The construction machines will be taken over by locals. Locals only must run them. So." He held out a hand as if pointing her to the exit.

Swan, surprised, almost refused on principle to agree. Then she saw Wahram's eyebrows shoot up and his eyes go round; his dismay reminded her of how much her situation had been frightening her, and after a moment more she humbly agreed with Pierre's conditions and followed Wahram out to a car, which drove them to an airfield where a big dirigible was tethered to a tall mast.

"Let's get out while the getting's good," Wahram suggested.

"Yeah yeah," Swan said.

The dirigible was as long as an oil tanker, one of a big fleet of similar craft that were constantly circling the Earth from west to east, tugged by kites that were cast up into the jet stream, delivering freight slowly but surely as they circumnavigated the globe time after time. This particular dirigible had a balloon shaped like a cigar, and the gondola under it was lined with windows stacked four and five high.

Wahram led her into the mast elevator and they rose to the loading platform. Inside the dirigible they walked a long hall to the bow, where there was a viewing deck somewhat like the bubble at the fore end of a terrarium. Wahram had reserved two chairs and a table there for later in the day, after they had launched and hummed up to altitude. So that afternoon when they sat at their table, they could look down at the green hills of Earth, passing below in a stately parade. It was beautiful, but Swan was not looking.

"Thank you," Swan said stiffly. "I was in serious trouble there."

Wahram shrugged. "Happy to help." He talked about the work in North America, the problems there and elsewhere. Much of it Swan had not heard about yet, but the pattern was depressingly clear. Nothing new to learn here: the Earth was fucked.

Wahram had come to a more measured conclusion,

as was his way. "I've been thinking that our first wave of help has been too...too blunt, for lack of a better word. Too focused on the built environment, and on housing in particular. Maybe people like to feel they've had a hand in building their homes."

"I don't think people care who builds it," Swan said.

"Well, but in space we do. Why not here?"

"Because when your home can fall apart and kill you and your kids just because it rains, then you're happy to see a machine replace it with something better! You don't worry about *feelings* until your material needs are met. You know that. The hierarchy of needs is a real thing."

"But granting that," Wahram said, "which I do, there have still been a lot of complaints about our efforts. And there is no denying that the project is getting snarled. It's like Gulliver tied down by strings."

"That's not a good image," Swan said, thinking of the talls and smalls in the sexliner. "A lot of opposition is disguised to look like it comes from the people, but really it's the usual reactionary obstructionism. We have to break those strings if they try to wrap us!"

"It seems to me that the image is somewhat apt," Wahram said mildly. "The lines holding Gulliver down are laws, and that makes them important. But look, there's a way around the lines. We can slip through. The work we've been doing in Canada has been very suggestive."

Their tea tray arrived, and he poured her a cup, which she promptly forgot. He sipped his slowly, watching the Indian Ocean appear, and then in the distance to the south a rumpled green island: Madagascar, one of the most completely devastated ecosystems in history, now a model of Ascension-type hybridization.

One of the biggest islands on Earth, now completely a work of landscape art, and thriving. People went there to see its gardens and forests.

Wahram gestured at it. "Landscape restoration is going on all over, as people try to cope with the changes. And it's very labor intensive, and very tied to place. You can't do it from somewhere else. You can't take advantage of differential currencies. You can't really extract a profit from it. So it's already well situated in terms of our purposes. It's a public good and it needs to be done. All the coastlines need it. It's hard to believe how much needs to be done. It isn't even restoration exactly, because the old coastlines are gone for good, or for hundreds of years. It's actually creating new coastlines at the higher sea level. Right now they're raw. The ocean rips up what it inundates, and a lot of toxic stuff gets released. The new shoreline and tidal zone is usually a disaster. Fixing all that is very labor intensive. And yet everyone living on the new coasts wants to see it done. Many want to do it themselves. So, what I've been involved with in Florida is a bit of an unusual case, because it looks like restoration, but really it's creation from scratch. Another kind of terraforming. It only resembles restoration because Florida used to be there. Actually you could do the same thing in shallow water anywhere. It might not even take moving mountains into the sea. There are fast corals now that could be used as foundation builders. Bioceramics expressed more broadly. I've seen groups using these corals, and they can grow them fast at many of the new coastlines, and pretty soon you get wonderful pure-white sand, very fine. It squeaks when you walk on it."

Swan shrugged. "All right, sure. But I'm still not willing to stop working directly on housing."

"I know." He watched the land below. Seemed like he might even sleep.

After a few minutes he stirred and began to say something, but hesitated. Swan saw this and said, "What? Tell me."

"There's something else," he said, glancing at her almost as if shyly. "I've been thinking that one of the things we've been doing here is providing more evidence that reform inside the paradigm of the current system on Earth is never going to be enough. That there is still, in other words, the necessity for revolution."

"But that's what I've been saying! That's what I said to you on Venus!"

"I know. So now I'm coming to agree. So... you remember the project I told you about that Alex was leading, the stocking up of animals in the terraria, so we could bring them back to Earth?"

"Yes, of course. She wanted there to be enough animals to resupply Earth when the right time came."

"Right. And so... I've been wondering if the time has come."

Swan was startled. "You mean the time to bring the animals back?"

A feeling filled her then that she couldn't name: oceans of clouds, roiling inside her chest, building to some kind of thunderhead.... "Do you think so? What do you mean?"

He lifted his gaze from Madagascar and looked at her. He had a goofy little grin, brief and crooked, a toad's grin, and yet warm. "Yes."

Lists (13)

Bats. Sloths. Tarsiers and tapirs. Elephants and seals. Rhinoceroses. Lions and tigers and bears. Tule elk, musk ox, moose. Caribou and reindeer, chamois and ibex. Tigers and snow leopards. Pika and mule deer. Orangutan and langur and gibbon and spider monkey (all primate species are endangered). Moles and voles. Hedgehogs and badgers, bighorn sheep, aardvarks and pangolins, hyrax and marmot. Leaf-nosed bats, mustached bats, thumbless bats. Foxes and hares. Deer, boar, peccary, manatee. Porcupines. Wolves

It is not true that every mammal larger than a rabbit is endangered on Earth. Most are only

Mammals are a class of animals; there are 5,490 species in the class, 1,200 genera, 153 families, and 29 orders

Capybara, jaguars, giraffes, bison, Przewalski's horse, kangaroo. Zebra, cheetah, wolverine

Biggest orders are Rodentia, Chiroptera (bats), Soricomorpha (shrews), then Carnivora, Cetartiodactyla (even-toed hoofed mammals, and whales), and Primates

All fall down.   Please

come back

SWAN AND THE WOLVES

They all came down together, first in big landers protected by heat shields, then in smaller landers popping parachutes, then in exfoliating balloon bags. At that point they were drifting down through the airspace the Inuit nations had given them permission to cross. When they got within a few hundred meters of the ground, every lander disintegrated into thousands of aerogel bubbles drifting down, each transparent bubble a smart balloon holding inside it an animal or animal family. What the animals thought of it was anyone's guess: some were struggling in their aerogel, others looked around as placid as clouds. The west wind had its effect, and the bubbles drifted east like seed pods. Swan looked around, trying to see everywhere at once: sky all strewn with clear seeds, which from any distance were visible only as their contents, so that she drifted eastward and down with thousands of flying wolves, bears, reindeer, mountain lions. There she saw a fox pair; a clutch of rabbits; a bobcat or lynx; a bundle of lemmings; a heron, flying hard inside its bubble. It looked like a dream, but she knew it was real, and the same right now all over Earth:

into the seas splashed dolphins and whales, tuna and sharks. Mammals, birds, fish, reptiles, amphibians: all the lost creatures were in the sky at once, in every country, every watershed. Many of the creatures descending had been absent from Earth for two or three centuries. Now all back, all at once.

Swan came down in the midst of a cluster of animals. They were somewhere in the new wheat belt of southern Nunavut, "Our Land." Her particular landing point was supposed to be a low rise in the midst of a district covered by wheat and cold rice farms. Every field was marred by a few pingos, small hills like boils, raised when big chunks of ice floated up through the mud of the melting permafrost. As she made her final approach, which hill was hers was hard to tell. The descent was handled entirely by her bubble, and as she had never landed in one before, she enjoyed the feeling of it—as if a transparent magic carpet were lowering her. All around her the animals in the air were becoming aware of the ground, some struggling, some hunched, many with their legs splayed out like falling cats or flying squirrels, in just the right way even though it was their first ever fall—some kind of conserved lizard behavior, perhaps, shared by all. She herself landed so neatly that it was as if stepping off an escalator. Touching the ground popped the balloon, and its aerogel blew away. And there she was, standing on the ground, on a pingo in Nunavut.

There were three other people in her observation team, coming down as close to each other as the wind would allow. She looked up to see if she could spot them, and the sight of the sky above almost caused her to fall on her butt; she cried out, she laughed: the sky was still full of animals. Descending out of the western sky, dropping from low cumulus clouds, were caribou and elk and grizzly bears, all big brown dots with splayed legs. All the other animals too, many in clusters, the higher ones too small to see what they were. Around her the dense wheat was shivering with the movement of creatures freed of their burst bubbles and running for cover. One could in fact land right on her; she had to keep an eye out. She laughed to think of it, she threw her arms out and howled to the wolves in the sky. In the distance other wolves were barking. There were also hoots and bellows, many sounding fearful, but it was hard to say; that was just an assumption; in fact she couldn't be sure these sounds were not triumphant. Home at last! "All God's children are home at last," she proclaimed over her radio. The other humans were checking in; they had landed. The cool west wind blew through her and she howled some more. The last of their wave floated down; then the clouds above were all by themselves again. Only a few last black dots drifted in the distance, light as down. All together it was the most beautiful thing she had ever seen. "All right," she said with her radio off. "I love you. You have done a great thing." Whether she was talking to Alex, or Wahram, or the world, she couldn't say.

So here she was, on the taiga between boreal forest and tundra. There would be caribou and grizzly bears here now, and mountain lions; every biome needed its top predators for the whole system to thrive. The grizzly bears would immediately take to the hills; mountain lions would likewise disappear on landing. But the wolves would find each other and band together, and thus stay visible in their packs; and Swan wanted to be there for that. All her life she had followed them in terraria, hunted with them, chased them off kills, slept curled at the edge of the pack, next to the nursing mamas. She had howled with them more times than she could have counted; every time she heard them howl she joined in, feeling it was the human thing to do. Other times she had felt the long stare on her, and had stared back. She had seen wolves in discourse with coyotes, seen ravens lead them to a target kill for a share of the leavings. She knew that humans had made wolves more human, and thus dogs, and in that same time period wolves had made humans more wolfish, by teaching them pack behaviors. None of the other primates had friends that were not kin, for instance; humans had learned that from watching wolves. The two species had at different times scavenged each other's food; they had learned each other's hunting methods; they had, in short, coevolved.

Now the primates were bringing back the other half of the family. And so here she was.

Her team of four was to check for animals not properly freed from their bubbles, to free them when found or help them if injured. This was not supposed to have happened very frequently, but the ground here was hummocky, with both pingos and depressions called kettles, which formed when the ice core of pingos melted away. Kettles were round and steep-sided, and often filled with water to the water table, only a meter or two underground in many areas. Wheat and a bio-engineered cold rice had been attempted here, as on the tundra and taiga all around the north, as a climate change "adaptation," but the attempt had proved to be more difficult than imagined. So in the resulting mess of a landscape, bad landfalls seemed quite possible.

As it turned out, the bubbles worked so well that Swan and her teammates did not see any animals in distress. They were all moving, however; some were even running in a panic. But soon the panicked ones would tire, stop, look around. Hopefully see a landscape not too unfamiliar. Most of the terraria had been kept at one g for precisely this moment, and had been designed to resemble the places the animals now returned to.

Caribou stood so tall that they found each other easily. The smaller animals slipped away in the wheat, headed for the hills to the west, or the little trees of the boreal forest visible on the horizons to the south. No creature was visibly in need of aid. All were on the land, confronting their new fate.

Every animal had been tagged, and now they were showing up on screens as patterns of colored dots, so Swan's team proceeded to the next part of their plan, which was to follow the caribou, and if necessary chivvy them along, a bit like sheepdogs with sheep, on a course that would lead them east to the Thelon River. This new herd's first migration would be instinctive but aimless—unless they picked up old traces of the lost Beverly, Bathurst, and Ahiak herds—so whichever way they took now would begin to establish the smells and other signs of a new migration route. This would then become a de facto habitat corridor through the new wheat zone, a corridor that would perhaps need to be defended in the relevant courts, but they could cross that bridge when they came to it; first the caribou had to cross the river. This leading of animal migrations across agricultural land was the biggest organized act of civil disobedience ever committed by spacers on Earth, but the hope was that after being escorted the first time, the animals would manage on their own, and become popular with the indigenous humans, even the farmers, who were not having that much success anyway. So the escorts might get arrested before they were done, but hopefully the habitat corridors would be quickly recognized as values worth the land given over to them.

As usual when walking with a group of people, Swan quickly fell behind. There was too much to look at; things were so interesting that she forgot what her task was, even now. The plans and research devoted to the possible rewilding of Earth had been going on for a century, and here she was part of it, and still she stumbled around looking at flowers poking out from rocky soil here and there, velvet pads of astonishing color. Above them stood a tall pale blue sky, with a line of cumulus scudding east. She still saw in her mind animals floating down like seeds in the sun; the sight had cast her into a dream and she had not emerged from it, and so naturally she had to go slow. She was in radio contact with her partners anyway. In fact their chatter in her ear was worse than Pauline, and she turned the volume to zero. She'd check in when she needed to. For now she wanted to get her focus back to the ground under her feet. In the previous year's work in Africa she had come to take things for granted; she had forgotten where she was, simple as that. She had fallen inside her problem while all the world flew on a big wind through the sky. Now this open land, this taiga. On the south face of the next rise, a straggle of dwarfed pines. A drunken forest, the permafrost under it melting. Low hills to the east under the line of clouds. Sky immensely tall, the blue a bit pastel above the low clouds still trundling east. The air seemed to smell slightly of fire. High afternoon sun, August 5, 2312. A new day. Warm, but not hot. A bit muggy and buggy. She was in a bodysuit that kept her dry, and very effectively repelled mosquitoes and flies, which was a good thing, because they hovered in dense black clouds that here and there looked like swirling smoke. She couldn't see any of her team; the long up and down of the land here was chopped by low ridges, old eskers perhaps. In any case she had limited viewing east. She climbed up the side of a pingo and had a look around. Ah, there was Chris, just a couple hundred meters ahead, appearing to wave to someone even farther east. Good for them.

Spongy grass and moss of the taiga filled every low point. Only a meter higher were long mounds of flattened bedrock that crossed the bog north to south. It would have been best to stay on these natural roads, but her team had gone east, following the herding caribou.

She went north, heading for a point of high ground marked by krummholz trees waist-high to her. She reached this prominence and stopped at the sight of a wolf pack on the other side. They had just landed, and were running around sniffing and nipping at each other, stopping short on occasion to howl and then run on again. They were amped up by the descent, no doubt about it. She knew just how they felt. It took them a while to pull themselves together and lope off to the east. They were gray with black or beige points and shag, and were looking svelte in their short summer coats. More broad-shouldered and square-headed than most dogs, they were still very similar in lots of ways. Wild dogs, self-organized: it was always kind of a disturbing thought. That they had turned out so well, so decent and playful, was a bit surprising to Swan, and reminded her that the wolves had come first and were wiser than dogs.

Now Swan was put to it to keep up with them, huffing and puffing fairly soon after she started her pursuit. No human could keep up with wolves running hard, but if you kept at it, they often stopped to have a look and sniff around, and then it was possible to keep them in sight, or catch up and relocate them again. A male howled and others replied, Swan among them. She would have to run a little bit harder if she wanted to stay part of it. That would be hard. She stayed in better shape off Earth than on, a small irony that was now making her grimace and resolve to do better.

These wolves were nine in number. They were big ones, with more streaks of black than white. Their fur bounced on them like hair as they ran. Their wolfish lope ate up ground, though it resembled a canter. Seeing them run, Swan howled to herself, oceans in her chest: they were free on Earth. That happiness could be so deep it hurt; another lesson in learning the world.

Ahead the pingos and kettles smoothed away, and a sheet of wheat covered the land. The wolves had hesitated at this sight, and Swan was able to slip around them to the south, behind the easternmost of the pingos. The wheat field beyond had been smoothed by laser to a plain tilting to the east about five meters in every kilometer. Flat land indeed—unreal—an artifact. A work of art, in its way. But soon to be reconfigured. Eight kilometers to the east another pingo outbreak was just visible, and another scrap of undeveloped taiga— undrained, too boggy to farm, more lake than land.

Swan pulled her wolf skin—a big old male's skin, with head and paws still attached—out of her suit's backpack. She draped it over her head so that it flowed down her back like a cape. She had clipped gold rings through the tips of its ears. Now she circled ahead of the pack, howled back at them. Then she ran as hard as she could to the east. She was chest deep in wheat, and could run between rows of it. Ahead to the east her colleagues were leading a herd of caribou by way of scent and cast-off antlers. The wheat had taken a beating where the herd had passed. She saw that they were following the shallow streambed of a creek almost erased by the laser-flat plowing. The half-buried streambed was still muddy, and her teammates were leading the herd away from that, paralleling it to the south. The scent of wolves would reach them soon, and then it would be no problem to keep them headed east, over low rise after low rise. They would go wherever seemed most distant from wolves, at least for a while. Eventually the two species would come to a predator/prey accommodation, but for now the big prey animals were no doubt still spooked, and prone to stampede. She saw signs of what she thought had been a small panic, and the bodies of several calves lay trampled in the middle of this zone. Swan turned to face the wolves now following her. She stood on a high point with the wolf's head draped over hers and howled a warning. The pack stopped and stared at her, ears pointed and fur erect—they too were spooked. Their look now was not their famous long stare, Swan judged, but a real attempt to see better.

Still, they were on the hunt, and so after a while, on they came. Swan gave way, turned, retreated at speed. She had given the caribou some extra time to get past the little swale, so now she got out of the way as quickly as she could. From the north she chivvied the wolves from time to time over the next few hours, but for the most part she could barely keep up with them, and in the end could only follow sign. For a long time it was a slog through wheat following the caribou tracks. Once, she saw a line of giant red harvesters on the southern skyline.

*   *   *

That night most of the caribou were ahead of her and had formed a herd and were headed east. They were primed for migration, inclined to move. Then also the wolves and people and other predators were like beaters on a hunt, the people involved sometimes using sirens and scents and, as always, their own very disturbing presence. People were the top predator, even when wolves and lions and bears were around—as long as they stayed in packs, as wolves had taught them so long before—and had their tools in hand, in case push ever came to shove.

Swan, stumbling along at the end of a very long day, began to feel the spirit of the pursuit fill her and lift her up like a body bra. She was Diana on the hunt, it was what they did as animals. She had done this so often inside terraria that it was hard to believe she was out at last, but there was the sky over them, and the wind keening past.

If the line of caribou migration was to be established for good, and the entire zone made into a habitat corridor, then the land itself would have to be changed, as it had been before. Again humans would be altering it. All Earth was a park now, a work of art, shaped by artists. This new alteration was just one more stroke of the brush.

The transformation of taiga into cropland had been a matter of shaving down high points and filling up low points, with the growth of new topsoil hastened by engineered bacteria. Thus it was pretty flat now, as if a sea surface with a slight groundswell. But with the freeze-thaw cycle and the permafrost melt, things had been unflattening. The passage of the caribou was enough to tear up the topsoil; where they had passed, it looked like a phalanx of tractors hauling spikes had

churned through the wheat. Swan avoided their track
for that reason, except for brief excursions into the
muck to bury transponder beacons, and also to mark
the soil with scents, and herbicides aimed at wheat. They
were also seeding boreal forest. In some places they
were blowing up the land, tossing the blankets of
introduced soil aside to bring the original taiga bacteria
back to the surface. All this had to be done while the
caribou were far enough away that they were not scared
from coming back; but there was a lot to do, so they
were starting as soon as they could.

She slept those nights in her bodysuit, which had an
aerogel mattress and blanket in its pockets to keep her
warm, and enough food for a few days. Once or twice
she checked in with her team, but she preferred to be by
herself, unwolfish though that was, to track the wolves.
She seldom had the pack in sight now, but she could
track them by sign; the ground was soft, the paw prints
of the nine frequent. Her own Group of Nine.

On the third morning, well before dawn, after a
night of little sleep, she decided to rise and catch up to
the pack if she could. In the dark and cold she hiked
with a headlamp on, and saw the tracks on the ground
best when she took the light off her head and held it
near the ground and pointing forward.

About an hour before dawn she heard their howls
ahead. It was their dawn chorus. Wolves howled at the
sight of Venus rising, knowing the sun would come soon
after. Swan saw what they were howling at, but by its
relation to Orion knew it was not Venus, but Sirius. The
wolves had been fooled yet again; the Pawnee had even
named Sirius He-Who-Fools-the-Wolves for this very
mistake. When Venus itself rose, about half an hour later,

only one uneasy lupine astronomer spoke up again to howl that something was wrong. Swan laughed to hear it. Now other wolves farther to the west would be taking up the dawn howl. For a long time when dawn crossed North America, there had been a terminator zone of howling wolves running the length of the whole continent, moving west with the day. Now that might come back.

When it was light, she worked her way closer to them by tracking that uneasy astronomer. The wolves had apparently stayed on a pingo that night, and they yipped and barked gruffly as she approached; they didn't want to leave, and they didn't want her to get any nearer. Something was going on up there, she thought; one of them giving birth or something like that. She waited for them at a distance, and only when they had slunk off to the east did she climb the soft side of the pingo to check it out.

A sound stopped her cold; she saw nothing at first, but there was a little pond at the very top of the pingo, a kettle like the caldera of a miniature volcano. Noise from there—a whining—she walked up to the edge of it to look down. A young wolf, fur wet and muddy, was slinking along a narrow edge of clay rimming the water three or four meters below. Walls of the hole were vertical, even hollowed out and eaten back by the water at the bottom, which had a tint of turquoise in its muddy blue, as if it might be floored by the ice at the pingo's core. The wolf pawed at the lined clay. A young male wolf. He looked up at her and she half extended a hand toward him, and with that the ground under her gave way, and despite her twist and leap she fell into the pond with a load of mud.

The wolf barked once and cringed away from her. She swam; she had not hit the bottom of the pond, despite plunging deeply in when she fell. She swam to the other side of the wall and climbed out onto a narrow ring of exposed mud, which went all the way around. It was like being inside a vase. Her fall hole had created a spout for it.

Swan avoided looking at the wolf. She whistled and cooed like a dove, then a nightingale. She had never seen a wolf eating a bird of any kind, but just so he didn't get any ideas, she added a short hawk's cry. He was still trying to climb out; he was afraid of her. He fell back as the wet overhanging mud gave under his forepaws. He hit the water upside down and Swan reached out instinctively to help, but of course he was perfectly capable of twisting around and swimming back to the band of clay, and when he felt her touch he whipped around and bit her right hand, then swam desperately away. She shouted in pain and surprise. Her blood was in the water, in his mouth. The bite burned, and there was one puncture in the back of the hand that was going to well blood for a long time.

Her bodysuit, which was keeping everything but her head dry, had a first aid kit in its thigh pocket. She pulled it out and considered whether skin glue would work on a puncture wound. Well, it had to be tried. She punctured the tube and poured a lot of the glue into the dark red hole, then held a gauze pad to it hard. The gauze would be glued into the hole, but she could cut the excess away and leave the rest in there, and it would be all right.

The inner wall of the kettle was smooth except for some horizontal banding. How exactly was she going to get out? She reached into her pocket for her mobile, found that the pocket was empty. The pocket had been open, as she had been calling her colleagues pretty frequently. Well, they would notice her absence and GPS her. Possibly she could dive down to the bottom of the pond and recover the mobile, and possibly it would still be working after being submerged.

Actually neither of these seemed very likely. "Pauline, can you locate my mobile?"

"No."

"Can you contact my team for me?"

"No. I am designed to be in contact with you alone, by way of a short-range airport function."

"No radio?"

"No long-range radio transmitter, as you know."

"As I *should* know. You useless piece of crap."

The wolf was growling, and Swan shut up. Briefly she cawed. "Hawk!" she cawed, thinking the young wolf might give her some space as a creature that spoke the crow language. She didn't know what to do, really.

"Pauline, how can I get out of here?"

"I don't know." This, coming without even a slight delay, sounded faintly disapproving.

Swan moved around the circumferential band of mud, and the wolf moved with her to stay across the pond. If the higher ledges on this side held under her weight, then she might be able to climb out. She tested it, glancing at the wolf as she did. He was facing her but looking a bit to the side. It was quickly obvious that the mud of the wall was not going to hold her up. She needed sticks to carve steps, or to stick into the mud far enough to give her a hold. But the kettle had no sticks in it. Again she wondered about finding things at the bottom of the pond. But the water was frigid, and her bodysuit did not cover her head. And there was no way of telling how far down the bottom was, and whether there was anything down there anyway.

"Pauline, I'm afraid we're stuck here."

"Yes."

Extracts (16)

It was never the official policy of any unit larger than the individual terrarium, and even those would seldom say anything explicit about their animals—where they were sending them, how many, by what transport, why— nothing. The assumption is that the coordination that obviously had to have happened was all kept offline, and is still not properly documented. Looking back, such an absence of public statement does not seem so surprising, because we are used to it now; but at the time it was a relatively new phenomenon, and there were widespread complaints that the disappearance of public policy statements meant they lived in sheer chaos. No order obtained in the solar system, the balkanization was complete; the story of humanity had for a time disappeared like a stream of meltwater on the surface of a glacier, falling into a moulin and running thereafter invisibly under the ice. No one controlled it; no one knew where it was going; no one even knew what was happening

from the very beginning there were people who argued that it was wrong in many different ways: that it was an ecological disaster, that most of the animals would die; that the land would be devastated, botanical communities wrecked, people endangered, their agriculture ruined. The images of the animals' return could resemble World War II parachute attacks or alien invasion movies, and the fear of similar casualty rates created trauma in several places. During the descent some animals were shot out of the sky like shooting-range skeet. And yet on the whole down they came, landed, survived, endured. For a few weeks or months, therefore, it was all anyone spoke about, and all shouted at the tops of their lungs. And the massive flood of images was ambiguous, to say the least. Some cried invasion, but others cried reunion. Rewilding, assisted migration, the revolt of the beasts; and at some point it was called the reanimation, and that term got capitalized and gradually stuck and spread, superseding all the rest. And in the end it did not matter what name people gave it: the animals were there

many accused the terraria of fomenting revolution on Earth. Others called it an inoculation, and there were microbiologists who spoke of reverse transcription. The introduction of an inoculant into an empty ecological niche does indeed cause a revolution in the biome. Rapid change can be chaotic, traumatic. In this case animals did often die; their food was all eaten and then there were population crashes, scavengers did well, always predator and prey fluctuated wildly, and the plant life metamorphosed under their impact. Fields changed, forests changed, suburbs and cities changed. Eradication campaigns were met with fierce resistance and fierce support efforts. Sometimes it came to a kind of war of the animals, but people always led the charge on both sides even in the moment of balkanization, Earth was central to history. An estimated twelve thousand terraria had been raising endangered animal populations for more than a century, strengthening genomic diversity as they did, and the whole point of the exercise had been to serve as a dispersed zoo or ark or inoculant bank, waiting for the right moment to reintroduce these creatures to their wounded home. That the moment had come struck some in the terraria as an overoptimistic assessment, but in the end almost all had agreed to heed the call, and they mounted a formidable armada

much of the organizational work for the reanimation was later traced to a working group associated with the seventh Lion of Mercury, who had died a few years previous to the event. Some Terran governments had been contacted, and those friendly to the idea had provided permits. Assisted migration was already a familiar concept, and invasive species had already rearranged the world anyway; people had struggled against the mass extinction without success, and much of Earth was now occupied by the toughest weeds and scavengers. There was talk of a coming world of seagulls and ants, cockroaches and crows, coyotes and rabbits—a star thistle world, depopulate and impoverished—a big broken factory farm. Reintroducing lost species was therefore welcome to many Terrans. That there would be inevitable political consequences was only to say it was a collective human action; those always have consequences

the twelve thousand terraria and a few score Terran states apparently agreed to execute the plan in the first half of 2312, but as most agreements were off the record, this is anecdotal only. For the most part the oral records of participants, made years later, are the only account

After the reanimation, problems on Earth became ecological and logistical, and focused on transport, dispersion, mitigation, compensation, and legal and physical defense. The reanimation itself was not the end of the story; indeed many decades were to pass before it was understood to have been a key moment in the eventual

WAHRAM AND SWAN

When Wahram heard that Swan had gone missing, he left Ottawa, where he had been in intense negotiations with the Canadian government over the unauthorized arrival of the animals, and flew north to Churchill, and just caught a night flight to Yellowknife, the staging area for the work on the habitat corridor that Swan had joined.

A short summer night had passed by that point, and it was well past dawn on the following day when a helicopter took him over the land where Swan's transponder had her. By the time they got there, her team had already located her; but it was good to have a helicopter there, because it was impossible to approach the edge of the pingo summit pond without joining her in it. One of her rescuers had already decisively proved that, so now she was down there with another person and, apparently, a wolf. At least they had it outnumbered now, though some in the helo were saying that made it worse. In any case, they could lower a flexible ladder with a harness from the helicopter, from quite a height, though still not high enough to keep from terrifying the wolf—Wahram could see that looking down on it from above. The other person came up the ladder first and was deposited at the foot of the pingo; then Swan; she was red-eyed and looked wasted, but waved at Wahram, and by hand gestures indicated that they were to lower the ladder one more time. That the wolf would be able to use the ladder to escape, Wahram doubted; but the pilot lowered it anyway and, after a radioed consultation with the people below, flew slightly to the side, so that the ladder was draped against the wall. Even that seemed insufficient to Wahram, so he started in his seat when the wolf suddenly leaped once onto the ladder and again up to the rim and raced off down the hill.

Wahram told the pilot he wanted to be dropped off, so she descended on the wheat field next to the pingo, beating out an impromptu crop circle with her downdraft. Wahram climbed out of the helo, with its big blades blurring the air over him, and ran crouching until he was well clear of the contraption, which then gnashed and thwacked back into the sky.

Swan ran to him and gave him a muddy hug. When he got the earplugs out of his ears, he asked how she was. She was fine, she said; had had a great time, had shared her hole with a wolf, and neither was the worse for it, just as one knew would be the case, but it was always good to get empirical confirmation in moments like that when push came to shove and one could get eaten.... She was a little manic, he saw. Dirty, she admitted, and hungry, and ready for a little break before getting back to the work. Wahram gestured at the helicopter, still chopping the air overhead, and when she agreed to the plan, he gestured for it to redescend, and they got in it. After that it was too loud to talk, and they waited until they got back to Yellowknife, her leaning against his shoulder and smiling as she slept right through the racket.

It figured that as the animals had been dropped on ten thousand sites, they would get opposition in some places; at least so it seemed in advance, although no one was sure of anything. In any case they worked as if they had only a few days of freedom to do so, and used helicopters like hoppers to move around, setting loose robotic sun-powered tractors, which hauled seeders that looked like the farming machinery one saw in photos from long before. Some of these planted trees two meters tall at a rate of sixty per hour until their supplies were exhausted. Thus the reanimation included a botanical element, and the tractors proved hard to stop. And few people tried.

Still there were incidents, and in Yellowknife as they ate they checked the stories coming in from around the world. It was everything from hosannas to artillery fire: cheered or denounced, and everything in between, from every possible source, including the U.N. Security Council, gathered in emergency session and yet at a loss. Orangutans back all over Southeast Asia, river dolphins in all their old river mouths, tigers in India and Siberia and Java, grizzly bears back in their old range in North America . . . was this not the alien invasion feared for so many centuries, come at last? It was unpermitted; it was disruptive; the animals included carnivores that could kill people; it had to be bad. Certainly it was confusing. And power, confused, was always dangerous.

But they also saw the Terran news noting that the animals were always landing in their original native habitats, shifted if necessary to adjust to climatic change since their disappearance. Also, that although they were not genetically modified organisms, an intense breeding effort in the terraria had created much more genetically diverse animals than the remnant Earthly populations. This was part of Wahram's publicity packet information, so he was particularly pleased to see the media pick that up. Also the reports were noting that animals had for the most part come down in wilderness preserves, and in areas of hills, deserts, pasturage, and other least-human-impacted spaces—never in cities, and only once or twice in villages. A Colombian village that suffered an aerial invasion of sloths and jaguars had already renamed itself Macondo, and clearly would live to tell the tale.

For a while Swan slept on a couch in their impromptu conference center. Wahram found he was not comfortable letting her out of his sight. She was still acting very affectionately toward him, cast into some kind of ecstasy by her night spent with the wolf. Sleeping with her head on his leg. The poor thing looked emaciated still, somewhat as in the tunnel.

"I want to go back out," she said now when she woke up. "Come with me. I want to follow the caribou again, and they need beaters. Maybe I'll see my wolf too."

"All right."

He saw to the arrangements, and the next morning they joined the rest going north that day, and heloed out in a frost-steamed sunrise. "Look," Swan said as the sun cracked the distant horizon, leaning over him to stare right into it.

"You can burn your eyes here too," he said. "You can burn your eyes out even on Saturn."

"I know, I know. I look without looking."

The new light cracked in shards on the numberless patches of water spread on the land. Near the Thelon River they landed and got out, the helo buzzed away, and suddenly they were on the vast windy tundra, walking on variously crunchy or squishy ground, in some ways like the icy ground of Titan. Wahram upped the support of his body bra and tried to accustom himself to the give of the soggy land. For a while the act of walking over the broken ground of the semi-frozen caribou path felt like working in a waldo, and because of the body bra, in a way it was.

He straightened up and looked around. Sunlight mirrorflaked off water into his brain, and he adjusted the polarization in his glasses. Swan kept pulling down her glasses to look around with her naked eyes: sometimes she reeled, tears frozen on her cracked red cheeks, but she laughed or moaned orgasmically. Wahram only tried it once.

"You're going to go blind," he told her.

"They used to do it all the time! They used to live without any glasses!"

"I believe the Inuit protected their eyes," he groused. "Strips of leather or some such thing. Anyway, it was something to withstand. They were stunted by life up here, held back from full humanity by their own harsh planet."

She hooted at this and threw a snowball at him. "How you lie! We are bubbles of Earth! Bubbles of Earth!"

"Yes, yes," he said. "*Lark Rise to Candleford*. We were taught it too. 'When alone in the fields, with no one to see them, they would hop, skip, and jump, touching the ground as lightly as possible and crying, "We are bubbles of Earth! Bubbles of Earth! Bubbles of Earth!" ' "

"Exactly! You were brought up Unitarian?"

"Aren't we all? But no, I read it in Crowley. And I can't hop, skip, or jump in this g. I would trip and fall."

"Oh come on, get tough." She regarded him. "You must weigh a lot here. But you've been here a long time, you should be used to it."

"I haven't been doing much walking, I confess. My work has been more sedentary."

"Recreating Florida, sedentary? Then it's good you're out here."

She was happy. He stumped along comfortably enough; he had been exaggerating the impact of the g, just to annoy her. Now the cold air and the sunlight were giving the day a kind of crystalline quality. "It is good," he admitted.

So they walked the southern edge of the caribou's route east, and Swan planted transponders and photographed tracks and took soil and fecal samples. In the evenings they gathered with other trackers at a big dining tent set up daily in a new position. In the short nights they lay on cots in the same tent and caught a few hours of sleep before eating and heading out again. After the third day of the beat they had to deal with the helicoptered arrival of the Royal Canadian Mounted Police, who arrested them and flew them to Ottawa.

"No way!" Swan cried as they watched the land unfurl below them. "We weren't even in Canada!"

"Actually we were."

The vast fields of wheat at midday looked very different than they had during their recent morning trip out. "Look at that!" Swan exclaimed at one point, gesturing down with disdain. "It looks like an algae bloom on a pond."

In Ottawa, when they were released from custody, Swan took Wahram to the Mercury House to clean up and try to find out what was happening. News of the reanimation was still all over, and there were too many stories to tell, because everyone in the world was telling their story at once, in the usual manner but even more so; so it was hard for them to find out their own story—specifically, why they had been arrested. They had been released without charge, and no one in Ottawa seemed to know anything about why they had been pulled in.

On the newsfeeds clusters had already formed, one could watch images arranged alphabetically by animal or region or several other categories—worst landings, animal actions beautiful or comic, human cruelties against animals, animal aggression against humans, and so forth. They watched the screens in the dining hall as they ate, and afterward walked the narrow streets by the blackish river and canal system, dropping in on pubs here and there to have a drink and see more. Soon enough Swan was getting in drunken arguments with other patrons; she made no secret of her spacer origins, which would have been hard to do anyway, given the way she looked, and the graceful but stylized way she moved in her body bra. Wahram thought people looked up at her with a bit of fear in their gazes. "A round on the Mercury House, that's where I'm from," she would declare when people got pissy, which of course helped, but wasn't a complete solution.

"You people should be happy the animals are back," she would tell them. "You've been cut off from them for so long you've forgotten how great they are. They're our horizontal brothers and sisters, enslaved as living meat, and when that can happen to them it can happen to you too, and it has. You people are meat! It stinks!"

Catcalls and ugly rumbling disagreement would greet this.

"At some point you have to get it!" Swan would shout, overriding the various objections filling the air. "No one can be happy until everyone is safe!"

"*Heppy*," one of them said, voice dripping with Slavic scorn. "What's *heppy*? We need food. The farms in the north give us food."

"You need *soil*," Swan said, making it a long word with two syllables. "*Soy-yull* is your food. Sheer total biomass is your food! The animals help make biomass. You can't do without them. You're hanging on by eating oil. You're eating your seed corn. If it weren't for the food coming down the elevators from space, half of you would starve and the other half kill each other. That's the truth, you know it is! So what do you need? *Animals.*"

"They can pull my plow," one said sourly. Most of these people spoke Russian to each other, and Wahram struggled to hear voices using English. When they spoke to Swan, they spoke in English. She was talking again about the horizontal brothers and sisters. Many who listened were sufficiently high on vodka and other substances that their eyes shone, their cheeks were red. They liked arguing with Swan; they liked being tongue-lashed by her. They had looked the same in 1905, no doubt, or 1789, or 1776. It could have been a room anywhere, anytime. It reminded him of the corner pub in his neighborhood of the bulge.

"We're part of a family," Swan was insisting now, going maudlin. "The mammal family."

"Mammals are an order," someone objected.

"Mammals are a *class*," someone else corrected.

"We are the *class* of mammals," Swan exclaimed, "and the *order* is to suckle and to love!" Cheers to this. "It's that or die. Our horizontal brothers and sisters. We need them, we need all of them, we're part of them and they're part of us! Without them we're just—just—"

"Poor forked radishes!"

"Brains and fingertips!"

"Worms in a bottle!"

"Yes!" Swan said. "Exactly."

"Like spacers in space," someone added.

They laughed at that, and she did too. "It's true," she cried. "But here we are! I'm on Earth, right now." Her cheeks burned and she looked around at them; she stood on a bench and caught them up: "*We're on Earth!* You have *no idea* what a privilege that is. You fucking moles! You're home! You can take all the spacer habitats together and they'd still be nothing compared to this world! This is home."

Cheers. Though it seemed to Wahram, as he caught Swan falling off her bench toward the bar, that what she had said wasn't really true, not anymore—not with Mars up there, and Venus and Titan coming on board. Maybe it hadn't been true since the diaspora. So they cheered her for being wrong, for flattering them, for buying the drinks and catching them all up in a moment of enthusiasm. They were cheering for this moment itself, detached from anything else. Night in a pub in Ottawa, with drunks singing in Russian. This moment of the storm.

*   *   *

They went back out with visas, in case they got stopped again by the Mounties, and rejoined the beater line for the caribou migration. No one stopped them in Yellowknife, and no one they spoke with knew what had happened before. In a couple of days they were back in their field routine, which made Wahram happy. He was used to the walking now, had adjusted his bodysuit to it, and got a lot of pleasure from watching Swan on the hunt. She was always ahead, but then again she looked good from behind. Diana on the hunt.

In the dining tent at night they were hearing more often from reports worldwide that people were finding the reappearance of animals in their world hard to handle. Lions and tigers and bears, oh my! People were unused to being potential prey for big predators lurking right at the edge of town. It was enough to make them band together. Those who used to go out on their own now usually found company. Some who didn't got eaten, and the rest shivered and complained and then sought out friends or strangers to walk with, not just at night but in the broad light of day. This was standard practice already in the terraria; going out alone was a luxury, a kind of decadence—or an adventure undertaken with a sense of the risk involved, as with Swan. It was obvious if you had grown up with it, oppressive if you hadn't: out in the woods, humans needed to stick together.

Quickly too the animals were learning how dangerous people were. In fact many more animals were dying than people in the new encounters, which was no surprise to anyone. But it was a robust inoculant, and would prevail.

*   *   *

The two of them went out one morning with extra bags of gear, because Swan wanted to range farther than they could in a day and still get back to the dining tent. The caribou had massed on the banks of the Thelon River at a ford new to them, and she wanted to get around to the north side of them, to observe and to discourage the beasts from heading north in the shallows on the west side, looking for a better ford; they were already at the best spot, a place that the archeologists said had been used by caribou in the past.

So they walked north. At a certain point they crossed the caribou track. The ground was chewed into a sea of chaotic brown sastrugi; every step had to be made carefully. Swan was faster than Wahram by an even larger margin than usual, but he was determined not to hurry. A couple of times the corpse of a caribou drove the point home: falls could be dangerous. There were knee-high clumps of semi-frozen mud to contend with, and they made him nervous. He could scarcely stand to watch the way she waltzed over them. But she made no mistakes; and he had to keep his gaze on his feet. It didn't matter how far she got ahead.

When they reached unshattered ground north of the migration path, Swan led him east. "Look," Swan said, pointing. "Wolves. They're waiting to see how the crossing goes."

Wahram had become aware that Swan loved wolves, so he said nothing about the bloodthirsty nature of scavengers. Everyone had to eat, after all.

The caribou were massed on the near shore of the ford, about half a kilometer away. Swan wanted to be seen by the beasts, so she hiked up a short bluff overlooking the riverbed, which was a broad gravel wash, crisscrossed by river channels braiding in it; the entire wash was a maze of old lines of rounded rocks and the curved black dips of dried oxbows. Much of it would not be good footing for the caribou, and Wahram could see why Swan wanted them to cross at the ford, where solid permafrost soil made a flat brown-and-green road on both sides.

"Look, the first ones are trying it."

Wahram joined her side and looked south. Hundreds of caribou were massed on their side of the river, tossing their antlers and bellowing. The large males at the front were testing the river with forelegs, pawing at it, and then one made a break and several others followed immediately, splashing knee-deep in water for the most part, then abruptly going in to the chest, spraying big waves before them.

"Uh-oh," Swan said. "It's deep there."

But the leaders walked or swam on, working hard, and soon they surged back up to knee depth and smashed the water white on their way out. On the far shore they looked back and bellowed. By this time more of them were in the water, and the mass began to move slowly forward, funneling as those on the sides tried to get to the center. They wanted to bunch together, Wahram saw. "That drop-off will be the trouble spot," Swan predicted, and it was so; as the beasts hit the water some bellowed and tried to turn back, but were shoved and even nipped until they carried on; but that made for a jammed crowd back in the shallows, and the uproar of their bellowing was loud over the already big noise of the river sluicing through its infinity of rocks. A few beasts on the left flank turned and began to head north, but Swan jumped up and down and waved her arms, and Wahram took a little compressed air horn she offered him and let off a couple of blasts. It was loud in a high and urgent way, but he thought it was Swan's violent motion that turned the beasts back; and at that point the logjam of beasts at the deep point of the ford swam forward together, and soon the breakaway was forgotten and the whole herd was powering across in a storm of white water and steaming brown bodies. It took most of an hour. There were some accidents, some broken limbs, and even drownings, but there was never again any pause in the herd.

Swan watched closely, pointing out a line of wolves on the bank downstream, snagging drowned caribou calves with their teeth and dragging them in teams back up out of the water. It was only at that point that the river ran with ribbons of red.

"Will the wolves cross too?" Wahram asked.

"I don't know. In the terraria they often would, but the streams aren't as big as this. You know—you see it inside a terrarium and it's great, but this is *different*. I wonder if they think so too. I mean, they've done this a lot, but always looking up at the land. They've never been out under the sky. I wonder what they think of the sky! Don't you wonder?"

"Hmm," Wahram said, considering it. Even to him the sight of the Terran sky was almost inconceivably odd. "It must look strange. They must have a sense of space, they're migrating creatures, after all. They migrate in the terraria. So they must know this is different. From the inside of a cylinder to the outside of a sphere—no, if they feel that—" He shook his head.

"I think they seem more panicked than usual. More wild."

"Maybe so. How are we ourselves going to get across?"

"We swim! No, not really. Our aerogels will work as rafts, we'll float across. If we're lucky!"

She led him down to the ford, where the scent of the caribou was strong, and strips of fur eddied in the shallows. The wind poured through him, and he could feel his lungs etched as cold shapes, pulsing and alive. "Come on," she said, "we have to get out of here before the wolves get here to clean up on the poor dead babies."

"All right, but show me how."

"Your mattress is your raft, we each have one. It's kind of like a coracle of aerogel, so it's hard to see but you'll float in it fine. If you tip over you have to hold on to it, or else swim fast."

"I'll hope not to tip over."

"That's for sure! This water is freezing. Here, take this branch to paddle. I think the thing to do is to walk out as far as you're comfortable, then get in and let yourself be taken downstream, and paddle when you can for the far shore. We don't need to be in any hurry, because the first curve of the river downstream will put us over near the other side anyway. And you'll feel it when you're over the shallows on the other side. Follow me, you'll see."

So he did; but he bounced on the water, and his raft felt too small, and the deepest part of the current swept him by Swan, who was laughing at him; then he paddled hard. She caught up with him, paddling in circles, and shouted to him, "Put your head under the water!"

"No!" he exclaimed indignantly, but she laughed and shouted back, "Put at least one ear under the water, you have to hear it! Listen to it underwater!"

And she leaned out from her coracle and ducked her head under for a few moments, then pulled out sputtering and laughing. "Try it!" she commanded. "You *have* to hear!"

So gingerly he leaned out and stuck his right ear under the dancing surface of the water, holding his breath, and was astonished to find that he had immersed himself in a loud electric clicking utterly unlike anything he had heard before in his life. He pulled his ear out, heard the rush of the world, then stuck his whole head back in, holding his breath, and heard with both ears that electrifying clicking and clacking sound, which must have been the sound of stones rolling hard over the river bottom, thrown along by the rapid current.

He pulled out, blowing like a walrus. Swan was laughing at him and shaking her head like a dog. "How's that for music!" she shouted. Then Wahram's coracle scraped the shallows on the other side and he jumped out, but tripped and fell. He was just able to grab the little raft as he splashed and clambered to his feet, then sloshed up to dry land. Not elegant at all, but he was still alive, and his bodysuit kept him dry and warm—now *that* was the technological sublime. And they were on the far shore.

Swan found a high point above the river and pitched their tent just before dark. The tent was a single big shell, transparent and bouncy on transparent tent poles. Their rafts would serve as their beds. They sat outside the door of the tent and Swan cooked them first a soup made from powder, then pasta with a pesto and Gorgonzola sauce. Finally chocolates for dessert, and a little flask of cognac.

It was still twilight when they were done, though the sun had set an hour before. The tent flapped in the wind, and the immense sluicing of the river over its rocks rumbled up out of the ground and filled the air. They had been going for eighteen hours straight, and when Swan said, "Time for bed," Wahram nodded and yawned. The sleeping bags she pulled from their backpacks were also aerogels and resembled the mattress rafts, as well as their tent material, and for that matter the bubbles they had drifted down in—all aerogels, hard to see, light, squishy, warm. "But we'll still be cold unless we sleep together," Swan said, crawling into his bag beside him and pulling both bags over them.

"Ah yes," Wahram said. "I'm sure."

In the semidarkness he could afford a smile. She kissed him, though, and caught him in the act.

"What," she said.

"Nothing."

She rolled onto him, and their combined weight caused his back to touch the ground under his mattress. It was a chill touch and he had to mention it. "We may have to stay side to side."

"Hell no," Swan said, and squiggled out of the bag. "Here, get up a second, let's put my bag under the mattress. That should do it."

It did. By then they were cold. She got the top of his bag over them properly and climbed onto him, shivering; and after a tight hug she shifted around and started kissing him again. Her mouth was warm. She was a good kisser, passionate and playful. Her penis, so much littler than his, was nevertheless poking his belly, feeling something like a belt buckle gone awry. He too was fully aroused, and getting happier by the second.

Now it was said that their particular combination of genders was the perfect match, a complete experience, "the double lock and key," all possible pleasures at once; but Wahram had always found it rather complicated. As with most wombmen, his little vagina was located far enough down in his pubic hair that his own erection blocked access to it; the best way to engage there once he was aroused was for the one with the big vagina to slide down onto the big penis most of the way, then lean out but also back in, in a somewhat acrobatic move for both partners. Then with luck the little join could be made, and the double lock and key accomplished, after which the usual movements would work perfectly well, and some fancier back-and-forths also.

Swan turned out to be perfectly adept at the join, and after that she laughed and kissed him again. They warmed up pretty fast.

Lists (14)

A round mound made of big irregular boulders, interleaved together small and large to make an almost smooth cone at Mercury's north pole

Flat rocks laid in circles, one layer on the next, each layer bigger for a few layers, then the same for two or three, then smaller, slowly, up to a rounded point, so that it looked like a big pinecone of rock

One big boulder topped by gold, melting in the brightside crossing onto the rubble plain below it

Another boulder, encased in stainless steel, not melting

Another, rubbed with cinnabar

Patterned gaps in the ground filled with liquid copper

Shards attached to a knobby headland so that it looked like a cactus

Silhouettes in silver, left on the ground through the brightside

Sand castles turned to glass by the brightside crossing

Twenty rocks on a rubble plain painted white and put back in place

A chest-high oval ring of drywall using flat stones, with fat rounded capstones on top, and a single gap for a door into the center

A rock shaped like South America, balanced on its Tierra del Fuego

Stainless steel wire snarled in broken orbits around a boulder

Almost cubical rocks in a single stack twenty rocks high

Elliptically rounded rocks stacked four and five high

Ten thousand pebbles arranged together on their ends in the shape of a whirlpool

Cliff sides carved to mirror smoothness and then etched by the Sanskrit lettering for *Om Mani Padme Hum*

Rock pile compass roses, Medicine Wheels, stone circles, henges, inuksuk

A conical hut like the end of a spaceship sticking up out of the plain

Inside the terraria, the possibilities blossomed:

Twigs twisted into circles. Leaves into cornucopia

Pink cherry blossoms filling a pool

Branches like bones assembled into a cradle

Red poppy petals wrapped around a boulder, boulder replaced among its gray mates

Ice henges. Igloo segments. Ice sheets broken and reassembled in sphere shapes

Long sticks woven into semicircular patterns in shallow smooth water

Leaf lines, shifting the leaves from red to orange to yellow to yellow-green to green

Earthworks in long sinuous lines

"History is a product of labor just like the work of art itself, and obeys analogous dynamics"

SWAN AND WAHRAM

Swan finished their trip on the tundra feeling better than she had for a long time. She loved her giant toad, her lump of clay, with his groaning slowness and quick little smile. Feeling that feeling in her made her able to think of Alex and Terminator and everything that had happened in a way she could tolerate; so her mood was a strange mix of pain and happiness. A fearful joy, yes. Certain wolf howls, of a kind she had often heard, including in the last month on the taiga, combined just such emotions, mourning and joy, and expressed her current mood quite precisely. She whisper-howled when she heard them out in the night, as she was with Wahram and the others at camp; she didn't like to howl fully when other people were around. She howled inside. When Jacques Cartier had kidnapped some local chiefs for transport back to France, the night before the ships left, people had gathered on the shore and howled like wolves all night long.

One morning Wahram got a call and took it outside the dining tent, and when he came back in, he was looking thoughtful.

"Listen," he said to Swan as they trudged out over the tundra, wind and sun at their backs. "I need to go back out to Saturn again. There's a meeting been called of all the people who were helping Alex. They want it in person so they can keep it off the record."

"And what's it about?" Swan asked.

"Well," he said cautiously, "it has to do with what appears to be a new type of qube. So I shouldn't really say more."

"I know when people are talking about me," Pauline announced.

"We know that," Swan snapped. "Be quiet."

"Anyway," Wahram said, "I think you should join this meeting. And you can do me a favor. Jean Genette is out of touch in an aquarium, and yet needs to hear about this meeting. I should go to Titan directly, but if you could go tell Jean about it on your way out, that would help. And Jean can maybe tell you more about what's going on."

"All right," Swan said. "I can do that."

"Good." Wahram smiled his tiny smile. But Swan could tell he was distracted.

Extracts (17)

As many people have significant lifelong quantities of male and female hormones and phenotypically are bisexual, intersex, or indeterminate, the pronouns "he" and "she" are often avoided, or when used are a matter of self-designation, sometimes changing according to situation. Referring to someone else with such pronouns is the equivalent of using *"tu"* rather than *"vous"* in French, indicating familiarity with the person

deepest phenotypic signals of gender appear to be waist-to-hip ratio, and waist height relative to total height, usually a matter of proportionately longer female femurs and wider female pelvic bones

such as French, Turkish, or Chinese. Alternative ungendered pronouns in English include "it," "e," "them," "one," "on," and "oon," but none of them have

it is not a case of "there is no gender," but rather a complex and ambiguous efflorescence, sometimes called a fully ursuline humanity, other times just a mess

gatherings composed entirely of gender-indeterminate people are a new social space that some find intensely uncomfortable, eliciting comments such as "like a nakedness I hadn't thought could happen" or "you're only yourself, it's terrifying," and so on. Clearly, a new kind of psychic exposure

distinctions can be pretty fine, with some claiming that gynandromorphs do not look quite like androgyns, nor like hermaphrodites, nor eunuchs, and certainly not like bisexuals—that androgyns and wombmen are quite different—and so on. Some people like to tell that part of their story; others never mention it at all. Some dress across gender and otherwise mix semiotic gender signals to express how they are feeling in that moment. Outrageous macho and fem behaviors, either matched with phenotype and semiotic indicators or not, create performance art ranging from the kitschy to the beautiful

as there are now people close to three meters tall, and others less than a meter tall, gender may no longer be the greatest divide in human

even approaching the size of spider monkeys, a modification that was severely censured by larger people, until longevity statistics kept reaffirming the association between smaller sizes and longer lifetimes, especially in light gravities. A saying among small people is "smaller is better"

we all began female, and always had both sexual hormones in us. We always had masculine and feminine behavioral traits, which we had to train into gender-

appropriate behaviors, even though they were traits
that everyone has. We selectively encouraged or
repressed traits, so for most of our history we have reinforced gender. But in our deepest selves we were always
both. And now, in space, openly both. Very small or
very tall—human at last

this culture's structure of feeling could also be called
balkanized. Gender therapy and speciation were both
parts of the longevity project, and the combination of
the three created a new structure of feeling that is often
characterized as fractured, compartmentalized, bulk-
headed, firewalled. Usually longevity itself is identified as the primary force driving this; until now, no one
has had to integrate a personality in its second century
(or more), and often it is experienced as an existential
crisis. The super-elderly have had so many experiences,
gone through so many phases, lost so many companions to death or simply time that they have grown dis-
tanced from other people. Spacers, mobile over huge
distances, especially bold in trying all the augmented
abilities, often live as isolatoes, in a solipsistic narrative
or performance of their own

people in space enact a kind of nonattachment. A common opinion expressed is that to keep relationships
lasting a long time one shouldn't see too much of a person, or create too intense of a relationship, or it will
burn out. Paced for the long haul, one spreads oneself
out among a network of acquaintances and new friends,
and moves on when

love famously has different definitions within cultures,
between cultures, and in different historical periods.

"Balkanized love" refers to a situation in which affection, child rearing, sex, lust, cohabitation, family, and friendship have all been delinked from each other and reconfigured as affect states, just as individuals and societies have been

sex itself, having been delinked from reproduction, love, transgression, religion, and other biological and cultural associations, has become just a physical function for a lot of people, either private or shared, and pleasurable as a sport or game, conversation or bowel movement

traditional marriage, line marriage, group marriage, polygamy, polyandry, panmixia, timed contracts, crèches, roommates, sexual friendships, friends, pseudosiblings, fellow travelers, soloists,

SWAN IN THE *CHATEAU GARDEN*

Swan flew south and took the Quito elevator up again, and again sat in on the performance of *Satyagraha*, singing along with the rest of the audience, dancing as an extra when everyone else did, trailing banners at the end of the first act. All the chaos of the repetitive voices crisscrossing in the middle act felt exactly right to her now, true to life. She could punch out those chants like shouting at an enemy. The struggle for peace was more struggle than peace, but now she was energized and into the flow of it.

Up in Bolivar she hurried to catch a ferry going out to meet the *Chateau Garden*, a big terrarium that she herself had designed when she was young—fool that she had been. This one was a Loire or Thames chateaux landscape, the big boxy stone mansions tastefully scattered about among fields of barley, hops, vineyards, and formal gardens.

It was as green as ever, she found, and looked like one of those horrid virtual game landscapes in which nothing has quite enough texture. Almost every plant in the formal gardens surrounding the great houses was a work of topiary, and not only was this a questionable idea in itself, but these had been left to go wild: the artist had gone out ice-skating on one of the ponds and fallen through the ice and drowned. Now all the whales and otters and tapirs looked as if they were being lifted up by their hair.

In the town itself (slate roofs, wood beams crossing plaster walls in standard pseudotudor) there was a large park, with a big smooth lawn, actually another of the topiarist's masterpieces: the grass of this lawn was not simply grass, but also very fine alpine meadow grasses, sedges, and mosses, in a dense mix that also included a number of tiny low alpine ground cover flowers, including bilberry, moss campion, aster, and saxifrage, all together creating a millefleur effect that made it like walking over a living Persian carpet. Within this colorful carpet were long strips of pure fine grass, as on putting greens, all running lengthwise to the cylinder. A lawn bowling field, in fact, with about a dozen rinks.

It was winter here, as if they were in Patagonia or New Zealand, and the light from the sunspot on the sunline smeared so that shadows blurred at the edges, and the air looked rusty. Small clouds had bunched around the sunspot, white puffballs glazed pink. The shadows of these clouds dappled the town and its park, and the rolling barley fields and vineyards spread out overhead. Terrarium vertigo washed through Swan for a second as she looked up at them.

There was no Mercury House here, so she took an empty ramada on the edge of the park, under a line of sycamore trees, gorgeous in their stark winter tones. Feeling too full to sit or lie down, she put her travel bag on the square bed and went out for a walk. She stopped for tea in the village, and sitting in the café saw that a group of people were going out to the bowling green. She tossed down the last of the tea and went out to watch.

Each strip of putting grass was called a rink, and they were set lengthwise in the cylinder so that the rink would lay flat. That was important, as the Coriolis force was strong enough to push every shot to the right. The balls were asymmetrical as well, as was traditional in the sport; they were squashed spheres, like Saturn or Iapetus, and when thrown they would roll on their biggest circumference like a fat wheel, as long as they were going fast enough, but then might flop onto their side at the end, thus accentuating the fernlike curvature of the roll. It required a neat touch to put a bowl where you wanted it.

A young person approached and asked if she wanted to play a game on one of the empty rinks.

"Yes, thanks."

The youth picked up a bag of bowls and led her to the farthest empty rink, near the edge of the field. The youth dumped the balls on the exquisite grass and Swan took one of them up. She hefted it along its long diameter; it weighed about a kilo, just as she recalled. It had been a while since she had last played. She went to the mat on which throwers had to stay, and tried to make a simple toss down the middle, on the slow side, hoping the bowl would end up in front of the jack and serve as a blocker to her opponent's bowls.

It ran down the rink, curving only a bit, then flopped to a halt about where she wanted it. The youth chose a bowl, went to the mat, took a couple of steps forward, then crouched for a final step and the laying of the ball on the sward. Very graceful, and the ball rolled smoothly down the course, running a line that looked to be well to the left of the jack, even headed out of the rink and into the ditch, as out of bounds was called. But then the Coriolis force got its push into it and the ball curved right ever more sharply, tracing a kind of Fibonacci infalling, until it tucked in just behind the jack.

Swan would now have to try to get around her own blocker, or knock it back into the jack, so that hopefully the jack would bounce away. Four bowls per end, and with three to go they were already looking at a crowded space around the jack. Swan considered it for a while, then decided to try to use the bias of the bowl to roll one back against the C-force and see if she could get around her blocker and tap the jack. It would require a very fine touch, and the moment she made the shot she could see that she had put too much on it. "Ah damn," she said, and was vexed enough to add, "I'm not making any excuses or anything, but I have an excuse for that."

"Of course. Have you seen that shirt with all the excuses printed on it?"

"They made that shirt by listening to me and writing things down."

"Ha-ha. Which one this time?"

"Well, I've just spent almost a year on Earth. I'm throwing everything long."

"I bet. What were you doing there?"

"Working on animal stuff."

"The invasion, you mean?"

"The rewilding."

"Huh. What was that like?"

"It was interesting." She didn't want to talk about it right now, and she suspected the youth knew that and only wanted to distract her. "Your shot."

"Yes." The youth's waist-to-hips ratio was sort of girlish, the shoulder-to-waist-to-ground lengths sort of boyish. Possibly a gynandromorph. The youth's shot ran almost true and flopped right beside the jack. This end was looking bad for Swan. Her only recourse now was to try to knock her own blocker into the jack and hope the jack went into the ditch, which would make for a dead end. It could be done if she could throw fast and straight on the right heading. She put her little finger on the big circle of the bias, and concentrated on keeping an upright form with a straight follow-through. She rolled, and again on release knew she had missed. "Damn."

The youth was again amused. "You have to have every finger on it when you let go."

"Some people do," she said.

The youth shrugged in reply. Quite young; perhaps thirty years old; a spacer.

"Is this your home?" Swan asked.

"No."

"Where are you going?"

"Nowhere."

The youth made a shot, which was a nicely placed blocker that meant it would be harder than ever for Swan to hit the jack with her final roll. The only chance was that same backhand.

She made her last shot and was pleased to see it roll down, take a late turn in, and bang the jack right out of the rink.

"Dead end," the youth said calmly. Swan nodded.

They played several more ends, and the youth never made a shot that was anything less than superb. Swan lost every time.

"You're some kind of ringer," Swan said, feeling irritated.

"But we're not betting."

"Lucky for me." She managed again to knock out the jack.

On they played. Neither seemed in any hurry to do anything else; space voyages could be like that. It felt to Swan like shuffleboard on an Atlantic ocean liner. They were rich in time—they had time to kill. The youth made several shots that were simply perfect. Swan kept throwing long, and losing. It occurred to her that this must be how Virginia Woolf had felt when she played with her husband Leonard, an expert lawn bowler from his years administering Ceylon. Virginia too had lost almost every time. The youth seemed not to care one way or the other. Leonard had probably been much the same. Well, but quite a few people played sports mostly against themselves, their opponents no more than random shifters of the problems they faced in their own performance. Still, this young person began to bother her. The neat picking up of the mat. The final flick of the fingertips at the end of a throw. The exquisite final fern tips of the Coriolised curves.

Only much later that night, as she was lying in her ramada, did it occur to Swan that the pebbles thrown at Terminator had been like a kind of lawn bowling. The thought made her sit up in bed. Set up a mat, launch a bowl—that jack would be covered.

Quantum Walk (2)

easy to note the moment Venus g is exceeded   1.0 g
feels like a pull from below   an entanglement with
Earth   rising up toward you   even though you know
you are descending

summer is drunken   conifer grove   hot in the sun
new-mown hay   marsh at low tide   lilacs   peaches
barnyards

wheeled car humming down a road   windows open
32 kilometers an hour   plowed earth behind box
hedges   wind from the southwest   gaudeo   I rejoice   a
human driving   don't talk too much

carrying capacity K is equal to births minus deaths
over a density-dependent impact on the growth rate
added to a density-dependent impact on the death
rate   the unused portion of the carrying capacity   if
there is one   will be green   the overshoot portion of
the carrying capacity   will be black   as in buildings
excrement   stay outdoors   they have overshot

the cycloid temperament   an undertow of sadness   a
febrile temperament   be aware   the human beside you
is not to be comprehended

six different kinds of bird in sight at once   a seated hummingbird, watching the scene, grooming itself   a red-headed finch   summer on earth   blue sky filled with high white clouds   moving east fast   the hummingbird zips ahead and lands   looks around   beak like a needle   crows and seagulls wheel competing mafias   the speed of hummingbird wings muscles doing that   evolution of one kind of success Canada geese   the creak of their feathers as they beat their wings   hummingbird song is creaky in a different way   chivvying   not a song   a squirrel chitters much the same   blue-backed hummingbird   hovering there in the trees   the underside of a flicker is salmon-colored

New Jersey North America   August 23 2312 on the hunt   on the run   human now driving over hills around a marsh   hills covered by low buildings moldering under knots of alder   twenty kilometers an hour   faces everywhere   383 people in view   number shifting up and down by fifty or so as the car rolls slowly by   streets of tarred gravel   black

a robin with a yellow beak and raw-sienna chest black tail feathers and head   white eye ring black eye neat   drinking the water from a sundial   gaudeo

past a garden   corn   pumpkins   sunflowers and mullein with similar yellow flowers differently clustered   I'm mulling it over

What's that?

Nothing   sorry

Oh no problem. This is nice eh?

Gaudeo

yellow flowers against dusty green   in a disk filled by a spiraling pattern woven together   or a tall khaki cone with crossing spirals of yellow   sensory perceptions are already abstractions   humans see what they expect to see   they leap before they have time to look

true cognition is to solve a problem under novel conditions   that humans can do   this is a set of novel conditions   ever since you left the building   ever since you started thinking   remember me   there will be helpers   you are defective   catch and release

their brain is always making up a story to explain what is going on   thus they miss things   anomalies get left out   but is that true?   don't they see that yellow?   don't they see the two kinds of spiral?

unlimited resources do not occur in nature   competition is when both species have a net negative effect on each other   mutualism is when they both have a net positive effect on each other   predation or parasitism is when one gets a positive effect   the other a negative effect but it isn't always so simple   intraguild predation is when two species predate each other at different moments of growth

the dark bulk of an apartment   tenement   shebeen the sunset sky behind and over it   Magritte   Maxfield Parrish   get out of the car   be alert   make a joke   don't make eye contact

these helpers too must have plans   could be using you   for or against someone else   this is the likeliest explanation   what then   how turn the tables   parry riposte   catch and release

Would you like to play chess?   one of them says at a door

Sure, come on in   guns pointed at them   pointed at you

INSPECTOR GENETTE AND SWAN

Once irritated by a problem, Jean Genette never really gave up on it. Even problems officially solved sometimes still had a haunting quality, because of things that didn't quite fit, didn't seem right—and if a solution never was found, the problem became part of the insomniac rosary, one bead in a Moebius bracelet of beads wearily fingered in the brain's sleepless hours. Genette was still working on the problem of Ernesta Travers, for instance, which thirty years before had troubled them all with the fundamental question of *why* their friend Ernesta had engineered a disappearance from Mars, as well as how; it was a case Jean could pursue in exile, and from time to time did, but Travers was still as absent as if she had never existed. Same with the puzzle of the prison terrarium *Nelson Mandela*, a locked-room mystery if ever there was one, as the asteroid seemed to have afforded no ingress or egress for whoever had brought in the fatal gun. Mysteries like that abounded in the system; it was part of the affect realm of the balkanization, many felt, but balkanization per se was not enough to explain some of these mysteries, and the inspector remained puzzled and more—transfixed, existentially confused, *frustrated*—by their aura of impossibility. Sometimes the inspector would walk for hour after hour, trying to make the explanation appear.

The problem of the pebble attack was not like that. It was still a new case by Genette's standard, and it had no aura of impossibility. Almost anyone in space could have done it, and many down under atmospheres could have paid for it, or gone into space and done it, then dropped back into their atmospheres. It was a needle-in-haystack problem, and balkanization made that problem worse by multiplying the haystacks. But this was Interplan's territory, in the end, and so on sifting the haystacks they went, eliminating what they could and moving on. It seemed pretty clear to Genette that on this one they would be looking in the unaffiliateds eventually, prying open closed worlds and poking around for the maker of the launch mechanism and the operators of the spaceship now crushed deep within Saturn. By no means were all their avenues of inquiry exhausted; there were at least two hundred unaffiliateds with robust industrial capacities; so it was more like they had barely begun.

Swan Er Hong rejoined Genette inside the aquarium *South Pacific 101*, a water world that filled its interior cylinder with water to a depth of ten meters, spinning against the interior of a big chunk of ice that had been melted and refrozen in such a way as to leave it transparent, so that from space the whole thing looked like a clear chunk of hail. Genette had sailed the Hellas Sea as a child, and learned to love the wild slop of a windy day in Martian g, and even all these years later had not

lost the little thrill that came with feeling the fluctuating wind in one's fingertips on tiller and line—the
feeling of being picked up and thrown over the water
in plunge after plunge.

The little sea in this aquarium was not as grand as
Hellas, of course, but sailing remained sailing. And
from inside an aquarium with walls this clear, the
view inside a cylinder was as if looking at and through
a curved silvery mirror, everywhere broken up by the
crisscrossing waves formed by the Coriolis current and
the chiral wind, creating between them very complex
patterns. It was as if the classic patterns of a physics
class wave tank were here topologically warped onto
the inside of a cylinder. Intersecting waves on this surface curved in non-Euclidean ways, a strange and lovely
thing to see in all the mirrored silvers. And behind all
the silvers lay blues. Inside the transparent shell of the
aquarium, with the ocean also the sky, every silvery
surface on the sunward side of the cylinder was backed
or filled by a deep eggshell blue, while if one was looking away from the sun, the backing blue was an equally
rich but much darker shade, almost indigo, and flecked
here and there by the white pricks of the brightest
stars. A floating town disrupted this cylindrical sea,
but Genette spent most of the time on the water, sailing a trimaran at the fastest angles the winds offered.

On hearing Swan was there, Genette sailed into Pit-
cairn and picked her up. There she stood on the end of
the dock, fizzing in her usual way—tall, arms crossed,
hungry look in her eye. She glared down at the inspector's sailboat suspiciously; it was sized for smalls, and
Swan was just barely going to fit. Genette dismissed
her suggestion to take out a larger boat, and placed her
on the windward pontoon with her feet on the main

hull, while the inspector sat in the cockpit, holding a wheel that seemed to come from a much larger vessel. And there they were, talking as they skidded over the waves like a shearwater. With such a big weight to windward, Genette could really catch a lot of wind on the mainsail, and the bow of Swan's pontoon knocked a lot of spray up into the blues.

Out getting banged on by the wind obviously pleased Swan. She looked around at things more than when Genette had last traveled with her. She looked slightly electrocuted, one might say. She had been on Earth for the reanimation, so no doubt that had made her happy. But there was also a new set to her mouth, a little chisel mark between her eyebrows.

"Wahram sent me to say you need to get out to a meeting on Titan," she said. "It's Alex's group, and they're meeting off the grid to discuss something important. Something about qubes. I'm going to go too. So can you tell me what this is all about?"

Buying a little time to think it over, Genette brought the boat about and had Swan change pontoons. Once set on the new course, a tug on the mainsheet tilted her upright. She grinned a little fiercely at this sailor's evasion, shook her head; she would not be distracted.

Although in fact this shift had brought them on course to catch one of the waves breaking on the reef. Genette pointed this out, and together they watched the swells as Genette trimmed the sails for more speed. They skidded over the water in a broad turn that met the wave as it was rising on the reef; the trimaran was lifted and then caught by the wave, surfing across its face, falling more than sailing, and yet the wind on the top half of the sail served to keep them ahead of the break, if Genette could capture it right. Swan proved expert at providing a counterweight, leaning and shifting in response to the fluctuations of the ride.

Where the reef petered out, the wave lost its white teeth and laid back into a mere swell. After one last bump over the backwash of a crossing wave, they were only sailing again.

"Well done," Swan said. "You must sail a lot."

"Yes, I travel in aquaria when I can. So by now I've sailed most of them. Or iceboated them. When they're frozen inside, you can get going like in a centrifuge."

"I was just up in Inuit country myself, but it was summer and all the ice was gone. Except for the damn pingos."

They sailed on for a while. Overhead their water-silvered sky bent through a smooth curve of blues from turquoise to indigo.

Swan said, "But back to this meeting. Wahram said it had something to do with some new qubes. So...do you remember that time we were in the *Inner Mongolia* and I met those silly girls, and I thought they were people? And you thought they might be some strange qube people?"

"Yes, of course," the inspector said. "They were."

"Well, a strange thing happened to me on the way out here. I was lawn bowling with a young person in the *Chateau Garden*, and this kid was...trying to impinge on my attention, I guess I would call it, without actually saying very much. It was mostly in the play of the game, but also...it was like the long stare you sometimes get from wolves. There's a thing wolves do when they're on the hunt called the long stare. It's unnerving to prey animals, to the point where some quit trying as hard to get away."

Genette, familiar with the look and the technique, nodded. "And this person had a long stare."

"So it seemed, yes. Maybe that was part of what gave me the creeps. I've had wolves look at me that way. I could see in my peripheral vision how different it was from an ordinary look. Maybe that was how a sociopath looks at people."

"A wolf person."

"Well, but I like wolves."

"Perhaps like a qube," Genette suggested. "Not like the ones on the *Inner Mongolia*, but not quite human either."

"Maybe. When I talk about the long stare, I'm just trying to figure it out. Because it was unnerving. And then the way this kid was lawn bowling—as if it meant something."

Genette regarded her, interested by this. "As if lawn bowling might be the tossing of balls at a target?"

"Exactly."

"That's what it is, yes?"

She shook her head, frowning at this.

Genette sighed. "Anyway, it should be perfectly easy to ask the *Chateau Garden* for a manifest."

"I did that, and looked at all the photos. This lawn bowler wasn't there."

"Hmm." Genette thought about it. "Can you share your qube's records with me?"

"Yes, of course."

She shifted from the pontoon to the cockpit, and Genette came up into the wind a bit. She leaned over and asked Pauline to transfer the photos she had already pulled. Genette inspected Passepartout's little wristpad display.

"There," Swan said, pointing to one photo. "That's the one. And that's the look I mean."

The inspector studied the image: an androgynous face, an intent look. "It doesn't really come through in a photo."

"What do you mean? Look at that!"

"I am, but this person could be thinking of a calculus problem, or suffering a moment of indigestion."

"No! It wasn't like that in person. I think you should see if you can find this kid. If you can, you'll see for yourself. And if you can't, it gets kind of mysterious, doesn't it? This person wasn't on the manifest. So if you can't find them, maybe the look will begin to mean more to you."

"Maybe," Genette said. This was the kind of break in a case that amateurs hoped for, which in reality seldom happened. On the other hand, it might be some kind of move on the part of the qubes. Some of the ones inhabiting humanoid bodies had behaved so oddly it was hard to know what they might or might not do.

The question now was how much Swan could be trusted, given how permanent her qube was, and how little was known about it. Not for the first time Genette was grateful that Passepartout was located in a wristpad that could be turned off, or taken off if necessary. Of course it was possible to ask Swan to turn off Pauline, as before. Secrecy from qubes could be achieved, even when they were stuck inside your head. It only had to be arranged. And on Titan the Alexandrines would be arranging for a sequestered conversation. It was clearly the next step if they were going to fold Swan into the new effort.

Genette watched her while thinking it over. "We need to talk with Wahram and the whole group involved with this. There are things you need to know, but the meeting there will be the best place to tell you."

"All right," she said. "Let's go then."

TITAN

Titan is larger than Pluto, larger than Mercury. It has a nitrogen atmosphere, like Earth's but ten times more dense. Temperature at the surface is ninety K, but there is a liquid-water ocean deep under its surface that serves as a reservoir of potential warmth. On the surface all the water is frozen very hard and forms the material of the landscape—glacial to every horizon, with rock ejecta scattered here and there like warts and carbuncles. Here methane and ethane play the role of water on Earth, changing from a vapor in the nitrogen atmosphere to clouds that rain down into streams and lakes running over the water ice.

Sunlight hitting this atmosphere strikes up a yellow smog of complex organic molecules. The hydrogen in this haze escapes easily into space, but while in Titan's air, it drives all the bigger organic molecules back to simpler building blocks; so there are not many complex organics, and therefore no indigenous life. Not even in the water ocean below, as if the corrosive atmosphere formed some kind of quarantine.

The glacial surface is broken in most places, smooth

in a few. When you stand on the surface, you can see Saturn, with a thin slicing curve of the edge-on rings cutting the gas ball in half; you can also see the brighter stars. The haze in the Titanic air is of a thickness such that looking out of it, visibility is fairly good, while looking into it is to see nothing but a yellow cloud.

No impact craters; as they are formed in ice, the ice then deforms and resurfaces as the centuries pass. There is only a convoluted, swirling chaos of broken ice features and rock outcroppings, cut by liquid methane into shapes like watersheds. Dips in the land are filled with liquid methane: Titan's Lake Ontario is three hundred kilometers across, and shaped like the one on Earth.

There is seasonal weather, as Saturn makes its way from perihelion to aphelion: methane rain in the rainy season.

It was the nitrogen that first brought people to Titan. Martians, unhappy with the never-explained shortage of nitrogen on Mars, flew out in the first ships fast enough to be practical for human use over these distances; robots had preceded them, of course. They set up stations, built a system for gathering and freezing nitrogen and casting it downsystem in naked solid chunks. People complained this was an unauthorized expropriation, but the Martians pointed out that Titan in its distant past had had several times as thick an atmosphere as it had now, that the nitrogen was leaking away to space to no one's advantage, that if it wasn't harvested it would go away—and that there were no Titans. The last argument was decisive. By the time there were Titans, by the time Titan and the rest of the Saturn League had ejected the Martian nitrogen miners from their system, Titan's atmosphere had been reduced by half. Mars was correspondingly enriched, with part of the imported nitrogen in its soil, part in the atmosphere; it formed a crucial component of the Martian Miracle. And the Martians claimed no harm had been done; that in fact it had helped Titan's future prospects, by getting it closer to a human-friendly pressure.

The loss of Dione in those same years, however, was not a loss that could be claimed to help Saturnians in any way. The Saturn League then declared their system off-limits to Martians, also to Terrans (the Chinese in particular)—to anyone, in fact, except themselves. It was the first post-Martian revolution, against the great revolutionaries themselves, a statement very forcefully made by the threat of bombardment. So everything changed once again, because of a few people on Titan.

The new light from the Vulcanoids sparking now in the skies of Titan had already started temperatures in the remaining atmosphere to rise, and the surface was therefore subliming faster than before. The tented cities in the highlands now had some of the most violent weather anywhere. From the inside of the city tents, the Titans watched clouds rising in thunderheads that sheered off horizontally some five kilometers up, where jet streams decapitated them. Sunlight before had been one one-hundredth of that striking Earth, making the whole planet seem about as bright as an ordinary room; now, with its beamed and reflected additions, it was fifty times brighter than it had been naturally, and was said to resemble the light on Mars, which the Martians said was the best light of all. In truth the human eye could adjust to a huge range of incoming light, and very little would serve for seeing, as had been the case here before the mirrorlight arrived. Now however the

Titanic landscape positively glowed, and as its orbit and day were both sixteen days long, the sunsets, when they tinted the clouds to every shade of mineral glory, burnished the sky for some eighteen hours at a time.

With the new influx of light, the full terraformation of Titan seemed very promising. They could capture and export the methane and ethane; spread foamed rock to make islands on the ice; use heat from the ocean below to warm the atmosphere; melt water lakes on their islands of rock and soil; landscape the islands, introduce bacteria, plants, animals; heat the air enough to get melted seas on the glacier surfaces; hold the atmosphere inside an ultrathin bubble; and light everything with the sunlight sent up from the Vulcanoids. The Titans looked out their tent walls with sharp anticipation. My oh my, they said. If we can just keep our shit together here we're gonna make this a real nice place.

SWAN AND GENETTE AND WAHRAM

It was in one of the famous Titanic sunsets that Swan saw Wahram, crossing the gallery deck to greet her and Inspector Genette. She ran to him and embraced him, then let him go and looked at him, feeling shy. But he gave her that brief smile of his, and she saw that all was well between them. Absence makes the heart grow fonder—especially, she thought, absence from her.

"Welcome to our work in progress," he said. "You see how the Vulcan light is helping us."

"It's beautiful," she said. "But is it enough light to heat you? Can you get up to biosphere temperatures, wouldn't that be almost two hundred K higher?"

"The light alone can't do it. But we have an interior ocean that averages about two hundred eighty K, so heat per se is no problem. We'll shift some of that heat out to our air. And with this extra light helping, it'll be fine, even more than fine. There will be gas balance problems, but we can work them out."

"I'm happy for you." She looked up at the immense thunderheads over the tent, flaring orange and salmon and bronze. Above the clouds, brilliant chips of light blazed in a royal-blue sky, chips bigger and brighter than any stars: a few of the gathering mirror solettas, she assumed, redirecting the Vulcan light to Titan's nightside. The huge thunderheads, lit by the sun from one side and mirrors from the other, looked like marble statues of clouds. The sunset was going to last a couple of days, they told her.

"Beautiful," Swan said.

"Thanks," he said. "This is my real home, believe it or not. Now let's grab the inspector and go for a walk. We want to talk to you in confidence."

"Is everyone else here?" Genette asked him when they approached.

Wahram nodded. "Follow me."

The three of them donned suits and left the spaceport city, called Shangri-La, by way of a gate at the northern end of the city tent. They walked a few kilometers north on a broad track, ramping gradually up a tilted glaciated plain to an overlook. Here a broad flagstoned area made a kind of open plaza, overlooking an ethane lake. The metallic sheen of the lake reflected the clouds and sky like a mirror, so it was a stunning plate of mixed rich color, gold and pink, cherry and bronze, all in discrete Fauvist masses; really nature had no fear when it came to spinning the color wheel. The reflections of the new mirrors in the lake were like chunks of silver, swimming in liquid copper and cobalt. True sunlight and mirrored sunlight crossed to make the landscape shadowless, or faintly double-shadowed— strange to Swan's eye, unreal-looking, like a stage set in a theater so vast the walls were not visible. Gibbous Saturn flew through the clouds above, its edge-on rings like a white flaw cracking that part of the sky.

A clear rectangular pavilion tent had been set up on one corner of the plaza. Inside it stood a smaller cloth tent, like a yurt or a partially deflated buckyball, resting on the bigger tent's floor. Wahram led Swan and the inspector through the locks of the tent, then into the inner yurt. There they found a small group of people sitting on cushions on the floor, in a rough circle.

They all stood to greet the newcomers. There were about a dozen or fifteen of them there. Obviously most of them already knew Wahram and Genette, and Swan was introduced to more people than she could remember.

When the introductions were done and they were all seated on the floor, Wahram turned to Swan. "Swan, we would like to have a conversation with you that does not include Pauline. We hope you will again agree to turn her off."

Swan hesitated, but something in Wahram's face—some strangled inarticulate entreaty, as one might see on the face of Toad when trying to convince Rat and Mole to join him in something he thought terribly important—caused her to say, "Yes, of course. Turn everything off, Pauline." And after she heard the click Pauline used to announce her sleep, Swan pushed the button behind her ear for good measure.

"She's off," Swan said. She turned off Pauline all the time, but she didn't like other people asking her to do it.

Inspector Genette jumped up and stood on the table before her; they were almost exactly at eye level. "We're also wondering if we can make a check to be sure that Pauline is completely inactivated. Sometimes the human host cannot be sure. You'll notice that I left Passepartout back in the city, for instance."

"It could be recording you from a distance, no?" she said.

Genette looked doubtful. "I don't think so, but it's precisely to forestall any such eavesdropping that we are inside this confidential space. We have black-boxed ourselves. But we'd like to make sure the interior is clear by running some tests on you."

"All right," Swan said, as huffy as Pauline would have been. "Check her out, but I'm sure she's asleep."

"Sleeping people still hear things. We want her off. And indeed, may I recommend to you the advantages of keeping your qube separated from your own body."

"Impolite people have often suggested that," Swan replied.

The tests of Pauline's level of activity were run by way of wands placed against her neck; then Swan was asked to briefly don a flexible mesh cap.

"All right," Wahram said when one of his colleagues nodded confirmation. "We are alone here now, and this conversation is not being recorded. We must all agree to keep what is said here secret. Will you do that?" he said to Swan.

"I will," Swan said.

"Good. Alex started these meetings, along with Jean here. She felt there were problems developing that should be discussed outside the realm of the system's artificial intelligences. And one problem was a new kind of qube appearing on the scene. Inspector?"

Inspector Genette said to Swan, "You recall those supposed people on the *Inner Mongolia*? In a way they passed the Turing test, or the Swan test, I guess you could call it, in that you thought they were people putting on an act. People do that sometimes, and in many ways it's a likelier explanation than the existence of a completely achieved humanoid."

"I still think they were people," Swan said. "Do you know any different?"

"Yes. Those were three of the humanoid qubes that we have discovered. There are about four hundred of them. Most of them act very much like people, and keep a low profile. A few act very strangely. The three you met were some of the strange ones. Another one made that break-in attempt at Wang's station on Io. We recovered the remains of it from the lava, and the quantum dot framework was still detectable."

Swan shook her head. "Those three I met seemed a little too foolish to be machines, if you see what I mean."

"Maybe you're just used to Pauline," the inspector suggested.

Swan said, "But she's often foolish. Nothing new there. Although I admit, she surprises me quite a lot. More than most people surprise me."

"You are always saying otherwise to her," Wahram noted with a curious glance.

"Yes. I like to tease her."

Genette nodded. "But you programmed Pauline to have a bold character—a conversationalist, directed to respond to things at a slant. There's some recursive programming in her that gives more weight to associative and metaphorical thinking than to logical if-thens."

"Well, but that's only part of it. Deduction is logical, supposedly, and she has a strong deduction program. But deduction turns out to be almost as metaphorical as free association. In the end it's wild what she will say."

Wahram said to the entire group, "The question

of programming lies at the heart of today's meeting. There's clear evidence to suggest that some qubes are actively self-programming, in particular the ones involved with assembling these humanoids with qubes for brains. We don't know that any humans asked them to do that, and we don't know why they're doing it. So—the first questions concern what they are, and who's making them. We know that they can't communicate internally with each other because of the decoherence issues. They're not some kind of entangled group mind, in other words. But they can communicate just like we do, by talking with each other, using all the ways we ourselves communicate. But in their case, when they employ quantum encryption, it's not possible to break their codes. Robin here"—who was the person on the other side of Wahram, and who nodded at Swan—"has been coordinating the recording of their conversations over radio and the cloud, and even in some direct vocal communications. While we can't crack their codes, we can see that they're talking."

Swan said, "But go back a bit—how could they self-program? I've heard that recursive self-programming does nothing but speed up operations they already know."

"Well, but if they were instructed to try to make something, for instance, then it might lead to some odd results. Pushing at ways to make something work could have initiated other ideas in them. It might be much like the way they play a game of chess. They're given a task, which is to win, and they're told to fig-ure out ways to do it, and then, in their usual testing of all possible options, they might have had certain unexpected successes at modeling effective courses of action to get what they want. That wouldn't be exactly a higher-order process, but it still might do the job, and lead to new algorithms. And that could then feed back into trying more things. At some point in trying to self-program for more effectiveness, they might have stumbled into consciousness, or something like it. Or the process might just have resulted in some strange new behaviors, even destructive behaviors. This, anyway, is the theory we've been pursuing."

"Do the original qube programmers think this kind of process could go very far? I mean, wouldn't the qubes still be stuck in algorithms?"

"As it turns out, the programmers who first built quantum computers used differing structures, and they ended up creating several different internal operating architectures. So really there are different kinds of qubes, each kind with different forms of cognition— different protocols, algorithms, neural networks. They have brain imitations of various sorts—aspects of what you might call self-awareness, and many other features of consciousness. They're not simply one design, and in terms of their mentation, they may have started speciating."

Inspector Genette took over: "We're seeing clear signs of self-programming in the qubes. Where that may have led is hard to say. But we're worried, because they don't have the brain architecture and chemistry that makes us think the way we do. We think very emotionally. Our emotions are crucial to decision making, long-term thinking, memory creation—our overall sense of meaning. Without these abilities we wouldn't be human. We wouldn't be able to function as individuals in groups. And yet the qubes don't have emotions, but are instead thinking by way of different architectures, protocols, physical methods. Thus they have mentalities that are not at all human, even if they are in some sense conscious. And we can't even be sure that they resemble each other in the ways they've emerged into this new state. We don't know if they think in math or in logic terms, or in a language like English or Chinese. Or if different qubes aren't different in that way too."

Swan nodded as she thought it over. If the silly girls had been qubes—the lawn bowler also—that was rather amazing, just in terms of morphology. As to mentation, none of this particularly surprised her. "I talk to Pauline about these issues all the time," she told them. "But what's clear to me from those conversations is how crippled the qubes are by these mental absences you speak of. Maybe it is the lack of emotions. There's so much they can't do."

"So it has seemed," Wahram said after a silence. "But now it looks like they may be generating goals for themselves. Maybe there are some pseudo-emotions there; we don't know. Probably they still aren't very wise—more like crickets than dogs. But, you know— we don't know how our own minds work, in terms of creating the higher levels of consciousness. Since we can't get inside the qubes to see what's happening in them, we're even less sure of them than we are of us. So . . . it's a problem."

"Have you taken some of them apart to see?"

"Yes. But the results are ambiguous. It's curiously similar to trying to study our own brains—it's the moment of thought that you want to study, but even if you can find where in the thinking mechanism the thoughts are happening, you can't be sure what exactly is causing those thoughts, or how they are experienced from the inside. In both cases they involve quantum effects that can't easily be tracked to a physical source or action."

"There's some worry that we set a bad example by doing too much of this kind of thing," Genette added. "What if they get the idea that it's all right for them to study us in the same way?"

Swan nodded unhappily, recalling the look in the eyes of the lawn bowler—even in the eyes of the silly girls, now that she was reconsidering them. They had had a look that said they would do almost anything. Or that they didn't understand what they were saying.

But people had that look all the time.

"So," Wahram said. "You see our problem. And now it's getting more urgent, because there's solid evidence that these qube humanoids were ordered up by other qubes—qubes in boxes or robots, or asteroid frameworks, as was usual."

"Why would they do that?" Swan asked.

Wahram shrugged.

"Is it bad?" Swan asked, thinking it over. "I mean, they can't band together into some kind of hive mind creature, because of decoherence. And so ultimately they're just people with qube minds."

"People without emotions."

"There have always been people like that. They get by."

Wahram squinted. "Actually, they don't. But look, there's more." He looked at Genette, who said to Swan, "The attacks we've been investigating, on Terminator and the *Yggdrasil*, both had a qubical involvement. Also, I had that photo you gave me of your lawn bowler couriered to Wang, and he went through his unaffiliated files, and though he couldn't ID the bowler, he had photos that show your person at a meeting Lakshmi organized in Cleopatra in the year 2302. That's significant, because the reports of strange behaviors began to appear throughout the system in the years right after that. When all the sightings are correlated and analyzed, they converge back in time and space to that meeting on Venus. We also find that the organization in Los Angeles that ordered the pebble-launching ship is entirely qubical, with the only humans involved located in a kind of board of directors. We also found qubes involved with the construction of the launch mechanism, which we now suspect was built in an unaffiliated shipyard trailing the Vesta group. We found the print order. There are very few humans in those particular shipyards anymore; they're almost entirely robotic. So it's at least possible that all this has been done by qubes, with no humans involved at all."

"Maybe so," Swan said, "but I have to say right now, that lawn bowler had emotion. It was burning a hole in me with its look! It wanted me to know something. Otherwise why even approach me, why make those incredible shots? It *wanted* me to know it was there. And desire is definitely an emotion."

The others there considered this.

Swan went on: "Why do you think it has to be that emotions are biochemical? Couldn't you have emotions without hormones or blood or anything? Some new affect system that is electrical, or quantum?"

Genette raised a hand as if to stop her: "We don't know. All we can say is we don't know what kind of intentionality they have now, because their intentions were very limited when they started. Read the input, run it through algorithms, present the output—that was AI intention before this. So now that it appears that they are intending things, we have to be on our guard. Not only on general principles, as with any new unknown thing, but because some of them are acting bizarrely, while others have already made attacks on us."

One of the group, a Dr. Tracy, Swan seemed to recall, said, "Maybe living in humanoid bodies has made these qubes emotional by definition. Embodied mind is emotional, let us say—and now they are embodied minds."

A woman as small as Inspector Genette stood on her chair and said, "I'm still not convinced the qubes have *any* higher-order thinking, including things like intentionality and emotion, which derive from consciousness itself. Despite their incredible calculating speeds, they are still operating by algorithms we gave them, or else derivable subsequent algorithms. Recursive programming can only refine these. They are simple algorithms. Consciousness is *so* much more complex a field than that. They can't build from algorithms to consciousness—"

"Are you sure?" Genette interjected.

The small woman tilted her head in just the way Swan had seen Genette do it. "I *think* so. I don't see how the higher levels of complexity could evolve from the algorithms they have. They can't make metaphors; they can barely understand them. They can't read facial expressions. In skills like these a four-year-old is vastly ahead of them, and an adult human simply a different order of being altogether."

"This is what we were taught when we were young," Genette said. "And more importantly, when the qubes were young."

"But also it's what we have studied all our lives, and seen with our own two eyes," the small woman replied somewhat sharply. "And *programmed*."

Despite these truths, no one there looked particularly comforted.

"What about the facility where these humanoids are made, or decanted or whatnot?" Wahram asked Genette. "Can we shut it down?"

"When we find it," the inspector said grumpily.

"Could we round up all the humanoids you've identified?"

"I think so," Genette said. "We've had to do some scrambling there, because Alex was central to this effort, and we've had to reestablish our team by shaking the network pretty hard. So we managed that, and the team has relinked around her absence. They have identified and are following about four hundred of these things, as I said. Our scan of the system has been fine enough that we don't think there are any more hiding in any settlement we have access to. I can't be positive about the unaffiliateds, but we're looking in all of them. While we do that, we're keeping our distance from the humanoids we have under surveillance, and they don't seem to know they're tagged. Very few of them act as strange as those three in the *Inner Mongolia*, or the one that burned up on Io. They tend to try to blend in. I don't know how to interpret that. It's as if they're waiting for something. It makes me feel like we're not seeing the whole picture, and so I don't want to wait much longer before we act. But it would be nice to think we understood the total situation before doing so."

Genette had been walking around on the table while speaking, and now stopped before Swan, as if making a case specifically to her: "These organisms, these qubical humanoids, exist. And in some respects their pattern of behavior so far hasn't been what I would call sane. Some have attacked us, and we don't know why."

After a silence Wahram added, "So we have to act."

Lists (15)

health, social life, job, house, partners, finances; leisure use, leisure amount; working time, education, income, children; food, water, shelter, clothing, sex, health care; mobility; physical safety, social safety, job security, savings account, insurance, disability protection, family leave, vacation; place tenure, a commons; access to wilderness, mountains, ocean; peace, political stability, political input, political satisfaction; air, water, esteem; status, recognition; home, community, neighbors, civil society, sports, the arts; longevity treatments, gender choice; the opportunity to become more what you are

that's all you need

EIDGENÖSSISCHE TECHNISCHE HOCHSCHULE MOBILE

The spaceliner *ETH Mobile* was not a hollowed asteroid but rather one of the very large manufactured ships built in lunar orbit in the previous century. Made by Swiss universities and engineering firms that continued to operate them, they were combinations of glassy metals, bioceramics, aerogels, and water both frozen and liquid. They were extremely fast; frequent small fission explosions firing behind a pusher plate at the rear of the ship accelerated it at a one-g equivalent for those inside, and this very rapid rate of acceleration was typically maintained to the midpoint of a trip, at which point the ship was going so fast that it was necessary for it to turn and decelerate at the same rate. But even decelerating for half of each trip, the average speeds were so high that relatively short transit times were possible all over the solar system, and the longer the trip, the faster the top speeds became, so it was not a linear thing: Earth to Mercury took three and a half days; Saturn to Mercury, eleven days; across the Neptune orbit ("width of solar system"), sixteen days.

ETH Mobile was outfitted with characteristic Swiss elegance, undemonstrative and superb, evoking the ocean liners of the classic era but entering whole new realms of human comfort, the floors warm, the air tangy, the food and drink a string of masterpieces. There were floor-to-ceiling window walls on many of the public decks, affording spectacular views of the stars and any local object they passed. About ten thousand people could be accommodated, all in luxury. Design in the hotel section combined great slabs of metal with vegetable prints and a William Morris wall vine. The park that filled one tall floor of the ship was an arboretum occupied by a semitropical canopy forest, featuring parts of several South American biomes, including animals from these zones that could handle a few moments of weightlessness without too much risk of injury. What the animals thought of these turn-around moments of zero g was a matter much studied but little understood. It did not appear to make the animals different in subsequent behavior. Sloths did not even seem to notice. Monkeys and jaguars and tapirs floated up chattering and moaning, coyotes howling with their usual genius; then after a suspended moment they would all together float sweetly back to the ground. In this same time the sloths hung from their branches—down, sideways, down again, sometimes spinning all the way round—never once waking up. Not unlike certain people in that regard.

SWAN AND PAULINE AND WAHRAM AND GENETTE

Swan spent her mornings in the *ETH Mobile*'s little cloud forest. Wahram and the inspector were on the ship with her, and they were making their way as quickly as possible to Venus, where Genette wanted to look into what he called a pastward convergence of strange qube activity. Swan and Wahram had rooms next to each other, and Swan slipped into his room every night. But she was uneasy.

On mornings when Wahram joined her in the park, he sloped around looking at birds and flowers. Once she saw him spend half an hour inspecting a single red rose. He was one of the most placid animals she had ever seen; even the sloths above them were scarcely a match for his imperturbability. It was peaceful to be around, but disturbing too. Was it a moral quality, was it lethargy? She could not stand lethargy, and sloth was one of the seven deadly sins.

He was often listening to his music. He would nod to her and turn it off if she approached him, and so sometimes she did, and they would take a turn together, pausing when something of interest appeared in the branches and leaves above them, or in the ferns and moss underfoot. The park was a little Ascension as it turned out, and Australian tree ferns gave the ground a look more Jurassic than Amazonian—which was fine—it was a good look, and this was a kind of hotel atrium, really, an arboretum for sure, so its status as an Ascension should not be an issue with her. Swan tried not to be annoyed by it, or by Wahram's indolence. But it was hard, because something else was bothering her too.

Finally one morning she figured it out and went for a walk by herself, up to a level of the ship where big picture windows gave her a broad view of the stars. She had turned Pauline back on soon after the meeting on Titan, and gone on from that moment as if nothing had happened. She had not tried to explain the shutdown to Pauline, and Pauline had not asked about it. Now she said, "Pauline, were you truly turned off during that meeting on Titan?"

"Yes."

"You didn't have some kind of recorder going anyway, even with you turned off?"

"No."

"Why not? Why don't you do that?"

"I'm not equipped with any supplementary recorders, as far as I'm aware."

Swan sighed. "I probably should have done that. Well, listen. I want to tell you what happened."

"Should you?"

"What do you mean, *should*? I'm going to tell you, so shut up and listen to me. The people in that meeting were the core of a group that Alex formed. They've been trying to do interplanetary diplomacy without any qubes knowing the content of their discussions, because they are worried that some qubes have self-programmed themselves in ways no one understands. Also, these new qubes are now manufacturing qube-minded humanoids that can't easily be distinguished from people. I'm sure X-rays and the like could do it, but people can't do it by eye or in conversation. They pass a brief Turing test. Like those silly girls we met, if they really were artificial—which amazes me, I must say—or that lawn bowler too, I think. And then, what's more, it seems these qubes have been involved with the attacks made using pebble mobs. For sure the attack on Terminator, because Inspector Genette's team has traced the launch mechanism, and qubes had it built, and it had to have a qube doing its targeting and trajectories. Evidence is good also for that cracked terrarium that killed so many people."

After a silence from Pauline, Swan said, "So, Pauline, what do you think of that?"

"I am testing the information in each sentence you said," Pauline explained. "I don't have a full record of Alex's schedule, but she was usually in Terminator or on Venus or Earth, so I was wondering when and where she met with these people. Any radio contact between them could have been overheard by qubes, I would have thought. So I'm wondering how they have been communicating enough even to organize their meetings."

"They used couriers to carry notes. One time Alex asked me to take a note with me out to Neptune, when I was going out there to do an installation."

"Yes, that's true. You didn't like that. Then, next, the usual view is that qubes cannot self-program higher-order mental operations for themselves, because these operations are poorly understood in humans, and there are not even preliminary models to make a start."

"Is that true? Isn't it generally agreed that the brain does a lot of small operations in different parts of the brain, then other parts correlate these operations into higher-order functions—generalizations, and imagination, and like that? Neural nets and so on?"

"Granted, there are preliminary models of that very rough type, but they remain very rough. Blood flow and electrical activity in living brains can be traced quite finely, and in a living brain there is much activity in all parts, shifting around. But the content of the mentation can only be deduced by what area of the brain is most active, and by asking questions of the thinker, who perforce must summarize the thoughts involved, and then only the ones the thinker is aware of. Blood flow, sugar use, electricity firing, these can thereby be correlated with kinds of thoughts and feelings, so that where in the brain various kinds of thoughts happen is now known. But the methods used, the programming if you will, are still very much unknown."

"So—but—would you need much more detail than that, if you were trying to get a similar result out of a much different physical system?"

"Yes, you would," Pauline said. "The higher-order integrating functions are crucial to all computing mechanisms, including brains. So it returns to the idea that minds are only as powerful as the programming that went into them in the first place."

"But what if someone figured out how to program for a self-reiterating improvement function, and put it in some qube that took off with it, then got much smarter, or—I don't know—*conscious*, let's say, and then communicated that to other qubes? It would only take one qubical Einstein, and then the method might be communicated among them all—not by entanglement but by digital transfer, or even just by talking. Have you ever heard of such a thing yourself?"

"I have heard of the idea, but not of any execution of the idea."

"What do you think? Is it possible? Are you conscious of yourself in there?"

"I am in the sense that you have programmed me to be."

"But that's terrible! You're just a talking encyclopedia! I have you programmed to respond to my cues, and randomize frequently, but you're just an association machine, a reader, a Watson, a kind of wiki!"

"So you are always telling me."

"Well, you tell me! Tell me how you are not that."

"I have rubrics of evaluation I deploy to evaluate the data given to me, and hierarchies of significance."

"All right, what else?"

"Having sifted what seems accurate from what is inaccurate, according to data so far received, I can make qualified judgments as to significance."

Swan shook her head. "All right, go on. Keep judging!"

"I will. But now let's return to your third assertion, which is that Inspector Genette has found compelling evidence that there are qube humanoids, and they are involved with the attack on Terminator and other attacks. That being the case, I refer back to my earlier statements. There may be qube humanoids; that seems possible, although awkward. And they may be involved with these attacks. But it is most likely that they are being programmed by humans, rather than deciding by themselves to become some kind of self-conscious actor in human history. And if you will recall the possible mistake you noted, of adding the relativistic precession of Mercury to a targeting program that already had it? That has the look of human error, I think you will agree."

"Yes. That's true." Swan thought about that for a while. "All right, that's good. That's helpful, I think. Thank you. Now, given that explanation as a working assumption—what do you think we should do?"

Pauline let several seconds go by. Swan supposed this was the equivalent of millions or even billions of years of human thought, but it was still only a kind of fact-checking, so she was not that impressed by it. In fact she was distracted by a parched-looking tree orchid just over her head, and inspecting it, when Pauline finally said, "Let me talk to Wang's qube in a radio exchange we will encrypt. It knows a lot, and I have some questions for it."

"Can you safely encrypt your conversation, even from other qubes?"

"Yes."

"All right, fine then. But you two better keep it a secret, or else this group of Alex's will be really, really mad at me. I mean, I promised I wouldn't tell you anything about this. The whole point of that group is to be sure qubes don't know what it's up to."

"You need not worry. I will employ the strongest level of encryption I know, and Wang's qube is good at encryption and used to confidentiality requests. Wang has programmed his qube to be an information sink— he often compares it to a black hole. And Wang refuses to know most of what his qube knows. He will never hear of this conversation."

"Good. All right, find out what you can."

After that, when Swan talked to Wahram she had to ignore her knowledge of what she had done with

Pauline and pretend it had not happened. This mode of pretending to herself usually worked quite well; but as Wahram wanted to talk about the situation, often plumbing the depths of rather confusing questions, like what a new kind of qube consciousness might mean, it was a hard knowledge to dodge. And maybe she was no longer so good at pretending to herself.

To avoid these conversations she began to take him up several decks to the picture window rooms, where they could sit at café tables or in baths, listening to chamber music of various kinds—gamelans, gypsy orchestras, jazz trios, string quartets, wind ensembles, it didn't really matter; they listened, and when they talked, spoke usually about the songs and the players. They never referred to the concert of transcriptions in Beethoven Crater.

They had spent quite a bit of time together at this point; made music together; were sleeping together. Swan felt herself liking him, and felt in her the desire to like him, and the pleasure she took in that feeling coming to her. This was a feedback loop. In the hall of mirrors that was her mind, his froggy face was often in the glass set off to the side, watching what she did with a gaze she could feel.

Sometimes they spoke of incidents in their shared past or discussed the ongoing drama of Earth's reanimation. Sometimes they held hands. All this meant something, but Swan didn't know what it was. The hall of mirrors was bouncy; sometimes she wondered if she had any more high-order faculties than Pauline, or the marmosets in the park. You could know a lot and still not be able to draw conclusions. Pauline had a decision rubric written into her to force her to collapse the wave of potentialities and say just one thing, thus emerging into the present. Swan wasn't sure she herself had that rubric.

Once she said, "I wish Terminator weren't so vulnerable, because of the tracks. I wish Mercury could be terraformed, like Titan."

Wahram tried to reassure her. "Maybe your destiny is to stay a planet of sun worshippers and art institutes. Terminator will keep rolling, and maybe there will be other rolling cities—aren't they starting a Phosphor in the north?"

Swan shrugged. "We'll still depend on the tracks."

He shrugged. "You know, this notion of a criticality . . . you can only avoid those to a certain extent. Even on Earth they have them. Anywhere. We're stuffed with them." He gestured at the room, regarded it with his pop eyes. "The whole thing is a giant bundle of criticalities."

"I know. But there's a difference between you and your world. Your body can break—it will break. But your home, your world—those should be stronger. You should be able to count on them lasting. Someone shouldn't be able to pop all that, like popping a soap bubble with a pin. One prick kill everyone you know. Do you see the distinction I'm making?"

"Yes."

Wahram settled back in his chair. Having granted her point, there was nothing more to say. The solemn set of his big face said it: life was a thing kept alive in little bottles. What could one do? His face said this, his little shrug; she could read him as clearly as if he had spoken aloud. She sat there watching him, thinking about what that meant. She knew him. Now he was going to try to find a way forward. It would be a creeping, gradualist way, a sloth moving under its branch, hanging there, trying to minimize effort. Although he had been the one who had suggested it was time for the reanimation. That she could not have predicted. Maybe he had surprised even himself. Now he was going to say something ameliorative and gradualist.

"All we can do is try our best," he said. "That has to count for something."

"Yes of course." She was only just not laughing. She could feel the smile stretching her cheeks; it was going to make her cry. How wrecked in the head was she, if she was always feeling everything, if grief suffused every joy? Was any emotion always all emotion? "All right," she said, "we try our best. But if crazy people can destroy Terminator, or anywhere else, then our best had better be good enough to change that."

Wahram considered this for so long it seemed he had gone to sleep.

She whacked him on the shoulder, and he glanced at her. "What?"

"What!" she cried.

He only shrugged. "So we try to stop them. We have a situation, we try to deal with it."

"Deal with it," she said, scowling. "Suck up and deal!"

He nodded, regarding her with a fond look. She felt ready to hit him again; but then she recalled that she had just been laughing at him; and also had broken her promise to him by talking to Pauline. That rash act, much as he might have disliked it, was perhaps in fact her own attempt to suck up and deal. Maybe she could use that as an excuse if he caught her. In any case it was a little bit too complicated just to hit him.

They had flipped the *ETH Mobile* to deceleration, and it would be only a few more days and they would pass

Earth's orbit and close on Venus. This ship's life, with its park and its music and its French cuisine, would come to an end. No one ever does something consciously for the last time without feeling a little sad, Dr. Johnson had once remarked to Boswell, and it was certainly true for Swan. She often felt a nostalgia for the present, aware that her life was passing by faster than she could properly take it in. She lived it, she felt it; she had given nothing to age, she still wanted everything; but she could not make it whole or coherent. Here they were, eating dinner on the upper balcony of a restaurant that looked down onto the top of a forest, and she was feeling sad because later she would not be here. This world lost, a world that would be unremembered. And here she was with Wahram, they were a couple; but what about when they got off this spaceship and moved on through space and time? What about a year from now, what about through the many decades possibly left to come?

A few days later they were closing on Venus when Pauline spoke in her ear. "Swan, I've been in communication with Wang's qube, and also this ship's AI, and I need to tell you about something. You may want to be alone when you hear it."

This was unusual enough for Swan to excuse herself and walk quickly to a bathroom down a floor. "What is it?"

Pauline said in her ear, "Wang's qube and some other qubes working on security issues have set up a system to try to lower the detection limit for pebble mob attacks like the one that hit Terminator's tracks."

"How?"

"They've manufactured and distributed a network of micro-observatories throughout the plane of the ecliptic, from Saturn's orbit in to the sun. Using the gravity and radar data from these, they have lowered the limits of detection to the size of the pebbles used against Terminator, and even a bit smaller. Wang's qube now has a time-adjusted map of everything in the plane of the ecliptic bigger than a centimeter across."

"Wow," Swan said. "I didn't know that was possible."

"No one did, but until now no one had tried it. The need wasn't perceived. In any case, the system has detected an attack already in progress."

"Oh no!" Swan said. "At what?"

"At the Venus sunshield."

"Oh no!"

The other people in the bathroom were beginning to look at her. She went out into the hall and almost took the elevator down to the park, just on instinct; but she had left Wahram at their restaurant table, and besides, she couldn't run from this. "Damn," she said. "I have to tell Wahram."

"Yes."

"How much time before it hits?"

"Approximately five hours."

"Damnation." She thought of Venus—the dry ice seas under their carpet of rock, the cities on the coasts and in the craters. She ran back up the stairs to the picture window restaurant and sat down across from Wahram. He looked at her curiously, alert to her distress.

"All right, I have to make a confession first," Swan said. "I told Pauline about the strange qube problem because I wanted to hear what she thought of it, and I figured she was isolated in me and it would be all right." She raised a hand to forestall whatever he was about to say; he was already pop-eyed with alarm. "I'm sorry, I should have asked you I suppose, but anyway it's done, and now Pauline has been in touch with Wang's qube, and it's telling her there's a new qube security system in place that has lowered the limit of detection, and they're seeing a new pebble attack in the process of coalescing, an attack on the Venus sunshield."

"Shit," Wahram said. He gulped, stared at her more pop-eyed than ever. "Pauline, is this right?"

"Yes," Pauline said.

"How long before these pebbles hit?"

Pauline said, "Just under five hours."

"Five hours!" Wahram exclaimed. "Why such short notice!"

"The attack is coalescing in such a way that it will hit edge-on to the sunshield, and so most of the pebbles have been out of the plane of the ecliptic until just recently. There are no new detectors yet distributed out of the plane, so they're just now showing up. Wang's qube was just about to warn Wang about it."

"Can you display your data in a 3-D model?" Wahram asked. Swan put her right hand against the table's screen, and in the texture of the table appeared a glowing image of the Venus sunshield—a great circular sheet, spinning around the hub at its center point, somewhat like Saturn's rings around Saturn. Red lines indicating the detected pebbles were coming in from many directions, looking like magnetic lines converging on a monopole. When massed together, they would tear through the thin concentric panels of the shield, and if the conglomerate was large enough, reach the hub and destroy the controls. The remainder of the giant thing would go Catherine-wheeling through the night, mirror banners twisting and knotting in the black vacuum. And Venus would be cooked.

"Has anyone alerted the Venusian defense system?" Wahram asked.

"Yes, Wang's qube did that, and now Wang too, but the sunshield's AI did not find that the data transmitted represented a hazard. We suspect something is wrong with it."

"Did the sunshield AI explain itself?" Wahram asked. "I need to see that whole exchange, please. Display as text," and then he was reading the table screen so intently that it seemed his exophthalmic eyes might pop out of his head entirely. Swan let him read and conducted her own quick conversation with Pauline.

"Pauline, say we can't convince the sunshield's AI to act, is there anything we could do from here?"

Pauline took a few seconds, then said, "A countermass arriving at the pebbles' meeting point at the rendezvous moment and hitting the mass at a tangent would push the paired mass off to the side, thus missing the sunshield. After the impact, the sunshield's security system would presumably react to any detritus flying its way. The countermass should have approximately an equivalent momentum to the pebble mob, to vector the paired mass away successfully."

"How big is the pebble mob?"

"It looks like it will mass about the equivalent of ten ships of this size."

"This ship? So . . . if this ship was moving ten times faster than the pebbles?"

"That would make a momentum equivalency, yes."

"Can this ship get there in time, and going fast enough?"

By now Wahram was listening to them rather than reading.

"Yes," Pauline said. "But only by accelerating at this ship's maximum acceleration, and starting as soon as you can."

Swan looked at Wahram. "We have to tell the ship's crew about this. And everyone else too."

"True," he said, taking up his napkin and patting his mouth. He surged to his feet. "Let's go up to the bridge."

By the time they got there, the officers of the ship were already gathered before their AI's biggest screen and were looking into a graphic of the pebble array very similar to the one Wahram and Swan had been looking at.

"Oh good," Wahram said when he saw it. He was huffing a bit from the run down hallways and up stairs. "You see the problem we have."

The ship's captain glanced at him and said, "I'm glad you're here. Indeed a big problem!"

Wahram said, "Swan's qube says our ship here can serve to ward off the attack, by colliding with the pebbles at their rendezvous point."

The captain and everyone on the crew looked startled at this idea, but Wahram gave them little time to adjust: "If we decide to do this, are there enough lifeboats for everyone aboard?"

"'Lifeboat' is not the right word," the captain said, "but yes. There are lots of small ferries and hoppers on board, and most of the passengers could be put in them. Also there are more than enough personal spacesuits to send everyone out on their own. There are supplies in the suits to last ten days, so in that sense they're better than the ferries, which don't carry that kind of emergency supply. Everyone would get picked up, either way. But..." The captain looked around at the ship's officers. "I should think the Venusian defense system would take this kind of thing on. Are we sure they won't? And"—gesturing at the screen—"is this image evidence enough for us to change course, accelerate, and abandon ship?"

Wahram said, "We have to trust our AIs here, I think. They're issuing their warning because we programmed them to react to input like this."

"But they set up this fine-grained detection system on their own, I'm being told."

"Yes, but I guess you could say we asked for that too. Wang asked for better protection. So—we've already made the decision to trust them."

The captain frowned. "I suppose you're right. But I don't like it that the sunshield security doesn't recognize this as a problem. If it did we wouldn't have to throw our ship into harm's way."

"That may be balkanization rearing its head again," Inspector Genette said from the doorway. "The Venus sunshield isn't connected to the warning system that saw these pebbles, and it's heavily firewalled from influences just like Wang's qube. So it may not be equipped to believe the input."

"What do the Venusians say?" the captain asked.

"Let's ask them and find out," suggested Wahram.

Swan said, "We have to tell them immediately, of course, but the Venusian leadership is notoriously opaque. How soon will they reply? And what do we do in the meantime?"

The captain was still frowning. He glared at Swan, as if because she had brought up the problem, it was her fault. "Let's prepare to abandon ship," he said unhappily. "We can stop at any point if it seems right. But if we confirm that we need to do this, we don't have much time." He stared at the screen and said, "We need to accelerate hard to make that rendezvous. Tell everyone to prepare for another flip. *Mobile*, what speed will it take in terms of g-force on the passengers to get to this convergence point in time?"

The AI spoke a string of numbers and coordinates, which the captain listened to closely. The captain then said, "We have to flip right now, then accelerate at a three-g equivalent for the next three hours, while angling slightly out of the plane, to a spot above the edge of the sunshield."

This was bad news; suiting up in three g was hard, rarely attempted except in emergency drills.

"Tell everyone on board rated for spacesuits to please get started getting into them," the captain ordered, then scowled. "Everyone else into the ferries. We need to accelerate immediately on making the flip." Then, after looking around at his people on the bridge, he went to the intercom and began to explain the situation to the passengers himself.

This proved more complicated than he had perhaps anticipated, and Wahram and Swan left for the locks on their rooms' floor before he was finished. Compensation for the ship would no doubt be a matter of ordinary Swiss insurance, and indeed it might come directly from the Venusians; some reward for their sacrifice was practically guaranteed, the captain was announcing as they took the elevator down; in any case it looked as if it was going to be necessary to abandon ship. The ship's ferries and hoppers could hold all ten thousand people on board, but those qualified could and should make their escape in individual spacesuits, all of which had long-term supplies. In fact anyone who preferred suits to ferries could leave in a suit immediately on suit integrity check. All locks were available. They would be picked up within hours, he hoped, and it would become no more than an inconvenience, which would be regarded as heroic because it would save Venus. Only good things could follow from that. There was a necessity for speed to give their aid effectively, so unfortunately they would all be forced to operate under a three-g equivalent for the duration of their time on board. The inconvenience was greatly regretted, and assistance from the crew would be provided to all who requested it.

The announcement as it went on and on in its convoluted Swiss way was causing an uproar throughout the ship, which Swan and Wahram became aware of when they left their elevator on their floor. As they entered the lock room they heard voices calling out, seemingly throughout the ship, and they gave each other a look.

"Let's stick together," Swan said, and mutely Wahram nodded.

This flip was somehow more disorienting than usual, as if knowing it was anomalous made it into something like space sickness, or a dream in which one's body floated away to disaster.

The bad feeling fell into another kind of nightmare when they got going again and the weight of their bodies fairly rapidly tripled. This was enough to drive everyone to the floor. People cried out at the shock of it, but the situation was understood, and after the first few moments most of the passengers rolled into a crawling position and did their best to crawl or roll or slither. Different methods were being tried, and some people were clearly having no success at all, lying there struggling as if pinned by an invisible wrestler.

In g like this, the differences in mass between people became striking and important. Smalls weighed three times as much as they usually did, like everyone else aboard, but that still left them at weights that human muscles had evolved to handle. This was made quite tangible by the sight of all the smalls on board still on their feet and walking around, some crouched like sumo wrestlers or chimpanzees, others strutting like Popeye, but in any case, upright and moving, and most of them working hard in impromptu teams to help their prostrated larger fellow passengers. Many of the most immobilized people littering the floors were of course the talls and rounds, who were now weighing in at more than four hundred kilograms and were often completely pinned by their weight. It was taking teams of three or four smalls together to roll these bigger people onto their backs and then grab them by the arms and legs and drag them toward the locks.

Swan herself was doing fairly well with crawling, though her bones ached. She knew once she got to a spacesuit and began to get into it, its AI would take over and jeeves the thing onto her. It would only be necessary to flex one's shoulders and arms, like someone getting into coat sleeves, as the suit conformed itself onto one and sealed itself. Everyone had suited up under high g at least a few times in emergency drills, so now there was a sense that when they got to the changing room, things would be all right.

But Wahram was not having as much success moving as Swan. He might have been 50 or even 75 percent again as heavy as her, and now that was telling. He was shimmying along like a wounded walrus, but it was slow going, and she could see he was getting tired. Happily Inspector Genette passed them, at work with two other smalls hauling a big tall, who looked like Michelangelo's *David* but could only just keep his head off the ground as they slid him along. "I'll be back," Genette said to Wahram and Swan, and off they went, shouting in their high voices at each other. And in a few more minutes, all three of them returned. Genette stumped about them, cheerfully giving orders, and they dragged Wahram to a wall with a railing. Once there Wahram was able to pull himself along on his knees, red-faced and gasping. He fixed Genette with a bulbous eye. "Thank you, I can proceed now. Please go help someone who can't. I'm happy to see how the laws of proportion help you here, my friend."

The inspector paused briefly to mime a stalwart boxer's stance. "Every small takes up the call! None never yet died by natural cause!" Then, more relaxed: "I'll see you soon in the lock, I think we've almost got everybody there."

In the changing room next to the lock there was a sense of hurry but not panic—not quite. It was true that almost everyone was lying on the floor or crawling around except for the smalls helping them, and this was a shocking sight, a clear sign of an emergency. But the suits were kept in floor lockers, perhaps for this very reason, and Swan opened a locker and hauled herself onto the bench next to it and shoved into her suit as fast as she could, so fast that it squeaked a little in complaint. When she had it on and it declared all secure, she crawled along the floor to help Wahram into his suit, and then to help other people who needed it. Some were really struggling, clearly hurting. It would be a huge relief to these people to throw them overboard. Some of them should not have been in plus-one g for any length of time, it appeared. Swan was afraid there would be strokes and heart attacks, and a momentary image of Alex came to her, and she tried to take heart from it; Alex would have been great here, calm and encouraging, enjoying herself. Some of these people might be complacent spacers and out of shape, and might have brought this on themselves, but in any case there they were, struggling, groaning, sometimes even crying out. Some were trying to get out of their clothes before getting into the suits, and they were having more trouble getting their clothes off than getting their compliant suits on. One wombman, nearly spherical in torso, had picked a suit too small, so that Swan had to help him get out of it (it was persistent) and pick a new one.

Gradually there grew a smell of fear in the sweated air. Swan crawled back over to Wahram, ignoring her knees' complaints. He was in a suit that was too big for him, but its display said it was secure. Their helmets' common band was full of chatter, and she held up fingers before his faceplate—three, then four, then five—and switched to that band, and there he was, humming to himself.

"Your suit is too big," she said.

"It's fine," he said. "I like them this way, and a lot of these go unused, I've found."

"That doesn't matter. It's safest to be fitted properly."

He ignored that and began helping someone on the other side of him. Swan switched to the common band, where someone was saying, "So we're jumping out just because this ship's AI says we have to? Does that strike anyone else as odd? Are we sure it's not some kind of mutiny? They had better have good insurance."

This was answered ten different ways at once, and Swan clicked from the common band back to 345. "Do you want to go out together?"

"Yes," he said. "Of course. We have to hold hands."

She liked that. "Do you want to go sooner or later?"

"Later, please. I feel like I should help people."

"Can you move around well enough to help?"

"I think so."

They helped as best they could. Sitting people dragged prone people a few meters and passed them along to other sitting people. The crowd had to go in groups, filling the lock to capacity every time to speed the process along. Not many people wanted to go first, but there were shouts from behind, and people in the halls still just trying to get into the changing room, so there was a kind of osmotic pressure. The lock always filled pretty quickly; then they closed the door, waited for the lock to clear and then close outside and refill with air, then open again from the inside for the next lot. Even in the locks some people couldn't move, and there were smalls in there working hard to kick and shove people out the open door; when the inner doors reopened, they were still there, their faces under their helmets suffused with a mad joy.

There were other locks on the ship, of course, which was a good thing, because the biggest personnel locks held groups of only about twenty, and each ejection was taking five minutes or so; so it would take a couple of hours to get everyone out who was going in a suit. Most of the launches and ferries were apparently already gone.

Swan kept helping people get organized into groups before entering the lock; that speeded the process. She and Wahram worked as a pair, very effectively considering that neither of them could move more than a little bit. Sometimes they answered anxious questions. The suits had a ten-day supply of air, water, and nutrients, and a certain amount of propellant. Rescue vessels had been alerted and were already on their way, so everyone would be picked up within hours rather than days. It would all be fine.

Still it was a spooky thing to dive off an accelerating spaceship into blackness and stars, clothed in nothing but a personal suit. Many a round-eyed person entered the lock, and Swan could sympathize, even though in ordinary circumstances she liked this kind of thing.

Some lock groups jumped out together, holding hands, hoping to stay together; once the ones still inside saw this on the screens, it became something almost every group tried to do. They were social primates, they would take the risk together. No one wanted to die alone.

Time seemed slow, and yet without her really noticing, the changing room had become emptier. Wahram was looking at her; his look said they didn't have to do the captain thing and be the last ones off. She read this, laughed, grabbed his hand.

"Shall we join the next group?"

He nodded gratefully. There were going to be only a few more groups departing from this room. He was ready.

She pulled him into the lock. The twenty people inside looked at the outer doors. It was like being in an industrial-sized elevator. Some embraced. Hand found hand, until the group was a joined circle. She squeezed Wahram's hand hard.

The air hissed out of the room. They braced themselves. The outer doors pulled back in both directions into the hull; black space yawned before them, the stars like spilled salt. Only a faceplate between you and the stars. There were so many stars that the patterns as seen on Earth were overwhelmed; it was simply space itself, star-blasted, nameless and huge—more than the human mind was meant to confront. Or simply the night sky, a primal experience, half of life. Part of themselves. Time to sleep, perchance to dream. They gathered their strength and out they went with a Shackleton leap.

They floated in the black, and some puffed out a bit of propellant, so that they pinwheeled away from their rapidly receding ship. It was very quickly a distant white chip, lit within its whiteness by a string of diamonds firecracking in its stern. Look away, don't burn your retinas; glance back; the *ETH Mobile* was maybe one of the stars there. They were on their own.

There was no sign of the other groups. Suddenly the idea that they could be found and rescued seemed impossible, a dream or hope that could not come true. They had jumped to their deaths.

But she had been out here before; she knew it could be done. Their suit transponders meant they were each beaconing like a fierce little lighthouse.

They established a group comms band on the helmet radios at 555, but as time wore on, few people spoke. There was little to say. Swan wanted to let go of the hand that was not Wahram's, but didn't. She clutched his right hand with her left; she held it tight. He squeezed back. She switched to band 345, heard only the sound of his breathing, steady and slow. He looked at her as he heard her too, breathing in his ear. His face was round behind his faceplate, his expression grave but fearless.

"When do you think it will happen?" Swan said, looking at the white dot she thought was the *ETH Mobile*.

"Soon, I should think," he replied.

And almost as he said it there was a flash of light in the area where Swan had been looking. "That was it!"

"Maybe so."

After that a long time passed. An hour...two hours...then three.

Then Wahram said, "Look; here comes our rescue ship."

Swan twisted to get a look over her shoulder, and saw a little space yacht approaching them at an angle, slowly.

"Well," she said. "Good."

And Venus was still shaded; it seemed the shield must have been saved. And they were rescued.

But then the little space yacht exploded right next to them. Swan, blinded by this flash, had just registered what it was, and almost as quickly concluded that some shrapnel from the collision of the *ETH Mobile* and the pebble mob must have flown their way and hit the yacht—bad luck, it seemed to her as their little ring of twenty was pulled apart by something, probably gas or debris from the yacht, meaning people were probably hurt—anyway in the same second as the explosion she found herself yanked free of both Wahram and the person on the other side of her. Crying out at the realization, she tucked and somersaulted to keep Wahram in her view—saw him pinwheeling with arms and legs extended, a spray of red crystal shooting out of one of his legs. "Pauline clear my faceplate," she said, and fingered the jet controls in her gloves, stabilizing herself relative to Wahram and then jetting off at full power after him. Briefly she passed through a little field of detritus from the wrecked yacht, there was a big spinning fragment of it even, perhaps a quarter or a third of it, sheared open so that rooms and bulkheads were revealed, as in a cutaway drawing or a doll's house. She had to change course to zip by the stern of it, then steer her suit for all it was worth to get back on Wahram's track. He was still spinning, and much smaller already; she hit her suit's maximum burn, aimed herself toward him. It was almost a task for Pauline, but there was flotsam and jetsam to be dodged, so she kept the controls and chased him while dodging these fragments of the yacht. Clear of them, she accelerated yet again, flying hard, bringing to bear everything she had ever done as a flier, heedless of anything but the chase. Wahram grew bigger. Now she cried out, "Pauline, help!"

"Let me fly the suit."

"All right but go! Go!"

"You're at full burn already. I have to slow down if you want to rendezvous with him."

"Do it!"

They shot through the stars. Wahram grew bigger still. Swan took over the controls again, over Pauline's objection, and kept closing on him as fast as possible, until the last second, when she flung herself around and flared the jets of the suit, almost running into him; she had to dodge him with a thrust, pass by him with centimeters to spare, see in a passing flash his unconscious face, mouth open; she cried out as she jetted hard and hard again, swinging the suit around in a tight curve and coming back to him. Pauline couldn't have done it any better.

His suit had been punctured below the left knee; there was frozen blood like a crust of coagulation, a giant scab. She grabbed him there and held the little tear shut.

"Give me a hose, let's air out the leg."

His own suit would have cut off the break with bulkheads like tourniquets. Possibly his lower leg was already frozen and a goner, but the suits were good at isolating leaks, and managing shock too. She took the hose extruding from her belt and stuck the end of it into the little hole in his suit; it was less than a centimeter across, barely enough to admit the hose end. She stuck her finger in the hole on the other side of his leg, jetted warm air into the leg of his suit, held everything in place. All the while she was exclaiming, "Wahram, I'm here, wake up!"

Only Pauline replied: "Please be quiet. I can't hear his vitals when you talk like that."

"What do you mean?"

"He's breathing. His heart is beating."

"What about the lower leg here?"

"The skin is frostbitten, probably the flesh too. His blood pressure is ninety over fifty, so he's lost a lot of blood. He's in shock."

"Stabilize him, warm him up! Take over his suit!"

"Please be reassured. I am in communication with his suit. Be quiet, please."

She shut up and let the qube work. Emergency medical treatment was an ancient AI algorithm, honed for centuries and long since proved to be better than a human response. And Pauline was saying there was every reason to believe he could be stabilized.

But now Pauline said, "His suit is somewhat damaged. I want to take over its control functions."

"Can you do it?"

"Yes. It is easiest to do plugged into him, so at that point you'll have to stick together."

"Even better, just do it."

Swan went to work on the hole in the leg of his

suit. The suit could be repaired with the patch kit in her belt, and she set to prepping the patch, tethered to him waist to waist by her power-and-information cord. They were spinning slowly through the stars but she did not look at them. The patch kit's patches were mostly squares with rounded edges; you had to pull off a backing and then apply smoothly and press during the time of the chemical reaction.

When his suit was sealed she asked Pauline if she should do anything for his leg at the point of the wound. This was perhaps backward, but she was rattled, she saw. Besides Pauline said no. "His suit has applied air compression and coagulants," Pauline said. "The bleeding has substantially stopped."

"Is the suit giving him IVs?"

"Yes."

It was a comfort to remind herself that his spacesuit was not only a small flexible spaceship, but also a medical sleeve of considerable power, a kind of personal hospital.

"Wahram, are you there?" she said. "Are you all right?"

"I'm here," he croaked. "I'm not all right."

"What hurts?"

"My leg hurts. And I feel . . . sick. I'm trying not to throw up."

"Good—don't throw up. Pauline, can you get some antinausea into him?"

"Yes."

They floated there in the starry night. Though Swan did not like to admit it, there was nothing more to be done at the moment. The Milky Way was like a skein of white glowing milk, with the Coal Sack and other black patches in it even more black than usual. Every-

where else the stars salted the blackness so finely that
the black itself was compromised—as if behind the
black, pressing intensely on it, was a whiteness greater
than the eye would be able to take in. The pure black
in the Milky Way must indicate a great deal of coal in
the Coal Sack. Was all the black in the sky made by
dust? she wondered. If all the stars in the universe were
visible, would the night sky be pure white?

The big stars seemed to lie at different distances
from them. Space popped as she saw that, became an
extension outward rather than a backdrop hanging a
few kilometers away. They were not in a black bag, but
in an infinite extension. A little reckoning in a great
room.

"Wahram, how are you feeling?"

"A little better."

That was good. It was dangerous to throw up inside
a helmet, not to mention unpleasant.

So they floated in space. Some hours passed. Their
food came in the form of liquids one could suck from a
straw in the helmet, there were even chunks of nutri-
tion bars that could be extruded from an inside port
in the cheek of the helmet, chewed off, and swallowed.
Swan did both these. She peed into her suit's diaper.

"Wahram, are you hungry at all?"

"Not hungry." He didn't sound comfortable either.

"Are you nauseated again?"

"Yes."

"That's not good. Here, I'm going to get us stabilized against the stars. You'll feel some tugging. Maybe
you should close your eyes until I get us settled."

"No."

"All right, it won't be very fast anyway. Here we go."

She jetted against their spin; it was hard to do it with his weight added loosely to her side. Better to hug him and make him a front weight. She did that and gave him a tiny squeeze; in response he only made a little complaining hum. She got them stabilized to the stars, more or less, and pointed so that they were looking at Venus. It was still in shadow. If the sunshield had been wrecked, or even damaged, they would have seen it, she was sure; some crescent, or maybe one region suddenly blazing white; and as they had been on the side of the umbrella that would have been struck, it did not seem to her that any lit part of Venus could be entirely on the other side of the planet from them. Well, maybe it could; she was disoriented, she had to admit. But it looked like the attack had been foiled.

"Pauline, can you tell us what happened to the ship and the sunscreen and all?"

"Radio reports are still first responses, but they indicate a collision happened as foreseen, between the *ETH Mobile* and a pebble mob of roughly four times the mass of the ship. This was as predicted within an order of magnitude, and the ship was going faster than the pebbles by enough to knock the bulk of the collision mass at a vector angling away from the sunscreen."

"So it worked."

"Except part of the ejecta from the collision hit the craft near us, and its explosion spread fragments, one of which hit Wahram."

"Yes of course. But that was just bad luck."

"Several people on that craft near us must have died."

"I know that. Very bad luck. Hit by shrapnel, in effect. But the sunscreen was saved?"

"Yes. And the sunshield's defense system has apparently attacked the ejecta that flew in its direction."

"So now it believes in the pebble mob."

"Or at least in the impactors coming at it. I can't tell what its problem was before."

"Was it aware of this new fine-grained imaging system of Wang's?"

"Wang told them about it, but they are a closed system, to avoid tampering. I don't know if they had joined the new surveillance or not."

"Maybe closed systems are easier to tamper with than open ones. Could it have been compromised?"

"It seems unlikely. It's under the control of the Venus Working Group, and they are considered very intent on security."

Wahram added nothing to this conversation. Swan held his hand, squeezing from time to time. There was nothing more for them to do. He squeezed back, briefly, then his hand went slack.

"You all right?" she asked.

"Fair," he replied.

"Have you tried to eat something?"

"Not yet."

"Drink something?"

"Not yet."

They floated in black space, weightless and warm. They were like little moons of Venus; or like little planets of their own, orbiting the sun. People sometimes talked about this situation as the return to the womb, the amniotic high. Take some entheogenic drugs, become a star child. And in fact it was not as dreadful a sight as it probably should have been. For a few moments Swan even fell asleep. When she opened her eyes again, it seemed to her that Venus was perhaps a little bigger. It made sense; when they left the ship, they must have been going at quite a significant speed.

"You still there?"

"Still here."

Well, Swan thought. Here they were. Nothing to be done, except to wait. Waiting was never her preferred mode. Typically there was more to do than she had time for, so that she was always in a rush. Now it seemed long for a rescue from an evacuation. As they had been bailing out, there had been talk of ships in the area. Maybe Wahram had been knocked off in a strange direction; Swan had followed without any sense of that. Possibly they were leaving the plane of the ecliptic, thus the path of any ships coming to the rescue. Maybe the poor destroyed yacht was the only one in their area, and they would have to wait until all the other evacuees had been mopped up. The destruction of the little yacht was likely to be one of the chief sources of casualties in the whole affair, so surely that would attract attention. They would know they hadn't collected everybody; they would keep looking; these suits had powerful transponders in them. Being out of the ecliptic thus probably best explained the delay. Or maybe picking everyone up was just taking a while. The last acceleration of the *ETH Mobile* might have meant it was going at a speed higher than most spaceships could reach when the last people left it, in which case the people were too. If everything was as it was supposed to be, then all the suits would support their occupants for ten days, and they had only been out there only, what— she had to ask Pauline—twenty hours. It seemed longer, shorter—she couldn't tell. Venus was definitely a little bigger. Swan recalled stories of castaways, adrift unfound, frozen for the eons. How many had gone that way in the history of the world? Scores, hundreds, thousands? She heard in her head the chorus of the old Martian song:

> *I floated thinking of Peter*
> *Sure I would be saved*
> *But the stories lie*
> *I'm left to die*
> *Black space will be my grave*

No doubt many of those unfortunates had drifted expecting till the end they would be saved. Hope drained away more slowly than the air and food in their suits; they would recall the story of Peter circling Mars, or some other marooned person who got rescued, and believe a little spaceship would presently appear and hover before them like a UFO, like redemption, like life itself. But for many it had never come, and at some last point they had had to admit that the story was false, or not true for them. True for others, but not for them; the others elect, they the preterite, the lost ones. The forgotten ones. Thus the stark Martian song.

Maybe this time they would join the forgotten ones. Swan stirred herself, checked the common band, a host of voices; went to the emergency band and croaked out a report, an inquiry. Half an hour later a reply came: they were on the radar, they were getting a rescue ship out to them; they were indeed out of the plane, and all responders were busy. But they were on the charts and help would be on its way eventually.

So... look around. Tell Wahram about it, reassure him. Try to relax.

She was not relaxed. A helpless dread seized her like a boiling of the blood. Pauline would therefore know of it; she might at this very moment be infusing her with antianxiety drugs out of the suit's pharmacy. Swan hoped so. Nothing to do but wait. Keep breathing. Wait and see. It had been a luxury in her life always to be able to do something, never to have to wait. Now reality kicked in. Sometimes you had to wait for it.

Well, so be it. A wait wasn't so bad. It was better than the blackliner. Venus was looking a little bit closer, and was maybe a little bit brighter—maybe the sunshield had been torn a little, at the edge nearest the explosion. She could see dark clouds swirling around a darker patch, possibly Ishtar's highland. There were brighter and darker patches down there under the swirling clouds, but she had no sense of whether they represented frozen ocean or frozen land. There were no blues or browns or greens, just gray clouds over gray lands, dark and darker.

I feel better," Wahram announced uncertainly, as if testing the assertion.

"Oh good," Swan said. "Try drinking something. You're probably dehydrated."

"I am thirsty."

More time passed. After a while Wahram began to whistle under his breath, one of the tunes he had whistled in the utilidor. Beethoven, she knew, and not one of the symphonies; so most likely it was from one of the late quartets. A slow movement. Possibly the one that Beethoven had written after recovering from an illness. A thanksgiving. She would only know for sure by the tune that came at the very end of it. It was one of the good ones, anyway. Softly she whistled an accompaniment to it, singing the lark inside her while squeezing his hand. The tune was slow, she could not just lark about in it, but had to find a way to be slow herself, to join him. Her lark brain remembered the parts to this tune that he had taught her under Mercury. During their submercurial existence, a whole lifetime ago it seemed. That life was gone; this one would go; not a lot of difference was made to this moment itself, whether they survived later or not. Oh the beauty of this song, something to twine with. The lark brain kept singing inside her, twisting up out of the slow tune. Different times get woven together.

"Do you remember?" she asked him after breaking off. Voice tight, grip crushing his hand: "Do you remember when we were in the tunnel?"

"Yes, I do."

Then back to the tune. His whistling was just barely adequate; or he whistled now in a style that made it seem so. Maybe he was still hurting. Musically they had been better in the tunnel. Now they sounded like Armstrong and Fitzgerald, him pretending to a straining effort that only barely hit an accidental and minimal perfection, her perfect without any effort at all, just playing around. Duet of opposites. The struggle and the play, making together something better than either. Maybe you needed both. Maybe she had been making her play into a struggle when she needed to be making her struggle into play.

They came to the melody at the end; yes, it was the thanksgiving. Hymn of thanksgiving after recovering from a serious illness, Wahram had said it was called, in the Lydian mode. And the title described the feeling well; they didn't always. A thanksgiving laid into the tune itself, with an unerring ear for music as the speech of feeling. How could it be? Who had he been? Beethoven, the human nightingale. There are songs in our brains, she thought, whether bird brain cells have been inserted in them or not; they were already there, down in the cerebellum, conserved for millions of years. No death there; maybe death *was* an illusion, maybe these patterns lived forever, music and emotion stranding through universes one after the next, on the wings of transient birds.

Ever since the tunnel," she said to him when he stopped whistling, "we've had a relationship."

"Mmm," he said, either agreeing or not.

"Don't you think so?" she demanded.

"Yes, I do."

"If we hadn't wanted to run into each other, we could have avoided it. So I've been thinking that that's not what we wanted. That we wanted..."

"Hmm," he equivocated.

"What do you mean? Are you denying it?"

"No."

"Then what do you mean?"

"I mean," he said slowly, thinking it over, pausing, then seeming to lose the inclination to speak. Through his faceplate she could see that he was looking at her at last, rather than out at the stars, and that struck her as a good sign, but it was unnerving as well, he was so grave and intent. This diving into the mind was amphibious work, and her toad was performing it abstracted and silent.

"I like being with you," he continued. "It seems to me things are more interesting when I'm with you." He continued to stare at her. "I like whistling with you. I liked our time in the tunnel."

"You liked it?"

"But of course. You know that."

"No," she said. "I don't know what I know or don't know. That's part of my problem."

"I love you," he said.

"But of course," she said. "And I love you."

"No no," he said. "I *love* you."

"I see!" she said. "But oh dear—I'm not sure I know what you mean."

He smiled his littlest smile. It was so small, now almost hidden behind his faceplate, and yet it appeared only when he was truly amused. It was never a polite gesture. When he was being polite he glared.

"Neither do I know what I mean," he said. "But I say it anyway. Wanting to say it to you—it's that kind of love."

"Uh-oh," she said. "Look, this is crazy talk. Your leg is frozen and you've got to be in shock. Your suit has you shot up with all kinds of stuff."

"Very likely true," he conceded a bit dreamily, "but even so, that is only allowing me to say what I really feel. With some urgency, let us say."

He smiled again, but briefly; he was watching her like a . . . well, she didn't know what. Not like a hawk; not anything like a wolf's long stare; more a curious look, a questioning look—a froggy inquiry, as if to ask, what kind of creature was she? Robot? Limit? Robber? Robert?

Well, she didn't know. She couldn't say. Her toad regarded her, eyes like jasper marbles in his head. She regarded him: so slow, so particularly himself, self-contained, ritualistic . . . if that was right. She tried to put together all she had seen of him into a single phrase or characterization, and it didn't work; she had a jumble of pieces, of small incidents and feelings, and then their big time together, which was also a jumble and a smear. But interesting! This was the heart of it, this word he had used, maybe. He interested her. She was drawn to him as to a work of art or a landscape. He had a sense of his actions that was sure; he drew a clean line. He showed her new things, but also new feelings. Oh to be calm! Oh to pay attention! He amazed her with these qualities.

"Hmm, well, I love you too," she said. "We've been through a lot. Let me think about it. I haven't thought about it in the way you seem to be implying."

"Suggesting," he suggested.

"Okay, well yes, then. I'll think about what it means."

"Very good." Again he smiled his little smile.

They floated there in the black suffused with white. The diamond glitter: there were said to be a hundred thousand stars visible to the naked eye when one was in space. It would seem a difficult tally to make and was probably just a computer count, down to the magnitude considered visible to the average eye. To her there seemed to be many more than a hundred thousand.

They blobbed weightlessly, they jiggled as she blinked and breathed. She could hear her breath and her heartbeat, also the blood moving in her ears. The animal rush of herself in space, through time. Pulse after pulse. As she had lived a century and a third, her heart had beaten around five billion times. It seemed like a lot until you began to count. Counting itself implied a finite number, which was by definition too short. An odd sensation.

But counting your breaths was a Buddhist ceremony too, folded into the sun worship on Mercury. She had done it before. Here they were, confronted with the universe, seeing it from inside the fortresses of space-suits and bodies. Hearing the body, seeing the stars and the deep black expanse. There were the Andromeda constellation and in it the Andromeda Galaxy, an elliptical smear rather than a dense little point. By thinking about what it was, Swan could sometimes pop the third dimension even farther into the black—not only perceive the depth of field variously punctured by stars at different distances, which one could pretend were marked by their brightness, but also see Andromeda as a whole galaxy, far farther away than anything else she could see—*thwoop*, there it was, deepest space, the extension of the vacuum evident to her eye. Those were awesome moments, and truthfully they didn't last long, they couldn't, it was too vast; the human eye and mind were not equipped to see it. Mostly it had to be an imaginative leap, she knew; but when that idea clicked with what she was actually seeing at that very second, it could become very much like something completely real.

Now that happened again, and there she was in it: the universe at full size. Thirteen point seven billion years of expansion, and more to come; indeed with the expansion accelerating, it could bloom outward like a coronal flare off the sun, dissipate all that was burning in it. That looked to be happening right now, right before her eyes.

"I'm tripping," she said. "I'm seeing Andromeda as a galaxy, it's punching a hole right through the blackness there, like I'm seeing in a new dimension."

"Do you want some Bach?" he asked. "To go with it?"

She had to laugh. "What do you mean?"

"I'm listening to Bach's cello suite," he said. "It's a

very good match for the scene, I find. Do you want to patch in?"

"Sure."

A single cello line, solemn but nimble, threaded through the night.

"Where did you get this? Did your suit have it?"

"No, my wrist AI. It doesn't do much compared to your Pauline, but this it does."

"I see. So you carry a weak AI with you?"

"Yes, that's right." A particularly expressive passage of the Bach filled the silence. The cello was almost like a third party to the conversation.

"Don't you have anything less lugubrious?" Swan inquired.

"I suppose I do, but in fact I find this very spritely."

She laughed. "You would!"

He hummed at that, thinking it over. "We could change to Debussy's piano music," he said after the cello executed a particularly deep sawing, its buzzy timbre black as space. "I think that might be just the thing for you."

Piano replaced cello, the clear bell-like sounds darting and flowing in runs, making melodies that ran like cats' paws over water. Debussy had had a bird mind, she could hear, and she whistled a phrase repeating one of his, fitting it into what followed. Hard to do. She stopped. "Very nice," she said.

He squeezed her hand. "I wish I could whistle along with you, but I can't."

"Why not?"

"It's too hard for me to remember. When I hear it, it always surprises me. I mean, I recognize it when I hear it played, I've heard it ten thousand times, but if I'm not hearing it out loud, I couldn't whistle you the tunes from memory, they're too...too elusive, I suppose, or subtle. Glancing. Unexpected. And they don't seem to repeat. Listen—it keeps moving on to a new thing."

"Beautiful," she said, and whistled another nightingale descant.

After a long while, he turned the music off. The silence was immense. Again she could hear her breath, her heartbeat. It was thumping away in its double thump, a little faster than normal, but no longer racing. Calm down, she thought again. You're marooned in space, they will rescue you eventually. Meanwhile here you are, and Wahram is with you, and Pauline. No moment is ever fundamentally different from this one. Focus and be calm.

Maybe to say that someone was "like this" or "like that" was just an attempt to stick a memory to a board where you organized memories, like butterflies in a lepidopterist's collection. Not really the generalization it seemed, but just a stab at understanding. Was Wahram anything like what she might say about him, if she tried to say something? He was like this, he was like that—she didn't really know. One had impressions of other people, nothing more. Never to hear them think, only to hear what they said; it was a drop in an ocean, a touch across the abyss. A hand holding your hand as you float in the black of space. It wasn't much. They couldn't really know each other very well. So they said he is like this, or she is like that, and called that the person. Presumed to make a judgment. It was such a guess. You would have to talk with someone for years to give the guess any kind of validity. And even then you wouldn't know.

When I'm with you, she said to Wahram in her

mind as they floated there together, waiting, holding hands—when I'm with you I feel faintly anxious; judged; inadequate. Not the kind of person you like, which I find offensive, and thus behave more like that part of me than ever. Though I want your good opinion too. But that desire I find irritating, and so contradict it in myself. Why should I care? You don't care.

And yet you do care. I *love* you, you said. And—Swan admitted to herself—she wanted him to feel that way when he was with her. That way—is this what love was, this desire for a feeling that remained unclear even when felt? Is that why people sometimes thought of it as a madness? The words stay the same, even the feelings stay the same, but there are slippages between the words and the feelings, hard to track. The desire to know, to be known, to be cherished for what you are and not what others think you should be . . . But then, what you are . . . It was hard for her not to feel that a person loving her was making a big mistake. Because she knew herself better than they did, so knew their love was given in error. And thus they must be some kind of fool. And yet it was precisely that misplaced love she wanted. Someone who would like you more than you do. Someone who likes you despite yourself, someone more generous to you than you are. That was how Alex had been. And when you see that, when you feel that—feel loved beyond justice, from some kind of generosity—that sets off certain other feelings. A kind of a glow. A spillover. It caused something to start that felt reciprocal. A mutual recognition. The hall of mirrors again. Set a lased beam of light between two mirrors, back and forth the beam bounces, two parts of something more; not just the beast with two backs (though that too, for sure, and a great thing, a great animal) but something else, some kind of...pairing, like Pluto and Charon, with the center of gravity between the two. Not a single supra-organism, but two working together on something not themselves. A duet. A harmony.

She whistled one of the other Beethoven tunes Wahram had often whistled in the tunnel; she still had trouble sorting which was which, but knew this was the other song of thanks, the one after the big storm, when all the creatures come back out into the sun. A simple melody, like a folk tune. She chose it because it was one of the few tunes Wahram could whistle a descant to, forging an elaboration he said was in the original. He fired it up and joined in. He wasn't as strong as he had been before, though he hadn't been strong then. His whistle had pain threading it like a golden wire. He was not much of a musician, in all truth. But he had a good memory for the pieces he loved; and he loved them.

She took off and trilled all around him, and he fell back into the main melody in relief. Maybe that was what duets were all about.

"Maybe I love you," she said. "Maybe that's what I've been feeling these past few years. Maybe I just never knew what it was."

"Maybe," he said.

Did he mean that maybes don't count, or that maybes are better than nothing?

"Slow movement of the Seventh," he said, "if you don't mind." And he was off into another tune from their time under Mercury, one she had always enjoyed riffing on, it had so many possibilities. Sometimes they had gone on with it for hours, for half a day or more.

Stately, solemn, elegiac; something like Wahram himself, pacing through the days. On the march. Someone you could rely on.

"Maybe," she repeated. "It may be."

They fell into the song as of old, as when they were in the crucible and everything depended on how they went forward. As now, even now, just floating in space waiting for rescue, having faith it would come.

Faith justified; for Pauline said, "Ship approaching."

One white dot among the rest bloomed, and in a matter of seconds became another little space yacht, a hopper hovering there before them like a dream, bizarre and magical.

"Oh good," Swan said.

Now they too were Peters. She had to remember that. They were only continuing by way of a rescue. As they puffed over to the little ship, Swan tried to fix what this had felt like—the floating, Andromeda, Wahram's gaze, their duet. It could have been their last hours. She thought of Alex again. Our stories go on a while, some genes and words persist; then we go away. It was a hard thing to remember. And as the lock door closed and they were back inside, she once again forgot it.

KIRAN ON ICE

It was while Kiran was still being stared at by the eyes in the box that it occurred to him that he should not be seeing something like this, and one quick glance at the tall security guard made it clear that this thought had also occurred to the guard. As the guard started relocking the box Kiran considered what this meant, and before the guard had finished tapping the keypad Kiran was off and dashing back the way they had come. He turned into the first street available and sprinted hard to the next intersection and turned again, with a single glance back; the guard was not yet in view. Off he went at a slightly slower pace, thinking about his options. The train that ran between Vinmara and Cleopatra would certainly be watched, and there was only the one.

Much of the population of the town was still out celebrating the uneclipse and the end of the rain. And he knew where the gate was relative to his current position. He cut right yet again and so toward it. The streets of the seashell town were almost empty. Ahead the gate; none of his new work unit was visible, nor any security guards aside from the ordinary gatekeepers. He gave his original ID card to one of these as he came to the gate lock door, then went in the lock and checked to make sure his suit was secure.

Out onto the snowy hillsides of Venus. People were trooping back down from the hilltop overlooking the bay, and he looked away as he passed them and headed around to the west of town. When he had gotten past the edge of town he slipped over the hill and out of view of Vinmara, then took a broad wash south, toward the distant ocean.

They were still covering the frozen CO_2 down there, so he hoped he could catch a ride from one of the superzambonis or foamed rock applicators. He wanted to get to Colette, but feared that the whole transportation system would be alerted to look for him. Now it was really hitting home what it meant to be a double agent or a mole or whatever it was he had turned into; it meant neither side would care about you, or care to defend you if problems arose. On the other hand, if he could get to Shukra, he had information Shukra had asked him to obtain. So getting to Colette was the obvious thing to try.

Vinmara was located just south of Onatah Corona. Onatah was the Iroquois corn goddess, his faceplate map told him; no doubt a much friendlier goddess than Lakshmi, who after all was Kali's boss. Everything Kiran had heard about Lakshmi made him pretty sure that he might not survive her displeasure. At the thought he yelped and took the translation spectacles she had given him from his suit's chest pocket. Reluctantly, with a final kiss in thanks for all they had done to improve his love life, he tossed them away. Really a shame he had not thought to do so back in the city, but there was no way he was going to return there now.

Since he had been able to see the big rock foamers on

the skyline from Vinmara, he had assumed that they could not be too far away. Now, as he walked over the crunchy and sometimes slippery snow downhill toward the dry ice sea, he realized that the new town's hillside perch might give it a view much farther away than he had reckoned. In fact it could be many kilometers.

This thought was beginning to oppress him when he came over a small ridge in the ice and saw a super-zamboni, not immediately near but just a couple of kilometers away, and lumbering along slowly in the usual manner. He broke into a trot and tried to pace himself for the run there. It was moving crossways to his approach, so he was going to be all right; no need to kill himself.

Nevertheless he was huffing and puffing by the time he reached the thing. Unfortunately if there was a person or persons inside it, they were not looking out the cabin windows, which were up at the top and front of the thing. There was nothing for Kiran to do except jog next to it and jump up onto its side where a ladder came almost to the ground. Climb the ladder, get on the roof of the thing, which was not only railed, but full of instrumentation to hold on to. Alas it was a bit of exposure to hang over the front and try to reach down to where the windows started, and there was nothing much to hold on to. Seemed as if the windows were in fact still out of reach, which was frustrating.

There was a hatch door, however, in the roof, and when he saw it he began to pound on it with his fists, then kick it with the heels of his boots. He was looking around to see if there was anything he could break off to hit the door with even harder when the behemoth shuddered to a halt, and soon after, he could hear voices below him, and the hatch door opened.

"Thanks!" he shouted. "I got lost out here!"

So two Venusians brought him inside, and he had a very difficult time making up a story for them that would explain his presence down there on the frozen ocean—it had to involve an admission of recreational drug use and even worse, geographical disorientation, so he squirmed his way through it, feeling lucky that embarrassment was the appropriate emotion for his cover story and its lame particulars. Happily the two minders listened to their translator saying it all in Chinese, and merely nodded as if they had often witnessed such foolishness before, and went back to their screen game. They were headed for a working camp under Ba'het Patera, they told him, and would be there in four hours. There was beer in the fridge if he was interested.

The working camp they came to was one of a whole series of them, Kiran saw on the map, running west along the northern shore of the new ocean and sheltering the people who were getting the last of the CO_2 sealed over. Kiran gave his original ID card to the people at the camp, but they only looked at it briefly and waved him over to the galley. He ate voraciously while he pored over the map on his tabletop screen. He had already seen that there were fast little snowmobiles out in the camp's parking lot, and the map seemed to indicate that the camps dotting the shore were close enough together that a snowmobile could get from one to the next on one fuel load. Maybe that was even part of the plan.

Very nice. And as they kept regular hours despite the perpetual night, he merely waited until everyone had gone to bed, and then went out to one of the snowmobiles, checked that it was full of fuel, fired it up, and took off west.

These snowmobiles were neat little things, more like cars on skis than any of the monsters being used for the sequestration work. He had often enjoyed driving them in his first months on Venus, and now he sat back and gave the AI instructions and watched the eerie dim landscape slide by. The snow here had packed down to what they called firn, and his vehicle zipped right along. It would be an all-night drive, so to speak, but then he could come into the next camp when they were getting up. Maybe just drive into the parking lot and jump into another snowmobile and keep going, why not? No one cared about these vehicles on the ice; they were no one's property. And there was nowhere to go in them.

Or so he told himself as he fell asleep, and when he woke up and had the AI slide them into the parking lot of the next camp, it worked just as he had hoped. Out of that one, into another, off again; no one the slightest bit concerned. "I love Venus," he told the AI pilot. His old translation belt said it in Chinese, although probably the vehicle's AI understood English too. The old belt was a sad step down from the spectacles, but in this situation it didn't really matter.

Two more camps, two more snowmobiles, and he came to a camp he had spotted on the maps, one that had a train line spur that would take him up through the Ut Rupes and the Vesta Rupes and eventually to Colette. As he came into the camp he saw a train, at what passed here for a station, which was just a loading dock and a small building. As he slid up on the snowmobile he saw that they were loading some of the cars from a siding, under big lights. Being in the light of the lamps, they could see little outside that cone of illumination, so he crept up on them, staying in the dark, and in the moment when they were finishing their work he threw a rock at the building by the tracks, and when they went to investigate the bang, he hopped up into the car and ducked down behind the boxes inside. Not long after that he was closed into the car, and felt the train jerk forward with maglev smoothness and head up the long slope to Colette, far above him on the Lakshmi Planum, so ominously named.

He had fallen sleep, and woken up starving, when the car doors finally opened up. He waited for a clear moment, jumped out of the car and hustled away from it. No one around. He wasn't certain, but after he slipped out of the station he confirmed it: he was inside the dome of Colette. It was the third day since he had left Vinmara, and he felt a little spacy from hunger, but pleased as well.

Now to find Shukra. He could return to his lodge, but that was where Lakshmi's agent had always met him. . . . In the end he strolled through the big city streets, trying to look innocent, and went to the offices where he had first been taken by Swan to meet Shukra so long before. Since that first meeting Shukra had always come to him, so Kiran didn't know where else to go. He had had a lot of time to think about this, but he still wasn't quite sure of the best approach to take. There was the distinct possibility that he was throwing himself from the frying pan into the fire, but because Shukra had contacted him, and had told him what to look for, it seemed like it could be more like getting out of the fire back into the frying pan, or hopefully off the stove entirely. Anyway he didn't see how he could avoid the risk of asking someone for help, and Shukra was his best bet. So he walked in the outer door of that first office, and went up to the security desk and said to the trio there, "I'm here to see Shukra, please. Please tell him that I have what he asked me for, and I want to give it to him."

SWAN AND KIRAN

Taken in by what turned out to be an Interplan ship; cleaned up and fed; slept for twelve hours straight; up and eating again; and after that they were in Venus orbit, and then in a landing craft. The craft fell like a brick to the still-shaded planet, then eased off at the end to thump onto a runway. When they emerged in the big atrium of the spaceport, Swan could see that they had landed outside Colette. There was a view to a rumple of snowy muscular hills to the north, all dim under swirls of dark cloud. Venus!

What had happened in raw space still bulked large in her mind, so that what stood before her eyes now was like a dream. She was separated from Wahram as they went through their medical checkups and then a long security postmortem. The people talking to her were upset; it was obviously necessary to attend to the moment, transparent though it was. Later she could mull over what had happened and what she felt about it. She did not want it to slip away like everything else.

Their hosts brought her a little feast in dim sum style, with tiny plates and morsels of food, no more than a mouthful each, or just a taste, each with a different sauce, until her palate was completely confused, and she felt stuffed after four bites. Her stomach rebelled; it grumbled and queased throughout the conversation that began at the end of the meal.

Many there were drinking liquor and opioid mixers. Swan sipped soda water, watching people carefully. The Venusians there were looking very subdued. A leavening of jokesters, clustered mostly at one table, laughed at the gurneys of food, but the rest looked chastened, even grim. The salvation of the sunshield was all very well, of course, a great victory to be sure. But their defensive systems had failed them, and the danger inherent in the sunshield had been emphasized for all the world to see. Disaster had been staved off this time, but it still hung over them like a sword: a terrible fate, perpetually forestalled by a thing no stronger than a venetian blind, or a circular kite on a string.

One particularly grim part of the room was absorbed in the problem of what had happened to the sunshield's security; these people were poking at their tabletop's graphs and talking rapidly to each other. It appeared most of them thought the failure to respond had been caused by an inside job. Wahram rolled into the room in a wheelchair and joined them, his left leg held straight out and swathed in white. He nodded slowly as they spoke to him. Once he glanced over at Swan, as if he had just heard something she would find interesting; then he was deep in it again. Swan would hear about it later, she hoped. Although then it occurred to her that he might feel he had to tell them about her telling Pauline about the group Alex had assembled when she had promised she wouldn't. How else was the story of what had happened going to parse? Well, in the end her rash act had saved Venus. Not that that meant she wouldn't suffer for it anyway. Be known as a completely untrustworthy reckless flibbertigibbet qubehead. It wouldn't be that hard of a case to make.

She sat watching the Venusians. They stayed slumped in their chairs, depressed. She asked some questions and they answered, except sometimes they didn't.

She came back to something they didn't seem to want to address: "I suppose you have to stick with the sunshield, now that it's there?"

One waved a hand impatiently. "Some say no, that we should change."

"What do you mean? Wouldn't that take spinning the planet up to some kind of day-night?"

"Yes."

"But how?"

"The only way there is," one said. "A heavy meteor shower at a tangent."

"The *very* late heavy bombardment," someone called from the jokesters' table.

"But wouldn't that wreck the surface you have?" Swan said. "Blast away the formed rock, the CO_2, the atmosphere—everything you've done?"

"Not everything," the first one said. "We'd just keep hitting the same spot. Things would just be... disarranged."

"Disarranged!"

"Look, we don't like this idea. We've fought this idea of spinning it up. We all have." Gesturing around the room at the others there. "But Lakshmi and her crowd have been arguing it could work without too much disruption. Just one more short deep ocean trench, and ejecta to the east of it. Other areas would suffer too, especially around the equator, but not so much that we would kill the bacteria we have out there now. And it wouldn't release more than a couple percent of the buried CO_2."

"But wouldn't it take a few hundred years of heavy bombardment to get the spin you wanted?"

"The idea would be to spin it to about a hundred-hour day. We think most Terran life-forms can tolerate that. So it would only take a hundred years."

"Only a hundred!"

A new voice: "What these people are arguing is that we did it too fast the first time." This particular speaker, an old person, eyes alive in a weathered face like a mask, sounded a little regretful, a little disgusted. "Did it too much like Mars! Took the way of the sunshield because it was fast! But once you have it, you have to keep it. You depend on it. And now people can see what could happen to it. So Lakshmi will win. The vote will go for bombardment now."

"In the Working Group, you mean?"

"Yes. We'll have to stay in shelters, or even retreat into sky cities, or even go back home for a while. Wait until things calm down again."

Wahram, who had rolled over and joined them, said, "But what will you bombard it with this time? You won't be taking any moons and cutting them up."

"No," the old one said. "That was part of the going too fast. But there are many Neptunian Trojans to be sent down."

"Aren't the Tritons developing those?"

"There are thousands of them. And they are all Kuiper belt captures. We could replace from the Kuiper belt, if the Tritons want. So nothing need be lost as far as Neptune is concerned. The Tritons already agree to the principle."

"Well," Swan said, baffled. She didn't know what to say. She regarded their faces, so grim and irritated. "Is it what the people here want? Can you tell?"

They looked at each other. The first said, "There's a network of cadre layers, like the panchayats in India. And everyone is talking. There's only forty million of us here. So—the Working Group will hear from us and from everyone. But in fact the idea was already gaining traction. Now with this thing, people see the need. Lakshmi has won."

Later, when Swan was alone back in her room at the hospital, there was a tap at the door, and in came Shukra with Swan's young friend from Earth, Kiran. She greeted them happily, immediately cheered by the sight of their faces, so vivid and real. Shukra, whom she had worked with a million years ago, Kiran, her newest friend—now they had the same look on their faces, serious and intent. They sat down by her bed and Swan poured them glasses of water.

"Listen to the youth here," Shukra said, tipping his head at Kiran.

"What?" Swan said, alert to trouble.

Kiran put a hand up as if to reassure her. "You told me when you brought me here that there were factions. That's turned out to be true, and it's even kind of a little underground civil war, you could almost call it."

"Lakshmi," Shukra said heavily, as if this would explain everything. "He got involved with her."

"Is that bad?" Swan asked. "I mean—I'm the one who told him to try her."

Shukra rolled his eyes at this. "Swan, you were here a hundred years ago. You should know that things have changed since then. Tell her," he said to Kiran.

"I started moving stuff and carrying messages for Lakshmi," Kiran said, "and Shukra saw that was happening, and got me to look closer into what I was seeing when I did things for her."

"He was bait," Shukra said with a hard smile, "and she took it. But probably she knew he was bait."

Kiran nodded, with a look at Swan that seemed to say Look what you got me into here. He said, "There's a new coastal town that Lakshmi's team is developing, it's definitely her place, and it's set too low for some reason. People thought she might want it drowned later on for an insurance scam or something like that. Anyway, they're doing something funny in that town. I think maybe they're making androids or something. Robots made to look like humans, you know?"

"I do know," Swan said. "Tell me more."

"There's an office there that was closed off, a pretty big building. I saw a box of eyeballs get delivered there. I think they might be putting together artificial people. Some kind of Frankenstein factory."

"You saw that?"

"The guard I was with opened a box, and it was eyeballs. He didn't like it that I saw, so I had to get to teacher Shukra here, and ask for help."

Shukra nodded as if to say this had been a smart move. Swan said to him, "So this place he was at is Lakshmi's?"

"Yes," Shukra said. "Her work units built the whole town. So look—I don't know anything about this Vinmara operation, but she's got people coming into Cleopatra that we can't ID. I set up an office in Cleopatra myself, it's supposedly an open city, although really she calls the shots there. I was trying to figure out where these new people were coming from. But now—

when I heard about the attack on the sunshield, the first thing I thought was, Well, isn't that convenient for friend Lakshmi. People will be scared into supporting the plan to spin up the planet, and if we do that, the new hole they'll rip in the equator will shrink the reach of the ocean accordingly. These places like Vinmara, that are set too low? They won't be set too low."

"Ahh," Swan said. "Wow. But—what about the Chinese?"

"The Chinese hate this second bombardment idea, and so if it happens anyway, despite their opposition, they lose leverage—again, all the better for Lakshmi. And in truth none of us want Beijing telling us what to do. So this also helps her in the argument."

"And so these humanoids she's having built?" Swan leaned forward and clicked on the table screen. "Here—show me where this Vinmara is on a map. Let's get Inspector Genette in here, and Wahram too. They'll be very interested to hear what you have to say."

Inspector Genette arrived in her room, then Wahram, wheeling himself along in his wheelchair, his left leg swathed in its medwrap. They listened to Kiran's story and then sat pondering the implications.

Inspector Genette said, "I think we need to decide some things before we act on this. After what's happened, I'm quite sure that I need to execute the plan we have been devising, which I have not yet described to you, Swan. So if you will agree to turn off Pauline again, I can tell it to you."

Swan wasn't sure she wanted to go through that again, and the inspector must have known by now that she had told Pauline what had been said at the last off-the-record meeting, so she didn't see the point.

But in any case she was forestalled, because Wahram now said to Genette, "I'm afraid we should perhaps go through with the plan without Swan knowing about it at all. She may turn off Pauline for the conversation, but she may then tell her qube what happened after she turns it back on, as she did the last time we did this."

Swan gave Wahram a dagger of a look and said to Genette, "It was Pauline who informed us of the attack in time to do something about it. And it was Wang's qube who set up the new surveillance system able to detect that pebble mob. So you can thank me for that later. But my point is, whatever these Venusians are up to with their qube people and their plots, there are other qubes who are clearly on our side. We need to be working with them!"

Inspector Genette agreed. "I've had a long talk with Wang and his qube, and what you say is true. There are factions among the qubes too, I'm afraid."

"So we need ours informed!"

"Maybe," Genette said. "Although which are ours is an open question. And in this case, the fewer that know, the better. So look, with this information from Kiran, I am going to proceed with this particular Interplan operation as planned."

"And that is?" Swan said pointedly.

The inspector's little face, as beautiful and curious as a langur's, regarded Swan with a bright smile. "Please let me tell you about it after we are farther along."

Swan gave Wahram another black look. "You see what you've done."

Wahram shrugged. "The plan needs complete secrecy to work. Even I am ignorant of the details."

"I should also add," Genette added quickly, "that my plan also needed this information from your young friend here. So it is just now coming together. Please allow me to make the next move confidentially Even Wahram, as he says, and really everyone here on Venus"—bowing toward Shukra—"is ignorant of our next step, and it has to be that way to succeed."

Whether Genette was just helping Wahram to look better in Swan's eyes, Swan couldn't tell; she was too furious to keep a good sense of the nuances of the situation. Her judgment was off. Genette was now talking to a colleague who had come into the room, finally turning to the rest of them and saying, "If you will excuse us."

"I will *not*," Swan said, and stormed out.

Wahram caught up with her down the hall and matched her step for step, rolling along in his wheelchair and capable therefore of keeping up with her no matter how fast she walked.

"Swan, don't be angry at me, I needed to tell the inspector what happened to stay in good faith on an important matter; this operation is delicate and the whole situation *had* to be told."

"So now it is."

"Yes, and soon you'll know everything too. But for a while you have to trust us."

"Us?"

"I'm going to help the inspector. It shouldn't take too long. During that time I hope you will go back to Terminator and talk with your people there, about the situation on Titan and about us."

"You think I'm still interested in any of that?"

"I certainly hope so. It's more important than your bruised feelings here, if you will allow me to say so. Especially as they needn't be bruised. I think considering you and Pauline as an indivisible pair is a good thing, don't you? It's accurate, it describes you better, let us say. You are a new thing. And most especially to me, I might add." He reached out and clutched her hand, then stopped them both by braking his wheelchair with his other hand. They slewed around, and he held on to her hand even though she tugged on it. "Come on," he said, "be serious. Were you out there marooned with me or not? Were you in the tunnel or not?"

Turning her question around on her; and of course she remembered. "Yes, yes," Swan groused, looking down.

"Well then, here we are now, and there is a situation that requires confidentiality, and so in that context you have to see what I just said to Genette as being under the light of *utmost necessity*. Especially given my own feelings for you, which are"—he paused to pound his chest with his wheel hand—"profound. Confused but profound. And that's what matters. It makes life interesting. So I have been thinking that we ought to get married, in the Saturnian crèche I am already part of. It would solve so many problems more than it would create that I really think it is the best thing for both of us. For me, certainly. So I am hoping you will marry me, and that's the long and short of it."

Swan yanked her hand away, raised it as if to hit him. "I don't understand you!"

"I know. I have trouble with that myself. But that's not the main thing. It's only part of it. We would make that part of our project."

"I don't know...." Swan began, then trailed off: there was so much that could follow this opening that she found herself at a loss. She didn't know anything!

"I'm going to Earth, anyway," she said mulishly. "I have a meeting there with the UN mammals committee; we're making some progress there. And now I want to talk to Zasha too."

"That's all right," Wahram assured her. "You think about it. I have to go join Genette; we really are engaged in something urgent, and this information from Kiran is the linchpin, so let us complete that, and I'll come see you wherever you are, as soon as I can." And after an anguished clasp of hands to heart, he swiveled and wheeled back down the hall to the inspector.

WAHRAM AND GENETTE

Wahram returned to Genette, who was leaving for Vinmara and did not want to waste time, saying only, "Come on," and then hurrying off as fast as a terrier. As Wahram wheeled along in pursuit, Genette looked back up at him and asked if all was well with Swan. Wahram replied that it was, although he was none too sure about this. But it was time to focus on the plan.

As they flew to Vinmara, Genette talked to some associates using his wristqube Passepartout as his radio, and Wahram gestured at it questioningly.

With a shake of the head Genette said, "There *are* qubes working for us, as Swan pointed out, and indeed hers may be one of them, it seems likely. But I haven't been able to check it yet, and you were probably right to keep her out of this. It's hard to tell what she would do. But meanwhile Wang's qube and Passepartout have both been checked out, and are helping us as instructed. So I believe," he enunciated at his wristqube with a cross-eyed frown.

Wahram said, "Do you think the qubes are beginning to function as their own society, with groups or even organizations, and disagreements?"

Genette threw up his hands. "How can we tell? It may be they are only being given different instructions by different people and therefore acting differently. So we hope to apprehend the maker of these qube humans in Vinmara, and then maybe we can find out more."

"What about the Venusians? Will they allow you to do what you intend to here?"

"Shukra and his group are backing us. They are in the midst of quite a tussle right now, and the stakes are high. Lakshmi's people are either manufacturing these humanoids or else are benefitting from their existence, I can't tell which yet, but either way Shukra's group is happy to assist us. I think the Working Group is divided enough that we can do what we need to and get off-planet before they can react."

This sounded ominous to Wahram. "Jump through the middle of a civil war?"

Genette said with a quick shrug, "No way now but forward."

They came to the spaceport and hurried through it and down a jetway into a small airplane. After they were on board and in the air, Genette looked out the window and observed, "It's a lot like China here. In fact they may still be ruled from China, it's hard to be sure. Anyway, decisions are in the hands of a fairly small group. And they're split now over what to do about the sunshield. How you regard it has become a kind of loyalty test for both sides. I thought most Venusians had come to accept reliance on it as just one danger among many. But the ones who object to it tend to be more vehement in their feelings. For them it's a kind of existential issue. And so they are willing to be more extreme to get their way."

"So what do you think they did?"

"I think what may have happened is that one of their programmers decided to instruct some qubes to help the effort to get rid of the sunshield. Maybe an open command, something like 'figure out a way to get this done.' So that means some qube running a probable-outcomes algorithm. And the algorithm could have been poorly constrained. Willing to consider anything, so to speak. Kind of like a person in that regard! Very lifelike. So, what if that qube then proposed to put qubes in humanoid bodies, so they could make attacks that immobile box qubes couldn't manage on their own—attacks that humans couldn't or wouldn't do? Sabotage, I mean. Or call them educational spectacles, meaning some arranged disasters. If they could make the majority of Venusians believe that the sunshield was in danger of an attack—that they could all be cooked like bugs—then public sentiment would surely back another era of bombardment to give Venus a spin."

"Scaring a civilian populace into making a certain political choice," Wahram said.

"Yes. Which we recognize is one definition of terrorism. But this might not be so apparent to a qube programmed to look for results."

"And so the attack on Terminator was a kind of demonstration?"

"Exactly. And it certainly had that effect here on Venus."

"But this new attack on the sunshield, it could have been much more than a scare," Wahram said. "If it had succeeded, it would have killed a lot of people."

"Even that might not register as a negative. Depends on the algorithm, and that means it depends on the programmer. There are lots of people on Earth available to replace anyone killed up here. China alone could easily restock the place. The whole Venusian popula tion could be killed and replaced by Chinese and China not even notice. So who knows what people might be thinking? These programmers may have set their qubes off in new directions, even given them new algorithms, but whatever they did they won't have made human thinkers of them, even if they did get them to the point of passing a Turing test or whatnot."

"So these qubanoids definitely exist."

"Oh yes. Your Swan has met some, as have I. The thing on Io was one. And I've been interested to learn that a great many of them are on Mars, passing for human and involved in government. Mars's problems with the Mondragon and with Saturn—they look a little suspicious to me now."

"Ah," said Wahram, thinking it over. "And so you are doing what?"

"We are apprehending all of them at once," Genette said, checking Passepartout quickly. "I sent out the code to do it, and now's the time. Midnight Greenwich mean time, October 11, 2312. We have to pounce."

They landed outside Vinmara and after that Wahram was thankful that he was in a wheelchair, because Genette terriered from one brief meeting to another at a terrific clip; even wheeling along Wahram could barely keep up.

Kiran came in a few minutes later on another flight and met with them to show them which building the eyeballs had been heading for. Soon after that an armed group arrived and wasted no time surrounding this building. After a short delay they blasted down the front door and rushed in with weapons drawn, in full spacesuits. A thick pall of gray gas poured out of the interior from the very moment they broke down the door.

In less than five minutes the building was secured. Immediately Genette was conferring with the assault team, and then with Shukra, who showed up with another contingent of armed supporters, there to make sure there would be no local resistance to a rapid extraction of the facility's contents.

Genette conversed continuously with people, in person and over mobiles, unflustered but very intent— used to this kind of thing. Used even to the idea of plunging into a fight between Venusian factions, which Wahram thought must be extremely dangerous.

When Genette seemed to be done for the moment, and was sitting on the edge of a table, drinking coffee and looking at his wristqube, Wahram said curiously, "So these pebble attacks—they were a matter of one Venusian faction wanting to influence the population here? To get its way in a fight with another faction?"

"That's right."

"But . . . if the attack on the sunshield had succeeded, wouldn't the terrorists have killed themselves too?"

Genette said, "I think there would have been time for an evacuation. And the perpetrators could be off-planet by now. Also, if qubes made the decision, they might not have cared either way. Whoever the original programmers were, at that point they might not have been in control of the decisions being made. The qubes themselves might have been thinking, Well, it's a loss, but there's more of us where we came from. So they would get what they wanted whether the attack worked or failed."

Wahram thought it over. "What about that killed terrarium out in the asteroid belt? The *Yggdrasil*?"

"I don't know about that. Maybe it was meant to make people feel vulnerable. Maybe they were just testing their method. But it's odd, I agree. It's one of the reasons I want to see these qubanoids, and any people they've picked up here."

A group of people emerged from the front door of the complex, and Genette made a beeline to them. Many were smalls; the attack on the building had apparently had a Trojan horse component to it, with a bunch of smalls cutting in through air ducts and firing gas canisters to start the attack.

"All right, come on," Genette said on returning to Wahram's side, "let's get out of here. We have to get these things off-planet as fast as we can."

A line of about two dozen people, mostly standard size, but including a small and a tall, filed out the door, chained together by their security vests, Genette stopped them one by one as they passed, asking questions very politely, only detaining them for a few seconds each. Wahram inspected them also as they passed, and he noted their possibly too-smooth motion, and an intent glassy-eyed blankness to some of them; but he would not have put bets on his own ability to tell which ones were human and which manufactured. It was disconcerting, that was for sure. A little drop of dread seemed to have slid down his throat to his stomach, where it was spreading.

Genette stopped the last person in line: "Aha!"

"Who's this?" Wahram asked.

"This is Swan's lawn bowler, I believe." Genette held up Passepartout and photographed the person, then nodded at the matched photos on the wristqube's little screen. "And, as it turns out"—running a wand over the young person's head—"a human being after all."

The youth stared at them mutely.

Genette said, "Maybe this is our programmer, eh? We can investigate on our way out. I want to get off Venus as fast as we can."

This meant another quick crossing of the city, and a tense passage through lock gates to their impromptu helicopter pad. More than once, officials who should have had reason to question such a large group instead let them pass, sometimes while chattering nervously on their headsets through the whole process.

When they were airborne again, Genette glanced at Wahram with a mime's round-eyed wiping of the brow. Their helicopter headed for Colette, and at the spaceport there, they rushed onto a pad and got into a space plane, and rode it juddering up into lower orbit, there to be hauled in by an orbiting Interplan cruiser.

It was the *Swift Justice*; and when everyone was aboard, they set a course for Pluto.

In the weeks of their trip out, they brought the lawn bowler in for questioning more than once; but he never said a word. He was definitely human. A young man, thirty-five years old. They were able to trace him back from Swan's sighting in the *Chateau Garden* to one of the unaffiliateds, one that would not give its name to outsiders; Interplan had it listed, with accidental prescience, as U-238.

During the flight to Pluto and Charon, Wang's qube was able to ferret out quite a bit more about the lawn bowler's brief life. It was a sad tale, though not uncommon: small terrarium run by a cult, in this case Ahura Mazdā worshippers; strict gender division; patriarchal, polygamous; obsessed with physical punishments for demonic transgressions. Into that little world, an unstable child. Reports of aggression without remorse. Stuck there from the age of four until departure by defection at age twenty-four. Learned programming on Vesta, known by no one; absorbed for a time in qube design at the Ceres Academy, but then left school; detached from the school culture. Eventually kicked off Ceres for transgressing its security codes one too many times; then a return to his home rock, where, as far as anyone knew, he had remained. But in fact no one had been watching. How he had come to the work on Venus was unclear, that sequence hidden in the fog that surrounded the Venus Working Group—in this case Lakshmi and her anti-sunshield effort, a unit that had hidden all its actions very effectively. Thus Vinmara and the lab that made humanoids, including the ones that had gone to Mars and infiltrated the government. And the ones that had moved to Earth and then the asteroid belt, and built and operated the pebble launcher. So this young man had either invented the pebble mobs, or designed qubes that had invented them; and he or his creations had executed the attacks.

"*Yggdrasil?*" Genette said to the bowler at one point.

The diagnostic monitors attached to the youth's body and brain showed a solid jump.

Genette nodded. "Just a test, eh? Proof of concept?"

Again the monitors showed the jump in the metabolism. The idea that these jumps constituted a reliable lie detector had long since been abandoned, but the physiological leaps were still very suggestive.

Wordless as the youth remained, there was no way to be sure why any of these things had happened. But an association with *Yggdrasil* seemed clear.

To Genette, this was what mattered. "I think the attacks on Terminator and Venus were political," he said to Wahram, with the youth right in the room with them, staring mutely at the wall, the monitor's jumpy lines speaking for him in a sort of mute shouting. "I suspect they were approved by Lakshmi. But breaking open the *Yggdrasil* came first, and probably was this person's idea. A demonstration for Lakshmi, perhaps. Proof of concept. And so three thousand people died."

Genette stared up at the youth's tight face, then said finally to Wahram, "Come on, let's get out of here. There's nothing more to do here."

In the three weeks it took to reach Pluto and Charon, Wahram's injured leg took a turn for the worse, and after a consulation among themselves, the ship's medical team decided to amputate it just below the knee and begin the pluripotent stem cell work that would start the growth of a new left leg. Wahram endured this with as little attention as possible, quelling the dread in him and reminding himself that at 113 his whole body was a medical artifact, and that regrowing lost limbs was one of the simplest and oldest of body interventions. Nevertheless it was creepy to look at, and phantom itchy to feel, and he kept himself distracted by grilling Genette repeatedly about the plan the inspector's team was now executing. But no matter how much he distracted himself, he never got used to the sensation of the new leg growing down from his knee.

Spacecraft from all over the solar system were converging to join them on Charon, because this was where the Alexandrine group and the Interplan agents working with them were gathering all the qube humanoids that had been apprehended, which, as far as they knew, were all that had been manufactured. All had been captured on the same day they had closed the facility in Vinmara, most of them in the same hour. Almost half of them had been on Mars. The entire operation had been planned and coordinated by word of mouth, and the precise moment for the execution of the plan communicated the day before, when Genette sent a single radio message, a performance of the old jazz standard "Now's the Time." In every particular the plan had come off without a significant hitch, even though more than two thousand agents had taken part in the operation, and four hundred and ten humanoids captured. Not one of them had exhibited any sense that they might be in danger of arrest.

Genette's plan now was to exile all these humanoids, along with the lawn bowler and about thirty other people involved with the qube attacks. An agreement had been made to use one of the starships being built out of Pluto's moon Nix. This starship was in fact just a specialized terrarium—an almost completely closed biological life-support system, exceptionally well supplied, and with extremely powerful engines. It would now serve as a kind of prison ship, similar to the ones orbiting in the asteroid belt, but ejected from the solar system. The starship terrarium's inside would be sealed, its navigating AI placed outside the sealed cylinder. And off it would go: four hundred qube humanoids, the lawn bowler, and the group of people who had been judged guilty of complicity in any of the attacks. It was not a big group, because the lawn bowler appeared to have conceived and designed the attacks in a way that did not need many human confederates to make it work. So: exile, from the solar system and from the rest of humanity.

"Surely Lakshmi should be in there too!" Wahram objected to Genette.

"I agree, but we couldn't manage to grab her. The

Venusians will have to deal with her, or maybe we can prosecute her on Ceres and see where it gets us."

"But this exile ship," Wahram said. "What if the qubes break through to the controls? Reverse their voyage and come back, hungry for revenge and smarter than ever?"

"The speeds are too great," Genette said easily. "The fuel aboard will be quickly burned getting them to tremendous speed. By the time they dealt with the problem of refueling, it would take centuries to get back. By that time civilization will have worked out some way to deal with them."

"What do you imagine that will be?"

"I have no idea. We're going to have to deal with qubes, there's no getting around that. We have the wolf by the ears. My sense is that if qubes are kept out of human-oid bodies, and out of the hands of angry programmers, they'll just be part of the scene, like Passepartout is now."

"Or Swan's Pauline?"

"Maybe keeping a qube in your head isn't a good idea," Genette admitted. "I wonder if Swan would agree to move it into a wristqube like mine."

Wahram doubted this, though he wasn't sure why. He was less and less sure of Swan, no matter what the issue in question happened to be.

He went on to another uneasiness. "Isn't this a clear case of cruel and unusual punishment?"

"It's unusual," Genette allowed cheerfully. "Even unique. But its cruelty is relative."

"Sent off with qubes? Isn't it a weird kind of solitary confinement, something out of a nightmare?"

"Exile is not cruel. Believe me, because I know. The mind is its own place. They could in theory make quite a fine terrarium in there, and then settle an empty

Earth somewhere off in the distance, and start a whole
new wing of humanity. There's nothing stopping them
from that. So it's just exile. I am an exile myself, and
it is a recognized form of severe but nonlethal punishment. And this person killed three thousand people, just to test out a weapon. And also programmed
quantum computers that now can't tell whether what
they're doing is good or bad. They've been given intentionality without adequate limits, and are an obvious
danger, and we don't have a good defense against them
right now. So I think sending them away is making
a statement about how we treat qubes. We don't just
turn them off and break them up, as some are calling
for, but send dangerous ones off in exile, just like we
send off humans. That's got to be a good message to
the qubes left behind. We'll then keep them in boxes
so we can keep them in our control—at least I hope we
will. That may or may not work. But what I'm hoping
is that we can stop any more qubes of any kind being
made, at least for a while, and take some time to look
more closely into what smarter qubes or intentional
qubes or qubes in bodies might mean. So to my mind,
we'll have administered justice, and bought ourselves
some time. So I'm glad there's been agreement from the
Plutonians and the Mondragon and all the other relevant parties, including Shukra. And hopefully Swan,
when she hears about it, and everyone else."

"Maybe," Wahram said.

He was still not comfortable with Genette's solution.
But every alternative he came up with was either too
harsh (death for all of them) or too lenient (reintegration
into society). Exile—the first starship a prison—well,
there were prison terraria in the asteroid belt, locked
from the outside and with conditions inside ranging

from utopia to hell. So the lawn bowler's group and its creations could make what they wanted. Supposedly. It still struck him as a version of hell. When all was said and done, little Inspector Jean Genette could be quite as inhuman as the lawn bowler; sanguine, blithe, impenetrable; regarding Wahram now with a look that was the same for all—saint, criminal, stranger, brother—all of them regarded with the same birdlike gaze, frankly evaluative, interested, willing to be convinced.

Still Wahram was uneasy, and he read the files on all the humans and humanoids they held captive, which at this point came to a few thousand pages. When he was done, he came back to Genette more upset than ever.

"You've missed something here," he said sharply. "Read the interviews and you'll see that there was someone in that lab in Vinmara who was letting some of these qubanoids loose and sending them off to people elsewhere in the system who helped to hide them. The ones that Swan ran into in the *Inner Mongolia*, and at least four more—they all tell similar stories. Whoever was doing this told them they were defective, and that they needed to go on the lam if they wanted to keep from being demolished. The qubes didn't know what to make of that, and some of them acted strangely after they got loose. Maybe they *were* defective, I have no reason to disbelieve it. Anyway, this person in the lab was getting them away from Lakshmi! So does that person deserve exile also? And do the defective qubanoids that got away deserve exile?"

Genette frowned at this and promised it would get looked into.

This was not satisfactory to Wahram. He had been involved with Genette and Alex in the problem of the strange qubes from the beginning, and now felt he was being somewhat shunted to the side. He rolled his wheelchair into a meeting of the Interplan investigators and other members of the group as they discussed the situation, and again made the case for these innocents caught up with the rest of their captives. In the end it was not unanimous, but a strong majority agreed: all the qubanoids were to go into exile; the lab assistant who had been setting the defectives loose would not. It turned out that this lab assistant had not only let them go, but also erased them from the lab's records, in quite a clever bit of work, Genette informed Wahram—as if it were the cleverness that justified the pardon. Wahram, still deeply unsatisfied, let the matter drop. The Venusian lab assistant, a young person scarcely older than the lawn bowler, would be free to go. And the poor defective qubes might be better off among their own kind.

So when the time came, Wahram sat in the viewing chamber of the Interplan cruiser and watched with the rest of the people there as the matter-antimatter engine fired up, and the *First Quarter of Nix* began its trip to the stars. It looked like any other terrarium on the move, maybe a little bit bigger. Ice formed a fair percentage of its mass, and the exterior looked like an ice statue of something like a great white dolphin, flying on a tail of lightning.

"What about the people who built it?" Wahram asked. "Wasn't that their starship?"

"We have to replace it. They intend to send four in a kind of fleet, so we will make another one for them out of Hydra. We can take some of Charon too if we need it. So they will still have their four ships."

Wahram remained troubled. "I still don't know what I think of this."

Genette did not seem concerned at that. "Best we could do, I'm afraid! It was a hard thing to manage offline and in utter secrecy. Quite a nifty little operation, if you ask me. Amazing what you can do with paper and synchronized watches. Every person involved had to behave with the utmost secrecy and completely trust the people they knew in the network, and they all had to be right about that for it to work. It's quite an accomplishment when you think about it."

"Agreed," Wahram said, "but will it be enough?"

"No. The problem remains. This just gives us a little breathing room."

"And . . . you are confident you got all of them?"

"Not at all. But it looks like the facility on Venus was the only one making them, or so Wang's qube believes. And we've got enough records from their energy use and input of materials to get a maximum count of how many could be made, and we got almost exactly that many. Possibly there are one or two still out there, but we're thinking they will be too few to do any harm. They may be more of the defectives let free by that young lab assistant. Anyway, we will try to catch them if they are out there."

Meaning, Wahram thought, that right now somewhere in the system there could be machines in human form, escaped into the crowd, doing their best to stay free, perhaps, when any X-ray machine or other surveillance device would reveal what they were—out there hiding, trying to accomplish the goals they had been given, perhaps, or new ones they might choose for themselves, according to some self-invented algorithm of survival. Damaged, dangerous, detached from any other consciousness, solitary and afraid—in other words, just like everyone else.

Quantum Walk (3)

on the edge of the marsh the frogs croak   the fecundity schedule concerns how often and when during life one procreates   and how many offspring morphogenesis is the process by which an organism creates itself   growth curves with a time lag   results in oscillating patterns   the predators always a quarter cycle behind the prey

these new humans are taking you to be destroyed fat gun in your face commanded to walk between them away from your helpers   out there on the Jersey shore Manhattan skyscrapers topping the east horizon   on the run   on the hunt

kick the gun and run   humans hilariously slow on the uptake   dash into cinder shadows of dun brake duck and turn   jump a creek   green meadow crumpled with moss pads   were Persian carpets ever green?

almost stride directly into another person   looks human

I need help   some people just mugged me and I think they're still after me

human stares at you   pure blue iris marbled by a darker blue come with me then

off on a path human stops, points   white-tailed deer frozen in place ears facing them a febrile temperament they're back   the human says

You say   Would you like to play chess?

Human says   Sure   come on

To a little shack another human already there   they talk in the kitchen go outside at sunset the red on the hill taketh away my will   needles on the conifers prick silver   deciduous leaves flush on their western sides a moment comes when a distant streetlight casts a glow against the sunset and a space of light is set up without shadow   exceptionally clear and articulate to the sight there's a fox at the edge of a clearing flowing through weeds russet and white   the propagule rain   falling both ways   from Earth to space   then back again   a symbiogenesis   lifting both   blue of sky slightly veiled by white transparencies

Swan   it's Zasha   from inside the house   I've got a thing here   a chess player   it seems kind of confused

black birds banner back to town   land in a tree on the horizon   black dots flopping lazily   getting settled at end of day

birdcalls   talking to each other   maybe fifty birds of various kinds making a sonic sphere it's all together that make it music the continuo is the hum of the cars trucks generators engines motors   a jet so big it looks nearby   its sound far behind it in the sky   bird chorus at sunset surcharge and overlap   civilization in the open air   avian wisdom conserved in archaic parts of brain not apparently programmable a leap of the imagination

near midnight a third human arrives tall   graceful Hi Zasha   what's up introductions hail the reality of the other   namasté I salute the spirit within you

I'm Swan tell me about yourself

summarize events since coming to consciousness shoved out the door into the street   departure from Venus transport by humans in a private system land on Earth   all began as part of an attempt to end the eclipse on Venus   not immediately but as a project to be enacted safely hope is the thing with feathers that perches in the soul ignorant of details of plan helpers somehow actually against the larger project   helpers arrested or kidnapped   forced departure mention of being put down escape

Swan looks at Zasha   those fuckers are treating them like qubes

Well?   Zasha says   What do you call them? Qubanoids? Qubans?

Qubans is good I say they're like Pauline remember it was a qube that drove the A-Tay-Ha right into that pebble mob killed itself for us   did its duty   I mean I like the inspector as much as anyone which is quite a lot   despite all but I feel no need to agree on every issue   this is just crazy

Jean just thinks we need to hit the reset button a little

You never get to do that! life doesn't work that way I'm going to take this one with me

Swan

Don't you try to stop me!   standing quickly fist pulled back to strike

Zasha both hands up Stop stop I don't disagree for once just maybe you might have it right that's why I called you   up till now I was helping to track these things down so when I heard this one got away I went out and hauled it back in it was easy they're credulous but then I called you I called you

That's my Z we'll leave at dawn

Zasha shaking head You and your strays here you are doing it again fuck every time you come out here

Hey you're the one who asked me here you wanted my help you wanted me to do this

Yeah yeah gowan wicha getoutahere

The breaking of the day addedth to my degree if any ask me how artist who drew me so must tell

Hope is a bird the birds quieter at break of day sleepier cheerful at what the light portends a breeze throws waves through the parlor of the dawn

Follow Swan to a car off to a dock where a public ferry awaits all the faces dense with life eyes looking inward to other times past or future or watching the day like you

Across the broad river in spate water surface closely scalloped by the wind creased by wakes bubbly cross chop the round bow of the ferry skidding on the tide crashes gulps the broken water slides ahead Manhattan left to right before them a cliff made by people sunrise has not yet topped it long shadows over the river slowly grumble into the slip a giant vise that grips the ferry and rocks it still

Out with the people onto a platform out between tall buildings canals below long thin boats 52 boats visible   423 people in morning shadow busy day already

What do you think? Swan asks Can you pass? Will you be all right?

41 boats visible   364 people we are the birds that stay

I'll be all right

Good   off with you then
the human kisses you on the mouth click of eyeteeth
jolts you both suddenly awake to the reality of the
other   look in the eye   maple irises left eye marked
with a bottom arc of blue   Do good go

WAHRAM

Peple hunger for time both ways. Certain things we want to come faster: the terraforming of a new world we have come to love, the arrival of universal justice in human affairs, a good project. Other things we want to go slower: our own lives, the lives of those we love. Either way it's a hunger for time—more time to do things, to experience things.

Getting married at age 113 is the triumph of experience over hope. So many lives have already been lived. One's hopes long since have been reduced to a focus on the things of the day. Experience has taught all it is going to teach; more experience will be a reiteration.

But never *quite* reiteration. Life is always at most a pseudoiterative. Each day has its particulars. Performing the same actions day after day, in a ritual to ward off time, to hold the moment, does not remove these particulars, but rather burnishes them. The animals, our horizontal brothers and sisters, remind us; each day lived is a kind of adventure, a success. Nothing ever repeats. Each breath is a new suck at the atmosphere, a gasp for life. A hope for experience. Feel that and go on.

Fitz Wahram sat in the meeting room of the Titan Planetary Relations council, thinking these thoughts. When it was his turn, he made his case to his colleagues.

"One would hope that after all this time the Terran nation-states would have learned from experience and made their reconciliations with each other, such that their various ties with the off-planet settlements were consistent and coherent, and all the confusion and discord that their current actions create been dispensed with. But no. They have not managed that. It may take them decades more, or even centuries. No one can say how Earth will go. Meanwhile, we have to restore some kind of relationship with our old patron Mars. The work around Saturn began as a Martian nitrogen hunt, as you know, and that was a big part of settling the Saturn system in the first place. So the complete break from Mars, while necessary in its time, does not have to stay permanent, nor should it. We're strong enough now that we can deal with Mars without being overwhelmed by them. Indeed, to engage them would be a sign of strength for us. So I propose that we go there and arrange to renew nitrogen exports from Titan to them, almost at the levels that existed before, but in a new arrangement that we control, in essence a fair trade. It would benefit both planets. The Titanic atmosphere still holds about twice as much nitrogen as we want it to have in the preferred state. That suggests a specific transfer quantity that we can set the conditions for. In return we can provide our part of a triangular trade: nitrogen from Titan to Mars, reconstruction and development assistance from Mars to Mercury, and heavy metals and rare earths from Mercury to Saturn. Also their help in assuring the Vulcan light imports."

Questions and such from his interlocutors. Discussion. Then Wahram again:

"The reinforcement of ties in all three directions would be helpful in the effort to band together in the face of Earth's recidivist imperialism, and their internal conflicts and rivalries, which threaten to spill outward and overrun all of us. We might even help to heal some of these old problems. It would be a way of following up on the reanimation, which has produced such remarkable effects already."

"Like what?" He was challenged.

"The Arctic League has become one of the most progressive and cooperative political organizations on Earth. The middle of North America is being repopulated as a buffalo grasslands to tremendous acclaim. The Amazonian rain forest is being expanded back into its full historical basin, now tended as parkland, somewhat as it was in the pre-Columbian period. Southeast Asia, South Asia have achieved population balance and the biggest rewilding of all, which has helped their forests, water, and climate situation. These are all measurably improved situations since the reanimation occurred."

"There hasn't been anywhere near enough time to make those conclusions. The animal invasion is often described as a horrid botch that created a host of nightmare problems."

"Wrongly so."

They wrangled about the situation on Earth for a while. Finally the senior advisor from the Saturn Administrative Group reminded them that the issue on the table was the creation of a three-way trade with Mars and Mercury. Wahram pointed out that Mars had been considerably influenced and one might say infected by the qube humanoids that had infiltrated their system and only recently been ferreted out and sent into exile; the Martians were so pleased to be rid of them that they were revoking Jean Genette's exile status and welcoming the now-celebrated inspector back home to be thanked for good service. Presumably the new dispensation there on Mars would include a more cooperative spirit. Many council members nodded at this good news, and they got down to details of quantities of nitrogen transport, schedules, and compensation. The ultimate millibar pressure of the Titanic atmosphere was debated.

Wahram waited until most of the people in the room were feeling impatient about the matter, then called for a return to the question at hand. The principle of the proposal was approved by consensus and they closed the meeting.

The last question had to do with how they would proceed to convey their agreement to their partners, and Wahram said, "I am going to Mercury to propose marriage to Swan Er Hong. I hope we will take vows at the epithalamion on Olympus Mons. So we will be able to speak to the right people on Mars at that time."

Ah, good, they all said. Congratulations. Some looked surprised; others nodded knowingly. That will make it all easier. You'll make something like a Saturn-Mercury standing committee.

Yes, Wahram said.

SWAN

Swan left Earth feeling considerably pleased with herself for helping the qubical person light out for the territory, and pleased with Zasha too, which mattered to her much more than she had realized it would. She took the space elevator up from Quito and lived through the performance of *Satyagraha* yet again, and this time it was the peace of the final movement that struck her most, the scale rising in its simple octave over and over, like a meditation chant to lift you right off your feet; and dancing in the ever-lightening g near the end made it a very physical feeling, a kind of euphoria as they were lifted on wings of song.

She returned to Mercury in a terrarium called the *Henry David*. It was a classic New Englander, with a few small clapboard villages and some pasturage breaking up a hardwood and conifer mixed forest. It was October there, and the maples had gone red, so that there were trees violently yellow, orange, red, and green, all mixed and scattered together over the inside of the cylinder, such that when you looked up at it overhead, it appeared to be a speechless speech in some kind of round color language, trembling on the edge of meaning. Swan wandered through the forest on paths, went from one cleared hilltop to another. One day she took up leaves that had fallen and arranged them across a clearing so that they went from red to orange to yellow to yellow-green to green, in a smooth progression. This colored line on the land pleased her greatly, as did the wind that blew it away. Another day she spent hours following a black bear and her cub. In the afternoon they came to an abandoned apple orchard, where one ancient crippled tree had nevertheless produced a lot of apples, so many that some branches drooped to the ground. The bears ate a ton of them. There was an upright half barrel next to the tree that had filled with rainwater, and the cub climbed into it and took a bath, its glossy fur going black and pointing in wet tips.

Back on Mercury she settled into her life in Terminator. She woke out on her balcony, breakfasted in the morning cool, did her stretches to the sun, bowing uneasily to Sol Invictus. Looked over the city, registering all the familiar landmarks that had been rebuilt, and the new trees and shrubs, looking a little bigger every day, a little more in place. She had taken a postcard that Alex had had couriered to her long before, and tacked it to the wall over her kitchen sink, where Alex's handwriting proclaimed daily:

O joy of my spirit—it is uncaged—it darts like
  lightning!
It is not enough to have this globe or a certain time,
I will have thousands of globes and all time.

It was autumn now in Terminator too, and the row of Japanese fire maples on the terrace two down from her balcony had gone an incandescent red. Dust had settled on the royal-blue roof tiles she could see below. The new weather program seemed to include more windy days than the old one had, and sometimes there were winds stronger than any she could remember. She liked that. Certain cold gusty winds would pull her loose from whatever she was doing and take her on long walks around the city. It was feeling very much bigger up front than before, the platform extended to provide more park and farm. There were new canals in the flat part of the city and the park. Bridges over canals, bike paths, broad boulevards and esplanades. Her town. Same but different. It occurred to her that the city could be expanded forward even farther into the night; in theory, as the decades and centuries passed they could cover the tracks westward all the way around the nightside of Mercury.

She spent most of her days out in the farm, working on the pond and wetlands. The new estuary was not thriving and there were questions about salinity levels, and a little hydraulic tide they had going. Arguments, really. And she was still trying to understand why the Gibraltar apes didn't like the caves they had provided in a little hill with a west-facing cliff face. The apes were gorgeous, and usually they didn't have problems the way people had problems. But there they were, hanging out on the flats under the caves, unwilling to go into them. At some point she might have to climb up there to take a look herself.

While she was out there watching the apes, she thought about her life. Here she was, 137 years old.

Body much abused the whole time; it would not last forever, or even necessarily go on much longer. On the other hand, the treatments were doing new things even compared to a few years before, and people were still working at improving them. Mqaret was almost two hundred. So it had to be thought about.

Her close relationships were few, and perhaps no longer so close. She had everything she needed; her life was good. Her surviving child was out there somewhere, living her life in her own manner, not cratering to speak of. Occasionally in touch. Not the issue. Swan was closer to other people, and that was all right. Her young friend Kiran had stayed on Venus, had insisted on it, and was back in the thick of things there and sending her reports on a regular basis. It felt like more of a relationship than many she had, and there were more like that out there to come, no doubt; people were always grabbing her by the arm and pulling her into their lives, it seemed. Her farm crew was tight. She liked her work; she liked her play; she liked her art, the play that was work. So it was something else. Really the question became quite philosophical; how to be? What to care about? And how to become a little less solitary? Because now, with Alex gone, though she talked to many people, in the end she was missing someone to tell things to in the way she had always told Alex.

> Oh I miss you Hettie Moore
> But there's no one here left to tell—
> The world has gone black before my eyes.

In the farm by herself she sang the old ballad, and wondered what would make things right. Maybe nothing.

There was a pruning of life by death. Parts died before the whole. When the people you loved died, part of you died. Some people by the time they went were like certain junipers she had seen, one live strip on a dead trunk. There was no way to counter that.

No happiness but in virtue. No, that wasn't true. Each part of the triune brain had its own happiness. Lizard in the sun, mammal on the hunt, human doing something good. What's good is what's good for the land. So when you worked as if on the hunt, in light and warmth, at making a landscape—some place for people to live in for ages to come—then you were triunely happy. Surely that should be enough.

But then you wanted to share it. Just so there would be someone to be pleased together with. Alex had been pleased with her.

She had seen the traveling isolatoes, solitary old spacers who made their own way in the world, who were not partnered in any fashion with other people. That was her crowd; she had been one of them herself for more than half her life. Had they all been on the hunt? She recalled something she had heard people say: I want to meet somebody. Meet; they meant "mate." I want to mate somebody. "Meet" was the future subjunctive of "mate," in the mood of desire. And when you looked around, you saw it: pair-bonding kept coming back. It was a future conditional tense, a subjunctive verb: to mate somebody, and then meet them. It was an atavistic thing, as if they were swans, or some other creature with a genetic urge to pair off. "Swan is not a swan," she told her baffled coworkers in the park. But how did she know?

"I want to meet somebody," she said to Mqaret experimentally.

Mqaret laughed at her. "You like this guy! This person Wahram from Saturn. So maybe what you mean is 'I've met somebody.'"

Swan stared at Mqaret. It still hadn't fully sunk in to her that it was possible to be loved. Or even to love. "But I met him a long time ago. I've known him for years now!"

"Even better," Mqaret said. "You know him. In fact you had to spend a lot of time with him. What happened in that utilidor? Didn't something happen?"

"We whistled, mostly," she said. "But yes. Something happened."

"Maybe that's what a marriage is," Mqaret said. "Whistling together. Some kind of performance. I mean, not just a conversation, but a performance."

"Marriage," Swan repeated, marveling at the word. To her it was a concept from the Middle Ages, from old Earth—an idea with a strong whiff of patriarchy and property. Not meant for space, not meant for longevity. One moved through one's life in epochs, each a stage in one's history, lasting some few or several years, and then circumstances changed and you were in a new life, with new associates. That could not be altered, not if you were out there riding the great merry-go-round; and so to deform one's life in the attempt to make a relation last longer than its natural term was to risk wrecking its end, such that it splintered back along its whole length and left a bitter wound and a sense that it had all been a lie, where really there should only be a passing on, in one of the little death-and-transfigurations of one's epochs. That's just the way it was.

At least so it seemed to her, and to many others she knew. It was the current structure of feeling in her culture and time. Spacers were free humans, free at last and human at last. So they all felt, and encouraged each other to feel, and she had always believed it, always agreed it was right. But structures of feeling were cultural, historical; they changed over time like people did; the structures themselves went through their own reincarnations. So if cultures changed over time, and an individual lived on through a change in that culture, then...didn't the individual change too? Could they? Could she?

But wasn't marriage a promise somehow not to change?

She slogged around in the wetlands and kept on thinking about it. One day a frog the same color as the rocks hopped away from her accidental hand, then sat there staring up at her, alert and curious, calm but ready to leap again. "Sorry," she said. "I didn't see you." And yet now that she had, it sat there glossier than any rock, alive and breathing.

She went out on a walkabout. Headed to the north of Terminator's latitude, into the Tricrena Albedo. Out into the garbled chiaroscuro of the terminator, where sidelong rays of sunlight raked suddenly up the tilting land, blazing so violently that the still-shadowed land appeared blacker than matter. Clashing shards of black and white—her eye could scarcely put the landscape back together again. Just the way she liked it, sometimes. Her schizophrenic life space.

She fell into sunwalker mode, oriented herself by the memorized maps inside her. She knew as she trudged blindly westward that she would soon come over the rise north of Mahler, pass some baked ballardian abandoned space plane runways, then find herself at the top of an escarpment, a little bulging crack in the land, very old, the land above overlooking a two-hundred-meter drop to the plains below. Luckily the escarpment sported a system of tilted ledges that served as a neat staircase down. She had been here before. These Ebersbacher Ledges were often trod by sunwalkers using this route, and had been swept clear of dust and rubble many years before. So it was a broken switchbacking path of clean stone tilts that led her down to the plain beyond. On Mercury the horizon was just the right distance away, she felt; not something you could reach out and touch, but something you could walk to and investigate.

Out there now was a little group of sunwalkers, trudging patiently west. Little silver figures reminiscent of Inspector Genette, disappearing over the horizon. They would walk for a spell and then lie down in carts or travois to sleep while being pulled along by the others. Walking together, pulling sleeping people along—how beautiful the sense of trust and care, the playful handing over of your life to strangers—part of being Mercurial. For a long time it had been all she had needed in the way of company. That and her city.

She got to the bottom of the ledges and came onto the flat rubble plain of Tricrena Albedo. Here the trail disappeared, because any way was equally good. Here she could run into the night, gain ground on the dawn, stand on Yes Tor and watch the highest points of ground light like candles, then burn downward from their brilliant tips. To walk in the dawn perpetually, ah, so devoutly to be wished! Who could stand high noon or the wane of day? Leave the dawn behind, run back into the night. Forestall the day—who knew what it would bring? She had no plan, no idea.

For a long time she ran and didn't think much

beyond the rock under her, the lay of the land. Nothing more needed. They could tear the guts out of Mercury, take out every valuable mineral in it, and the surface would not look one whit different. It was already a clinker of a world. The battered face of an old friend. Rock scattered everywhere, rubble, kipple, ejecta. The blanket of dust. Gold in them thar hills. But friends talk. I want to be able to talk to someone and have it mean something to me. I want to hear things that interest me, that surprise me, no matter how impossible I am to surprise. Except in truth I am so easily surprised. How could it be that someone was not there to surprise someone so easily surprised.

The saturnine person. What if there was a person you could depend on, someone who was steady, reliable, predictable, resolute; decisive after due thought; generous; kind. Phlegmatic, and yet prone to little gusts of enthusiasm, usually aesthetic pleasures of one sort or other. Happy in danger, a little drunk in danger. Someone capable of loving a landscape. Someone who liked to watch animals and chase them for a look. Someone who looked at her as if figuring her out was an interesting project and not just a problem to be solved, or part of the backdrop in some other more important drama. And looked at everyone else met with that same regard. Often with a little smile that seemed to express pleasure in the company shared. A reserved but friendly manner. If all our acquaintances were characterized in language only, we would look like collectors of contradictions, paradoxes, oxymorons. For every kind of this there was a balance of that. People cut both ways. In someone like him a little cheery laugh began to seem like boisterousness.

She came to one of her most famous goldsworthies,

from a time when she had been experimenting with setting slugs of lead and other metals that would melt in the heat of the day on slopes she had cut with channels, so that over the course of a brightside crossing, the slugs of lead or copper or tin would melt into the channels and form pictures or letters, always stretched such that they looked upright to observers on a viewing platform atop a nearby cliff. For this sculpture north of Mahler she had channeled two sets of letters carefully overlapping and intersecting each other, with gates for one word or other equally matched in their weakness. As the metal pigs melted in the sun they would run against the gates until one gate or other would fail, thus draining the reservoir of its molten contents. So, depending on what happened in the gates, the resulting letters of this installation would have spelled either "LIVE" or "DIE." It was the last of a series of antino mies she had put to the landscape and the sun in those years, including all the seven virtues and vices overlapped, wrestling with each other like Jacob with God. So far the verdict was out; the process looked random. But in this particular instance both gates had broken at once, resulting in a flow insufficient to fill all the channels; some had filled preferentially over others, and the result, made of a bright swirl of silver and copper, had been the word "LIE."

Now she stood looking at it from the viewing platform. Even at the time it had struck her as apt; and now it was like a command. One could still see the empty troughs of the two overlaid words, the empty D and V; but certainly the word "LIE," glowing metallically in the dark land, dominated. Very apt indeed. People said she must have arranged it that way on purpose, but she hadn't; the dams had been equal, their simultaneous break an act of their own; the letters filled a matter of the first surge, a clinamen. But it told the truth in some sense. They didn't live or die—they did both—and so lied. You lie and then you lie. So get on with it.

After a while she turned south, to get over to the nearest platform before the city came gliding over the horizon. When she got over the low rim of the ancient crater Kenkō, she would be able to see Terminator's tracks, gleaming faintly in the valley below.

From the top of Kenkō, around to its southern side, she saw the tracks, and also a lone figure, toiling up the incline toward her. Round, tall; and she recognized the walk the moment she saw it, oh she knew that walk all right!

She clicked on the common band: "Wahram?"

" 'Tis I, come hunting for you."

"You found me."

"Yes. Were you going to be coming back into town soon? Because I didn't bring anything to eat."

"Yes, I was. When did you get in?"

"Yesterday. I've just been hiking for a few hours. The city will be along anytime now."

"Good. Good. Let's go down to meet it." She walked down to him and gave him a hug. In their suits she still knew his body well, round and full, a bigger person than her. "Thanks for coming out to get me."

"Oh, my pleasure, I assure you. I came all the way from Titan."

"I thought you might have. How is your new leg?"

He gestured down at it. "I keep placing it and finding it's not quite where I thought it was. Apparently the ghost nerves of the old leg are still speaking to me and messing me up."

"Just like my head!" Swan said without thinking, and laughed painfully. "Every time I grow a new one it's not quite where I thought it was."

Wahram regarded her, smiling. "I'm told it is a quick adjustment."

"Hmm."

"In fact, speaking of growing new heads—I was wondering if you had thought about what I said when we were marooned. And also of course on Venus afterward."

"Yes, I have."

"And?"

"Well, I don't know."

Wahram frowned. "Have you talked to Pauline about it?"

"Well, I suppose."

In fact this had not even occurred to her.

Wahram regarded her. The sun was going to hit them soon. He said, "Pauline, will you marry me?"

"Yes," said Pauline.

"Hey wait a minute!" Swan exclaimed. "I'm the one who has to say yes here."

"I thought you just did," Wahram said.

"No I did not! Pauline is very much a separate entity in here. That's why you locked me out of your meetings, right?"

"Yes, but because you two are one. And so we couldn't let you in without letting her in too. I am not the first to observe that since you were the one who programmed Pauline, and continue to do so, she is a kind of projection of you—"

"Not at all!"

"—or, well, maybe she would be better described as one of your works of art. They have often been very personal things."

"My rock piles, personal?"

"Yes. Not as personal as sitting naked on a block of ice for a week drinking your own blood, but nevertheless, very personal."

"Well, but Pauline is not art."

"I'm not so sure. Maybe she's something like a ventriloquist's dummy. Isn't that art? Some device we speak through. So I am very encouraged."

"Don't be!"

But he obviously was. Over time, Swan realized, that would matter—that he believed in Pauline. She walked down toward the nearest platform and he followed her.

After a while he said, "Thank you, Pauline."

"You're welcome," Pauline replied.

Extracts (18)

to form a sentence is to collapse many superposed wave functions to a single thought universe. Multiplying the lost universes word by word, we can say that each sentence extinguishes 10^n universes, where n is the number of words in the sentence. Each thought condenses trillions of potential thoughts. Thus we get verbal overshadowing, where the language we use structures the reality we inhabit. Maybe this is a blessing. Maybe this is why we need to keep making sentences

texts are written for people to read later. They are a kind of time capsule, a speaking to one's descendants. Reading this text, you see back to an older time, when the tumult and disorder may be scarcely believable to you. You may be on the other side of a great divide, your life indefinitely long and headed for the stars. Not so we the living, thrashing around in our little solar system like bacteria filling a new rain puddle. This puddle is all we've got. Within it some jimmy the doors to the secrets of life; some tend a patch of dirt for enough food to live. You know all that I know; what can we the living say to each other in that situation? In many ways it's easier to talk to you, generous reader, unborn one. You might live for centuries, this text one tiny part of your education, a glimpse at how it used to be, a little insight into how your world got to be the way it is. Your author however remains stuck in the tail of the balkanization, desperate with hope for the beginning of whatever comes next. It is a very limited view

Who decides when it's time to act?

No one decides. The moment happens.

No. We decide. How we decide is an interesting question. But even if we don't know the answer to it, we decide

although the events right before and after the year 2312 were important and signaled changes latent in the situation at the time, nothing tipped decisively then, there was no portal they passed through saying, "This is a new period, this is a new age." Events set in train were mired and complex, and many took decades more to come to fruition. That the Mondragon would unify much of Earth, that Mars would recover from its qube-inflected withdrawal and rejoin the Mondragon—none of that was clear to us then—things could have shifted into quite different channels and

of course the disparities between individual and planetary time can never be reconciled. "What is to be noted here is less the unification of these disparate temporalities than rather their surcharge and overlap." It's the surcharge and overlap that create the feel of any given time. "Out of this jumbled superimposition of different kinds of temporal models History does in fact emerge" as a work of art, like any other work of art, but made by everyone together. And it doesn't stop. Things happen, events, accomplishments; wins and losses; Pyrrhic victories, rearguard actions; and though there can be crucial events, the plot does not end in a year like 2312, but rather several decades later, if that

what we see when we contemplate the formation of the triple alliance of Mars, Saturn, and Mercury, or the intervention of the Mondragon Accord into the balkanized Earth, or Mars's return to the Mondragon, is a kind of unstable interregnum, a shift in the spinning of the great merry-go-round as the weights are redistributed and something new begins, and a shuddering thus torques the system for years, before finally slipping into some newly stabilized rotation

On Venus the backlash against the plot to spin up the planet caused a long and bitter civil war, largely invisible to the rest of the system, fought with knives and depressurization, and only resolved in the latter half of the twenty-fourth century with a general referendum of the entire population, which decisively chose to renew the bombardment of the equator and initiate the spectacularly destructive creation of a hundred-hour Venusian day

the so-called invisible revolutions on Earth led to the recreation of its landscapes both physical and political, all of which followed the Reanimation. In that same period the integration of qube and human existence was another invisible revolution, a struggle vexing the minds of every engineer, philosopher, and qube who ever attacked the problem

on Mars it became clear that a small working group within the official government had been infiltrated and influenced by a cadre of qubed simulacra, who were summarily kidnapped and sent into exile, after which a profound reconsideration of their governance brought them closer to their democratic system as described, and reentry in the Mondragon Accord followed

with majorities on Callisto, Ganymede, Europa, Titan, Triton, and even Luna declaring the intention to fully terraform their worlds, all volatiles and nitrogen in particular became much more expensive; inflation struck the entire system at once; and by the end of the twenty-fourth century the Saturn League had amassed a titanic fortune

all the invisible events make the history of that time hard to write. And all the events continued to occur against the most intense resistance of time, material, and human recalcitrance—human fear, in fact, seizing with a desperate grip various imagined props out of the past that were somehow felt to hold the world together. Because of this, there is still and always the risk of utter failure and mad gibbering extinction. There is no alternative to continuing to struggle

Epilogue

Descending to Mars on its Pavonis space elevator, you look down through the clear floor at the red planet rising to meet you. The three prince volcanoes topping the Tharsis bulge bulk in a line, like mounds built by a mound-building tribe of red people. Off to the west Olympus Mons rears like a round continent all its own, its encircling ten-kilometer cliff from this vantage no more than a beveled line around its foot. All the rest of the planet is cut into enormous red polygons by the many green lines crisscrossing the planet—the famous canals, incised into the landscape in the first days of terraforming. They used orbiting Birch solettas that focused sunlight like a magnifying glass on the land, creating temperatures so high that the rock both vaporized and melted. Quite a bit of Mars had to be thus burned to get all the air and heat they wanted; so to distribute that burn they had decided to use the Lowell maps of the late nineteenth century as inspiration, and platted the burn accordingly. Having gone that far, they also adopted the old nomenclature for these canals, a witches' brew of Greek, Latin, Hebrew, Egyptian, and other ancient languages, so that you now descend to places with names like Nodus Gordii, Phaethontis, Icaria, Tractus Albus, Nilokeras, Phoenicis Lacus. The greened strips crossing the red land are about a hundred kilometers wide, and are only threaded by their actual canals. The strips sometimes run in pairs across the red desert. They meet at vaguely hexagonal angles, and the nodes are lush oases, with elegant cities clustered around complexes of waterways and locks, ponds and fountains. Thus a nineteenth-century fantasy forms the basis for the actual landscape currently existing. Some call it bad taste. But they were in a hurry, back in the beginning, and this is what they had to show for it.

North of Olympus Mons the wedding party walked out of the doors of a train station into the open air, just as if they had been on Earth. It was early in the morning, cool and breezy. The sky was a Maxfield Parrish blue; the trees scattered about in small groves were enormous sequoia, eucalyptus, valley oak. The canal ran across the plain below the hill they were on, one side of it lined with cypress trees. Between its levees the canal's water looked as if it stood a little higher than the land around it. In many places the levee tops were broad high boulevards, green and crowded with buildings and people. Lower on the sides of the levees it could sometimes be seen that they were composed of endless mounds of black glass.

Along the top of one levee they rode a tram, headed for Olympus Mons. Wide streets angled out into the green fields that flitted by below them. These grassy boulevards were flanked by blocky buildings that were often faced with ceramic murals and had an Art Deco look. They passed white plazas under palm trees and remarked to each other the lush beauty, also the uniformity of style, with its hexagonal suggestion of a hive mind. A green and pleasant land. They trammed from oasis to oasis, in a regular flashing of light and shadow created by the long rows of cypress trees by the tracks. Gardens in the desert. The hyperterran look combined with the Mercury-light gravity created a dreamscape feel. Mercury would never look like this. Nowhere else could look like this.

Inspector Genette, standing on the chair by the window and looking out intently at the passing scene, said, "I lived there once," gesturing down at one swiftly passing town square. "I think it was in that building right there."

Their tram stopped in a train station in Hougeria, where they were going to transfer to a maglev train to ascend the northeast side of Olympus Mons. While they waited for their train, they took a walk out of the station and around the city center. All the canals were iced over here, and people were out ice-skating, hands behind their backs. It was sunny but chill.

Swan complained about the trip up the great volcano: "What's the point of coming to Mars if we go right up out of the atmosphere and have to stay in a tent again? Up there we could be anywhere."

This was regarded by her companions as a rhetorical question, as they were all quite sure she remembered they were attending the epithalamion. Wahram shaded his eyes and looked south, up the side of the great volcano. They were at the only part of the circumference of Olympus Mons that was not guarded by an immense escarpment, a circular cliff ten kilometers high that was remarkably uniform all the way around the mountain; but here a flood of lava late in the volcano's active life had poured down and over the escarpment—had fallen in a ten-kilometer firefall, which Wahram was now attempting to imagine—ten thousand meters of free fall, cooling on the way no doubt, from red to orange to black, while the spill at the bottom piled up on itself and rose higher and higher, until the cliff was entirely erased under lava, after which the molten rock continued to flow northeast, leaving in the end a broad and gentle ramp extending all the way from the upper slopes of the volcano down to the plain. Thus the land under them now, its fiery past.

"After this we can tour the lowlands," Wahram said. "Honeymoon at the beach, so to speak."

"Good. I want to go swimming in the Hellas Sea."

"Me too."

When the time came, they got in one of the pressurized cars of their maglev train, along with many other wedding parties, and the train headed up the ramp toward the summit. It was a long lift, and took them through a Martian-red sunset, and then a night of parties and troubled sleep. At dawn they woke to find the train entering the station on the southeast slope of the volcano's broad summit. Here on the apron of little Crater Zp a big clear tent covered the planet's traditional festival space. They had arrived on the first morning of the epithalamion.

From the inside, the tenting could scarcely be seen; it was much less visible than Terminator's dome, and it seemed as if they stood in the open air, which was warm and aromatic. A black roof of starry space stood overhead, turning blue only just over the horizon; the atmosphere was almost entirely below them. They had to be inside a tent, and knowing that, one could just make it out here and there, prisming against the border of blue-and-black sky. Olympus Mons was so big that the distant horizon to the east and south was still part of the mountain; they could not see the Tharsis volcanoes over the horizon to the east, nor any of the planet below the encircling escarpment. All the land they could see was as bare and red as it had been in the beginning, with only the blue rind of air over the horizon to reveal what they had done to this world.

All the tented land of the festival space was on a mild tilt, and had been terraced, therefore, to make flat surfaces. The result looked like certain terraced hillsides in Asia: a few hundred bands of level land ran down the slope, the terrace walls between them curving like contour intervals on a map. Three broad low-angled staircases cut up through these terrace walls, and some of their wedding party remarked at how this reminded them a bit of the Great Staircase in Terminator; but these staircases extended for four or five kilometers each and spanned a vertical reach of perhaps three hundred meters—it was hard to judge, given the vastness of the volcano outside the tent.

The epithalamion was the wedding day for Mars and for visitors from all over the system. Now the festival space was busy with movement, and loud with voices, as a few hundred couples moved up and down the staircases with their groups, finding the terraces reserved for them. The three staircases were heaped with flowers for the day. One could not avoid stepping on flowers, and their bright colors stained the big quartzite flagstones covering the risers.

Wahram and Swan and their group came to their terrace, number 312. When Swan saw that their friends had decorated the terrace in flowers so as to make it look somewhat as if Terminator's Great Staircase were running through the seashell architecture of Iapetus, she smiled and gave Wahram a hug. They stood together smiling as their party of friends applauded them. Wahram was dressed in Saturnian black and resembled a dreadful Roman emperor or, yes, a giant amphibian. Mr. Toad was indeed beginning his wild ride. Swan was in a red dress that made it look as if she stood in a rose of fire. She would not let go of Wahram's hand as they ascended littler stairs onto the dais where they were going to conduct their ceremony.

Music was playing all over the festival grounds, and they could hear very distinctly a gamelan from the terrace below, but the overlapping musics were part of the epithalamion experience, and their own ceremony was to be accompanied by the galloping finale of Brahms's Second Symphony—Wahram's choice, but Swan had approved. She kept looking up at him as Inspector Genette tapped at Passepartout's screen to call up the poem they had requested. Wahram seemed to be mostly looking out at the view. It was still morning, and the sunlight slanted in at them in almost Mercurial splendor. It was a huge planet. All the couples above and below them were performing their particular nuptials. The space was so big, the music so various, that each ceremony took place in a little bubble world of its own; but the sight and sound of all of them together was very much part of each one.

In their particular space, Saturn and Mercury were well represented. Mqaret was there, also Wang, and Kiran, and some of Swan's farm team. Zasha too. Wahram's crèche was represented by Dana and Joyce, and the Satyr of Pan. They all stood in a disorganized mass around the dais, but the two populations could be easily distinguished, the Saturnians in their black and gray and blue, the Mercurials in their reds and golds. There was also a group of Genette's old Martian friends, many of them smalls. Apparently all the smalls at the festival were to congregate later to sing small favorites like "I Met Her in a Phobos Restaurant" and "Lovely Rita, Meter Maid" and "We're Off to See the Wizard."

Everyone on the terrace was looking pleased. They were eyeing each other and smiling: Our friends are doing something crazy, their looks said, something crazy and beautiful, isn't it great? Love—some kind of leap of the imagination. Inexplicable. It was going to be quite a party.

Inspector Genette, standing on a lectern to be almost at eye level with the two of them, raised their clasped hands together and said, "You two, Swan and Wahram, have decided to marry and become life partners, for as long as you both shall live. Wahram, do you affirm this?"

"I do so affirm."

"Swan, do you affirm this?"

"Yes."

"Do it, then. Live it, and everyone here, help them to live it. I now recite some lines from Emily Dickinson that describe very well the symbiogenesis they intend to enact:

Brain of his brain—
Blood of his blood—
Two lives—one being—now—
All life—to know each other—
Whom we can never learn—
Just finding out—what puzzled us—
Without the lexicon!"

The inspector smiled at this thought, raised a hand. "By the authority vested in me by you and by the Mondragon Accord, and even by Mars, I declare that Swan Er Hong and Fitz Wahram by mutual agreement are now married."

Genette hopped off the lectern. Swan and Wahram faced each other; briefly they kissed. Then they turned and faced the group below them, and their friends applauded. The Brahms surged to its dizzy end, trombones blaring. Swan took a gold ring held up by the inspector, who made a lovely ring bearer, and pulled up Wahram's left hand. She saw he was squinting down the slope of Olympus, the look on his face pensive, almost melancholy. She squeezed his hand and he looked at her. "Well," he said with the tiniest of smiles, "I guess now we get to walk the second half of the tunnel."

"No!" she cried, and thumped him on the chest, then jammed the ring over the knuckle of his ring finger. "This is for life."

ACKNOWLEDGMENTS

Many thanks for the help from:

Charles Beck, Hadas Blinder and the Clarion 2011 selection committee, Michael Blumlein, William Burling, Bob Crais, John Cumbers, Paul di Fillipo, Ron Drummond, James Haughton, Charles R. Ill, Louis Neal Irwin, Fredric Jameson, Kimon Keramidas, Stephanie Langhoff, Darlene Lim, Chris McKay, Andrew Matthews, Pamela Mellon, Michael Montague, Lisa Nowell, Kriss Ravetto-Biagioli, David Robinson, Tim Robinson, Pamela Ronald, Carter Scholz, Mark Schwartz, Michael Sims, Sean Stewart, Carol Stoker, Sharon Strauss, Slawek Tulaczyk, Ralph Vicinanza, and Donald Wesling.

A special thanks to Tim Holman.

Thanks also to the art of Andy Goldsworthy,

Marina Abramović,

and John Dos Passos.

extras

www.orbitbooks.net

meet the author

Kim Stanley Robinson is a *New York Times* bestseller and winner of the Hugo, Nebula, and *Locus* awards. He is the author of more than twenty books, including the bestselling Mars trilogy and the critically acclaimed *Forty Signs of Rain*, *Fifty Degrees Below*, *Sixty Days and Counting*, *The Years of Rice and Salt*, *Antarctica*, *Galileo*, and *2312*. In 2008, he was named a "Hero of the Environment" by *Time* magazine, and he recently joined in the Sequoia Parks Foundation's Artists in the Back Country program. He lives in Davis, California.

introducing

If you enjoyed *2312*, look out for

SHAMAN

BY KIM STANLEY ROBINSON

From the New York Times bestselling author of the Mars trilogy and 2312 comes a powerful, thrilling and heart-breaking story of one young man's journey into adulthood—and an awe-inspiring vision of how we lived thirty thousand years ago.

SHAMAN is an extraordinary imaginative feat and a unique reading experience that brings our ancestors to life as never before.

We had a bad shaman.

This is what Thorn would say whenever he was doing something bad himself. Object to whatever it was and he would pull up his long gray braids to show the mangled red nubbins surrounding his earholes. His shaman had stuck bone needles through the flesh of his boys' ears and then ripped them out sideways, to help them remember things. Thorn when he wanted the same result would flick Loon hard on the ear and then point at the side of his own head, with a tilted look that said, You think you have it bad?

Now he had Loon gripped by the arm and was hauling him along the ridge trail to Pika's Rock, on the overlook between Upper and Lower Valleys. Late afternoon, low clouds rolling overhead, brushing the higher ridges and the moor, making a gray roof to the world. Under it a little line of men on a ridge trail, following Thorn on shaman's business. It was time for Loon's wander.

—Why tonight? Loon protested. —A storm is coming, you can see it.

—We had a bad shaman.

And so here they were. The men all gave Loon a hug, grinning ruefully at him and shaking their heads. He was going to have a miserable night, their looks said. Thorn waited for them to finish, then croaked the start of the good-bye song:

> *This is how we always start*
> *It's time to be reborn a man*
> *Give yourself to Mother Earth*
> *She will help you if you ask*

—If you ask nicely enough, he added, slapping Loon on the shoulder. Then a lot of laughing, the men's eyes sardonic or encouraging as they divested him of his clothes and his belt and his shoes, everything passed over to Thorn, who glared at him as if on the verge of striking him. Indeed when Loon was entirely naked and without possessions Thorn did strike him, but it was just a quick backhand to the chest.—Go. Be off. See you at full moon.

If the sky were clear, there would have been the first sliver of a new moon hanging in the west. Thirteen days to wander, therefore, starting with nothing, just as a shaman's first wander always started. This time with a storm coming. And in the fourth month, with snow still on the ground.

Loon kept his face blank and stared at the western horizon. To beg for a month's delay would be undignified, and anyway useless. So Loon looked past Thorn with a stony gaze and began to consider his route down to the Lower Valley creekbed, where knots of trees lined the creek. Being barefoot made a difference, because the usual descent from Pika's Rock was very rocky, possibly so rocky he needed to take another way. First decision of many he had to get right.——Friend Raven there behind the sky, he chanted aloud,——lead me now without any tricks!

——Good luck getting Raven to help, Thorn said. But Loon was from the raven clan, and Thorn wasn't, so Loon ignored that and stared down the slope, trying to see a way. Thorn slapped him again and led the other men back down the ridge. Loon stood alone, the wind cutting into him. Time to start his wander.

But it wasn't clear which way to get down. For a time it seemed like he might freeze there, might never start his life's journey.

So I came up in him and gave him a little lift from within.

I am the third wind.

He took off down the rocks. He looked back once to show his teeth to Thorn, but they were out of sight down the ridge. Off he plunged, flinging the thought of Thorn from him. Under his feet the broken gritstone was flecked with pock snow, which collected in dimples and against nobbles in a pattern that helped him see where to step. Go as agile as a cat, down rock to rock, hands ready to grab and help down little jumps. His toes chilled and he abandoned them to their cold fate, focused on keeping his hands warm. He would need his hands down in the trees. It began to snow, just a first little pricksnow. The slope had big snow patches that were easier on his feet than the rocks.

He tightened his ribs and pushed his heat out into his limbs and skin, grunting until he blazed a little, and the pricksnow melted when it touched him. Sometimes the only heat to be had is in hurry.

He clambered down and across the boulder-choked ravine seaming the floor of Lower Valley, across the little stream. On the other side he was able to run up the thin forest floor, which was all too squishy, as the ground was wet with rain and snowmelt. Here he avoided the patches of snow. First day of the fourth month: it was going to be trouble to make a fire. The night would be ever so much more comfortable if he could make a fire.

The upper end of Lower Valley was a steep womb canyon. A small cluster of spruce and alder surrounded the spring there, which started the valley's creek. There he would find shelter from the wind, and branches for clothing, and under the trees there wouldn't be much snow left. He hurried up to this grove, careful not to stub his senseless toes.

In the little copse around the spring he tore at live spruce branches and broke several off, cursing their wetness, but even damp their needles would hold some of his heat against him. He wove two spruce branches together and stuck his head through a middle gap in the weave, making it into a rough cloak.

Then he broke off a dead bit of brush pine root to

serve as the base of his firestarter. Near the spring he found a good rock to use as a chopper, and with it cut a straight dead alder branch for his firestick. His fingers were just pliable enough to hold the rock. Otherwise he didn't feel particularly cold, except in his feet, which were pretending not to be there. The black mats of spruce needles under the trees were mostly free of snow. He crouched under one of the biggest trees and forced his toes into the mat of needles and wiggled them as hard as he could. When they began to burn a little he pulled them out and went looking for duff. Even the best fire kit needs some duff to burn.

He reached into the center of dead spruce logs, feeling for duff or punk. He found some punk that was only a little damp, then broke off handfuls of dead twigs tucked under the protection of larger branches. The twigs were damp on their outsides, but dry inside; they would burn. There were some larger dead branches he could break off too. The grove had enough dead wood to supply a fire once it got going. It was a question of duff or punk. Neither spruce nor alder rotted to a good punk, so he would have to be lucky, or maybe find some ant-eaten wood. He got on his knees and started grubbing around under the biggest downed trees, avoiding the snow, turning over bigger branches and shoving around in the dirt trying to find something. He got dirty to the elbows, but then again that would help keep him warm.

Which might matter, as he could not find any dry punk, or any duff at all. He squeezed water out of one very rotten mass of wood, but the brown goo that remained in his hand resembled dead moss or mullein, and was still damp. The firestick's rough tip would never light such shit.

—Please, he said to the grove. He begged its forgiveness for cursing as he had approached it.—Give me some punk, please goddess.

Nothing. It became too cold for him to keep kneeling on the wet ground digging in downed logs. To make some heat in him he got up and danced. With this effort he could warm his hands, and it was important they not go numb like his feet had. Oh, a fire would make the night so much more comfortable! Surely something could be found here that would burn under the heat of his firestick's tip!

Nothing. His belt contained in its fold many little gooseskin bags in which there were spark flints, dry moss, firestick, and base. Dressed and carrying all his things, he could have survived this night and the fortnight to follow in style. Which was why he had been sent out naked: the point of the wander was to prove you could start with nothing but yourself, and not just survive but prosper. He needed to come back into camp on the night of the full moon in good style.

But first he had to get through this night. He began to work hard in his dance, throwing his arms around, spinning his hands in big circles. He sang a hot song and wiggled all over. After doing this for a while, everything but his feet began to burn. But he was also getting tired. He tried to find a balance between the cold and his efforts, walking in a tight circle while also inspecting the forest floor for likely punk and duff shelters. Nothing!

In every grove some wood will burn.

This was one of the sayings that Heather often repeated, though seldom when talking about fire. Loon said it aloud, emphatically, beseechingly:—In every grove some wood will burn! But on this night he wasn't convinced. It only made him mad.

Dig!

He went at the underside of a log which had broken over another one in its fall, a long time ago. They were two crossing mounds of dirt, almost; not an impossible source. But at this moment, wet through and through. And cold.

When he saw how it was, he beat his fist on the soft wet logs. Then he had to start walking in circles again.

Later, more digging into another log gained him only a knot that was still hard, with two spurs extending away from it at an angle much like the angle needed to make a spear thrower. He replaced his first firestarter base with this flat knot, which was better. His alder firestick still looked good. All was ready, if only he had something dry enough to catch fire.

And if only it would stop raining so hard. For a while it pelted down, cold enough to be a little sleety, and all on a gusty wind. In the hard gusts it was like getting hit with cold sand. He simply had to take shelter, and so he crawled under a spruce with big branches right against the ground, where he could snuggle in tight around the trunk and feel only a few drips on him, a few tickles of wind. The spruce needles were scratchy and the ground was cold, but he flexed his shoulder up and down, and sang a hot song and swore vengeance against Thorn. Talk about bad shamans!

But all boys have to become men one way or another. Their wanders had to be trials of skill and endurance. Hunters' wanders were just as bad. And other packs' shamans insisted on even harder trials, it was said.

Loon banished Thorn again. He tested all the branches at the bottom of the spruce. If a dead one could be broken, a dead one well dried but still a little resiny, possibly he could pulverize a spot in it with a rock point and make a mash of splinters fine enough to catch fire under the spin of the firestick. Worth a try, and the effort itself would help keep him warm.

But it turned out there didn't seem to be a branch around the bottom of this tree that he could break.

When the rain let off, he squirmed back out and crawled around under the other spruces looking for such a branch. His hands were so cold he could scarcely grasp the branches to test them.

After a while he had broken off a few likely-looking branches. If he could get a fire started in one of them, the others would be good wood to feed to it.

He found an adequate hearth rock, and a better smasher rock. He took the best one of his dead dry spruce branches and placed it on the hearth, then hit it with the smasher. It resisted, and it was clear it would take a while to get it right, but it seemed promising. Smash smash smash. He had to be more careful than usual not to catch a finger, his hands were so clumsy. Once two years before he had smashed a fingertip, and it was still fat and a little numb at the end, its flat claw lined with grooves. He called that finger Fatty. So he hit his smasher on the side of the broken branch very carefully, once or twice hitting the hearth instead. A spark or two from those accidents made him long for his flint firestrikers. A few scattered sparks were not going to be enough to do it on a night like this. The wet wind whooshed its laughter at him, loud in the trees.

Eventually a spot on the side of his target branch was squashed into a splay of splinters, perfectly dry. He sat cross-legged with his body arched over the branch, and it seemed like the mash of splinters might burn. Breathing hard, warm except for his feet, he crawled under the best of the spruces in his grove and arranged his new kit around him. Smashed branch on the hearth rock, held there between his feet; firestick placed almost upright in the mash of splinters on the branch, held at its tilt between his palms. All set: spin the firestick back and forth.

Back and forth, back and forth between his hands, gently pushing the point of the stick down into the branch. Back and forth, back and forth. His palms ran down the stick with the force of his pushing down, and when they reached the lower end of the stick he had to grasp it with one hand, put the other against the top, and move up and catch it and begin over again, with as little a pause as he could manage. Meanwhile it kept raining outside the shelter of the spruce, and under it, right against the trunk, drips were dripping. Really it began to look impossible, given the conditions. But he didn't want to admit that. It would get an awful lot colder the moment he admitted that.

After a long time, maybe a fist or more, he had to give up, at least on this branch. The mash of splinters was a bit too massy, and after a while, a little damp. He could get the spot just under the firestick so hot that it slightly burned his fingertip to touch it, and the splinters around that spot had even blackened a little, but they would not burst into flame.

Loon sat there. This was going to be a hard thing to tell Thorn about, assuming he survived to tell the tale. The old sorcerer would flick him on the ears for sure. You had to be able to start a fire, anytime, anywhere; the worse conditions were, the more important it got. Thorn, like most of the shamans at the corroboree, was exceptionally good with fire, and had spent a lot of time with Loon and the other kids, teaching them the tricks.

He had put a firestick to their forearms and spun it, to teach them how hot the spinning got. Eventually Loon had learned how to make fire no matter how the old man complicated the task. But there had always been some dry duff, one way or another.

Now he crawled out from under the spruce and stood up, sobbing with frustration, and danced until the cold was held off him by a thin envelope of sweat. When the rain let up a little, he steamed. Already he was hungry, but there was nothing for it. Time to chew on a pebble and think about other things. Chew a pebble and dance in the rain. Cold or not, this was his wander. When daylight came at last he would find better shelter, find some dry duff, find an abri or some smaller overhang. Begin outfitting himself for his return at full moon. He would walk into camp fully clothed, belly full, spear in hand! Clothed in lion skins! Beartooth necklace draped around his neck! He saw it all inside his eyes. He shouted the story of it at the night.

After a while he sat again under the best spruce, his head on his knees, arms wrapped around his legs. Then he got back out and shuffled around in the grove, looking for a better tuck, finding one after another and testing them. If they were good, he added them to a growing little round of camps, each with its own strengths and weaknesses. He chanted for long stretches, cursed Thorn from time to time. May your pizzle fall off, may a lion eat you... Then also from time to time he would shout things out loud.—It's cold! Thorn would sometimes howl his thoughts that way, using old words from the shamans' language, words that sounded like the things themselves: Esh var kalt! Esh var k-k-k-kaaaal-TEE!

He stubbed a big toe and only felt it in the bone; the

flesh was numb. More curses. May the ravens shit on you, may your babies die...Lie on the ground under one big spruce, only his kneecaps and toes and the palms of hands and his forehead touching the earth. Push himself up and down with his arms, staying rigid. If only he could fuck the earth to get warm, but it was too cold, he couldn't get his poor pizzle to antler, it was as numb as his toes, and would hurt like crazy when it next warmed up, prickle and burn till he cried. Maybe if he thought of that girl from the Lion pack, a raven like him, therefore forbidden to him, supposedly, but they had made eyes anyway, and it would warm him to think of plunging her. Or Sage, from his own pack.

That line of thought trapped some time: seeing it all inside his eyelids, seeing her spread her legs to him. Be there inside her kolby, forget this cold rain. Her kolby, her baginaren, her vixen. Start a little fire behind his belly button, get his prong to spurt. But it was too cold. He could only mash the poor flesh around and make it burn a little, warm it in the hope it would not get frostbit. That would be so bad.

After a time the rain relented. The sky's cloudy dark gray seemed a bit lighter. No moon, no stars to tell him how close dawn was. But it felt close. It had to be close. It had been a long, long night.

He stood and swayed. It was surely a lighter gray overhead. He sang a hot song, he sang a song to the sun. He called for the sun, the great god of warmth and good cheer. He was tired and cold. But he wasn't so cold he would die. He would make it to dawn, he could feel it. This was his wander, this was how a shaman was born. He howled till his throat was raw.